photograph by Berenice Abbott

Margaret Anderson

THE
LITTLE REVIEW
ANTHOLOGY

By Margaret Anderson

MY THIRTY YEARS' WAR

THE FIERY FOUNTAINS

THE "LITTLE REVIEW" ANTHOLOGY

THE UNKNOWABLE GURDJIEFF

THE STRANGE NECESSITY

THE

LITTLE REVIEW

ANTHOLOGY

Edited by

MARGARET ANDERSON

HORIZON PRESS   NEW YORK

CONTENTS

The Editor's commentary between the selections is set in italics.

PREFACE	11
The New Note—SHERWOOD ANDERSON	13
How a Little Girl Danced—NICHOLAS VACHEL LINDSAY	15
I Went Down into the Desert—NICHOLAS VACHEL LINDSAY	17
Man and Superman—GEORGE BURMAN FOSTER	18
The Milliner—SADE IVERSON	21
The Swan—F. S. FLINT	22
Bright Sunlight—AMY LOWELL	23
A Young American Poet—RICHARD ALDINGTON	24
Au Vieux Jardin—RICHARD ALDINGTON	28
John Cowper Powys on Henry James	28
"So We Grew Together"—EDGAR LEE MASTERS	31
The American Family—BEN HECHT	37
Autumn Song—BEN HECHT	42
Portrait of Theodore Dreiser—ARTHUR DAVISON FICKE	45
Theodore Dreiser—JOHN COWPER POWYS	46
Rupert Brooke—ARTHUR DAVISON FICKE	52
Poems—RICHARD ALDINGTON	52
THE READER CRITIC	55
The Struggle—SHERWOOD ANDERSON	55
Two Poems—CARL SANDBURG	59
Reversals—MARGARET C. ANDERSON	60
Letters from Prison—EMMA GOLDMAN	62
Jottings—JANE HEAP	65
Chinese Poems—TRANSLATED FROM LI PO	66
Paderewski and Tagore—JANE HEAP	67

Mr. Powys on Dostoevsky 69
"The Compleat Amateur"—HAROLD BAUER 71
A Decadent Art—JANE HEAP 73
Mary Garden—JANE HEAP 75
Isadora Duncan's Misfortune—MARGARET ANDERSON 80
THE READER CRITIC 81
On a Certain Critic—AMY LOWELL 82
THE READER CRITIC 84
Push Face—JH 85
Editorial—EZRA POUND 99
Eeldrop and Appleplex—T. S. ELIOT 102
The Week-end—LOUIS GILMORE 109
Poems—WILLIAM BUTLER YEATS 109
Imaginary Letters—WYNDHAM LEWIS 110
The Hippopotamus—T. S. ELIOT 128
James Joyce—JANE HEAP 129
Japanese Plays—EZRA POUND 131
THE READER CRITIC 134
Cantelman's Spring-Mate—WYNDHAM LEWIS 137
A Song—WILLIAM BUTLER YEATS 144
Poems of Po Chu-i—TRANSLATED BY ARTHUR WALEY 144
Summary—EZRA POUND 145
THE READER CRITIC 146
Sketches—JH 148
In Shadow—HART CRANE 149
Women and Men—FORD MADOX HUEFFER 150
Villon's Epitaph—WITTER BYNNER 159
Scarron's Epitaph—WITTER BYNNER 160
Improvisations—WILLIAM CARLOS WILLIAMS 160
A Study in French Poets—EZRA POUND 164
Broken Necks—BEN HECHT 176
Three Illuminations of Rimbaud 183
Cooperation—EZRA POUND 185
You Say You Said—MARIANNE MOORE 187
Marianne Moore and Mina Loy—EZRA POUND 188
Mefk Maru Mustir Daas..ELSE VON FREYTAG-LORINGHOVEN 189
The Chinese Written Character—ERNEST FENOLLOSA
and EZRA POUND 190
Poems—EZRA POUND 206

6

THE READER CRITIC 211

Temple Inscriptions (In China)—WITTER BYNNER 215

"Exiles": A Symposium 215

Henry James—ETHEL COBURN MAYNE 221

In Explanation—EZRA POUND 225

Henry James and the Ghostly—A. R. ORAGE 230

In Memory—T. S. ELIOT 232

Phanopoiea—EZRA POUND 232

The Valet—DJUNA BARNES 233

Three Professional Studies—WILLIAM CARLOS WILLIAMS 240

Poems—WALLACE STEVENS 247

Prohibition and Art of Conversation—JOHN BUTLER YEATS 248

Snow Scene: Puppet Booth—MARK TURBYFILL 254

De Gourmont: A Distinction—EZRA POUND 255

Poem—ELSE VON FREYTAG-LORINGHOVEN 258

Landscape with Trees—CARLOS A. V. KRAL 260

Affectionate—ELSE VON FREYTAG-LORINGHOVEN 269

Breviora—EZRA POUND 269

THE READER CRITIC 272

Tales of a Hurried Man—EMANUEL CARNEVALI 275

THE READER CRITIC 283

A Visit (from the French of Vildrac)—WITTER BYNNER 285

W. H. Hudson—Some Reminiscences—FORD MADOX HUEFFER 287

Hudson: Poet Strayed into Science—EZRA POUND 295

Sunday Afternoon—MALCOLM COWLEY 295

On Trial for "Ulysses" 297

I Cannot Sleep—JANE HEAP 311

Brancusi—EZRA POUND 312

"Gardening with Brains"—JH 316

B.B. or the Birthplace of Bonnes—GERTRUDE STEIN 317

The Art of Madness—EVELYN SCOTT and JH 322

Aesthetic Meditations—GUILLAUME APOLLINAIRE 326

THE READER CRITIC 328

"Ulysses" Again—JH 329

Dialogue—MARGARET ANDERSON 331

Mr. and Mrs. Elliott—ERNEST HEMINGWAY 332

To Mark Anthony in Heaven—WILLIAM CARLOS WILLIAMS 335

Ornament in Jean Cocteau's "Le Grand Ecart" 336

Abstraction and Time in Music—GEORGE ANTHEIL 336

7

Waiting—WILLIAM CARLOS WILLIAMS   339
Notes—JANE HEAP   339
Machine-Age Exposition—JANE HEAP   341
The Machine—FERNAND LEGER   343
Paris at One Time—JANE HEAP   345
"A Rotten Corpse"   346
Noces—TRISTAN TZARA   348
THE LAST NUMBER OF THE "LITTLE REVIEW"   349
LETTERS   380

ACKNOWLEDGMENTS

I am glad to record my indebtedness to the various publishers and agents or estates who have permitted the use in this anthology of prose writings or poems copyrighted or controlled by them. My cordial thanks for permission to reprint are given to:—

Richard Aldington: For "A Young American Poet," "Au Vieux Jardin," and "Poems from the Greek of Myrrhine and Konallis";

Witter Bynner: For "Villon's Epitaph," "Scarron's Epitaph," "Temple Inscriptions (In China)," and "A Visit";

Harcourt, Brace and Company, Inc.: For "The Hippopotamus" from *Collected Poems 1909-1935* by T. S. Eliot, copyright, 1936, by Harcourt, Brace and Company, Inc.;

Henry Holt and Company, Inc.: For "Gone" and "Graves" from *Chicago Poems* by Carl Sandburg, copyright, 1916, by Henry Holt and Company, Inc., copyright, 1944, by Carl Sandburg; used by permission of the publishers;

The Houghton Mifflin Company: For "Bright Sunlight" and "On a Certain Critic" from *Pictures of the Floating World* by Amy Lowell, used by permission of the publishers, Houghton Mifflin Company;

Alfred A. Knopf, Inc.: For "Nuances of a Theme by Williams" and "Anecdote of Canna" from *Harmonium* by Wallace Stevens, copyright, 1923, 1931, by Alfred A. Knopf, Inc., and for "The Harper of Chao" and "On the Way to Hangchow" from *Translations from the Chinese* by Arthur Waley, copyright 1919, 1941, by Arthur Waley; reprinted by permission of Alfred A. Knopf, Inc.;

Liveright Publishing Corporation: For "In Shadow" and "Garden Abstract" from *The Collected Poems of Hart Crane*, copyright 1933 by Liveright, Inc., and for "The Valet" from *A Book* by Djuna Barnes, copyright renwed 1950 by Djuna Barnes;

PREFACE

THERE is nothing stronger than the force of a conviction. It will drive you to success.

My conviction in founding the *Little Review* was that people who make Art are more interesting than those who don't; that they have a special illumination about life; that this illumination is the subject-matter of all inspired conversation; that one might as well be dead as to live outside this radiance. I was sure that I could impose my conviction by creating a magazine dedicated to Art for Art's sake.

I see, today, that I succeeded.

William Carlos Williams once wrote me: "As always, most of the stuff the *Little Review* prints is bad, I suppose, but the *Little Review* is good." How right he was. But it is only by condensing the *Little Review* to its quintessence that one can see how good it was.

I know now the sources of this "goodness." Much of it came from Ezra Pound and his genius for discovering and aiding the important artists of our time; much of it came from my own flair for distinguishing between the "interesting" and the "uninteresting"; but most of it came from Jane Heap and her possession of that special illumination.

Someone has defined great Art as a struggle for communication. As I read through the files of the *Little Review* I feel more strongly than anything else this "strange necessity" to communicate those matters that lie just beyond the range of common understanding. Jane and I, to all who came, were those good companions whose talk led to exaltation.

It is ironic that this magazine of my high purpose should have lacked, in two of its three phases, the very quality it was created for

—Art. Its first phase was enthusiasm, presented in bad writing—I knew nothing of the art of writing in those first years. Its last phase (after I had actively withdrawn) was that dead-end of intellectual obscurantism which is the fashion today and which I abhor. It was in its middle phase—in its commentary on Art, on the nature and function of the artist—that it fulfilled my conviction. That is why, in spite of all its deficiencies, it became a legend. It was like those conversations that fly, while others remain anchored to the ground.

To reduce fifteen years of a magazine's life to 135,000 words demands ruthless editing. I have omitted entirely an early play by Aldous Huxley, one by Dreiser, one by Lady Gregory; a too-long poem, "The Cape of Good Hope," by Cocteau. Certain things, like Yeats's very beautiful "Seven Poems to a Dying Lady," have been left out because of excessive reprint prices, or because of copyright complications. Sherwood Anderson's "New Testament" does not appear, though there is a paragraph in it that I would rather have reprinted than anything else he ever wrote. In some cases the authors themselves have chosen to be represented by pieces which I don't consider their best.

My apologies to all those whose names, because of space restriction, do not appear at all.

In the interest of variation and change of pace I have kept no very strict chronological order. All I have hoped to do is to trace that luminous line of "interest"—the artist's mental-emotional clairvoyance.

MARGARET ANDERSON

THE LITTLE
REVIEW
ANTHOLOGY

I feel no compulsion to begin this Anthology by quoting my first editorial. The emotions I expressed in it were basic, laudable, and identical with those I feel today; my expression of them was incredible. I prefer to begin with an article from the first number written by Sherwood Anderson, entitled appropriately "The New Note":

The New Note
SHERWOOD ANDERSON

THE new note in the craft of writing is in danger, as are all new and beautiful things born into the world, of being talked to death in the cradle. Already a cult of the new has sprung up, and doddering old fellows, yellow with their sins, run here and there crying out that they are true prophets of the new, just as, following last year's exhibit, every age-sick American painter began hastily to inject into his own work something clutched out of the seething mass of new forms and new effects scrawled upon the canvases by the living young cubists and futurists. Confused by the voices, they raised also their voices, multiplying the din. Forgetting the soul of the workman, they grasped at lines and solids, getting nothing.

In the trade of writing the so-called new note is as old as the world. Simply stated, it is a cry for the reinjection of truth and honesty into the craft; it is an appeal from the standards set up by money-making magazine and book publishers in Europe and America to the older, sweeter standards of the craft itself; it is the voice of the new man, come into a new world, proclaiming his right to speak out of the body and soul of youth, rather than through the bodies and souls of the master craftsmen who are gone.

In all the world there is no such thing as an old sunrise, an old wind upon the cheeks, or an old kiss from the lips of your beloved; and in the craft of writing there can be no such thing as age in the souls of the young poets and novelists who demand for themselves the right to stand up and be counted among the soldiers of the new.

. . . Be ready to accept hardship for the sake of your craft in America—that is craft love.

. . . Given this note of craft love all the rest must follow, as the spirit of self-revelation, which is also a part of the new note, will follow any true present-day love of craft.

. . . Why do we so prize the work of Whitman, Tolstoy, Dostoevsky, Twain, and Fielding? Is it not because as we read we are constantly saying to ourselves, "This book is true. A man of flesh and blood like myself has lived the substance of it. In the love of his craft he has done the most difficult of all things: revealed the workings of his own soul and mind?"

To get near to the social advance for which all moderns hunger, is it not necessary to have first of all understanding? How can I love my neighbor if I do not understand him? And it is just in the wider diffusion of this understanding that the work of a great writer helps the advance of mankind. I would like to have you think much of this in your attitude toward all present-day writers. It is so easy for them to bluff us from our position, and I know from my own experience how baffling it is constantly to be coming upon good, well-done work that is false.

In this connection I am tempted to give you the substance of a formula I have just worked out. It lies here before me, and if you will accept it in the comradely spirit in which it is offered I shall be glad. It is the most delicate and the most unbelievably difficult task to catch, understand, and record your own mood. The thing must be done simply and without pretense or windiness, for the moment these creep in your record is no longer a record, but a mere mass of words meaning nothing. The value of such a record is not in the facts caught and recorded but in the fact of your having been able truthfully to make the record—something within yourself will tell you when you have it done it truthfully. I myself believe that when a man can thus stand aside from himself, recording simply and truthfully the inner workings of his own mind, he will be prepared to record truthfully the workings of other minds. In every man or woman dwell dozens of men and women, and the highly imaginative individual will lead fifty lives. Surely this can be said if it can be said that the unimaginative individual has led one life.

The practice of constantly and persistently making such a record as this will prove invaluable to the person who wishes to become a true critic of writing in the new spirit. Whenever he finds himself baffled in drawing a character or in judging one drawn by another, let him turn thus in upon himself, trusting with child-like simplicity and honesty the truth that lives in his own mind.

If this practice is followed diligently, a kind of partnership will in time spring up between the hand and the brain of the writer. He will find himself becoming in truth a cattle herder, a drug clerk, a murderer, for the benefit of the hand that is writing of these, or the brain that is judging the work of another who has written of these.

. . . I would like to scold every one who writes, or who has to do with writing, into adopting this practice, which has been such a help and such a delight to me.

Nicholas Vachel Lindsay, who had already appeared in Poetry, *gave us a poem for the first number.*

How a Little Girl Danced

NICHOLAS VACHEL LINDSAY
Being a Reminiscence of Certain Private Theatricals
(Dedicated to Lucy Bates)

> Oh, cabaret dancer,
> *I* know a dancer
> Whose eyes have not looked
> On the feasts that are vain.
> *I* know a dancer,
> *I* know a dancer,
> Whose soul has no bond
> With the beasts of the plain:
> Judith the dancer,
> Judith the dancer,
> With foot like the snow
> And with step like the rain.
>
> Oh, thrice-painted dancer,
> Vaudeville dancer,
> Sad in your spangles,
> With soul all astrain:
> *I* know a dancer,
> *I* know a dancer,
> Whose laughter and weeping
> Are spiritual gain;
> A pure-hearted, high-hearted

Maiden evangel
With strength the dark cynical
Earth to disdain.
Flowers of bright Broadway!
You of the chorus
Who sing in the hope
Of forgetting your pain:
I turn to a sister
Of sainted Cecelia,
A white bird escaping
The earth's tangled skein!—
The music of God
In her innermost brooding!
The whispering angels
Her footsteps sustain!

Oh, proud Russian dancer:
Praise for your dancing!
No clean human passion
My rhyme would arraign.
You dance for Apollo
With noble devotion:
A high-cleansing revel
To make the heart sane.
But Judith the dancer
Prays to a spirit
More white than Apollo
And all of his train.

I know a dancer
Who finds the true God-head;
Who bends o'er a brazier
In Heaven's clear plain.
I know a dancer,
I know a dancer,
Who lifts us toward peace
From this Earth that is vain:—
Judith the dancer,
Judith the dancer,
With foot like the snow,
And with step like the rain.

Later we printed several other Lindsay poems, of which I quote only one:

I Went Down Into the Desert

I went down into the desert
To meet Elijah—
Or some one like, arisen from the dead.
I thought to find him in an echoing cave,
For so my dream had said.

I went down into the desert
To meet John the Baptist.
I walked with feet that bled,
Seeking that prophet, lean and brown and bold.
I spied foul fiends instead.

I went down into the desert
To meet my God,
By Him be comforted.
I went down into the desert
To meet my God
And I met the Devil in Red.

I went down into the desert
To meet my God.
Oh Lord, my God, awaken from the dead!
I see you there, your thorn-crown on the ground—
I see you there, half-buried in the sand—
I see you there, your white bones glistening, bare,
The carrion birds a-wheeling round your head!

*Our first mention of Gertrude Stein appeared in the first number.
It was written by George Soule who later became a member of* The
New Republic *staff.*

. . . Has the cubist literature of Gertrude Stein awakened echoes
in Chicago? I have read it without understanding before this. But
one night my host—a great, strong, humorous, intelligent hulk of a
man, himself a scoffer at cubism—read part of her essay on Matisse so
that it was almost intelligible. His inflection and punctuation did
it. Her chief characteristics seem to be an aversion to personal pronouns and a strict adherence to simple declarative statements, un-
troubled by subordinate clauses or phrases of any kind. Her
thought, therefore, resolves itself awkwardly in a four-square way.
The multiplicity of her planes becomes confusing after a page, but
each plane stands alone. Thus—(I quote inaccurately)—"Some ones

knew this one to be expressing something being struggling. Some ones knew this one not to be expressing something being struggling. This one expressed something being struggling. This one did not express something being struggling." Which, of course, is the cubist way of saying that "Some thought he was trying to express struggle in an object, others thought the contrary. As a matter of fact, he sometimes did express struggle; sometimes he did not."

But it seems her early work is now getting too obvious, so she is in the throes of a later phase. In her "Portrait of Miss Dodge" she has eliminated verbs and sentence structure entirely, flinging a succession of image-nouns at the reader. One can surely not accuse her of "prettiness."

Since we were a revolutionary magazine, Nietzsche was naturally our prophet. I asked Dr. George Burman Foster, professor of philosophy at the University of Chicago, to do a series of articles on Nietzsche. They ran for perhaps a year, and I quote parts of the first one:

Man and Superman
GEORGE BURMAN FOSTER

In his voluptuous vagabondage Rousseau at length halted at Paris, where he managed to worry through some inconstant years. The thing that saved the day for him was the fragment of a pamphlet that blew across his path in one of his rambles, announcing a prize to be awarded by the Academy of Dijon for the best answer to an extraordinary question. Had the renascence of the arts and sciences ennobled morals? That was a flash of lightning which lit up a murky night and helped this bewildered and lonely wanderer to get his bearings. Thoughts came to him demoniacally which shaped his entire future and won him no small place in the history of humanity.

Answer is "No!" said Rousseau. And his answer was awarded the academic prize.

It seems strange that the history of his times sided with Rousseau's "No." Certainly it was the first fiery meteor of the French revolution. It pronounced the first damnatory sentence upon a culture that had already reached the point of collapse. In his own body and soul Rousseau had bitterly experienced the curse of this culture. It was largely responsible for his heart's abnormal yearning whose glow was consuming him. Instead of ennobling morals this culture had inwardly barbarized man. Then it galvanized and painted the outside of life. And then life became a glittering lie.

Thus Rousseau became prophet in this desert of culture, and called men to repentance. "Back from culture to nature," was his radical cry; back from what man has made out of himself to what nature meant him to be. Nature gave man free use of his limbs; culture has bound them with all sorts of bindings, until he is stiff, and short-winded, and crippled. According to nature man lives his own life; man is what he seems and seems what he is; according to culture he is cunning, and crafty, and mendacious.

The eighteenth-century man of culture hearkened with attentive soul to the dirge in which one of its noblest sons vented his tortured heart. The melancholy music bruised from this prophet's heart silenced the wit and ridicule of even a Voltaire, who wanted to know, however, whether "the idea was to go on all fours again." In a few decades the feet of revolutionary Frenchmen were at the door ready, with few and short prayers, to bear to its abode that culture whose moral worth even a French Academy had called in question and for whose moral condemnation had awarded the first prize.

Now it was from an entirely different side, indeed it was from an entirely different standpoint, that Friedrich Nietzsche contemplated modern culture, particularly the national culture of the German Fatherland. What horrified him was not simply the *content,* but the *criterion,* of our culture. He sharply scrutinized the *ideals* which we set ourselves in our culture. He found not simply our achievements but our ideals, *ourselves* even, so inferior, so vulgar, so contemptible, that he began to doubt whether even the Germans could be recognized as a culture people or not. Hence Nietzsche became the most ruthless iconoclast of our culture. Unlike the majority, unlike the scholars, the philanthropists, the philistines, Nietzsche was not moved by the misery of the masses, by the great social need of our time. He did not regret that the boon of our culture was shared by so few, inasmuch as, in his opinion, this boon was of very doubtful value. He found our life so barbarous, so culture-hostile, that he still missed the first elements of a true culture among us.

Hence Nietzsche lunged against *status quo.* He did what he himself called *"unzeitmässig,"* untimely. He flung a question, more burning than any other, into our time—more burning than even the social question, constituting indeed the main part of that question. It was the question as to how *man* fared in this culture—the question as to what *man* got out of it and as to what it got out of man.

Never before had this question been put as Nietzsche put it. We should recall that Nietzsche was not one of those who had experienced the extremes of either plenty or want, nor was he one of those who filled the wide space between the two. To him, the pessimism of the discontented and the optimism of the fortunate and the satisfied were alike superficial, if not impertinent. It was not a question of "happiness" at all. In bitter, biting sarcasm he says, with reference to the English utilitarian "happiness morality": "I do not seek my happiness; only an Englishman seeks his happiness; I seek my *work*."

No; his was a question which his conscience put to culture. Was it a "culture of the *earth*, or of *man*?" Here Nietzsche probes home. And he alone did it. The most diverse censors of our time had not seen and said that no matter how desirable, no matter how gloriously conceived the new order of things might be, *man* must be the decisive thing; *man* must tip the scales. It was this that went against the grain. Mightier machines, larger cities, better apartments, bigger schools, what was the good of it all, *et id omne genus*, if new and greater men did not arise? So said Nietzsche. And he said it with high scorn to a generation which had forgotten that man is not for "culture," but culture for man; of man, by man, for man.

. . . And yet had there been no Nietzsche there would still remain Cicero's warning: "Woe to a people whose wealth grows but whose men decay." But there was a Nietzsche and he dared to call even his Fatherland Europe's "flat country"—flat was a hard word for a land that could once boast of so many poets and thinkers. . . . With a fury and a fire that literally consumed him, he dedicated himself to the task of leading men up out of this flatness, away from this leveling—up to an appreciation of the potential—not the actual —greatness of man's life. Greatness is not yet man's verity but his vocation, his true and idiomatic destiny. Greatness? This is a man's strength of will; the unfolding of a free personality. To say *I will* is to be a man. All human values are embraced in this *I will*. To produce men who can say *I will* is at once the task and the test of culture. This *I will* is the climax and goal of man. In this *I will* vanishes every fearsome and disquieting *I must*, every compulsion of outer necessity. Not the passive adjustment of man to nature, but the ac-

20

tive adjustment of nature to man; nature outside of him and nature inside of him—that is human calling and human culture.

. . . That is the meaning of the Superman of Friedrich Nietzsche.

An unknown name appeared in an early issue—one of the two or three unsolicited manuscripts we printed in all the years. It was signed to a poem which arrived with a modest little note: "Something about your magazine—perhaps the essential actuality of it— has moved me to make the 'simple confession' which I enclose. Print it if it is good enough; throw it in the waste-basket if it is not."

The Milliner
SADE IVERSON

All the day long I have been sitting in my shop
Sewing straw on hat-shapes according to the fashion,
Putting lace and ribbon on according to the fashion,
Setting out the faces of customers according to fashion.
Whatever they asked for I tried to give them;
Over their worldly faces I put mimic flowers
From out my silk and velvet garden; I bade Spring come
To those who had seen Autumn; I coaxed faded eyes
To look bright and hard brows to soften.

Not once, while they were looking in the glass,
Did I peep over their shoulders to see myself.
It would have been quite unavailing for me,
Who have grown grey in service of other women,
To have used myself as any sort of a model.
Had I looked in the mirror I should have seen
Only a bleached face, long housed from sunshine,
A mouth quick with forced smiles, eyes greyly stagnant,
And over all, like a night fog creeping,
Something chill and obscuring and dead—
The miasmatic mist of the soul of the lonely.

When night comes and the buyers are gone their ways,
I go into the little room behind my shop.
It is my home—my silent and lonely home;
But it has fire, it has food; there is a bed;
Pictures are on the walls, showing the faces
I kissed in girlhood. I am myself here;
All my forced smiles are laid away with the moline
And the ribbon and roses. I may do as I please.

If I beat with my fists on the table, no one hears;
If I lie in my bed, staring, staring,
No one can know; I shall not suffer the pity
Of those who, passing, see my light edge the grey curtain.
One night, long ago, merely for madness
I stripped myself like a dancing girl;
I draped myself with rose-hued silks
And set a crimson feather in my hair.
There were twists of gold lace about my arms
And a girdle of gold about my waist.
I danced before the mirror till I dropped!
(Outside I could hear the rain falling
And the wind crept in beneath my door
Along my worn carpet.)

       I folded my finery
And prayed as if kneeling beside my mother.
Whether there was listening I cannot say.
There was praying! There was praying!
Never again shall I dance before the mirror
Bedizened like a dancing girl—never, my mother!

I have a low voice and quiet movements,
And early and late I study to please.
As long as I live I shall be adorning other women,
I shall be decking them for their lovers
And sending them upon women's adventures.
But none of them shall see behind this curtain
Where I have my little home, where I weep
When I please, and beat upon the table with my fists.

*In the summer of our first year we printed one of the new group
of poets who were becoming known as Imagists:*

The Swan

F. S. FLINT

Under the lily shadow
and the gold
and the blue and mauve
that the whin and the lilac
pour down on the water,
the fishes quiver.

Over the green cold leaves
and the rippled silver
and the tarnished copper
of its neck and beak,
toward the deep black water
beneath the arches,
the swan floats slowly.

Into the dark of the arch the swan floats
and into the black depth of my sorrow
it bears a white rose of flame.

. . . and in the same number Richard Aldington sent a statement of the Imagists' tenets:

I. Direct treatment of subject. We convey an emotion by presenting the object and circumstance of the emotion without comment. For example, we do not say, "O how I admire that exquisite, that beautiful, that—25 more adjectives—woman." But we present that woman, we make an "Image" of her, we make the scene convey the emotion. . . .

II. As few adjectives as possible.

III. A hardness as of cut stone. No slop, no sentimentality. When people say the Imagiste poems are "too hard" . . . we know we have done something good.

IV. Individuality of rhythm. We make new fashions instead of cutting our clothes on the old models.

V. The exact word. We make quite a heavy stress on that. It is most important. All great poetry is exact. All the dreariness of nineteenth century poetry comes from their not quite knowing what they wanted to say and filling up the gaps with portentous adjectives and idiotic similes.

Here is a definition by Ezra Pound which helps us: "An Image is that which presents an intellectual and emotional complex in an instant of time."

At the beginning of the Little Review's *second year Amy Lowell sent us the first of the many poems of hers we were to print:*

Bright Sunlight

AMY LOWELL

The wind has blown a corner of your shawl

Into the fountain,
Where it floats and drifts
Among the lily-pads
Like a tissue of sapphires.
But you do not heed it,
Your fingers pick at the lichens
On the stone edge of the basin,
And your eyes follow the tall clouds
As they sail over the ilex trees.

. . . and Richard Aldington wrote an article on "H. D." (Hilda Doolittle) who was a leader in the Imagist group:

A Young American Poet

RICHARD ALDINGTON

IT is the defect of English, and in a lesser degree of American, criticism that such criticisms as are not merely commercial are doctrinaire. The critic, that is to say, comes to judge a work of art not with an open mind but with a whole horde of prejudices, ignorances, and eruditions which he terms "critical standards." "A work of art," you can hear him say, "must be this, must be that, must be the other," when indeed a work of art may well be no such thing. Just now the cry is all for "modernity," for lyrical outbursts in praise of machinery, of locomotion, and of violence. And the "critics" obediently fill their minds with these prejudices until at length you discover them solemnly declaring that a work of art has no value except it treat of machinery, of locomotion or of kindred subjects! I have yet to find the critic who approaches his job in the right spirit; who asks himself first, What has the artist attempted to do?, and then, Has he succeeded? The commercial critic is of course the more reprehensible; the doctrinaire critic is nevertheless a serious menace to that liberty of the arts of which one cannot be too jealous. In England especially the doctrinaire critic reigns. Yesterday it was all Nietzsche; then Bergson; now there is a wild fight between a dozen "isms," combats between traditional imbeciles and revolutionary imbeciles. So that one spends half one's time becoming an "ist" and the rest of the time in getting ride of the title.

The neglect of the poems of the young American poet—H. D.— who is the subject of this article, is due, I think, to the following facts. The author, who apparently possesses a great degree of self-criticism, produces a very small bulk of work and most of it is lost in magazines; such work as attained publicity was judged, before being read, from its surroundings; the work, being original, seemed obscure and wantonly destructive of classic English models (you must remember that there are very, very few people in England who have the faintest idea of what is meant by vers libre); the use of initials rather frightened people; and the author had no friends among the professional critics.

Now America has this advantage over most European countries that its inhabitants are mostly willing to accept a fresh view of things. The lack of a "tradition" has advantages as well as disadvantages. An American author, then, is less likely to see things in a conventional way, and is less likely to be deterred from any novel and personal method of expression. (For in 1911, when H. D. began to write the poems I am considering, vers libre was practically unheard of outside France.)

If I were asked to define the chief quality of H. D.'s work I should say: "I can only explain it by a paradox; it is a kind of accurate mystery." And I should go on to quote the ballad of Sir Patric Spens in which from a cloudy, vague, obscure atmosphere, where nothing is precise, where there is no "story," no obvious relation between the ideas, certain objects stand out very sharply and clearly with a very keen effect, objects like "the bluid-red wine," "the braid letter," the young moon in the old moon's arms, and the ladies with "their fans intil their hands." And then I should go on to say that this "accurate mystery" came from the author's brooding over—not locomotives and machinery—but little corners of gardens, a bit of a stream in some Pennsylvanian meadow, from memories of afternoons along the New Jersey coast, or of a bowl of flowers. Curious, mysterious, rather obscure sort of broodings with startling and very accurate renderings of detail. And then I should explain the author's use of Hellenic terms and of the rough unaccented metres of Attic choruses and Melic lyrics—like those fragments of Alcaeus and Ibycus and Erinna—by pointing out that it is in those poems—the choruses in the Bacchae, for example—that this particular kind of brooding over nature found its best expression.

Let me quote a portion of a poem to illustrate these qualities: the quality which I have called "accurate mystery," the quality of brooding over nature and the quality of spontaneous kinship with certain aspects of Hellenic poetry. I take it that, if one liked to be specifically

modern, the poem could be called "Wind on the New Jersey Coast."
But the author's innate sense of mystery, of aloofness, just like that
of the anonymous author of Sir Patric Spens, makes her place the
action in some vague, distant place and time. Though it be contrary
to current opinion I hold that the poem gains by this.

HERMES OF THE WAYS

The hard sand breaks,
And the grains of it are clear as wine.

Far off over the leagues of it,
The wind,
Playing on the wide shore,
Piles little ridges,
And the great waves break over it.

But more than the many-foamed ways
Of the sea,
I know him
Of the triple path-ways,
Hermes,
Who awaiteth.

Dubious,
Facing three ways,
Welcoming wayfarers,
He whom the sea-orchard shelters from the west,
From the east
Weathers sea-wind;
Fronts the great dunes.

Wind rushes
Over the dunes,
And the coarse, salt-crusted grass
Answers.

Heu,
It whips round my ankles!—etc., etc.

I am not willing to have that poem read quickly and cursorily,
as one reads a column of newspaper print. It must be read with some
of the close, intense attention with which it was written. Each word
and phrase were most carefully considered and arranged. The

reader must remember that the object of such writing is not to convey information but to create in the reader a mood, an emotion, a sense of atmosphere. Mr. Yeats is right when he complains that newspapers have spoiled our sense of poetry; we expect poetry to tell us some piece of news, and indeed poetry has no news to tell anyone. Its object is simply to arouse an emotion, and no emotion is ever aroused in a person who skims through a piece of poetry as he skims through a journal.

When I read that poem I have evoked in me a picture—like a picture of Courbet or Boudin—of a white sea roaring on to yellow sands under a bright sky, with the wind sweeping and whistling in the dunes. And I have a feeling that it is a magic sort of picture, of somewhere a great way off, where it would not surprise me to find the image of a god at the cross-roads, with the offerings of simple people about the pedestal. And at the same time I always remember bathing from some sand-dunes near Rye, in Sussex, on a very windy afternoon, when the sand blinded me and the sharp grass cut my ankles as I ran down to the water.

I cannot, of course, tell what sort of effect such writing has on other people. It may be that I am especially sensitive to it. But let me quote another of the author's poems, conveying a totally different mood.

SITALKAS

Thou art come at length
More beautiful than any cool god
In a chamber under Lycia's far coast,
Than any high god who touches us not
Here in the seeded grass.
Aye, than Argestes,
Scattering the broken leaves.

If you ask me to say precisely what that "means" I could only explain it in this way. When I read that poem I experience the emotions I should expect to receive if I were lying in a sunny meadow on some hot late September afternoon—somewhere far inland, where there would be a great silence broken very gently by the rustle of the heavy headed grass and by the stir of falling beech leaves—somewhere so far inland, somewhere so hot, that it would come as a shock of delighted surprise to think of a "cool god in a chamber under Lycia's far coast." It does not annoy me that I have never been to

Lycia, that I have no more idea who Sitalkas and Argestes were than who Sir Patric Spens was; it is all one; I get my impression just the same, which, I take it, is what the author aimed at. And indeed the odd unknown names give it a very agreeable sense of mystery and of aloofness.

Such are some of the qualities of the work of the young American who hides her identity under the initials H. D. I believe her work is quite unknown in America, though, before the war, I remember seeing some comment on it in a French literary paper. It was in another French review that a critic complained that this author was not interested in aeroplanes and factory chimneys. Somehow I feel quite coldly about factory chimneys when I read sudden intense outbursts of poetry like those I have quoted and like this:

> The light of her face falls from its flower
> As a hyacinth,
> Hidden in a far valley,
> Perishes upon burnt grass.

I couldn't resist reprinting Aldington's own poem from the Imagist Anthology which I have always considered his best:

Au Vieux Jardin

RICHARD ALDINGTON

> I have sat here happy in the gardens,
> Watching the still pool and the reeds
> And the dark clouds
> Which the wind of the upper air
> Tore like the green leafy boughs
> Of the divers-hued trees of late summer;
> But though I greatly delight
> In these and the water lilies,
> That which sets me nighest to weeping
> Is the rose and white colour of the smooth flag-stones,
> And the pale yellow grasses
> Among them.

John Cowper Powys on Henry James

(Jottings from a lecture)

HENRY JAMES is a revealer of secrets, but never does he entirely draw the veil. He has the most reluctance, the most reverence of all the great novelists. He is always reluctant to draw the last veil. This great, plump-handed, moribund figure, waits—afraid. All of his work is a mirror—never a softening or blurring of outlines, but a medium through which one sees the world as he sees it. In reading his works one never forgets the author. All his people speak in his character. All is attuned to his tone from beginning to end.

He uses slang with a curious kind of condescension,—all kinds of slang,—with a tacit implicit apology to the reader. So fine a spirit—he is not at home with slang.

His work divides itself into three periods—best between 1900 and 1903. In reading him approximate 1900 as the climacteric period.

His character delineation is superb. Ralph in *The Portrait of a Lady* is the type of those who have difficulty in asserting themselves and are in a peculiar way hurt by contact with the world. Osborne—in the same book—is one of those peculiarly hard, selfish, artistic, super-refined people who turn into ice whatever they touch. He personifies the cruelty of a certain type of egoism—the immorality of laying a dead hand upon life. Poe has that tendency to lay a dead hand upon what he cares for and stop it from changing. Who of us with artistic sensibilities is not afflicted with this immorality? This is the unpardonable sin—more than lust—more than passion—a "necrophilism," to lay the dead hand of eternal possession upon a young head.

Nothing exists but civilization for H. J. There has been no such writer since Vergil. And for him (H. J.) there is but one civilization—European. He is the comopolitan novelist. He describes Paris as no Frenchman does! Not only Paris, but America, Italy, anywhere the reader falls into a delicious passivity to the synthesis of nations. He knows them all and is at home in all. He is the novelist of society. Society—which is the one grand outrage; it is not pain—it is not pity; it is society which is the outrage upon personality, the permanent insult, the punishment to life. As ordinary people we hate it often—as philosophers and artists we are bitter against it, as hermits we are simply on the rack. But it is through their little conventionalities that H. J. discovers people, human beings, in society. He uses these conventionalities to portray his characters. He hears paeans of liberation, hells of pity and sorrow and distress as people signal to one another across these little conventionalities. He fills the social atmosphere with rumors and whispers of people toward one another.

In describing city and country he is equally great. He does not paint with words, but simply transports you there. Read *The Am-*

bassadors for French scenery! Everything is treated sacramentally. He is the Walter Pater of novelists with an Epicurean sense for little things—for little things that happen every day.

There is another element in his work that is psychic and beyond—magnetic and beyond. His people are held together by its vibrations. Read *The Two Magics*.

H. J. is the apostle to the rich. Money! that accursed thing! He understands its importance. It lends itself in every direction to the tragedy of being. He understands the art of the kind of life in which one can do what one wants. He understands the rich American gentleman in Europe—touches his natural chastity, his goodness, the single-hearted crystalline depths of his purity. Read *The Reverberator*.

To appreciate the mise en scène of his books—his descriptions of homes—read *The Great Good Place*. He has a profound bitterness for stupid people. He understands amorous, vampirish women who destroy a man's work. Go to H. J. for artist characters—for the baffled atrophied artists who have souls but will never do anything.

Read *The Tragic Muse*. Note the character of Gabriel Nash who is Whistler, Oscar, Pater all together and something added—the arch ghost—the moth of the cult of art.

The countenance of H. J. says that he might have been the cruelest and is the tenderest of human beings. To him no one is so poor, so unwanted a spirit but could fill a place that archangels might strive for. James is a Sennacherib of Assyria, a Solomon, a pasha before whom ivory-browed vassals prostrate themselves. He is the Solomon to whom many Queens of Sheba have come and been rejected, the lover of chastity, of purity in the natural state.

He is difficult to read, this grand, massive, unflinching, shrewd old realist, because of his intellect—a distinguished, tender, subtle spirit like a plant. And in the end I sometimes wonder whether H. J. himself in imagination does not stroll beyond the garden gate up the little hill and over to the churchyard, where, under the dark earth, he knows that the changing lineaments mold themselves into the sardonic grin of humanity.

Edgar Lee Masters' "Spoon River Anthology" had appeared in the St. Louis Mirror. *He often came to the studio to talk and laugh—we called him "Thackeray" because of a striking resemblance. One day he brought me the following:*

"So We Grew Together"

EDGAR LEE MASTERS

Reading over your letters I find you wrote me
"My dear boy," or at times "dear boy," and the envelope
Said "master"—all as I had been your very son,
And not the orphan whom you adopted.
Well, you were father to me! And I can recall
The things you did for me or gave me:
One time we rode in a box-car to Springfield
To see the greatest show on earth;
And one time you gave me red-top boots,
And one time a watch, and one time a gun.
Well, I grew to gawkiness with a voice
Like a rooster trying to crow in August
Hatched in April, we'll say.
And you went about wrapped up in silence
With eyes aflame, and I heard little rumors
Of what they were doing to you, and how
They wronged you—and we were poor—so poor!
And I could not understand why you failed,
And why if you did good things for the people
The people did not sustain you.
And why you loved another woman than Aunt Susan,
So it was whispered at school, and what could be baser,
Or so little to be forgiven? . . . .

They crowded you hard in those days.
But you fought like a wounded lion
For yourself I know, but for us, for me.
At last you fell ill, and for months you tottered
Around the streets as thin as death,
Trying to earn our bread, your great eyes glowing
And the silence around you like a shawl!
But something in you kept you up.
You grew well again and rosy with cheeks
Like an Indian peach almost, and eyes
Full of moonlight and sunlight, and a voice
That sang, and a humor that warded
The arrows off. But still between us
There was reticence; you kept me away
With a glittering hardness; perhaps you thought
I kept you away—for I was moving

In spheres you knew not, living through
Beliefs you believed in no more, and ideals
That were just mirrors of unrealities.
As a boy can be I was critical of you.
And reasons for your failures began to arise
In my mind—I saw specific facts here and there
With no philosophy at hand to weld them
And synthesize them into one truth—
And a rush of the strength of youth
Deluded me into thinking the world
Was something so easily understood and managed
While I knew it not at all in truth.
And an adolescent egotism
Made me feel you did not know me
Or comprehend the all that I was.
All this you divined. . . . . .

   So it went. And when I left you and passed
To the world, the city—still I see you
With eyes averted, and feel your hand
Limp with sorrow—you could not speak.
You thought of what I might be, and where
Life would take me, and how it would end—
There was longer silence. A year or two
Brought me closer to you. I saw the play now
And the game somewhat and understood your fights
And enmities, and hardnesses and silences,
And wild humor that had kept you whole—
For your soul had made it as an antitoxin
To the world's infections. And you swung to me
Closer than before—and a chumship began
Between us. . . . . .

   What vital power was yours!
You never tired, or needed sleep, or had a pain,
Or refused a delight. I loved the things now
You had always loved, a winning horse,
A roulette wheel, a contest of skill
In games or sports . . . long talks on the corner
With men who have lived and tell you
Things with a rich flavor of old wisdom or humor;
A woman, a glass of whisky at a table
Where the fatigue of life falls, and our reserves

That wait for happiness come up in smiles,
Laughter, gentle confidences. Here you were
A man with youth, and I a youth was a man,
Exulting in your braveries and delight in life.
How you knocked that scamp over at Harry Varnell's
When he tried to take your chips! And how I,
Who had thought the devil in cards as a boy,
Loved to play with you now and watch you play;
And watch the subtle mathematics of your mind
Prophesy, divine the plays. Who was it
In your ancestry that you harked back to
And reproduced with such various gifts
Of flesh and spirit, Anglo-Saxon, Celt?—
You with such rapid wit and powerful skill
For catching illogic and whipping Error's
Fangéd head from the body? . . . . .

        I was really ahead of you
At this stage, with more self-consciousness
Of what man is, and what life is at last,
And how the spirit works, and by what laws,
With what inevitable force. But still I was
Behind you in that strength which in our youth,
If ever we have it, squeezes all the nectar
From the grapes. It seemed you'd never lose
This power and sense of joy, but yet at times
I saw another phase of you. . . . . . .

        There was the day
We rode together north of the old town,
Past the old farm houses that I knew—
Past maple groves, and fields of corn in the shock,
And fields of wheat with the fall green.
It was October, but the clouds were summer's,
Lazily floating in a sky of June;
And a few crows flying here and there,
And a quail's call, and around us a great silence
That held at its core old memories
Of pioneers, and dead days, forgotten things!
I'll never forget how you looked that day. Your hair
Was turning silver now, but still your eyes
Burned as of old, and the rich olive glow
In your cheeks shone, with not a line or wrinkle!—

You seemed to me perfection—a youth, a man!
And now you talked of the world with the old wit,
And now of the soul—how such a man went down
Through folly or wrong done by him, and how
Man's death cannot end all,
There must be life hereafter! . . . . .

As you were that day, as you looked and spoke,
As the earth was, I hear as the soul of it all
Godard's *Dawn,* Dvorák's *Humoresque,*
The Morris Dances, Mendelssohn's *Barcarole,*
And old Scotch songs, *When the Kye Come Hame,*
And *The Moon Had Climbed the Highest Hill,*
The Musseta Waltz and Rudolph's Narrative;
Your great brow seemed Beethoven's
And the lust of life in your face Cellini's,
And your riotous fancy like Dumas.
I was nearer you now than ever before
And finding each other thus I see to-day
How the human soul seeks the human soul
And finds the one it seeks at last.
For you know you can open a window
That looks upon embowered darkness,
When the flowers sleep and the trees are still
At Midnight, and no light burns in the room;
And you can hide your butterfly
Somewhere in the room, but soon you will see
A host of butterfly mates
Fluttering through the window to join
Your butterfly hid in the room.
It is somehow thus with souls. . . . . .

This day then I understood it all:
Your vital democracy and love of men
And tolerance of life; and how the excess of these
Had wrought your sorrows in the days
When we were so poor, and the small of mind
Spoke of your sins and your connivance
With sinful men. You had lived it down,
Had triumphed over them, and you had grown
Prosperous in the world and had passed
Into an easy mastery of life and beyond the thought
Of further conquests for things.

As the Brahmins say no more you worshipped matter,
Or scarcely ghosts, or even the gods
With singleness of heart.
This day you worshipped Eternal Peace
Or Eternal Flame, with scarce a laugh or jest
To hide your worship; and I understood,
Seeing so many facets to you, why it was
Blind Condon always smiled to hear your voice,
And why it was in a green-room years ago
Booth turned to you, marking your face
From all the rest, and said "There is a man
Who might play Hamlet—better still Othello";
And why it was the women loved you; and the priest
Could feed his body and soul together drinking
A glass of beer and visiting with you. . . . . .

        Then something happened:
Your face grew smaller, your brow more narrow,
Dull fires burned in your eyes,
Your body shriveled, you walked with a cynical shuffle,
Your hands mixed the keys of life,
You had become a discord.
A monstrous hatred consumed you—
You had suffered the greatest wrong of all,
I knew and granted the wrong.
You had mounted up to sixty years, now breathing hard,
And just at the time that honor belonged to you
You were dishonored at the hands of a friend.
I wept for you, and still I wondered
If all I had grown to see in you and find in you
And love in you was just a fond illusion—
If after all I had not seen you aright as a boy:
Barbaric, hard, suspicious, cruel, redeemed
Alone by bubbling animal spirits—
Even these gone now, all of you smoke
Laden with stinging gas and lethal vapor. . . . . .
Then you came forth again like the sun after storm—
The deadly uric acid driven out at last
Which had poisoned you and dwarfed your soul—
So much for soul!
The last time I saw you
Your face was full of golden light,
Something between flame and the richness of flesh.

You were yourself again, wholly yourself.
And oh, to find you again and resume
Our understanding we had worked so long to reach—
You calm and luminant and rich in thought!
This time it seemed we said but "yes" or "no"—
That was enough; we smoked together
And drank a glass of wine and watched
The leaves fall sitting on the porch. . . . . .
Then life whirled me away like a leaf,
And I went about the crowded ways of New York.

And one night Alberta and I took dinner
At a place near Fourteenth Street where the music
Was like the sun on a breeze-swept lake
When every wave is a patine of fire,
And I thought of you not at all
Looking at Alberta and watching her white teeth
Bite off bits of Italian bread,
And watching her smile and the wide pupils
Of her eyes, electrified by wine
And music and the touch of our hands
Now and then across the table.
We went to her house at last.
And through a languorous evening.
Where no light was but a single candle,
We circled about and about a pending theme
Till at last we solved it suddenly in rapture
Almost by chance; and when I left
She followed me to the hall and leaned above
The railing about the stair for the farewell kiss—
And I went into the open air ecstatically,
With the stars in the spaces of sky between
The towering buildings, and the rush
Of wheels and clang of bells,
Still with the fragrance of her lips and cheeks
And glinting hair about me, delicate
And keen in spite of the open air.
And just as I entered the brilliant car
Something said to me you are dead—
I had not thought of you, was not thinking of you.
But I knew it was true, as it was
For the telegram waited me at my room. . . . . .
                I didn't come back.

I could not bear to see the breathless breath
Over your brow—nor look at your face—
However you fared or where
To what victories soever—
Vanquished or seemingly vanquished!

One of the first stories brought in by Ben Hecht was this one:

The American Family

BEN HECHT

THE dead fingers of spent passions, spent dreams, spent youth clutch
at the throat of the rising generation and preserve the integrity of
the American family. Not that there is a typical American family.
There is only the typical struggle between the dead and the living,
between the inert and hideous virtue of decayed souls and the rebel-
lious desires of their doomed progeny.

The ambitious and educated American mother is a forceful creature, a strong, powerful woman. As an individual she is dead. Once
she knew and had the desire for beauty. Dead fingers reached into
her heart and killed it. The force of which she was doomed to become a part crushed her. The conventions of the world are stronger
than its natural destinies. Those conventions—the conventions of the
family—are not of the man's making. Woman attends to her own
subjugation. She preserves the spirit of the family, struggles and
labors to keep it a unit, to keep its members alike. Moaning with
the tyrannical lust for possession she enfolds her daughter in her
arms. There are certain things in her daughter which must be killed.
There is a dawning of love for "impossible" things in her daughter's
heart. There is an awakened mental curiosity, a perceptible inclination to break from the oppressiveness of the surrounding dead. In
the night the daughter wonders and doubts. She would like "to get
away"—to go forth free of certain fiercely applied restrictions and
meet a different kind of folk, a different kind of thought. She would
like to be—to feel the things she is capable of. It is all vague. Always
revolt is vague and intangible for the daughters of women. Revolt
is for souls still living, and the living are weaker than the dead. The
living soul is a lone, individual force, its yearnings are ephemeral
and undefined. The mother knows what they are. The dead always
know what it is they have lost. And in this knowledge the mother
is strong. But the living cannot say to itself what it wishes to gain,
what it reaches to attain. Only in the stray geniuses of time has the

37

individual soul fought desperately and triumphantly for its preservation. And there is no genius in the daughter. There is merely the divine and natural instinct for self-realization. Once the mother felt it and it was killed. Now the daughter has caught the dread disease—the contamination which starts a cold sweat under the corset stays of society; the thing which brings down upon it for its destruction the phalanxes of fierce fatuities—the moribund mercenaries employed by the home for its defense and preservation.

Something happens to crystallize the revolt. It is a man outside the pale, a good man, a bad man. It is a book. It is a friend. Often the struggle is fought through little things too numerous to mention and the struggle itself too casual to classify. Sometimes it wages without a word; at other times there are blows. And at such times the enshrouding veils are torn aside. One can see the dead rise up, their pasty limbs dragging with the mould and slime of their couch. One can see them reaching their dead arms out, with the bloodless flesh hanging from them in shreds. One can watch them crawl on their bony feet and as they come close—these dead—the foul odor that issues from their sightless, twisted, rotted faces hangs like a grey smeared canopy above them.

They come. They take their stand at the mother's back. And the pitiful struggle is on.

It is the mother who strikes the blows. Her first weapon (she uses it like a poison) is her love. She calls it that. "You are my only happiness," she cries. "I have given you everything, a part of me, all you have needed. I have sacrificed everything for you. All my dreams have been for you. O, how can you permit anything to come between us?"

The daughter listens. There is a selfish ring to it. But love must be forgiven for selfishness. In the schools and the churches the preliminaries of the struggle have been insidiously fought. Children owe duties to their parents and not to themselves. It was what the daughter learned at school. It is what she read between the lines of her books and heard from the lips of all around her. And now it is the murmur that rolls into her ears. It is the odor of the dead.

Day after day the mother strikes with this weapon. Her red, furious eyes dripping tears, she moans it out. Her voice is like the yelp of a frantic animal. Her voice is like the whine of a woebegone face. Her voice is cold and hard and hollow like the echo in a tomb.

The beauty that has come to her daughter is a fragile thing. The

loveliness she visioned is the most delicately mortal of life's treasures. Fiercely the mother hurls herself against it, hurls the reproaches of her dead soul, the recriminations of her entombed spirit—the odors of the dead . . . And her weapons are tangible things. They are sentences. They are the moral perversions with which the family unit always has fought for its preservation. They are tried things, prophetic precedents. And the beauty in the normal being is an indefinite force—a vagueness. It has no weapons with which to strike. Triumphant revolt is only for martyrs and artists. It is the losing force in normal existence.

Gradually it becomes clouded in the daughter's soul. She feels unclean. She imagines it is the beauty which is unclean. She does not know that it is the uncleanliness of the dead—the uncleanliness of her mother revealed to her in her heart by the divine light that is dying within herself. An agony comes into her. The struggle narrows to pain. Cold things reach at her heart. It leaps and flutters. She stands, her face white and a look of uncanny suffering about her eyes. The dead fingers grip fast.

The mother, moaning, shuddering, her eyes gleaming, enfolds her daughter in her arms. "I dare you to take her from me," she cries out to the man, to the friend, to the book, to the world of beauty, whatever it is toward which her daughter inclined for the divine instant of awakened soul. "I dare you. I dare you."

"Nothing can ever take me from you," the daughter weeps. Death.

Tears, a form of decomposition now, roll from her cheeks. The struggle is over. The unit has been preserved and now one may look at the unit and see what it is. The rotted figures of the dead have dragged their shredded flesh back to the graves.

There are different kinds of families. Only in the struggle between the dead and the living do they become the same even when the contestants differ. I will describe only one type. Perhaps it is *the* American family; perhaps it is not.

It is the family which considers culture a matter of polished fingernails and emotional suppression and dinner table aphorisms, puns and the classics in half morocco. It has bound volumes of *The Philistine* or some other mawkish philosophical twaddle on view in the bookcase. It—the spirit of this family—knows the titles of books memorized from literary reviews in current magazines and will discourse bitingly on the malicious trend of these radical volumes from the sweeping knowledge she has of their titles. In the matter of music the spirit of this family "plays safe." It will characterize as "tinkly" or "syrupy" anything melodious which secretly pleases it. The rather humorous falseness of its culture is inexhaustible.

Introspection is an indecent as well as impossible thing to the spirit of this family. To look into her soul and see the diseased and dead things that fill it is naturally impossible and naturally indecent. Dostoevsky calls man an animal who can get used to anything. And a man's adjustment to hideous things is not so final as a woman's.

For the spirit of this family to reveal an honest reaction when it is contrary to the approved artificial demands of a situation is as heinous an exhibition of bad taste as to uncover a thigh. But luckily this concealing of honest feeling is not often required. The spirit of this family is incapable in the main of honest feeling. That is a part of the beauty killed long ago in her, a part of the beauty she killed in the daughter, a part of the beauty the daughter will strangle in her own children. And one of the compensations for dead souls is that they naturally feel dishonest feeling and do not have to suffer with a realization of hypocrisy.

This family thinks of virtue in terms of legs. This family regards art and truth with a modulated leer. It is crudely cynical of everything outside its range. It sneers and pooh-hoos, it ostracizes and condemns. It is vulgarly contemptuous of the factors in life superior to it. The spirit of this family would have shrieked in outrage at the presence of Verlaine in its home—unless he could have reflected social distinction on it. It would have closed the doors to Ibsen,— except for the social distinction,—to every triumphant soul that had escaped the dead fingers and realized itself. And by some inexplicable trick of self-adjustment the spirit of this family looks upon thought as an undesirable affectation.

Social success means to this family a speaking acquaintance with any wealthier unit which originally considered itself "above" this family. Moral success means to this family an exemption from the prosecution of the forces it has reared for its own protection—keeping out of jail, out of scandal-monging newspapers, out of the malicious after-dinner gossip of its friends.

Of an evening you will find this family in the living room. The husband and father reads a newspaper. He has worked in his office all day and is tired. Life long ago ceased to mean anything to him. He is an animal husk in fine linen. He has his little prejudices and his little conventions. Indeed, he is a part of the system of the unit

40

but not much interested in it. He never was possessed of the capacity for beauty which his women folk once had and which they found it necessary to kill in each other. Man is a more natural part of the world's ugliness. He is coarser stuff in general. For him it is not necessary to wage any struggle. He accepted matrimony because of a concentrated physical curiosity in one woman, and because it was the thing to do at his age. Love suffered epileptic dissolution in the nuptial couch. Honor toward his woman expired when the mysteries of her flesh paled. Obedience is his natural state—that is, long ago he established a line of least resistance and inoculated his women folk with the fable that adherence to *this* line was the obedience and respect he owed them. If a latent instinct awakens suddenly in him he indulges himself. He finds it rather difficult to be immoral, but as he hesitates a latent strength overcomes his fear and thus he is able to be immoral and unfaithful to his own convenient restrictions in a natural manner and with no great loss of sleep.

One man in ten thousand inherits the beauty of the woman who bore him and he becomes an artist. It is not necessary for him to revolt. His fathers have taken care of that. There is an assured place in the world for him—not in the living room here in front of the fireplace but elsewhere, in places of which poets sing.

The family man keeps posted. He knows what is going on in the world but does not understand it. He is not capable of understanding. But sometimes understanding and reason coincide with his prejudices and he is then as liable to hold minority views as not. He is dry, sometimes clever. But always he jogs, jogs, jogs along. He can even sleep night after night in the same bed with his wife without feeling annoyance. His bluntedness is complete. Dostoevsky is right.

His wife and the mother of his children is a part of the furniture of existence for him. In his own way he is quite dead, but it was not necessary to kill him. If his son revolts, the instinct of his mother is communicated to him and he fights. He borrows the mother's weapons and he blasphemes in a half-hearted way about the duty to parents. But the beauty which the mother found easy to kill in the daughter usually discovers a hardier citadel in the son and usually he carries it safely into the world.

The room—this living room—is dimly and "artistically" lighted. The fire in the grate glows. The daughter sits in a corner speaking to a friend. At the other side sits the father—reading blankly. The wife enters. She surveys the scene from the doorway with a feeling of warm satisfaction. She comes in and sits down. They talk about nothing, they think about nothing. The daughter and the young man, beneath the smooth surface of the artificial moments, are playing at the eternal indecency. The mother leads the conversation. Neighbors are discussed. Friends are derided. Social inferiors are laughed to scorn. Social superiors are spoken of with adulation and veneration. At last the father climbs to his bed like an ox. He is tired, poor fellow. The mother follows him into the bedroom. A victor, utterly triumphant, she hugs her dead soul to herself and smiles. The daughter retires after being desperately kissed by the physically curious young man, and she lies awake a while wishing in moments of provoked sex that she too was married and meditating in calmer spaces upon the advantages of the family unit, the fireplace, the party calls. O, this daughter! She is the one who had the vision of beauty. She is the one whose soul sang for a day with the capacity for all the world's loveliness. Honesty, purity, fineness burned in her with their divine radiance. The lights are turned out. Death reigns supreme.

But two months later Ben Hecht was writing lyrically of "the white face of a dead love . . . a white face like a dim sorrow":

Autumn Song

BEN HECHT

MY heart scatters tears over the dark day. The dull silvered poplar leaves float in the air like dead butterflies.

It is the autumn come again, speaking with its soft-tongued winds to the trees and to me.

It is cold. I have lost my warmth. I have lost thee. And the autumn has come again to tell me of it.

Listen to the sad-tongued winds. See the storm faltering in the street. It is cold.

It is the autumn come again, the autumn in whose wild sad treasures we once laughed; once when your hot hands reached out to me like a bright cry mocking the somber lisping of the twilight season.

Where are the songs I sang, the songs that leaped out of flame? Do they echo still in your listening ears? Do they fall like warm tears in your heart?

See the winds droop wearily into the trembling tree arms. See the street grows pale. A dying panoply drifts across the grey-girthed sky.

Ho, Life, I have still a song for you. Though you come whispering to me from the golden tombs of youth, from the scarlet graves of love, I will make of the lament you bring me—music. I will make of the dull tears you bring me—lyrics. I will clothe the grey ghosts of sorrow in rich trappings.

For it is only she who hath died. It is only she whom I loved with all my soul. Though my heart scatter tears over the dark day they are the tears of plenty. For her death hath enriched me.

For the autumn is come again speaking with its soft-tongued winds to the trees and to me things I have never heard before; things that her white breasts never told me; things that her burning lips never said to me; wild, sad things that the flame from whence my songs once leaped never held for me.

The dull silvered poplar leaves float in the air like dead butterflies, and they are beautiful.

In my enthusiasm for the Imagists I composed an article which consisted entirely of their sharp pictures. John Gould Fletcher wrote that it was "a splendid thing to have done."

Imagism

MARGARET ANDERSON

SEA orchards, and lilac on the water, and color dragged up from the sand; drenched grasses, and early roses, and wind-harps in the cedar trees; flame-flowers, and the sliding rain; frail sea-birds, and blue still rocks, and bright winds treading the sunlight; silver hailstones, and the scattering of gold crocus petals; blackbirds in the grass, and fountains in the rain; lily shadows, and green cold waves, and the rose-fingered moon; pine cones, and yellow grasses, and a restless green rout of stars; cloud whirls, and the pace of winds; trees on the hill, and the far ecstasy of burning noons; lotus pools, and the gold petal of the moon; night-born poppies, and the silence of beauty, and the perfume of invisible roses; white winds and cold sea ripples; blossom spray, and narcissus petals on the black earth; little silver birds, and blue and gold-veined hyacinths; river pools of sky, and grains of sand as clear as wine. . . .

. . . dream-colored wings, and whispers among the flowering rushes; of moonlit tree-tops, and the gaiety of flowers; brown fading hills, and the moving mist; sea rose, and the light upon the poplars;

43

shaken dew, and the haunts of the sun, and white sea-gulls above the waves; bright butterflies in the corn, and a dust of emerald and gold; broken leaves, and the rose and white flag-stones; sea iris with petals like shells, and the scent of lilacs heavy with stillness; scarlet nasturtiums, and dry reeds that shiver in the grasses; slim colorless poppies, and the sweet salt camphor flowers; gold and blue and mauve, and a white rose of flame; pointed pines, and orange-colored rose leaves; sunshine slipping through young green, and the flaring moon through the oak leaves; wet dawns, and a blue flower of the evening; butterflies over green meadows, and deep blue seas of air, and hyacinths hidden in a far valley. . . .

. . . harsh rose and iris-flowers painted blue; white waters, and the winds of the upper air; green wine held up in the sun, and rigid myrrhbuds scented and stinging; the lisp of reeds, and the loose ripples of meadow grasses; mists on the mountains, and clear frost on the grass blade; frail-headed poppies, and sea-grass tangled with shore-grass; the humming brightness of the air, and the sky darting through like blue rain; strewn petals on restless water, and pale green glacier-rivers; somber pools, and sun-drenched slopes; autumn's gold and spring's green; red pine-trunks, and bird cries in hollow trees; cool spaces filled with shadow, and white hammocks in the sun; green glimmer of apples in an orchard, and hawthorn odorous with blossom; lamps in a wash of rain, and the desperate sun that struggles through sea mist; lavender water, and faded stars; many-foamed ways, and the blue and buoyant air; grey-green fastnesses of the great deeps; a cream moon on bare black trees; wet leaves, and the dust that drifts over the court-yard; moon-paint on a colorless house.

. . . Pagan temples and old blue Chinese gardens; old pagodas glittering across green trees, and the ivory of silence; vast dark trees that flow like blue veils of tears into the water; little almond trees that the frost has hurt, and bitter purple willows; fruit dropping through the thick air, and wine in heavy craters painted black and red; purple and gold and sable, and a gauze of misted silver; blue death-mountains, and yellow pulse-beats in the darkness; naked lightnings, and boats in the gloom; strange fish, and golden sorceries; red-purple grapes, and Assyrian wine; fruits from Arcadia, and incense to Poseidon; swallow-blue halls, and a chamber under Lycia's coast; stars swimming like goldfish, and the sword of the moonlight; torn lanterns that flutter, and an endless procession of lamps; sleepy temples, and strange skies, and pilgrims of autumn; tired shepherds with lanterns, and the fire of the great moon; the lowest pine branch drawn across the disk of the sun; Phoenecian stuffs and silks that are outspread; the gods garlanded in wistaria; white grave goddesses, and loves in Phryggia; wounds of light, and terrible rituals, and temples soothed by the sun to ruin; the valley of Aetna, and the Doric singing. . . .

. . . The moon dragging the flood tide, and an old sorrow that has put out the sun; whirling laughter, and the thunder of horses plunging; old tumults, and the gloom of dreams; strong loneliness, and the hollow where pain was; the rich laughter of the forest, and the bitter sea; the earth that receives the slanting rain; lost treasure, and the violent gloom of night; all proud things, and the light of thy beauty. . . . Souls of blood, and hearts aching with wonder; the kindness of people—country folk and sailors and fishermen; all the roots of the earth, and a perpetual sea. . . .

Portrait of Theodore Dreiser

ARTHUR DAVISON FICKE

There were gilded Chinese dragons
And tinkling danglers of glass
And dirty marble-topped tables
Around us, that late night-hour.
You ate steadily and silently
From a huge bowl of chop-suey
Of repellent aspect;
While I,— I, and another,—
Told you that you had the style neither of William Morris
Nor of Walter Pater.

And it was perfectly true . . . .
But you continued to occupy yourself
With your quarts of chop-suey.
And somehow you reminded me
Of nothing so much as of the knitting women
Who implacably counted stitches while the pride of France
Went up to death.

Tonight I am alone,
A long way from that Chinese restaurant,
A long way from wherever you are.
And I find it difficult to recall to my memory

The image of your large laboring inexpressive face.
For I have just turned the last page
Of a book of yours—
A book large and superficially inexpressive,—like yourself.
It has not, any more than the old ones,
The style of Pater.
But now there are passing before me
Interminable figures in tangled procession—
Proud or cringing, starved with desire or icy,
Hastening toward a dream of triumph or fleeing from a dream
   of doom,—
Passing—passing—passing
Through a world of shadows,
Through a chaotic and meaningless anarchy,
Under heavy clouds of terrific gloom
Or through ravishing flashes of knife-edged sunlight—
Passing—passing—passing—
Their heads haloed with immortal illusion,—
The terrible and beautiful, cruel and wonder-laden illusion
   of life.

Theodore Dreiser

JOHN COWPER POWYS

IN estimating the intrinsic value of a writer like Theodore Dreiser, it is advisable to indulge in a little gentle introspection. . . . It is true that all criticism resolves itself ultimately into a matter of taste; —but one has to discover what one's taste really is; and that is not always easy.

Taste is a living thing, an organic thing. It submits to the laws of growth; and its growth is fostered or retarded by many extraneous influences. In regard to the appreciation of new and original works of art, it belongs to the inherent nature of taste that it should be enlarged, transmuted, and undergo the birth-pangs of a species of re-creation. In the presence of a work of art that is really unusual, in an attempt to appreciate a literary effect that has never appeared before, one's taste necessarily suffers a certain embarrassment and uneasiness. It suffers indeed sometimes a quite extreme discomfort. This is inevitable. This is right. This means that the creative energy in the new thing is getting to work upon us, unloosening our prejudices and enlarging our scope. Such a process is attended by exquisite intellectual excitement. It is also attended by a certain rending and tearing of personal vanity.

One is too apt to confuse the existing synthesis of one's aesthetic instincts with the totality of one's being; and this is a fatal blunder; for who can fathom the reach of *that* circumference? And it is of the nature of all syntheses to change and grow.

Yet, on the other hand, nothing is more ridiculous and ineffective than the kind of hand-to-mouth criticism which attempts to eliminate its own past, and to snatch at the glow and glamour of a work of art, as it were *"de vacuo,"* and out of misty clouds. If one wishes to catch the secret of true criticism; if one's criticism is to be something more than a mere howl of senseless condemnation or yawp of still more senseless praise; one must attempt to do what Goethe and Saint-Beuve and Brandes and Pater were always doing: that is to say, to make every use of every tradition, *our own,* as well as that of classical authority;—and then carry all this a little, just a little, *further;* giving it the shudder and the thrilling interest of the process of organic growth. . . .

In dealing with a creative quality as unusual and striking as that of Theodore Dreiser, it is of absolutely no critical value to content ourselves with a crude physical disturbance on the surface of our minds, whether such disturbance is favorable or unfavorable to the writer. It is, for instance, quite irrelevant to hurl condemnation upon a work like The *"Genius"* because it is largely preoccupied with sex. It is quite equally irrelevant to lavish enthusiastic laudations upon it because of this preoccupation. A work of art is not good because it speaks daringly and openly about things that shock certain minds. It is not bad because it avoids all mention of such things. . . .

The *"Genius"* is an epic work. It has the epic rather than the dramatic quality; it has the epic rather than the mystic, or symbolic, quality. And strictly speaking, Dreiser's novels, especially the latter ones, are the only novels in America, are the only novels, as a matter of fact, in England or America, which possess this quality. It is quite properly in accordance with the epic attitude of mind, with the epic quality in art, this reduction of the more purely human episodes to a proportionate insignificance compared with the general surge and volume of the life-stream. It is completely in keeping with

47

the epic quality that there should be no far-fetched psychology, no quivering suspensions on the verge of the unknown.

Dreiser is concerned with the mass and weight of the stupendous life-tide; the life-tide as it flows forward, through vast panoramic stretches of cosmic scenery. Both in respect to human beings, and in respect to his treatment of inanimate objects, this is always what most dominatingly interests him. You will not find in Dreiser's books those fascinating arrests of the onward-sweeping tide, those delicate pauses and expectancies, in backwaters and enclosed gardens, where persons, with diverting twists in their brains, murmur and meander at their ease, protected from the great stream. Nobody in the Dreiser-world is so protected; nobody is so privileged. The great stream sweeps them all forward, sweeps them all away; and not they, but *It,* must be regarded as the hero of the tale.

It is precisely this quality, this subordination of the individual to the deep waters that carry him, which makes Dreiser so peculiarly the American writer. Perhaps this is one of the reasons why he has had a more profoundly appreciative hearing in England than in the United States. It was so with Walt Whitman in his earlier days. To get the adequate perspective for a work so entirely epical it seems necessary to have the Atlantic as a modifying foreground. Americans—so entirely *in it* themselves—are naturally, unless they possess the Protean faculty of the editor of Reedy's *Mirror,* unable to see the thing in this cosmic light. They are misled by certain outstanding details—the sexual scenes, for instance; or the financial scenes,— and are prevented by these, as by the famous "Catalogues" in Whitman, from getting the proportionate vision.

The true literary descendants of the author of the *Leaves of Grass* are undoubtedly Theodore Dreiser and Edgar Masters. These two, and these two alone, though in completely different ways, possess that singular "beyond-good-and-evil" touch which the epic form of art requires. It was just the same with Homer and Vergil, who were as naturally the epic children of aristocratic ages, as these are of a democratic one.

Achilles is not really a very attractive figure—take him all in all; and we remember how scandalously Aeneas behaved to Dido. The ancient epic writers, writing for an aristocracy, caught the world-stream from a poetic angle. The modern epic writers, writing for a democracy, catch it from a realistic one. But it is the same world-stream; and in accordance with the epic vision there is the same subordination of the individual to the cosmic tide. This is essentially a dramatic, rather than an epic epoch, and that is why so many of us are bewildered and confused by the Dreiser method.

The *"Genius"* is a long book. But it might have been three times as long. It might begin anywhere and stop anywhere. It is the Prose-Iliad of the American Scene; and, like that other, it has a right to cut out its segment of the shifting panorama at almost any point.

And so with the style of the thing. It is a ridiculous mis-statement for critics to say that Dreiser has no style. It is a charming irony, on his own part, to belittle his style. He has, as a matter of fact, a very definite and a very effective style. It is a style that lends itself to the huge indifferent piling up of indiscriminate materials, quite as admirably as that gracious poetical one of the old epic-makers lent itself to their haughtier and more aristocratic purpose. One would recognize a page of Dreiser's writings as infallibly as one would recognize a page of Hardy's. The former *relaxes* his medium to the extreme limit and the latter *tightens* his; but they both have their "manner." A paragraph written by Dreiser would never be mistaken for anyone else's. If for no other peculiarity Dreiser's style is remarkable for the shamelessness with which it adapts itself to the drivel of ordinary conversation. In the Dreiser books—especially in the later ones, where in my humble opinion he is feeling more firmly after his true way,—people are permitted to say those things which they actually do say in real life—things that make you blush and howl, so soaked in banality and ineptitude are they. In the true epic manner Dreiser gravely puts down all these fatuous observations, until you feel inclined to cry aloud for the maddest, the most fantastic, the most affected Osconian wit, to serve as an antidote.

But one knows very well he is right. People don't in ordinary life —certainly not in ordinary democratic life—talk like Oscar Wilde, or utter deep ironic sayings in the style of Matthew Arnold. They don't really—let this be well understood—concentrate their feelings in bitter pungent spasmodic outbursts, as those Rabelaisian persons in Guy de Maupassant. They just gabble and gibber and drivel; at least that is what they do in England and America. The extraordinary language which the lovers in Dreiser—we use the term "lovers" in large sense—use to one another might well make an aesthetic-minded person howl with nervous rage. But then,—and who does not know it?—the obsession of the sex-illusion is above everything else a thing that makes idiots of people; a thing that makes them talk like

Simple Simons. In real life lovers don't utter those wonderful pregnant sayings which leap to their lips in our subtle symbolic dramas. They just burble and blather and blurt forth whatever drivelling nonsense comes into their heads. Dreiser is the true master of the modern American Prose-Epic just because he is not afraid of the weariness, the staleness, the flatness, and unprofitableness of actual human conversation. In reading the great ancient poetic epics one is amazed at the "naivete" with which these haughty persons—these gods and demi-gods—express their emotional reactions. It is "carried off," of course, there, by the sublime heightening of the style; but it produces just the same final impression,—of the insignificance of the individual, whether mortal or immortal, compared with the torrent of Fate which sweeps them all along.

And the same thing applies to Dreiser's attitude towards "good and evil" and towards the problem of the "supernatural." All other modern writers array themselves on this side or that. They either defend traditional morality or they attack it. They are anxious, at all costs, to give their work dramatic intensity; they struggle to make it ironical, symbolical, mystical—God knows what! But Dreiser neither attacks morality nor defends immorality. In the true Epic manner he puts himself aside, and permits the great mad Hurly-Burly to rush pell-mell past him and write its own whirligig runes at its own careless pleasure. Even Zola himself was not such a realist. Zola had a purpose;—the purpose of showing what a Beast the human animal is! Dreiser's people are not beasts; and they shock our aesthetic sensibilities quite as often by their human sentiment as they do by their lapses into lechery.

To a European mind there is something incredibly absurd in the notion that these Dreiser books are immoral.

Unlike the majority of French and Russian writers Dreiser is not interested in the pathology of vice. He is too deeply imbued with the great naive epic spirit to stop and linger in these curious by-paths. He holds Nature—in her normal moods—to be sufficiently remarkable.

It is the same with his attitude towards the "supernatural." The American Prose-Epic were obviously false to reality if the presence of the supernatural were not felt. It is felt and felt very powerfully; but it is kept in its place. Like Walt Whitman's stellar constellations, it suffices for those who belong to it, it is right enough where it is—we do not want it any nearer!

Because the much-tossed wanderer, Eugene Witla, draws a certain consolation, at the last, from Christian Science, only a very literal person would accuse the author of The "Genius" of being a convert to the faith. To omit Christian Science from any prose-epic of American life would be to falsify the picture out of personal prejudice. Dreiser has no prejudices except the prejudice of finding the normal man and normal woman, shuffled to and fro by the normal forces of life, an interesting and arresting spectacle. To some among us such a spectacle is not interesting. We must have the excitement of the unusual, the shock of the abnormal. Well! There are plenty of European writers ready to gratify this taste. Dreiser is not a European writer. He is an American writer. The life that interests him, and interests him passionately, is the life of America. It remains to be seen whether the life of America interests Americans!

It is really quite important to get the correct point of view with regard to Dreiser's "style." The *negative* qualities in this style of his are indeed as important as the positive ones. He is so epical, so objective, so concrete and indifferent, that he is quite content when the great blocked-out masses of his work lift themselves from the obscure womb of being and take shape before him. When they have done this,—when these piled-up materials and portentous groups of people have limned themselves against the grey background,—he himself stands aside, like some dim demiurgic forger in the cosmic blast-furnace, and mutters queer commentaries upon what he sees. He utters these commentaries through the lips of his characters—Cowperwood, say, or Witla—or even some of the less important ones;—and broken and incoherent enough they are!

But what matter! The huge epic canvas is stretched out there before us. The vast cyclopean edifice lifts its shadowy bulk towards the grey sky. The thing has been achieved. The creative spirit has breathed upon the waters. Resting from his titanic labor, what matter if this Demiurge drowses, and with an immense humorous indifference permits his characters to nod too, and utter strange words in their dreams!

In the spring of 1915 Rupert Brooke came to Chicago. Though he could not give us any poems, being under contract to an English publisher, we spent many evenings with him and I took him to Eugene Hutchinson's studio in the Fine Arts Building to be photographed. The result was a classic.

51

The following poem is a memory of an evening in the studio. "Maurice" is Maurice Browne, director of the Little Theatre in Chicago.

Rupert Brooke

(A Memory)

ARTHUR DAVISON FICKE

One night—the last we were to have of you—
High up above the city's giant roar
We sat around you on the generous floor—
Since chairs were lame or stony or too few—
And as you read, and the low music grew
In exquisite tendrils twining the heart's core,
All the conjecture we had felt before
Flashed into torch-flame, and at last we knew.

And Maurice, who in silence long has hidden
A voice like yours, became a wreck of joy
To inarticulate ecstasies beguiled.
And you, as from some secret world now bidden
To make return, stared up, and like a boy
Blushed suddenly, and looked at us, and smiled.

Poems

(From the Greek of Myrrhine of Mitulene, and Konallis; translated by Richard Aldington)

I

Hierocleia, bring hither my silver vine-leaf-carved armlet and the
  mirror graven with two Maenads,
For my heart is burned to dust with longing for Konallis;
And this is the silver armlet which pressed into her side when I held
  her,
And before this mirror she bound up her golden-hyacinth-curled
  hair, sitting in the noon sunlight.

II

I, Konallis, am but a goat-girl dwelling on the violet hills of Korinthos,
But going down to the city a marvellous thing befell me;
For the beautiful-silver-fingered hetaira, Myrrhine, held me night-
  long in her couch,
Teaching me to stretch wide my arms to receive her strange burning
  caresses.

52

Fair young men have brought me presents of silver caskets and white
     mirrors,
Gold for my hair and long lemon-colored chitons and dew-soft per-
     fumes of sweet herbs.
Their bodies are whiter than Leucadian foam and delicate are their
     flute-girls,
But the wild sleepless nightingales cry in the darkness even as I for
     Konallis.

IV

We, Konallis and Myrrhine, dedicate to thee, Proserpine, two white
     torches of wax,
For thou didst watch over our purple-embroidered couch all night;
Was it thou who gavest the sweetness of sharp caresses?
For at midday when we awoke we laughed to see black poppies
     blooming beneath our eyes.

V

The doves sleep beside the slow-murmuring cool fountain, red-five-
     petalled roses of Paestum strew the chequered marble;
A flute-girl whispers the dear white ode of Sappho, and Hierocleia
     by the pool
Smiles to see the smooth blue-sky-reflecting water mirror her shining
     body;
But my eyelids are shunned by sleep that is whiter than beautiful
     morning, for Konallis is not here.

VI

O reeds, move softly and make keen bewildering music,
For I fear lest Arkadian Pan should seize Myrrhine as she comes
     from the city;
O Artemis, shed thy light across the peaks to hasten her coming,
But do thou, Eros, hold back thy white radiance till love be content.

VII

Last night Zeus sent swift rain upon the blue-grey rocks,
But Konallis held me close to her pear-pointed breasts.

VIII

Sappho, Sappho, long ago the dust of earth mingled with the dust of
     thy dear limbs,
And only little clay figures, painted with Tyrian red, with crocus,
     and with Lydian gold,

Remain to show thy beauty; but thy wild lovely songs shall last for
ever.
Soon we too shall join Anaktoria and Kudno and kiss thy pale
shadowy fingers.

IX

When Myrrhine departed I, weeping passionately, kissed her golden-
wrought knees, saying:
"O, Myrrhine, by what god shall I keep the memory of thy caresses?"
But she, bending down like golden, smiling Aphrodite, whispered
to me;
And lying here in the sunlight among the reeds I remember her
words.

X

Hierocleia, do thou weave white-violet-crowns and spread mountain-
haunting lilies upon my couch,
For Konallis comes! and shut the door against the young men for
this is a sharper love.

XI

This is the feast of Iacchus; open wide the gates, O Hierocleia;
Fill the kraters and kuathoi with sweet unmixed wine and snow;
bring thyrsus-wands,
And crowns of pale ivy and violets; let the flute-players begin the
phallic hymn
While the ten girl-slaves, drunken with the god, dance to the young
men.

XII

Hedulia now lies with Myrrhine who aforetime was my lover,
But seeing Hedulia she forgot me, and I lie on the threshold
weeping.
O marble threshold, thou are not so white nor so hard as her breasts,
receive my tears
While the mute stars turn overhead and the owls cry from the
cypresses.

XIII

Wandering in tears about the city I came to the dark temple of
Priapus;
The tall, naked, scented-tressed priestesses taught me the mysteries,
And I lay between Guathina and Leuke and afterwards Chrusea and
Anthea;

54

But now I worship the god on the mountain slopes, yet not unforgetful of Myrrhine.

XIV

This is the tomb of Konallis; Korinthos was her city and Kleobulina
    bore her,
Having lain in sweet love with Sesocrates, the son of Menophiles.
I lived three and twenty years, and then sudden sickness bore me to
    Dis
So they laid me here with my silver armlets, my gold comb, my chain
    and with little painted figures.
In my life I was happy, knowing many sorts of love and none evil.
If you are a lover, scatter dust, and call me "dear one" and speak one
    last "Hail."

Telos.

The Reader Critic

Witter Bynner, Windsor, Vermont:

I wish I could honor the Imagists as you do. Hueffer wrote *On Heaven* (not imagistic); and Pound wrote well before he affected a school . . . Pound has a rhythm he can't kill. But none of them, except Hueffer, says anything worth mentioning. They build poems around phrases, usually around adjectives. George Meredith has thousands of imagist poems incidental to each of his novels. But he knows their use and their beauty. These people wring tiny beauties dry. I can imagine a good poet using their methods on occasion, but he wouldn't be so damn conscious about it. On the whole, the Imagists strike me as being purveyors of more or less potent cosmetics, their whole interest being in the cosmetic itself, not even in its application. Poetry gave signs of becoming poetry again and of touching life—when these fellows showed up, to make us all ridiculous.

"The Struggle" is not the first story Sherwood Anderson gave us, but I have chosen it as the first to represent him.

The Struggle

SHERWOOD ANDERSON

THE story came to me from a woman, met on a train. The car was crowded, and I took the seat beside her. There was a man in the offing, who belonged with her,—a slender, girlish figure of a man, in a heavy brown canvas coat such as teamsters wear in the winter. He moved up and down in the aisle of the car, wanting my place by the woman's side, but I did not know that at the time.

The woman had a heavy face and a thick nose. Something had happened to her. She had been struck a blow or had a fall. Nature could never have made a nose so broad and thick and ugly. She talked to me in very good English. I suspect now that she was temporarily weary of the man in the brown canvas coat, that she had travelled with him for days, perhaps weeks, and was glad of the chance to spend a few hours in the company of some one else.

Everyone knows the feeling of a crowded train in the middle of the night. We ran along through western Iowa and eastern Nebraska. It had rained for days and the fields were flooded. In the clear night the moon came out and the scene outside the car-window was strange and in an odd way very beautiful. You get the feeling: the black bare trees standing up in clusters as they do out in that country, the pools of water with the moon reflected and running quickly as it does when the train hurries along, the rattle of the car-trucks, the lights in isolated farmhouses, and occasionally the clustered lights of a town as the train rushed through it into the west.

The woman had just come out of war-ridden Poland, had got out of that stricken land with her husband by God knows what miracles of effort. She made me feel the war, that woman did, and she told me the tale that I want to tell to you.

I don't remember the beginning of our talk, nor can I tell you of how the strangeness of my mood grew to match her mood, until the story she told became a part of the mystery of the still night outside the car-window and very pregnant with meaning to me.

There was a company of Polish refugees moving along a road in Poland in charge of a German. The German was a man of perhaps fifty, with a beard. As I got him, he was much such a man as might be professor of foreign languages in a college in our country, say at Des Moines, Iowa, or Springfield, Ohio. He would be sturdy and strong of body and given to the eating of rather rank foods, as such men are. Also he would be a fellow of books and in his thinking inclined toward the ranker philosophies. He was dragged into the war because he was a German, and had steeped his soul in the German philosophy of might. Faintly, I fancy, there was another notion in his head that kept bothering him, and so to serve his government with a whole heart he read books that would reestablish his feeling for the strong, terrible thing for which he fought. Because he was past fifty he was not on the battle-line, but was in charge of the refugees, taking them out of their destroyed village to a camp near a railroad where they could be fed.

The refugees were peasants, all except the woman in the American train with me and her mother, an old woman of sixty-five. They had been small land-owners and the others in their party were women who had worked on their estate. Then there was the one man, my companion's lover, weak in body and with bad eyes.

Along a country road in Poland went this party in charge of the German, who tramped heavily along, urging them forward. He was brutal in his insistence, and the old woman of sixty-five, who was a kind of leader of the refugees, was almost equally brutal in her constant refusal to go forward. In the rainy night she stopped in the muddy road and her party gathered about her. Like a stubborn old horse she shook her head and muttered Polish words. "I want to be let alone, that's what I want. All I want in the world is to be let alone," she said, over and over; and then the German came up, and putting his hand on her back pushed her along, so that their progress through the dismal night was a constant repetition of the stopping, her muttered words, and his pushing. They hated each other with whole-hearted hatred, that old Polish woman and the German.

The party came to a clump of trees on the bank of a shallow stream. The German took hold of the old woman's arm and dragged her through the stream while the others followed. Over and over she said the words: "I want to be let alone. All I want in the world is to be let alone."

In the clump of trees the German started a fire. With incredible efficiency he had it blazing high in a few minutes, taking the matches and even some bits of dry wood from a little rubber-lined pouch carried in his inside coat-pocket. Then he got out tobacco, and, sitting down on the protruding root of a tree, smoked, and stared at the refugees, clustered about the old woman on the opposite side of the fire.

The German went to sleep. That was what started his trouble. He slept for an hour, and when he awoke the refugees were gone. You can imagine him jumping up and tramping heavily back through the shallow stream and along the muddy road to gather his party together again. He would be angry through and through, but he would not be alarmed. It was only a matter, he knew, of going far enough back along the road, as one goes back along a road for strayed cattle.

And then, when the German came up to the party, he and the old woman began to fight. She stopped muttering the words about being let alone and sprang at him. One of her old hands gripped his beard and the other buried itself in the thick skin of his neck.

The struggle in the road lasted a long time. The German was tired and not as strong as he looked, and there was that faint thing in him that kept him from hitting the old woman with his fist. He took hold of her thin shoulders and pushed, and she pulled. The struggle was like a man trying to lift himself by his boot-straps. The two fought and were full of the determination that will not stop fighting, but they were not very strong physically.

And so their two souls began to struggle. The woman in the train made me understand that quite clearly, although it may be difficult to get the sense of it over to you. I had the night and the mystery of the moving train to help me. It was a physical thing, the fight of the two souls in the dim light of the rainy night on that deserted muddy road. The air was full of the struggle, and the refugees gathered about and stood shivering. They shivered with cold and weariness, of course, but also with something else. In the air, everywhere about them, they could feel the vague something going on. The woman said that she would gladly have given her life to have it stopped, or to have some one strike a light, and that her man felt the same way. It was like two winds struggling, she said, like a soft yielding cloud become hard and trying vainly to push another cloud out of the sky.

Then the struggle ended and the old woman and the German fell down exhausted in the road. The refugees gathered about and waited. They thought something more was going to happen, knew in fact something more would happen. The feeling they had persisted, you see, and they huddled together and perhaps whimpered a little.

What happened is the whole point of the story. The woman in the train explained it very clearly. She said that the two souls, after struggling, went back into the two bodies, but that the soul of the old woman went into the body of the German and the soul of the German into the body of the old woman.

After that, of course, everything was quite simple. The German sat down by the road and began shaking his head and saying he wanted to be let alone, declared that all he wanted in the world was

58

to be let alone, and the Polish woman took papers out of his pocket and began driving her companions back along the road, driving them harshly and brutally along, and when they grew weary, pushing them with her hands.

There was more of the story after that. The woman's lover, who had been a school-teacher, took the papers and got out of the country, taking his sweetheart with him. But my mind has forgotten the details. I only remember the German sitting by the road and muttering that he wanted to be let alone, and the old tired mother-in-Poland saying the harsh words and forcing her weary companions to march through the night back into their own country.

Two Poems

CARL SANDBURG

GONE

Everybody loved Chick Lorimer in our town.
    Far off
    Everybody loved her.
So we all love a wild girl keeping a hold
    On a dream she wants.
Nobody knows now where Chick Lorimer went.
Nobody knows why she packed her trunk: a few old things
And is gone. . . .
    Gone with her little chin
    Thrust ahead of her
    And her soft hair blowing careless
    From under a wide hat,
Dancer, singer, a laughing passionate lover.

Were there ten men or a hundred hunting Chick?
Were there five men or fifty with aching hearts?
    Everybody loved Chick Lorimer.
      Nobody knows where she's gone.

GRAVES

I dreamed one man stood against a thousand,
One man damned as a wrongheaded fool.
One year and another he walked the streets,
And a thousand shrugs and hoots
Met him in the shoulders and mouths he passed.
    He died alone

And only the undertaker came to his funeral.

Flowers grow over his grave anod in the wind,
And over the graves of the thousand, too,
The flowers grow anod in the wind.

Flowers and the wind,
Flowers anod over the graves of the dead,
Petals of red, leaves of yellow, streaks of white,
Masses of purple sagging . . .
I love you and your great way of forgetting.

I suppose I must include at least one of my typical ravings or be accused of discrimination. Here it is—it was written during my anarchist period:

Reversals

MARGARET C. ANDERSON

Now I see the secret of the making of the best persons.
It is to grow in the open air, and to eat and sleep with the earth.
—Whitman.

What do you call the place you live in?
I will describe it to you. Perhaps you can find a new name for it.
It is a place where men do not hold up their heads and look free.
Where many men work and starve, and many work and turn into cabbages, and many steal and turn into rats, and a few own the land and turn into hogs.
Where nature is not as important as law.
Where love is never as strong as things.
Where age is decay rather than more life.
Where art is encouraged but not recognized.
Where revolt is the strongest of emotions and the weakest of actions.

What do you call this strange place where it is immoral to take life deeply, and moral to be a half-thing?
Where it is beautiful to have theories of living, and ugly to apply them.
Where ignorance is a virtue and knowledge a crime.

Where reputation is more vital than character.

Where sociability is a goal instead of a vice.

Where indirection is known as unselfishness and self-direction as egotism.

Where genius, "being youth and wisdom," is sent to school to learn— (Never mind; I can't remember what).

Where impulse is assassinated before it can prove its worth.

Where one must achieve in gloom or be suspected of "lightness."

Where beauty comes only when one has struggled beyond the need of it.

Where sex is known as the greatest human experience, and experience in sex as the greatest human sin.

Where religion is known to be an unfolding, but experience in unfolding looked upon as irreligious.

What do you call this fantastic place where age that is weak rules youth that is strong?

Where parents prescribe life for children they cannot understand.

Where politicians and prostitutes and police and the press are despised but honored, and great spirits are suspected of greatness but feared and cast out.

Where nations go to war for things they do not believe in, and individuals will not go to revolution for things they do believe in.

Where birds that fly are put into cages and men who soar are put into jails.

What do you call this incredible place where men go inch by inch to death in jails? Where they cease to hear and see and feel and smell and talk and walk and sing and sleep and work and play and think and be—not by order of gods or monsters but by order of men?

What do you call this awful place where every great spirit walks not only in rebellion and misunderstanding and isolation but in persecution?

Where there are no heroes to make an end of horrors.

Where even to live outdoors cannot clean men.

Where there is no imagination and no faith.

Where there is no silence. . . .

Do you call it an asylum of crazed beings who annihilate each other? Not at all. You call it the world. You say it is "a good old

world, after all." And you resent the "freak" who tells you your
world is upside down.

*In 1916 Emma Goldman was sent to prison for advocating that
"women need not always keep their mouths shut and their wombs
open." She wrote me many letters and I quote a few fragments:*

Letters from Prison
EMMA GOLDMAN

> *Queens County Jail,*
> *Long Island City, New York.*
> *April, 1916.*

WHAT am I doing? I am watching human misery. There is no misery
so appalling as imprisoned misery. It is so helpless, so humiliated.

Yes, I think the prisoners do love me, at least those who have been
thrown in with me. It is so easy to get their love. The least bit of
kindness moves them—they are so appreciative. But what can one do
for them?

Do you remember that passage from Galsworthy's *Justice* in which
some one says to Falder: "No one wishes you harm"? Therein lies
the pathos. No one wishes these social victims harm. The Warden
and Matron here are exceptionally kind. And yet the harm, the ir-
reparable harm, is done by the very fact that human beings are
locked up, robbed of their identity, their self-respect, their self-hood.

Oh, I am not sorry I was sentenced. In fact I am glad. I needed to
get to these pariahs who are the butt of all the horrors. It would be
well if every rebel were sent to prison for a time; it would fan his
smouldering flame of hate of the things that make prisons possible.
I am really glad.

. . . We are awakened at six and unlocked at seven in the morning. Then comes breakfast, of which I have so far eaten only oatmeal
with what pretends to be milk. The coffee or tea I have not managed
to get down. At seven-thirty we are taken out into the yard. I walk
up and down like one possessed, to get the exercise. At eight-thirty
we are back, and the women keep themselves busy scribbling; but
my girls will not let me do that; I must talk to them. (The Warden,
by the way, is reading my *Anarchism*, and the Matron my *Social Significance of the Modern Drama*). In fact, I seem to have more devotion here than on the outside. At eleven we have dinner, and at four

in the afternoon supper—which I will describe to you when I come out. Then we are locked up until seven A. M.—fifteen hours, the hardest of all to bear. Do you remember the line in *The Ballad of Reading Gaol:* "Each day a year whose days grow old"? To me it is "each night a year whose nights grow long." I have always loved the night, but jailed nights are ghastly things.

The lights are on until nine P. M., and we can read and write all day—which is a god-send. Also this prison is one of the cleanest in the country.

. . . What on earth have I done that people should go into such ecstasies? No one raves because you breathe; why rave if you take a determined stand when that means the very breath of life to you? Really I feel embarrassed with all the love and devotion and adulation for so little a thing, so infinitesimal compared with the truly heroic deeds of the great souls. My only consolation is that the fight is not at an end and that I may yet be called upon to do something really great. But for the present it is hardly worth the fuss.

Today is Sunday and we were taken out to the yard for a walk. It was a glorious day, marred only by the monotony of the stripes and the spiritless slouching figures. Yet the sky excluded no one; its glorious blue spread over them all, as if there were no sorrows in all the world and man was never cruel to his kind.

The days pass quickly between the study of my fellow prisoners, my letters, and other writing. The evenings are taken up with reading. But jailed nights are so oppressive. They lie like stone upon your heart. The thoughts, the sobs, the moans that emerge like pale shadows from every human soul. It is stifling. Yet people talk of hell. There is no more threatening thing in all the world than the hell of jailed nights.

Good morning. Another crazing night has gone. . . . E. G.

In the spring of 1916 Jane Heap, whose mother was Norwegian and looked like a viking, whose father was English and looked like a scholar, joined the staff of the Little Review. *In "My Thirty Years' War" (page 102) I have described this event as the most interesting thing that ever happened to the magazine.*

Jane's talk was the best—psychologically the best—that I had ever heard. I wanted it for the Little Review, *though Jane protested that she couldn't write. I began jotting down things she said, and finally forced her to take on a department of critical comment. As it turned out, I was always more interested in Jane's talk about art than I was in Ezra Pound's, when he became foreign editor of the magazine in 1917. And as I look back over the files I find a new confirmation of this 1916 evaluation.*

But before Jane consented to write at all, we decided to take the Little Review *to San Francisco for the summer ("Thirty Years' War," page 110). We established ourselves in a ranch house in Mill Valley, California, and prepared to talk ourselves to death—about art of course. The first thing I suggested was that we publish an issue of the magazine made up of blank pages, stating that since no art was being offered we would publish nothing. Jane drew some cartoons of our activities, and I announced that we would wait for the "miracle" of art before we brought out another number.*

In the next issue we printed reactions to our blank-page number. Frank Lloyd Wright wrote from Chicago:

> The less money *The Little Review* has the better it *looks* anyway! Your resolve is interesting—but it looks like the end. . . . I don't see where you can find the thing you need.
>
> But miracles do happen—I wish I had a million or a pen.

I answered a subscriber's objections by writing:

> But what did I say about wanting only the perfection of art and none of its strivings? I said—Art. That includes the strivings, doesn't it? Surely we needn't go back to definitions. Ezra Pound has a nice analysis somewhere—to this effect: In such measure as an artist expresses himself truthfully, he will be a good artist; in such measure as he himself exists, he will be a great one. I want a record of the process of that "existing" from as many artists as possible. The process of each will include many things that are not perfection, but who ever told you that perfection and Art are synonymous terms? Some one sent me a sketch, in answer to my editorial, with this note: "You said you wanted Beauty. I am sending you something which I think has it." I thought it had beauty, too; but it had no Art. What do you people think I meant by the "miracle"? . . . Flint's *London My Beautiful* has it. The prin-

cipal trouble is that miracles usually have to be explained to be recognized. It's like the painter who took a friend to hear Powys. The friend went to hear what Powys had to say—"and I told her what he looked like," said the painter.—*M. C. A.*

Jane made a few jottings as an effort to start writing:

John Cowper Powys?

Powys should never write anything. People like Q. K. in the *New Republic* come about as near to getting Powys as they would come to catching a comet. Powys is not for culture-snatchers, matinee girls, or glorifiers of the obvious. He is merely for those possessed enough of their imaginations to fall for a miracle when they see one. Who goes to hear a lecture on Nietzsche and Dostoevsky to find out what Powys thinks of those men? You go—hoping through the gloom of Nietzsche and Dostoevsky to catch a flash of Powys. Powys is the best thing that has come to us—that mad wolf! I always feel sorry for Velasquez that he never had a chance at him.

"The Brook Kerith"

Lord Alfred Douglas has sued George Moore for blasphemy. The Queensberrys were born to be fools: whenever art appears in England they become Wilde-eyed.

Whoever started the tradition of George Moore's naughtiness? *The Brook Kerith* is as reverent as Mr. Moore is chaste. A long time ago we used "psycho-analysis" on Mr. Moore and knew then that he could never get out of the world without writing a book about religion. *The Brook Kerith* is the story of the Christian religion made out of Mr. Moore's religion, which is Art.

Tagore

Rabindranath Tagore is coming back to America to lecture. Go, if you have never seen that slight presence with features drawn of air—with eyes that seem never to have looked out—and let him put that white spell of peace upon your complex futility.

You sometimes wonder why men like Dr. Coomaraswamy come telling us border-ruffians of Art about Ajanta frescoes and sculpture and the music of India. Perhaps they know our homesickness and know that alone we can't even find the road.

Sarah Bernhardt

Bernhardt is coming again. Well, that's all right, too. And those who jeer at her age never could have appreciated her youth. But you, young ones, see her; and have the double joy of seeing her now; and, if you have it in you, you will see her then, too.

"Windy McPherson's Son" by Sherwood Anderson

Here is another man who hasn't written the great American novel.

Where did the superstition arise which makes writers, dramatists, painters, feel that the goblins will get them if they don't hold to American subjects to make American art? It's as funny as if they should say: let's use only American-made materials and we'll have an American art. Landscape and atmosphere effect about the only difference of temperament in nations. At least Art is so universal that the temperament of your nation is the only thing that can stamp your Art. You might write about pink pagodas in China and have American art. The temperament in these American novels would make this country seem all a western plain under a steely sky. It's the same with their style: it's like going through underbrush, tough and tangled and scratchy, not like walking through rich old orchards or wandering in terraced gardens.

They all sound as though they had been written in the morning.

These writers want their novels to be strong. They are: strong like an ox, not like a tiger. And they don't even know about these American things they are writing of. Dreiser doesn't know what a genius is (I mean, what is a genius), so he makes one: a home-made genius who comes out like home-made clothes.

These writers want their books to be homely—the great American vice: made from the people, by the people, for the people. It's merely another form of the glorification of sockless senators, etc.

They can't even name their books:

"Sister Carrie"!

"Jennie Gerhardt"!

"Windy McPherson's Son"! etc., etc.

Chinese Poems

Translated from the Chinese of Li Po by Sasaki and Maxwell Bodenheim

WHOSE DAUGHTER?

Fling me harp-notes almost soundless,
From your hidden white window.
Your coming is like a flower petal
Wavering down from the sky.
Walk after me, across the water
Like a drifting flower.
You sing of So-land, and speak of Ko-land.
You seem older than you are
And that opens my love.
I take your hand and we walk past many springs.

I GO TO VISIT A SEMI-GOD

A group of mountains, like blue screens,
Scrape the sky.
Nothing is written upon the blue screens.
I walk over them, pushing apart the clouds
And search for a slender road.
I lean against a tree
And hear rushing springs, and see warm flowers.
A green cow lies amid the warm flowers
And white cranes sleep on the tops of pine trees.
Twilight rises from a lake below the mountains,
And meets a cold haze from the mountain-tops.

Before we left Mill Valley Jane wrote her first article for the Little
Review:

Paderewski and Tagore

San Francisco, October 1.

This morning I lay in bed looking at the ceiling and thinking
about cats. How *elegante* they are, and impenetrable, and with what
narrow slant-eyed contempt they look out upon the world. Perhaps
that's the way it looks through little black perpendicular slits. . . .
Anyway I thought of cats, and of violin strings made of catgut, and
wondered about cats and music. Is it because violins are made of
living things—wood and catgut and mother-of-pearl and hair,—that
they make the most beautiful music in the world?

This afternoon we crossed the hills and the bay to the theatre
where Paderewski was to play. We knew that Tagore was in the city
too, and all the way over we speculated prayerfully as to whether he
would be at the concert.

67

We bought standing room, and stood waiting in the foyer near the table, where Mme. Paderwska was selling her dolls for the benefit of destitute Poland. I looked at those dolls and wanted one so much that I was afraid I couldn't enjoy the concert. They were masterpieces! I shall make myself one—perhaps like the Polish Faust, a gorgeous man with fawn-colored kid boots; or perhaps like the Zaza, a little girl of pale pink sateen with somewhat the look of Mlle. Pogani in the Cubist exhibition. She had hair of red-brown silk thread, and her dress was emerald green. She had little pellets of bright pink satin sewed on to make cheeks,—"and she seets always on the piano when Mr. Paderewski practices."

I wandered back to my standing-room and looked indifferently at the crowded house. There were too many people, I thought. And then with tears hurting my eyes and an ache in my throat choking me I called out: "There—there's Tagore—in the third box!"—and made them look quickly so they wouldn't see me cry. There he sat in the first chair in a robe the color of grass-cloth and a pale violet cap upon his head. From where we stood it looked like a high forage-cap, but soft; and he wore great glasses made of horn. There were some East Indians with him, and two Americans—just men. I watched him until I was almost in a trance: the angle at which his head was put on, the cheek bones that were like an extra feature. . . . Everything that lies beyond the reach of thought and wonder seemed concentrated in that dark Stranger. I trembled, frightened by my imagination and a little melancholy.

At last Paderewski came out to his piano, *elegante* and impenetrable. I seemed to see him quite differently beside Tagore—a bright heaven beside a still universe. I was so filled there was no room left in me for the music. Once he came back and played Schumann's *Warum:* a nice touch: Warum for that great Wonderer. What could our *Warum* sound like to him?

All the while I watched Tagore who sat so motionless, not seeming to be there, until Paderewski began some brilliant harsh thing of Liszt's, when he smiled and leaned forward. Was he thinking "What wonderful children these are?"

After the concert we ran down to the front row for the encores. The theatre was filled with all its noises of banging seats and slamming doors and people moving. Paderewski looked out at them as he played, eyes narrowed, watching with contempt: a great cat! He stopped, waiting in silken rage for quiet, then smiled, raising his hand and striking the keys with a sheathed paw.

Tagore went behind, and we waited to see him by the stage entrance, in a narrow paved alley under hanging iron stairways. How he came out through the dusk, not looking, walking alone! And he went away on foot, simple and mysterious, into the crowds.

With that spell upon us we went back into the dark theatre. Under the one light, chattering women were packing the dolls and a man went about slamming up seats. An expressman came, the trunks were taken away, and the women left as noisily as they had come. The doors were closed, and we waited in front of the theatre under a blazing white light. A great limousine rolled up; a laughing group came from the stage entrance: Paderewski in a high silk hat, a loose cape about his shoulders. He got into the lighted car, waved his farewells to the group on the sidewalk, touched a slight kiss to someone, and was driven away into the bright city.

Mr. Powys on Dostoevsky
(A reader sent us these jottings from one of Mr. Powys's lectures)

Shudders of life. . . .

I have only one thing to do—to bring you into a strange mass of palpable darkness with something moving in it. Dostoevsky is really a great mass, a volume, not a cloud nor a pillar of fire nor a puff of smoke, but a vast, formless, shapeless mass of darkness, palpable and drawing you towards itself.

Reading him is dangerous because of the inherent sense of fear likely to be accentuated in those who are a little mad and whose madness takes on the form of fear. We go on a visit to a mad house, to hospitals with Dostoevsky. But with him this whole world suddenly changes into a mad house. It is all haunting mad houses and hospitals filled with us maniacs of the particular fear we are subject to.

In Dostoevsky we suddenly realize that these Russians are ourselves. If the religion, mysticism, liberalism, despotism they possess were only Russian there are excellent books written by travellers in Russia for us to read. But Dostoevsky is different. If I could but mesmerize you . . . It is like reading the gospels in childhood, being overrun and overthrown by fate and then, after one has lived, meeting the words of the childhood situations and making associations.

I do not think of him as an artist, though he is a great one. You do not *think* of him . . . In ordinary life we suppress half the things and more we might say. Vanity and fear are the ultimate things. In Dostoevsky the people tug and scrape at one another's vain nerves with adder's poison. He gives one the sensation of discovering one's self and betraying one's self. He reveals as friends talking and discussing in the small hours of the morning reveal themselves to one another. The talk may be a describing of the animal functions of the human body. But in reality it is the psychic tingling, electric vibrations which the physiological structure exerts upon mind! Mind! Mind! Dostoevsky is interested in what people actually feel. He is more with people who have written diaries than with so-called realistic novelists. One gets from him a sense of perversion of human imagination . . . He is the most important of novelists; full of ripples and vibrations of imagination. Everybody has imagination. The things we do are nothing. Imagination is the only thing over which Will has no power.

Nietzsche says that he got all his contemporary philosophy from Dostoevsky. He got from him even his idea of the inner circle of aristocratic souls who really rule the world, are themselves unhappy, and take others to places which they (these others) cannot enter. Dostoevsky thinks that the secret of the world is in abandonment, perversion; Nietzsche in hardness, stiffness, the gay, the strong, the beautiful, aristocratic, dominant . . . Nietzsche with all his reality does not describe life as it is. Zarathustra is a dream—impossible perhaps. But Dostoevsky does describe life. Nietzsche's man is absolutely alone—has his own hell. Dostoevsky's has that too, but in a different way. He gives the feeling of a third person where two are alone. Do not think that Dostoevsky is a mystic. The essential thing is that you have this sense of a third person to which genius appeals. Dostoevsky is a stronger as well as a truer one than even Nietzsche himself.

Nietzsche is as a skater upon the ice, a dancer upon a tight rope who remains a white, balanced figure on the surface. Dostoevsky plunges—into a darkness full of voices. You must get there by a form of perversion. Every one of his characters is incurably hurt. Nietzscheans harden their hearts and live on the surface. All Dostoevsky people are weak. He thinks that only out of weakness will redemption come; abandonment to every emotion. In that he is Dionysian . . . Dostoevsky I cannot put into words. Perversion; Disease; God is Disease; God is Pain; Dostoevsky depicts how Disease gives one illumination. We have an idea that we must be well. Even Nietzsche says that. The Greeks said it ages ago. Dostoevsky says "No; I offer you a new value." He has a lust for fools—understands the mania that people have of making fools of themselves. God is Folly; God is Cruelty—perhaps an epicene God.

Dostoevsky is a cerebralist. His specialty is imaginative reactions. All the lusts that have stretched their wailing arms, all the hopes, all the goblins . . . In sex as in everything else people are not what they are doing; they are in that vortex of what they imagine themselves. Dostoevsky understands all that. Those frank-spoken people who think they know sex are puritans on the other side. They have no imagination.

We can overestimate what Dostoevsky has from Russia and not attribute what he is to himself. Other Russians are Russians—Turgeniev, Tolstoy, Andreyev, Chekhov, Gorky—but they are not as big as he is; perhaps they are more of the broader stamp.

. . . Constance Garnett's translations are masterpieces. The French are too artistic to translate Dostoevsky. . . . No one can approach Dostoevsky in creating a saint. Russia as the spiritual bringer-back of the world to Christianity—this runs through his works. He is *the* Christian. His books are full of translations from Scripture. He understands the underlying psychology of the gospels. Nietzsche said that putting the gospels with the art of the Old Testament was a crime in the name of Art. The Old Testament is undoubtedly finer art, but the New is psychology—masterly.

Harold Bauer followed the Little Review's *fortunes with great interest, always came to see us when he was in Chicago, and often played for us on my Mason & Hamlin grand piano.*

"The Compleat Amateur" or How Not To Be An Artist
HAROLD BAUER

(No, I cannot write you an article. And I add to this the expression of my fervent hope that no Amateurs are going to be allowed to scribble for THE LITTLE REVIEW. *Speaking as a subscriber, I haven't the least desire to read any of H. Bauer's clumsy attempts to express himself in a medium that is foreign to him. Let him stick to his business. . . . You must write the article you have in mind yourself. From the depths of your artistic intuitions draw forth the material*

*and give away the secrets—which are no secrets. Moreover, don't con-
fine yourself to music, much less to piano playing; take in the whole
field of art and call it "The Compleat Amateur, or, How Not To Be
An Artist." I suggest the following headings.—Extract from a letter
of the Author.)*

I. *"Le Style fait l'homme"*

If you want to become an author, give up your life to the study of
calligraphy, if a painter, devote yourself to the manufacture of
paints and brushes, if a composer, commit to memory the number of
notes in every standard classical work, and if a singer or instru-
mentalist, spend your whole energy in the establishing of a "sound
technical foundation." Emotional expression can then, if desired,
be subsequently smeared like treacle on bread over all these different
stylic bases, this operation requiring neither skill nor expression.

II. *"Means to an End"*

The amateur must learn that technique represents an obstacle to
be overcome and a set of tools to be acquired. It has nothing to do
with expression. Only an imaginative artist like Maeterlinck would
suggest that the road along which the student travels towards his
destination is in reality a link, a connection joining one with the
other—an umbilical cord partaking of the nature and attributes of
both traveler and goal. To a perfectly rational person the road is
merely a distance to be covered, a separation.

III. *Personality, or, as some authorities have it: Individuality*

This is the greatest asset of the Amateur. An artist is like everybody in the world. The book we read, the picture we see or the
music we hear which renders tangible our own dimly-felt thoughts
and emotional stirrings show that we are in reality one with the
artist and with the universe of which these expressions are but re-
flections of unseen and unheard forces. An artist combines the
power and responsibilities of the aristocrat with the feelings of an
anarchist, he is the guardian of privilege and the destroyer of authority, the leveler of barriers and the creator of the superman, the
leader and the servant of humanity and . . . the Arch Enemy of
the Amateur! The artist is like all humanity, but the Amateur is not
like the Artist. The Amateur must hang on for dear life to his precious soul and resist to the last gasp the incursions of any outside
force in which he can trace the semblance of his own nature, for if

anything gets in something may get out and he won't be able to sort himself out afterwards. Hence the Amateur must be an Individualist; otherwise he is doomed to extinction. The Amateur's business is to interpret the universe in terms eternally incomprehensible to anyone but himself, and to compromise with the necessity for intercourse with his fellow-creatures by the adoption of an artificial language which can convey thoughts and feelings of a superficial character, but nothing more.

The tale that points a moral, the picture that suggests a tale, and the music that evokes a picture; these are the vehicles for "personality" and your fine amateur must cultivate the pride that the realization of an exclusive understanding of these things gives. If Hamlet had been an amateur instead of being an artist he would never have suggested that a cloud was like a camel, a weasel, or a whale; he would have pointed out its resemblance to a mathematical calculation or a treatise on political economy, and Polonius would have been far more impressed—for this would have shown Great Individuality.

IV. *The Mission of Amateurism*

A true Amateur must learn the value of success, the immense importance of achievement, the inward meaning of gratified self-conceit. Praise from small minds represents the highest possible attainment of accomplished Amateurism. The object of Amateurishness is, like the puzzle pictures in the daily papers, to present a pretty little problem with a perfectly simple and obvious solution, thus giving effortless pleasure and satisfaction to all concerned.

The opportunities afforded by collective Amateurism for the repression of Art are invaluable and as the study of the subject is within the reach of all, including those who are congenitally afflicted with artistic talent, it devolves upon everyone who holds the opinion that this is the best of all possible worlds, to make it his life's occupation and aim to be a "compleat amateur."

A Decadent Art

JANE HEAP

WE have had grand opera in Chicago for several weeks. I am going to write here of grand opera, not of singing classes.

Grand opera, like a great hand whose fingers are the different arts, is trying to give us what the closed hand holds. Galli-Curci has

73

undone the critics for adjectives of praise, has fulfilled the hopes of managers, and filled the Auditorium with the sleep-walking public. We have had Muratore with his beautiful voice and his treacle personality. We have had efficient and awful Wagnerian singers. We have had satisfaction in our opera. And now comes Mary Garden, so surcharged with life that she sends a thrill of it before her—Mary Garden who outsings the composer in her feeling, who outpaints the painter in her acting, who outsculpts the sculptor with her body. Mary Garden gives us grand opera; she gives what the closed hand holds.

And so the fight will begin again and the old favorite record will be put on all the cheap human talking machines: "Of course Mary Garden can't sing, but she can act."

Grand opera by its very character is outside such simple criticism as this; it is outside all talk of voice production or singing off key or distracting the conductor. There is a measurable value in the component parts of any art, but the test that cannot be analyzed lies in the unity of these parts. This unity is the principle of Art. But grand opera is a composite of the arts, and the true test for it should lie in the unity of the employed arts, not in weighing any part of any one art. People will rave for days if Mary Garden fails in a note, although the aesthetic and emotional experience of the whole was unmarred; but the same people will never be disturbed if Galli-Curci moves about the stage like a lost cloak-model and breaks up the picture of the whole illusion by holding her body in positions not possible in human awkwardness; and is so intent on breathing that she almost forgets to attend to Juliet's funeral. So long as she sings according to a fixed standard she need go no further than a moving-picture screen. And Mary must be decried, though her performance hold in color like a tapestry and move in rhythm like a frieze.

When anything is as far from life as sung dialogue it must have a different treatment than either pure song or pure drama. Decoration should be the design for opera: a libretto that is a dramatic poem, music working itself out in a decoration for the poem, scenery a design of the matter and feeling of the libretto, and actors that can point the design not in the realistic day-life manner of the drama but with decorative acting. With this we might have great grand opera. One thing we have now: the great decorative actress *and* singer, Mary Garden.

Mary Garden is the biggest thing on our horizon today. To think that flesh could be so intelligent! She gives as generously of her undraped body as a Rodin statue; and the audience gives her back their applause, grudgingly, not knowing the great art of her. To put Rodin into inspired motion, but to do more than that even—! In the next issue I shall try to write of all she does,—Mary Garden,

> . . . . . "This Cyprian
> She is a million, million changing things.
> She brings more joy than any god; she brings
> More pain. I cannot judge her. May it be
> An hour of mercy when she looks on me."*

At the beginning of 1917 we moved the Little Review *to New York, and began what was for me the most interesting period of its life.*

. . . The famous article on "that pinnacle of earthly glory" appeared in the March 1917 number. Carl Van Vechten announced that he had bought a hundred copies to send to his friends.

Mary Garden

JANE HEAP

WHAT did the critics mean when they used to say that never again in our generation would there come another Bernhardt? They didn't mean that there would be no other great actresses because they were writing of actresses, all the time, whom they considered great. In an argument they would talk largely of Bernhardt's personality. Let them call it personality if they are using the better Oriental meaning of the word: Individuality. But I fear they mean only to limit something unknown so that it may be understood. The more external nullities they bring to prove it personality the more its unknown nature is emphasized. The more talk there is of arresting qualities of person, acts, and dress, of frankness and ferocity, tears and terror—the more talk there is of all its eccentric sanities, the more it recedes and becomes definitely itself, aloof and unnamed.

Arthur Symons tried to express it when he wrote of Bernhardt: "Two magics met and united, in the artist and in the woman." But after all it is only that through the woman you feel the imminence of something as great and impersonal as the sweep of sea and the

* Euripides.

growth of flowers. In all the arts, whenever the magic of the artist has been united with this other magic the possessor has been of the first great. Michael Angelo and the dark troubled magic of him. . . .

I wonder why, even in those people to whom has come some appreciation of the magic of the artist, there is still so often such strong resentment and distrust of this other magic. Because of their adventures in the great emotions, those who have it loosen new forces of life; they recreate the great passions; *they add something to Fate*.

Everyone feels that he has a right to a share in that which the millions are working together in uproar to add to existence. Many long for a share in that which the artists are making in silence for the soul. But who is there except the artist who is willing to feel in this thing the imminence of something beyond life and personality? Who else in the world except the lonely insane, because of their adventures in illusions and hallucinations, ever add anything to Fate? How easy to say that genius is akin to madness. All great antitheses are akin: all unknown things are mysteriously akin, as all known things are naturally akin. But how poignantly akin are the known and unknown! Why does anyone exclude himself from any connection with the infinite?

When I was a little child I lived in a great asylum for the insane. It was a world outside of the world, where realities had to be imagined and where, even through those excursions in illusions and hallucinations, there ran a strange loneliness. The world can never be so lonely in those places where the mind has never come as in a place where the mind has gone. There were no books to read in this place except the great volumes in the Patients' Library; and I had read them all. There was no one to ask about anything. There was no way to make a connection with "life." Out there in the world they were working and thinking; here we were still. Very early I had given up every one except the Insane. The others knew nothing about anything, or knew only uninteresting facts. From the Insane I could get everything. They knew everything about nothing, and were my authority; but beyond that there was a silence. Who had made the pictures, the books and the music in the world? And how had they made them? And how could you tell the makers from just people? Did they have a light around their heads? Were there any of them in the world now? And would I ever see one? One day a name came to me suddenly. Some one was talking of a "wicked French actress" who was touring America:—"Sarah Bernhardt." Even when *they* said it the name had a light around it! She would come as far as St. Louis. I would go at once. But I was too little. I had no money. . . . I would run away. I would walk the whole distance to her. But she would be gone before I could get there. . . . Some day I would go to Paris. Other people had got that far. I would go on living for that.

And then she came again! I was there, the first night, sitting in the balcony with some other art students. We had sold our futures to sit so close. I was burning with hot excitement and shaking with cold fear until the moment—it was *Camille*—when the long french doors opened and she came languidly and as if from a great distance; hands extended as if balancing her exquisitely upon an enchanted atmosphere, her suave voluptuous tawny head bent slightly down. I threw myself mind and soul into the waves of that caressing fiery magic which swept out to us.

After this came a new agony: the critics had said there would never be another. There was Duse, whom I have never seen; but she has always filled me with a restless trouble. What artist has ever so dared to offend Art? Never in all her life as an actress did she choose a play in which her great art could come into its own. It always seems that there is more laid upon the artist than a willingness to serve; it is almost a command to serve. Did Duse deny the command and by so doing add the martyrdom of Art to a great personal tragedy? Or was it because she tried to create an art out of nature itself that Art revenged itself upon her through nature? As an actress she had "no resources outside simple human nature." As a woman she had no resource in Art.

Then a new name came across the world, with a new radiance. Not with the glow of Duse's halo, nor with the threat of Bernhardt's heat-lightning, but with the radiance of the Northern Lights it shone above the horizon. . . . *Mary Garden!* Her magics have this kind of splendor. She has brought a new temper into the drama— something not Latin, not English. Duse could never be unnatural; Bernhardt can never be unsophisticated, un-French; English actresses can seldom be unconventional. But Mary Garden . . . She brings a sharp new ecstasy of life, an inexorable sadness of love; she brings an energy that is grace and a calm that is energy; she brings a frankness that is mystery. There is something Norsk about Mary Garden. In her the pure metal of the mind seems to have been annealed by an Oriental fire, adding to it a passion without vehemence. There is something unconquered about her, as if she came from that land where the sun shines at midnight; from that race which never made for itself a beneficent God.

I don't know where to begin to write about Mary Garden's art. There is art within art within art, and then there is Mary Garden.

First of all, she seems to be the only singer who knows that all the arts come from the same source and follow the same laws. Critics love to say that pure song and pure music do not express human emotion, although drama, poetry, painting and sculpture do. What logic! Pure music and pure song express exactly what drama, poetry, painting and sculpture express. But none of them expresses human emotion; they express the *source* of human emotion. To express the emotions of life is to live; to express the life of emotions is to make art.

I wish I could tell beautifully what a great creative artist Mary Garden is. It is one thing for the artist to create a character within the outlines definitely or indefinitely drawn by the composer; to put himself in the place of the character and act as he would act. But the creative artist *takes the character to himself* and then creates from his imagination in his own image—the image of his soul. The more universal the artist, the greater his power to reveal his soul in different images. What an infinite thing Mary Garden has shown her soul to be: Thaïs, the Jongleur, Monna Vanna, Carmen, Griselidis, Tosca, Mélisande, Salome!

And so when she creates a character she recreates the opera. Mary Garden is the only singer in opera to whom song is speech. Because in opera song and music have been fused with drama, the voice must become a medium for creating character, thought and emotion, together with the hands, face and body of the actor-singer. There is no need to discuss here what has or what has not been accomplished toward the creation of a new art by this fusion of the arts. You have but to hear and see Mary Garden in *Pelléas and Mélisande* to find poetry, music, singing and acting united so that the essence of each art comes to us with a rarer flavor than when free. No perfect thing can lose by being united with another perfect thing. However, it is no small task to do this in those older compositions in which music has been written to melodrama, to be sung by elaborate musical instruments. When the music carries beyond the true emotion of the drama, or when it does not reach to the limits of the drama, it is only an artist with flawless intelligence who can break over the barrier of the score and hold the music to the emotion with a backward line of the voice or carry it on by sheer genius to its full task.

And what a voice! You can't quite stand it when Mary Garden sings words like "amour," "pitié," "éternel." It breaks your heart in a strange way, because she makes you feel more precisely our brief longing, our frail tenderness and our deceiving hope. Many people don't like it—the same ones who don't like modern painting, the Imagists, Scriabine, and the rest. They have no idea that it is a new kind of instrument, to which they must bring new ears. They say: Why does she sing at all? Why doesn't she go into straight drama?—never realizing for a moment that she has a longer reach than Bernhardt, a stronger grasp than Duse. There is not enough resistance for her in pure drama. She must paint the canvas full.

Once before I called Mary Garden a great decorative actress. I am using decoration in the sense in which it is used in painting, where elimination and not elaboration is used to emphasize the intention of line and color. She carries this same idea into her costumes: she can give you the whole spirit and atmosphere of an historical costume by a mere silhouette of its lines. And she can draw in the whole psychology of a scene with one line of her body—the line of her walk. If she is to dominate a situation with her intellect or her beauty she walks from the center of her intelligence, which is the head, giving a length of line that makes the slightest step a stride; if it is a matter of the soul she walks from the center of her presence, which is the top plane of the chest, moving like a Presence—not like a being; when it is love she walks straight from her heart, with a line that repeats a pain; when it is passion she sinks the line to a point lower than the hip, and prowls destructively. In *Thaïs,* when she is trying to enthrall the monk, she winds about the stage and him, bending slightly in hip and knee. Later, in a scene of contest with him, she lifts the line to her consicousness and stands to the height of her belief in her own beauty and power. When she goes over to the nuns, she moves away with that beautiful unconsciousness of action which is never so mysteriously perfect a thing as in Mélisande.

There is nothing so thrilling in life to me as to watch this living painting which moves in rhythm like a frieze. How I should love to see her working out her designs against a background that has car-

79

ried out the line of intention of a poem. Imagine Mary Garden in the *Tristan* Liebestod, coming in upon a scene in which the short lines of a truncated castle rise from the endless planes of a black and purple sea; a fleet of violins in the orchestra singing the Love Death and Mary challenging all this dark negation with the one word "Tristan," in a voice which is a singing pain. But most of all I wish some one would make operas for her of those exotic things that lie outside of common experience, but which have their place in life: nature too heavily laden or too fantastically free or too weirdly true; bright precious hidden things, corroded jewels, heavy-hanging flowers of sleep—moon-flowers of the day. How passionately and reverently she performed that ritual of dark heat and sex savagery which is *Salome*.

The electric abundance of life in Mary Garden and the splendor of her body are dazzling at first. But it is a stillness of soul, an exaltation of passion which really stamp her. There is something inviolate about her. Other actresses may be soulful, grave, or innocent; but Mary Garden has authentic purity.

But why talk of all these things? I only want to say, "Ah, Conchobar, have you ever seen her, with her high laughing turbulent head thrown backward?"—this Aphrodite of the North, this bacchante from the sea, this viking of the soul. There is no other who has all beauty.

(Jane was wrong about Duse. If she had seen her, as I did lately, in an old Italian film shown at the Museum of Modern Art, she would have seen her "moving in rhythm like a frieze." I have rarely beheld anything more sculptural than Duse's silent performance. —M. C. A.)

Isadora Duncan's Misfortune

MARGARET ANDERSON

I HAVE waited five years to see Isadora Duncan. I went to the Metropolitan expecting to see the Dionysian, "the feet of the Centaur trampling the stage," etc. . . . Well, this is what I saw:

Isadora Duncan ran, jumped and skipped and stamped and swooned about the stage, dragging with her a body that was never meant to move in rhythmic line, turning music into stories of war and religion, illustrating the stories with obvious gesticulations toward the heavens or maudlin manouverings toward the grave, using the same gestures for the sweetness of Schubert as for the sacraments of César Franck, moving always *inside* the music, never dominating it, never even controlling it, never holding or pushing it to an authentic end. . . . Isadora felt a great deal. She shook her head and arms in such a fury of feeling that she appeared to be strangling; and when there was no way of reaching a further intensification she shook her whole body in a kind of spasm of human inability to bear the grief of the world. And every move was a futile and pitiable one because never once did her body become that mould through which a design is to shape its course and flow into its ultimate form. If the music made a wide swinging curve she made a cramped sudden curve; if it made a descending line she interpreted that, for some mysterious reason, by reverently clutching her abdomen and looking to God.

"Oh," they say, "you are talking about technique."

No, no, no! I am not talking about technique. I am almost never talking technique.

If you were much moved by what Isadora suggested to you—"the trampling feet of the Centaur, the look in her face as though she could drink blood"—why not realize that you can feel these emotions, if you feel like it, in the performance of the cheapest amateur. But that is no criterion of Art. In fact the more of those feelings you have the more you will know that what you are viewing is not Art. Because in the presence of Art you feel almost nothing, you imagine nothing, you are like a being in a vacuum, your mind in that mysterious instant Shelley likened to a fading coal.

You are talking only of what Isadora made you feel, not what Isadora *made*.

The Reader Critic

New York subscriber:

How we have looked forward to seeing Isadora Duncan dance! . . . But——! It's because I wonder if any people felt the way I did the night of March 6 at the Metropolitan that I am writing you. . . .

I was grateful, of course, for the César Franck—what human movements will express this, I wondered. . . . This was only the first—I was willing to wait. Then Ave Maria . . . the figure assumes some rather statuesque poses: arms uplifted, one arm uplifted, head thrown back, the line of her thigh and leg heavy—the modern sculptors have taught us to believe it good. Then a Giotto figure she seemed; a minute later Mrs. Flynn coming up from her wash-tub in the basement; a chord from the orchestra and the Statue of Liberty is before us. Encore; and Botticelli's nymph hastens to Venus: she bows and a wilted Easter lily bud which never knew full blossom is before us. Tschaikowsky's Pathetique . . . those must be real flowers she is using to scatter about. Second encore—posing for the public with an uplifted white rose—this the great dancer!

With the strains of the *Marseillaise* she appeared from the rear, right, in scarlet. . . . Well, the audience rose and Isadora (we're feeling chummy by this time) pointed! At the finish of the air— which surmounted all despite the figure on the stage—she disclosed what we suspected was there: an American flag! And the orchestra played *Star Spangled Banner* and she kissed the flag, and the audience sang; and after "Bravos" she "danced" the *Marseillaise* again and the audience shrieked; and the orchestra played *America* off key and swung to *Star Spangled Banner* again and she unwound the flag from off her and danced the thing they were playing,—in that costume of dark red she had worn when she danced the Call to Battle and the Lamentations Following Triumph of the *Pathetique;* and trampling on the red which was France, waving the flag which was the U. S. A., in the costume representing Poland—she pointed! And because she had *pointed* skyward, earthward and battleward, all in the course of one evening, we left, saying: "Well, we have seen Isadora Duncan dance!"

On A Certain Critic

AMY LOWELL

Well, John Keats,
I know how you felt when you swung out of the inn
And started up Box Hill after the moon.
Lord! How she twinkled in and out of the box bushes
Where they arched over the path.
How she peeked at you and tempted you,
And how you longed for the "naked waist" of her
You had put into your second canto.
You felt her silver running all over you,
And the shine of her flashed in your eyes,
So that you stumbled over roots and things.

Ah! How beautiful! How beautiful!
Lying out on the open hill
With her white radiance touching you
Lightly,
Flecking over you.
"My Lady of the Moon,
I flow out to your whiteness,
Brightness.
My hands cup themselves
About your disk of pearl and fire;
Lie upon my face,
Burn me with the cold of your hot white flame.
Diana,
High, distant Goddess,
I kiss the needles of this furze bush
Because your feet have trodden it.
Moon!
Moon!
I am prone before you.
Pity me,
And drench me in loveliness:
I have written you a poem;
I have made a girdle for you of words;
Like a shawl my words will cover you,
So that men may read of you and not be burnt as I have been.
Sere my heart until it is a crinkled leaf,
I have held you in it for a moment,
And exchanged my love with yours
On a high hill at midnight.
Was that your tear or mine, Bright Moon?
It was round and full of moonlight.
Don't go!
My God! Don't go!
You escape from me,
You slide through my hands.
Great Immortal Goddess,
Dearly Beloved,
Don't leave me.
My hands clutch at moon-beams,
And catch each other.
My Dear! My Dear!
My beautiful far-shining lady!
Oh! God!

I am tortured with this anguish of unbearable beauty."
Then you stumbled down the hill, John Keats.
Perhaps you fell once or twice;
It is a rough path,
And you weren't thinking of that.
Then you wrote
By a wavering candle,
And the moon frosted your window till it looked like a sheet of
    blue ice.
And as you tumbled into bed, you said:
"It's a piece of luck I thought of coming out to Box Hill."

Now comes a sprig little gentleman,
And turns over your manuscript with his mincing fingers,
And tabulates places and dates.
He says your moon was a copy-book maxim,
And talks about the spirit of solitude,
And the salvation of genius through the social order.
I wish you were here to damn him
With a good, round, agreeable oath, John Keats.
But just snap your fingers;
You and the moon will still love
When he and his papers have slithered away
In the bodies of innumerable worms.

The Reader Critic

WAR ART

B. C., Kansas:
The Little Review is the only magazine I have laid eyes on in
months that hasn't had a word in it about this blasted war. How do
you do it?

[Perhaps it's because none of us considers this war a legitimate or
an interesting subject for Art, not being the focal point of any
fundamental emotion for any of the peoples engaged in it. Revolutions and civil wars are different . . . but that is a long story.
There never has been a real revolution yet: peoples have revoluted
but they have never seemed to hold on to what they have fought
for. By the time the revolution gets to be history they are back behind where they started, staggering under the same kind of bur-
dens. They are really hunch-backs, but they think that which bends

their backs can be unloaded. And civil wars, whatever their pretext, seem always to be the fight of the self-righteous uncultivated against the cultivated and the suave.—jh]

I urged more and more writing upon Jane who, for me, could express more clearly than anyone else what I wanted the Little Review *to be.*

Someone writing from Washington, D.C., also expressed my own feeling:

I have been trying to articulate the unusual impression that the *Little Review* gives me. I placed it against the background of the other reviews. They fell away into two groups: those that have had their life and are dissolving, and those that are self-consciously becoming. The *Little Review* was clear against this parting and these opposite movements. It seemed not to move. It was (is). And then I recalled your own word, "Existences." That's it: *Little Review* is an existence. It is itself germinal. It needs no anterior functioning to explain it. It is the fulfillment of its own seed. It seems not to move, yet it does move. It is vibrant within itself, as all balanced life is. As art is . . .

In the following pages I have collected a number of Jane's commentaries. She published them under the title of

Push-Face   jh.

I

It is a great thing to be living when an age passes. If you are born in an age in which every impact of its expression is a pain, there is a beautiful poetic vengeance in being permitted to watch that age destroy itself.

What other age could have so offended? Instead of pursuing the real business of life, which is to live, men have turned all their denials and repressions into the accumulation of unessential knowledge and the making of indiscriminate things. Other ages have taken out their repressions in religious frenzies, but this age has taken everything out in motion. It is an elementary fact of sex knowledge that rhythmic motion is part of sex expression. Isn't it ironical and immoral that those nations which have prided themselves most on their virtue, and have hugged tightest to themselves the puritanic ideal, are the ones that have gone maddest over motion? America, being the most virtuous, obviously has the least sense of humor and has exceeded herself. From the cradle to the turbine engine, from the rocking-chair to the spinnings and whirlings of a Coney Island, she has become a national mechanical perpetual whirling Dervish.

The wheels became rollers which have rolled life out thin and flat.

Then Art cried out with all her voices. In the last few years we have had a return to the beginnings of all the Arts. If there ever comes a time in the world when men will give their attention to the life of Art and understand its movement, they will find it alert and inevitable. Life would follow it trustingly if it were not for the intrusions and hindrances of men. The Thing had happened: Life had made its protest through Art. But this consciousness never reached the unendowed mind. It (the unendowed mind) forced Life to avenge itself by flying into war.

The Price of Empire

Richard Aldington's two poems, with their frail reticent sadness, were sent to us from the trenches. Why do poets keep on singing in a world which doesn't value them? Why does the moon keep on shining? Surely it isn't obligation!—jh.

Wuzzed Thinking

Anonymous:

Recall to mind the ultimatum of Max Eastman: ". . . Our literary intellectuals will have to go to work. (!) Otherwise we shall merely have to enjoy them like a song. They will have to *pass their examinations.* (!) Science holds the power to make all intellectual literature mere dilettantism and nothing but resolute giants of brain with feeling can prevent it." Reflect the philosophy of the age, and you will have served Art. Do not attempt to rise precipitously and gaze rapturously into the Blessed Isles, floating without our sphere, situate in the fourth dimension. Come to Jesus!

[Reflecting the philosophy of the age has no more to do with Art than holding the mirror up to nature.—jh.]

Art for Whose Sake?

"What is *your* definition of art? You say: Art for Art's sake; that is only a phrase." Etc., etc.

[What is this you're telling us about Art? "The greatest and freest human *intellects*" in the past have never created Art. Intellects do not have aesthetic experiences. (You might as well ask a gas-engine to run a human being instead of that indefinable force called life.) The dreamers, the ones of imagination, have the whole vision—the outside and the inside, and the vision of the two working together with all things. Why do you want to limit them to one—the social vision? You say that Art has always been the handmaiden of oppression and superstition, that the Church has used all forms of Art to hold men to it. True. Let me salute the far-seeing and mighty wisdom of the Catholic Church that has so recognized the power of Art. If you who are trying to extend the social vision could learn that one lesson, what a strength you could add unto yourselves:—the only strength.

You say "Look less on the empty form and more on the animating truth which agrees with reality and life." Form is the only thing that remains forever: truth changes every day; form gives a thing its truth in Art and in life. Even the great social movement will have no truth until it has Form.

And for whom is *The Little Review* published? God knows.—jh.]

"What Is Art?"

When Tagore first gave his lecture on Art in Chicago I was not here, and all I could read about it or find out about it by asking was that it was anti-Tolstoyan. But I got the whole truth of it in a sentence when I asked a pupil of Tagore's, a young artist, "What does Mr. Tagore say in his lecture on Art?"

"What does he say? Oh, he just says what it is, this Art."

Every layman in this country who finds it necessary to establish himself a critic of Art and artists should hear that lecture and try to understand it if only in parts. But I suppose they wouldn't accept Tagore's word for it because he doesn't take them in on the ground floor, in the manner of *The Seven Arts,* for instance.

I can't quote directly, as the lecture is not yet published, but he has said all the things that one longs to say oneself. He defines the artist as one who says to the world: "I see you where you are what I am." Art is the most personal thing in the world. Man reveals himself and not his objects in Art. Matter and manner find their harmonics in our personality. The artist does not particularize through peculiarity, which is the discord of the unique, but through the personality, which is its harmony. Art is man's answer to the "Supreme Person." Art is personal and beyond science. So, too, is beauty. Beauty is not a fact but an expression. "Facts are like wine-cups that carry it." To all the confusion and misconceptions about beauty in Art he answers: The creation of beauty is not the object of Art. Beauty in Art has merely been an instrument and not its complete and ultimate significance. And to those who demand teaching or utility in Art there is this answer: The stage of pure utility is like a state of heat which is dark; when it surpasses itself it becomes white heat and then it is expressive; and when man thwarts his desire for delight, wanting to make it into good or into knowledge, it loses its bloom and healthiness.

Taking up the old controversy of Art for Art's sake, the fact that the phrase has fallen into disrepute is a sign of the return of the ideals of the puritanic age when enjoyment as an end in itself was held to be sinful. The idea of Art for Art's sake had its origin in a surplusage of life, not in asceticism or decadence. When our personality is at its flood-tide with love or other emotion it longs to express itself for the sake of expression, and we forget the claims of usefulness and the thrift of necessity.

After all the fighting and arguing one has to do up and down the world over what is Art, and Art for Art's sake, one comes from this lecture feeling: "He leadeth me beside the still waters; he maketh me to lie down in green pastures; he restoreth my soul."—jh.

Phases of Crazes

H. L. C., Chicago:

I wish you didn't have such a craze for foreigners and self-exiled Americans. I think you have missed your chance right here in your own country. I am sure there are writers if you would go after them who, if they couldn't write so well, would on the other hand be writing in a familiar manner about subjects known to us and in so doing be creating a literary tradition of our own.

I am tired of these floods of Russian, French, Scandinavian, Irish and Hindoo stuff that have swept the country. The war will probably reduce the importation of foreign books, and I for one think this will be a good thing. . . .

[I should think there might be room in America for one magazine which will print work just because it is good, no matter where it is produced. All we ask in this is to be allowed a choice of crazes.

To us it seems that there is an indiscriminate craze in the theatre, in books, in magazines, and even in exhibition rooms, for the American product with all its sins upon it. Let your fears for the contamination or stifling from abroad of American letters be at rest. Congress and the established publisher have attended to all that. Ignorance is protected from invasion far better than the country itself.

Each generation in this country is spared the shock of contemporary foreign masterpieces. When a masterpiece reaches America, a generation late, Time has tempered it to the shorn. I happen to know something of Tagore's experience with this protection. When Tagore was first "discovered" in America—(he had been published in London and had with him only a few personal copies of his work) —he sent to his London publishers for extra copies to meet the requests of his friends. Aside from a terrific tariff, the red tape and the questioning as to the integrity of his purpose in importing his own books proved too wearing an experience: the idea was abandoned. On his recent trip he brought with him a small collection of very gentle Indian water colours, with no other motive than to create if possible an understanding of Indian art in this country. His pictures were held up at the port of Seattle, he was called again and again before inspectors, made to swear all kinds of oaths, and to deposit a fabulous sum (some forty thousand dollars, as I remember) to assure the government that his intentions were all right.

As he was leaving the country some one asked him if he ever intended making another visit,—(there had been some agitation before this about including the Hindoo in the Oriental Immigration laws) —and Tagore replied, "I do not know. You will make a law against the Hindoo coming to your country. You have now a law against books. It may be you will make a law against poets coming too?"

When the western nations have finished making the world safe for democracy, if it wouldn't be too satirical the Orient might wage a world war to make the world safe for Art.—*jh*.]

Rolland's "Colas Breugnon"

At frequent and repeated intervals in America it becomes necessary to take oneself to a cyclone-cellar while a storm of enthusiasm for a new book or author sweeps the country. Because it is part of the storm to believe that a book by a frenchman is more "literary," it

89

places one more definitely to read him. "Jean Christophe" was one of these touchstones. I have been asked a thousand times if I have read "Jean Christophe." When I answer "No, I fear I am not one of Mr. Rolland's audience," instead of it being left as a compliment to him I am emphatically told that there are some good things in "Jean Christophe." A super-artist, it would seem, to have achieved so much in ten volumes.

All this is very well as another little game, but when it is looked at squarely it is rather depressing. Nine tenths of these cyclones are raised about second-rate men or men who are not artists at all; there is little chance for the true artist to get a hearing, and appreciation never.

Men like Rolland, grown in a country where the literary soil has been fertilized for centuries, are a very different product from the second-rate men in a country like America. Fertilization does not change the species; civilization should not be confused with genius. I cannot say any more of "Colas Breugnon."—*jh*.

Harold Bauer's Hands

Have you ever noticed how Bauer brings his hands in when he comes out to play? He carries them as if he didn't want to brush them against anything, for fear they would strike out music from whatever they touched. Or as if they were precious violins that might be broken.—*jh*.

A Blow!

Imagine what it did to us to have Harriet Monroe say in *Poetry* that there is too much art in Amy Lowell's *Men, Women and Ghosts?* Too much art!

I can imagine a book having all sorts of too much, but art means not too much or too little of anything. How does Miss Monroe expect Amy Lowell to write, if not like Amy Lowell? She has not come the way of Masters or of Dreiser. She is really the first poet in America to express in her writing something of that leisure from which they tell us Art flowers best.—*jh*.

Moore and More

I have been reading Frank Harris in *Pearson's* on George Moore's *The Brook Kerith*. What Mr. Harris really does is to jump on

George Moore for not writing a history of the life of Christ—the sociology, biology, and geology of Jerusalem.

Only in books of information and science does the writer have to submerge his personality and let the facts have first place. But Mr. Moore thought he was making a work of art, and here no one will deny the first right to the personality of the artist. Mr. Harris cavils about types, landscapes, customs, etc.

Almost the only presentation of Christ outside the Bible has been in painting. Have those painters "defiled our most sacred spiritual possessions" who, from the day when Florence knelt in her streets before Cimabue's Madonna, have painted every incident in the life of Christ and of the Holy Family in every setting from an Italian pasture to a Medici palace, using Italian types, Italian dress, Italian gestures? Has the great El Greco defiled the Christian religion because he painted Spanish Christs and saints in tomb-damp colors? Did Michael Angelo dethrone God because in his *Creation* he painted him with beard and flowing robe on his own authority? And the Germans and the Dutch? They must have been all leagued together to "misrepresent through ignorance," according to such critics as Mr. Harris. But who can say that they have not raised the tradition to a height the old Jews dared not dream?—*jh.*

Mr. Mencken, Philistine

To a person who has not had the advantage of American ancestry and American traditions, it is at first a little confounding, but later it becomes quite right and logical, that Mr. Mencken should be the critic of just the men and things he has chosen to criticize. His treatment of Henry James does not seem to me an error but rather the stamp of the true democratic inability to distinguish "breeds" of things.

Beginning with the egg of a dinosaur, has there ever been anyone who has known less about art and letters than Menken?

He has never known the creative artist as a fellow artist, but as a critic and as the hired editor of a commercial magazine: that gulf could never be explained to any critic, editor or layman . . . of all the first-raters that I know, I don't know one who would just naturally send his best or strongest work to the *Smart Set* . . . that is a part of the thing that makes them first-raters. Somewhere in "Prefaces" Mencken tells just how cagey he has always been about accepting Mss. . . . "before ever I give any thought to its artistic merit and suitability is the question whether its publication will be permitted" . . . does he think that the artists have been less cagey in sending him their work? "I have a long list of such things by American authors, well-devised, well-imagined, well-executed, respectable as human documents and as works of art, but never to be printed in mine or any other American magazine." I should like to see those documents of wronged American art . . . I am willing to wager that they are no better "art," whatever he calls them, than half the stuff that pours into this office—nor any more so-called obscene than teething-ring prattle compared to the things we have peaceably published. BUT we are not *free* to publish them nor were the writers *free* to write them, as far as America was concerned. Now that everything is free we will wait impatiently for Mr. Mencken to release this flood of genius in his new journal. Also—right here let us take up the herd of perfect "wood-sawing" artists loose somewhere between here and Chicago, known only to Mencken. "There is a group which says little and saws wood . . . they are sophisticated, disillusioned, free from cant . . . out of this dispersed, ill-defined group, I believe something will come." Of course disillusioned, sophisticated, free from cant is a pretty poor recipe for the true creative artist, but all sorts of things are done: cripples' races, blind juggling, etc. There are no unknown geniuses, there is no artist anywhere unknown to other artists . . . this is one of the simplest axioms about the nature of the artist. If Mr. Mencken can pull artists out of the middle-west he must use the same formula as the magician with his rabbit. But I am not doubting that they "saw wood."

I have never been able to read Mencken except for his slang. I have found that amusing when he was "whamming" some second-rate bad thing (has he ever slain a first-rate bad thing?); but when he endorses I feel much the same delight in his criterion as I feel when a salesperson assures me that "they are the smartest—I wear them myself."—*jh.*

A Letter

It is no part of my intention to start an argument with you or with any one over the art of Mary Garden. I hate controversy. It is a social vice. This note then is not to answer you but to show you why discussion is futile. We do not exist in the same world. Your concern is with education and the drawing-room, mine with creation, life and the individual.

92

Your slogan is moderation in all things. This is an intrusion on your part. You might leave moderation to the voluptuary. When I come into such close contact with the miserly disposition of the puritan race, the indisposition or inability to spend even a gesture of emotion, the tightness of natures that can never praise or curse splendidly or freely,—the impossibility of discussing any subject becomes to me appalling, and I have no other interest than to strike through the subject to the tensely fundamental differences in people.

You greet any spoken or written statement or observation by me with either a sigh or a laugh. "You are so extravagant, so superlative, so violent." This generosity of my nature is well known to me; so much so that I pity all who have come under it either for approval or disdain. And you are always sure that it has some personal direction. Why not admit your miserly dealings with these matters, and grant that my "outbursts" may be impersonal, even though you yourself suffer under the curse of the personal-outlook in all things.

I am rather hopeless about this, though. Even in our last discussion you took some of my remarks to yourself and talked vaguely about friendship and my offending your religion. I had given you no friendship. Friendship does not lie in my experience. I had not said more against your religion than to imply that the Christian virtues could not stand the wear and tear of my nature. You have known me well enough to know that I should always have respected your religion with silence, if silence is all the respect that you demand. But here was your religion influencing your attitude toward Art, and therefore the discussion. You were expounding Art: I was not attacking Christian Science.

You pretend to an interest in and a love for the arts. Yet you have never given an hour of your time in your whole life to the study of the arts. You have read neither criticism nor theories of Art. But you "love" Art and yet you have not enough respect for it to protect it from your own ignorance. You "love" it and you try to make a utility of it, to apply it to your living and your system of education with no more thought than if you were applying polish to your shoes, and for the same effect. And *I* have insulted *your* intelligence because I refuse to discuss Art in your terms! I thank the gods there are places where insults may not reach.

If I must say what I think about Christian Science: it is the greatest achievement of mediocrity and white corpuscles of the age, and a very necessary adjunct to our great American Index Filing

System. That is all. You recognize as Art only those works of art or so-called works of art that have been considered in good taste, or as innocuous enough to be countenanced in all educational institutions. You know nothing of primitive, ancient, or modern art. You laugh the same laugh at an African negro sculpture and at a Brancusi. If you admit your complete blindness to every form of modern art, including painting, music, poetry, what, may I ask, gives you your sight when you come to the drama as presented by Mary Garden?

You say that she is no actress, that she has no psychology, no intelligence, that she does not create real characters but moves through an opera in a series of beautiful poses like the figures in a dance. And you think this is damning what she does! You are speaking of "Monna Vanna" and this is your criticism because the jeunes filles sitting beside you didn't know, when it was over, whether Monna Vanna was a "pure woman" or not. Can such a lack—the lack of living, the lack of imagination about life—measure the psychology, the intelligence, the art of Mary Garden?

You say you can see that she is very beautiful. She is not. Not with that limited personal beauty you are praising. But there is an over-beauty which she creates out of herself like the beauty created out of a poem or a picture or a piece of sculpture by itself if it possesses the eternal quality of Art. I should have been slightly surprised to find you granting her beauty if I did not know that your kind always trusts its physical sight when it judges beauty as it trusts its taste when it judges Art.

While I knew, before your criticism, what you would do about her Art I must confess I had a curiosity about what she herself would do to you. Whether the timbre of her great existence would reach you.

You say you cannot accept anything that your reason will not accept, that does not meet standards of taste and does not measure with contemporary achievement. By this statement you have cut yourself off forever from the life of the emotions.

In creation of this kind the feelings can be the only judge. The audience can no longer rely upon standards: it must learn slowly a new telegraphy of Art. All comparison with contemporary achievement is drowned in this element of the eternal quality. In creation of this kind all apparent and unimportant details, all questions of opera singing or stage acting must go down before the aesthetic aim of the

94

woman. The exaggerations, the liberties, the distortions,—all the flexibility about which you have so many reservations, are indications of great creation: the main composition is as steady and sustained as a flame in a windless place.—*jh.*

Continuing the Subject

The part of my article you criticise was an attempt to strike through externals to suggest a psychology of anatomy,—a psychology founded on a theory that the definitive lines of the body take their intention from something more fundamental than will power. I have not read Dr. Adler's theory of the "fictitious goal." But I have learned from my study of the human body, in drawing from it, and from that eternal observation of it which becomes a tireless and almost unconscious preoccupation of the painter,—I have learned that it is possible for even the slightly intelligent to stamp his body with all the movement, bearing, and spirit of some cherished ideal or some protective coloring of himself which he wishes to present to the world. In great stress or in crises where the entire will power is overthrown or engaged elsewhere the body, like the mind, assumes its true lines and presence. On the stage this is a very simple way of unmasking a character,—you will say, an obvious way. Then why may not the fictitious role be obvious to the painter,—not a matter of "mere externals" but a legitimate thing to seize upon as a subject for satire or what you choose? This class of people—those of the fictitious role—are really the richest material for Art. It is only in cases where there is creative power back of the fictitious role that the thing itself becomes an art: in poets, musicians, painters, etc., when the fictitious becomes a thing created, where with mind and body they have created a wholly new, unshakable, well-designed character from themselves.

Byron, the unwanted, spiritless, club-footed child who created from this material a brilliant symbol of romantic manly beauty, "flashing a flaming heart across Europe."—*jh.*

Notes on Books

The critics here are like country doctors who carry on their entire business with proprietary or patent medicines.

They have no scent which will lead them to discover for themselves work of exception and creation, and, when bad stuff is put before them with the good, no principles from which they may strongly declare or damn.

They are merely practising reviewers who write carefully-gleaned comments upon two kinds of things: things that come from Europe heralded and stamped with the approval of some well-known critic over there, or things in this country recommended by Mrs. Atherton or Colonel Roosevelt.

When I am offended or amused by some exceeding stupidity or sentimentality I feel a momentary impulse to do something about it; but "I am a man who does not kill mosquitos."

I could never be a useful critic because I can never see myself taking any interest in anything beyond the work of art itself. It is of no interest to me whether the public comes to it early or late or never. If it were I should not try to lure or lead or goad or shame them to accept it. But to prevent my suffering I should entrench me in some creed of reincarnation and rest, knowing that they will have to come.

I have no militant opinions of the offensive kind. I have formed a few principles out of some intelligence that I contained at birth and I have kept them in spite of so-called education and training. I am quite conscious of their operating independently of my thoughts. I cannot understand Ezra Pound and Margaret Anderson when they become impatient with the American public because it won't take Art. I believe if you leave the right kind of food out the right kind of animals will get it—if they are hungry!

It is never a matter of impatience to me when people fail to use their brains; but I am sometimes puzzled when they give no sign of instincts or emotions. I should never be very angry or surprised at an automobile if it refused to go if the gasoline tank were found to be empty, but I would be slightly dashed if the gasoline, properly ignited, gave no action. Water in the gasoline would be the obvious answer to that, I suppose, and Puritanism in the blood the obvious answer to the life in America. This last seems to me more of a question than an answer. It goes back to the kind of people who could adopt a religion so opposed to life, no matter against what they were revolting. Some fundamental lack chose the religion and then chose a place to flourish. Some seeds are blown upon the rocks and are forced to take root there; they soon die, starved or burned out. Others choose the rock because it is all they need. It is cheap and sentimental to talk about the nation being so young. Savages have and are producing significant and permanent Art. Americans always talk and act as if all individuality, all nationality and race-consciousness were inevitably washed away, in the Atlantic, from everyone who dared to come to America. If there is to be Art in America, no fear: Art will have its way. The appalling and unholy thing is a nation that is satisfied and thinks it can exist without Art. It has no precedent, no parallel in history.—jh.

Amy Lowell's Loose Criticism

Miss Lowell showed a nice touch in naming her latest book *Tendencies in Modern American Poetry*. I flared up for just a second on opening it not to find Eliot or Pound included. But when I did not find Amy either I calmed down and discovered the reason: Pound is a force, not a tendency; Eliot sprang full-fledged perhaps; and Amy Lowell has answered for herself in her work. It's a little hard on H. D. to put her in such company. . . .

I am not going into a discussion of the book. My ideas of life and art are so opposed to those expressed by Miss Lowell that to do the thing properly I should have to write another book perhaps longer than hers.

The first sentence in the preface I think has been proved untrue by many artists by whom I think we can judge values. Yeats has not known there was a war. Jean de Bosschere, a Belgian of whom I shall write later, has created well without mentioning the war. I should say from where I stand that Art and the war have only this relation: the war is only a disturbance, a distant dust raised in the road by a mighty Passing. Art preceded the passing.

Miss Lowell believes she can understand and criticise these poets better because she knows them personally. Miss Lowell believes in friends and enemies in Art. I thought we were so far beyond the personal-life criticism of a man's work that all the people who ever did it were long dead. Our only concern is with the poetry. The poetry, if it be art, contains the ultimately differentiating stamp of the man.

Miss Lowell has become the guide, philosopher and friend of her contemporaries. In one place in the book she gently warns them against "seeing life through the medium of sex." In a recent article T. S. Eliot also took a rap at "those American poets who study Freud." Why warn them or jeer them about Freud? If it has taken all the men of science all the ages to discover something of what the first poet knew, why fear for the poets? I believe these scientists have depended entirely upon Art for their researches. Life is so short—to live at all. But to live one's life and one's immortality at once is what the artist must do. To be an artist one must be born containing an intense vision of the spirit of life; he must grip the fundamental qualities in the work of the past and in the little space of a life master a method or form of presenting himself.

If American writers have to study Freud to discover the spirit of life,—in other words, if they have to make themselves poets before they can begin to make poetry, it isn't warnings and jeerings they need: it's pity. Life is so short. But if reading Freud will influence any one in this country to believe that the force which produced him regulates his whole life, if anything can make the rawness in the general attitude toward sex a little less raw, boil the whole nation in Freud!

Miss Lowell's book is a book of loose thinking, of what I might call *cliché* phychology. When she compares poets to painters or dilates on the effects of environment she is as indiscriminate as a clubwoman.—*jh.*

In April, 1916, Ezra Pound had written from London: "Thanks for the last number of the Little Review. *The magazine seems to be looking up . . . though it seems to me rather scrappy and unselective. I thought you started out to prove Ficke's belief that the sonnet is 'Gawd's own city.' However, he seems to have abandoned that church. I still don't know whether you send me the magazine in order to encourage me in believing that my camp stool by Helicon is to be left free from tacks, or whether the paper is sent to convert me from error.*

"I am glad to see in it some mention of Eliot, who is really of interest.

"The Egoist is about to publish Joyce's A Portrait of the Artist as a Young Man *in volume form (since no grab-the-cash firm will take it) and do Lewis's* Tarr *as a serial. I think you will be interested in the two novels, and I hope you will draw attention to them, and to the sporting endeavor of* The Egoist *to do in this dark isle what the* Mercure *has so long done in France, i. e., publish books as well as a magazine."*

By May, 1917, I had asked Pound to become our foreign editor.

Editorial

EZRA POUND

I HAVE accepted the post of Foreign Editor of *The Little Review:* chiefly because:

I

I wished a place where the current prose writings of James Joyce, Wyndham Lewis, T. S. Eliot, and myself might appear regularly, promptly, and together, rather than irregularly, sporadically, and after useless delays.

My connection with *The Little Review* does not imply a severance of my relations with *Poetry* for which I still remain Foreign Correspondent, and in which my poems will continue to appear until its guarantors revolt.

I would say, however, in justification both of *Poetry* and myself, that *Poetry* has never been "the instrument" of my "radicalism." I respect Miss Monroe for all that she has done for the support of American poetry, but in the conduct of her magazine my voice and vote have always been the vote and voice of a minority.

I recognize that she, being "on the ground," may be much better fitted to understand the exigencies of magazine publishing in America, but *Poetry* has done numerous things to which I could never have given my personal sanction, and which could not have occurred in any magazine which had constituted itself my "instrument." *Poetry* has shown an unflagging courtesy to a lot of old fools and fogies whom I should have told to go to hell tout pleinement and bonnement. It has refrained from attacking a number of public nuisances; from implying that the personal charm of the late Mr. Gilder need not have been, of necessity, the sign manifest of a tremendous intellect; from heaping upon the high-school critics of America the contempt which they deserve.

There would have been a little of this contempt to spare for that elder generation of American magazines, founded by mediocrities with good intentions, continued by mediocrities without any intentions, and now "flourishing" under the command and empery of the relicts, private-secretaries and ex-typists of the second regime.

Had *Poetry* been in any sense my "instrument" I should years ago have pointed out certain defects of the elder American writers. Had *Poetry* been my instrument I should never have permitted the deletion of certain fine English words from poems where they rang well and soundly. Neither would I have felt it necessary tacitly to comply with the superstition that the Christian Religion is indispensable, or that it has always existed, or that its existence is ubiquitous, or irrevocable and eternal.

I don't mind the Christian Religion, but I can not blind myself to the fact that Confucius was extremely intelligent. Organized religions have nearly always done more harm than good, and they have always constituted a danger. At any rate, respect to one or another of them has nothing to do with good letters. If any human activity is sacred it is the formulation of thought in clear speech for the use of humanity; any falsification or evasion is evil. The codes of propriety are all local, parochial, transient; a consideration of them, other than as subject matter, has no place in the arts.

I can say these things quite distinctly and without in the least detracting from my praise of the spirited manner in which Miss Monroe has conducted her paper. She is faced with the practical problem of circulating a magazine in a certain peculiar milieu, which thing being so I have nothing but praise for the way she has done it. But that magazine does not express my convictions. Attacks on it, grounded in such belief, and undertaken in the magnanimous hope of depriving me of part of my sustenance, can not be expected to have more than a temporary success and that among ill-informed people.

Blast, founded chiefly in the interest of the visual arts, is of necessity suspended. With Gaudier-Brzeska dead on the field of battle, with Mr. William Roberts, Mr. Wadsworth, Mr. Etchells, and Mr. Wyndham Lewis all occupied in various branches of the service, there is no new vorticist painting to write about. Such manuscript as Mr. Lewis has left with me, and such things as he is able to write in the brief leisure allowed an artillery officer, will appear in these pages.

It is quite impossible that *Blast* should again appear until Mr. Lewis is free to give his full energy to it.

In so far as it is possible, I should like *The Little Review* to aid and abet *The Egoist* in its work. I do not think it can be too often pointed out that during the last four years *The Egoist* has published serially, in the face of no inconsiderable difficulties, the only translation of Remy de Gourmont's *Chevaux de Diomedes;* the best translation of Le Comte de Gabalis, Mr. Joyce's masterpiece *A Portrait of the Artist as a Young Man,* and is now publishing Mr. Lewis's novel

Tarr. Even if they had published nothing else there would be no other current periodical which could challenge this record, but *The Egoist* has not stopped there; they have in a most spirited manner carried out the publication in book form of the *Portrait of the Artist,* and are in the act of publishing Mr. Eliot's poems, under the title *Mr. Prufrock and Observations.*

I see no reason for concealing my belief that the two novels, by Joyce and Lewis, and Mr. Eliot's poems are not only the most important contributions to English literature of the past three years, but that they are practically the only works of the time in which the creative element is present, which in any way show invention, or a progress beyond precedent work. The mass of our contemporaries, to say nothing of our debilitated elders, have gone on repeating themselves and each other.

II

Secondly, there are certain prevalent ideas to which I can not subscribe. I can not believe that the mere height of the Rocky Mountains will produce lofty poetry; we have had little from Chimborazo, the Alps or the Andes. I can not believe that the mere geographical expanse of America will produce of itself excellent writing. The desert of Sahara is almost equally vast. Neither can I look forward with longing to a time when each village shall rejoice in a bad local poetaster making bad verse in the humdrum habitual way that the local architect puts up bad buildings. The arts are not the mediocre habit of mankind. There is no common denominator between the little that is good and the waste that is dull, mediocre. It may be pleasing to know that a cook is president of the local poetry society in Perigord,—there is no reason why a cook should not write as well as a plowman,—but the combination of several activities is really irrelevant. The fact remains that no good poetry has come out of Perigord since the Albigensian crusade, anno domini twelve hundred and nine. There being a local poetry society has not helped to prevent this.

The shell-fish grows its own shell, the genius creates its own milieu. You, the public, can kill genius by actual physical starvation, you may perhaps thwart or distort it, but you can in no way create it.

Because of this simple fact the patron is absolutely at the mercy of the artist, and the artist at the cost of some discomfort—personal, transient discomfort—is almost wholly free of the patron, whether this latter be an individual, or the hydraheaded detestable vulgus.

There is no misanthropy in a thorough contempt for the mob. There is no respect for mankind save in respect for detached individuals.

In this first number under Pound's editorship T. S. Eliot appeared in the Little Review *for the first time.*

Eeldrop and Appleplex

T. S. ELIOT

I

EELDROP and Appleplex rented two small rooms in a disreputable part of town. Here they sometimes came at nightfall, here they sometimes slept, and after they had slept, they cooked oatmeal and departed in the morning for destinations unknown to each other. They sometimes slept, more often they talked, or looked out of the window.

They had chosen the rooms and the neighborhood with great care. There are evil neighborhoods of noise and evil neighborhoods of silence, and Eeldrop and Appleplex preferred the latter, as being the more evil. It was a shady street, its windows were heavily curtained; and over it hung the cloud of a respectability which has something to conceal. Yet it had the advantage of more riotous neighborhoods near by, and Eeldrop and Appleplex commanded from their windows the entrance of a police station across the way. This alone possessed an irresistible appeal in their eyes. From time to time the silence of the street was broken; whenever a malefactor was apprehended, a wave of excitement curled into the street and broke upon the doors of the police station. Then the inhabitants of the street would linger in dressing-gowns, upon their doorsteps: then alien visitors would linger in the street, in caps; long after the centre of misery had been engulphed in his cell. Then Eeldrop and Appleplex would break off their discourse, and rush out to mingle with the mob. Each pursued his own line of enquiry. Appleplex, who had the gift of an extraordinary address with the lower classes of both sexes, questioned the onlookers, and usually extracted full and inconsistent histories: Eeldrop preserved a more passive demeanor, listened to the conversation of the people among themselves, registered in his mind their oaths, their redundance of phrase, their various manners of spitting, and the cries of the victim from the hall of justice within. When the crowd dispersed, Eeldrop and Appleplex returned to their rooms: Appleplex entered the results of his inquiries into large note-books, filed according to the nature of the case, from A (adultery) to Y (yeggmen). Eeldrop smoked reflectively. It may be added that Eeldrop was a sceptic, with a taste for mysticism, and Appleplex a materialist with a leaning toward scepticism; that Eeldrop was learned in theology, and that Appleplex studied the physical and biological sciences.

There was a common motive which led Eeldrop and Appleplex thus to separate themselves from time to time, from the fields of their daily employments and their ordinarily social activities. Both were endeavoring to escape not the commonplace, respectable or even the domestic, but the too well pigeonholed, too taken-for-granted, too highly systematized areas, and,—in the language of those whom they sought to avoid—they wished "to apprehend the human soul in its concrete individuality."

"Why," said Eeldrop, "was that fat Spaniard, who sat at the table with us this evening, and listened to our conversation with occasional curiosity, why was he himself for a moment an object of interest to us? He wore his napkin tucked into his chin, he made unpleasant noises while eating, and while not eating, his way of crumbling bread between fat fingers made me extremely nervous: he wore a waistcoat cafe au lait, and black boots with brown tops. He was oppressively gross and vulgar; he belonged to a type, he could easily be classified in any town of provincial Spain. Yet under the circumstances—when we had been discussing marriage, and he suddenly leaned forward and exclaimed: 'I was married once myself'— we were able to detach him from his classification and regard him for a moment as an unique being, a soul, however insignificant, with a history of its own, once for all. It is these moments which we prize, and which alone are revealing. For any vital truth is incapable of being applied to another case: the essential is unique. Perhaps that is why it is so neglected: because it is useless. What we learned about that Spaniard is incapable of being applied to any other Spaniard, or even recalled in words. With the decline of orthodox theology and its admirable theory of the soul, the unique importance of events has vanished. A man is only important as he is classed. Hence there is no tragedy, or no appreciation of tragedy, which is the same thing. We had been talking of young Bistwick, who three months ago married his mother's housemaid and now is aware of the fact. Who appreciates the truth of the matter? Not the relatives, for they are only moved by affection, by regard for Bistwick's interests, and chiefly by their collective feeling of family disgrace. Not the generous minded and thoughtful outsider, who regards it merely as evidence for the necessity of divorce law reform. Bistwick is classed among the unhappily married. But what Bistwick feels when he wakes up in the morning, which is the great important fact, no detached outsider conceives. The awful importance of the ruin of a life is overlooked. Men are only allowed to be happy or miserable in classes. In Gopsum Street a man murders his mistress. The important fact is that for the man the act is eternal, and that for the brief space he has to live, he is already dead. He is already in a different world from ours. He has crossed the frontier. The important fact is that something is done which can not be undone—a possibility which none of us realize until we face it ourselves. For the man's neighbors the important fact is what the man killed her with? And at precisely what time? And who found the body? For the 'enlightened public' the case is merely evidence for the Drink question, or Unemployment, or some other category of things to be reformed. But the mediaeval world, insisting on the eternity of punishment, expressed something nearer the truth."

"What you say," replied Appleplex, "commands my measured adherence. I should think, in the case of the Spaniard, and in the many other interesting cases which have come under our attention at the door of the police station, what we grasp in that moment of pure observation on which we pride ourselves, is not alien to the principle of classification, but deeper. We could, if we liked, make excellent comment upon the nature of provincial Spaniards, or of destitution (as misery is called by the philanthropists), or on homes for working girls. But such is not our intention. We aim at experience in the particular centres in which alone it is evil. We avoid classification. We do not deny it. But when a man is classified something is lost. The majority of mankind live on paper currency: they use terms which are merely good for so much reality, they never see actual coinage."

"I should go even further than that," said Eeldrop. "The majority not only have no language to express anything save generalized man; they are for the most part unaware of themselves as anything but generalized men. They are first of all government officials, or pillars of the church, or trade unionists, or poets, or unemployed; this cataloguing is not only satisfactory to other people for practical purposes, it is sufficient to themselves for their 'life of the spirit.' Many are not quite real at any moment. When Wolstrip married, I am sure he said to himself: 'Now I am consummating the union of two of the best families in Philadelphia.'"

"The question is," said Appleplex, "what is to be our philosophy. This must be settled at once. Mrs. Howexden recommends me to read Bergson. He writes very entertainingly on the structure of the eye of the frog."

"Not at all," interrupted his friend. "Our philosophy is quite irrelevant. The essential is, that our philosophy should spring from our point of view and not return upon itself to explain our point of view. A philosophy about intuition is somewhat less likely to be intuitive than any other. We must avoid having a platform."

"But at least," said Appleplex, "we are . . ."

"Individualists. No!! nor anti-intellectualists. These also are labels. The 'individualist' is a member of a mob as fully as any other man: and the mob of individualists is the most unpleasing, because it has the least character. Nietzsche was a mob-man, just as Bergson is an intellectualist. We cannot escape the label, but let it be one which carries no distinction, and arouses no self-consciousness. Sufficient that we should find simple labels, and not further exploit them. I am, I confess to you, in private life, a bank-clerk. . . ."

"And should, according to your own view, have a wife, three children, and a vegetable garden in a suburb," said Appleplex.

"Such is precisely the case," returned Eeldrop, "but I had not thought it necessary to mention this biographical detail. As it is Saturday night, I shall return to my suburb. Tomorrow will be spent in that garden. . . ."

"I shall pay my call on Mrs. Howexden," murmured Appleplex.

II

The suburban evening was grey and yellow on Sunday; the gardens of the small houses to left and right were rank with ivy and tall grass and lilac bushes; the tropical South London verdure was dusty above and mouldy below; the tepid air swarmed with flies. Eeldrop, at the window, welcomed the smoky smell of lilac, the gramaphones, the choir of the Baptist chapel, and the sight of three small girls playing cards on the steps of the police station.

"On such a night as this," said Eeldrop, "I often think of Scheherazade, and wonder what has become of her."

Appleplex rose without speaking and turned to the files which contained the documents for his "Survey of Contemporary Society." He removed the file marked *London* from between the files *Barcelona* and *Boston* where it had been misplaced, and turned over the papers rapidly. "The lady you mention," he rejoined at last, "whom I have listed not under S. but as Edith, alias Scheherazade, has left but few evidences in my possession. Here is an old laundry account which she left for you to pay, a cheque drawn by her and marked 'R/D,' a letter from her mother in Honolulu (on ruled paper), a poem written on a restaurant bill—'To Atthis'—and a letter by herself, on Lady Equistep's best notepaper, containing some damaging but entertaining information about Lady Equistep. Then there are my own few observations on two sheets of foolscap."

"Edith," murmured Eeldrop, who had not been attending to this catalogue, "I wonder what has become of her. 'Not pleasure, but fulness of life . . . to burn ever with a hard gem-like flame,' those were her words. What curiosity and passion for experience! Perhaps that flame has burnt itself out by now."

"You ought to inform yourself better," said Appleplex severely, "Edith dines sometimes with Mrs. Howexden, who tells me that her passion for experience has taken her to a Russian pianist in Bayswater. She is also said to be present often at the Anarchist Tea Rooms, and can usually be found in the evening at the Cafe de l'Orangerie."

"Well," replied Eeldrop, "I confess that I prefer to wonder what has become of her. I do not like to think of her future. Scheherazade grown old! I see her grown very plump, full-bosomed, with blond hair, living in a small flat with a maid, walking in the Park with a Pekinese, motoring with a Jewish stock-broker. With a fierce appetite for food and drink, when all other appetite is gone, all other appetite gone except the insatiable increasing appetite of vanity; rolling on two wide legs, rolling in motorcars, rolling toward a diabetic end in a seaside watering place."

"Just now you saw that bright flame burning itself out," said Appleplex, "now you see it guttering thickly, which proves that your vision was founded on imagination, not on feeling. And the passion for experience—have you remained so impregnably Pre-Raphaelite as to believe in that? What real person, with the genuine resources of instinct, has ever believed in the passion for experience? The passion for experience is a criticism of the sincere, a creed only of the histrionic. The passionate person is passionate about this or that, perhaps about the least significant things, but not about experience. But Marius, des Esseintes, Edith . . .'"

"But consider," said Eeldrop, attentive only to the facts of Edith's history, and perhaps missing the point of Appleplex's remarks, "her unusual career. The daughter of a piano tuner in Honolulu, she secured a scholarship at the University of California, where she graduated with Honors in Social Ethics. She then married a celebrated billiard professional in San Francisco, after an acquaintance of twelve hours, lived with him for two days, joined a musical comedy chorus, and was divorced in Nevada. She turned up several years later in Paris and was known to all the Americans and English at the Café du Dome as Mrs. Short. She reappeared in London as Mrs. Griffiths, published a small volume of verse, and was accepted in several circles known to us. And now, as I still insist, she has disappeared from society altogether."

"The memory of Scheherazade," said Appleplex, "is to me that of Bird's custard and prunes in a Bloomsbury boarding house. It is not my intention to represent Edith as merely disreputable. Neither is she a tragic figure. I want to know why she misses. I cannot altogether analyse her 'into a combination of known elements' but I fail to touch anything definitely unanalysable.

"Is Edith, in spite of her romantic past, pursuing steadily some hidden purpose of her own? Are her migrations and eccentricities the sign of some unguessed consistency? I find in her a quantity of shrewd observation, an excellent fund of criticism, but I cannot connect them into any peculiar vision. Her sarcasm at the expense of her friends is delightful, but I doubt whether it is more than an attempt to mould herself from outside, by the impact of hostilities, to emphasise her isolation. Everyone says of her, 'How perfectly impenetrable!' I suspect that within there is only the confusion of a dusty garret."

"I test people," said Eeldrop, "by the way in which I imagine them as waking up in the morning. I am not drawing upon memory when I imagine Edith waking to a room strewn with clothes, papers, cosmetics, letters and a few books, the smell of Violettes de Parme and stale tobacco. The sunlight beating in through broken blinds, and broken blinds keeping out the sun until Edith can compel herself to attend to another day. Yet the vision does not give me much pain. I think of her as an artist without the slightest artistic power."

"The artistic temperament—" began Appleplex.

"No, not that." Eeldrop snatched away the opportunity. "I mean that what holds the artist together is the work which he does; separate him from his work and he either disintegrates or solidifies. There is no interest in the artist apart from his work. And there are, as you said, those people who provide material for the artist. Now Edith's poem 'To Atthis' proves beyond the shadow of a doubt that she is not an artist. On the other hand I have often thought of her, as I thought this evening, as presenting possibilities for poetic purposes. But the people who can be material for art must have in them something unconscious, something which they do not fully realise or understand. Edith, in spite of what is called her impenetrable mask, presents herself too well. I cannot use her; she uses herself too fully. Partly for the same reason I think, she fails to be an artist: she does not live at all upon instinct. The artist is part of him a drifter, at the mercy of impressions, and another part of him allows this to happen for the sake of making use of the unhappy creature. But in Edith the division is merely the rational, the cold and detached part of the artist, itself divided. Her material, her experience that is, is already a mental product, already digested by reason. Hence Edith (I only at this moment arrive at understanding) is really the most orderly person in existence, and the most rational. Nothing ever happens to her; everything that happens is her own doing."

"And hence also," continued Appleplex, catching up the thread, "Edith is the least detached of all persons, since to be detached is to be detached from one's self, to stand by and criticise coldly one's own passions and vicissitudes. But in Edith the critic is coaching the combatant."

"Edith is not unhappy."

"She is dissatisfied, perhaps."

"But again I say, she is not tragic: she is too rational. And in her career there is no progression, no decline or degeneration. Her condition is once and for always. There is and will be no catastrophe.

"But I am tired. I still wonder what Edith and Mrs. Howexden have in common. This invites the consideration (you may not perceive the connection) of Sets and Society, a subject which we can pursue tomorrow night."

Appleplex looked a little embarrassed. "I am dining with **Mrs.** Howexden," he said. "But I will reflect upon the topic before I see you again."

The Week-end

LOUIS GILMORE

Is anything more tedious
Than a blue sky
And a gravel-walk
Between trees

Except the white
Woman at my side
Who is pretending
That I love her!

Poems

WILLIAM BUTLER YEATS

THE WILD SWANS AT COOLE

The trees are in their autumn beauty
The woodland paths are dry
Under the October twilight the water
Mirrors a still sky
Upon the brimming water among the stones
Are nine and fifty swans.

The nineteenth autumn has come upon me
Since I first made my count.
I saw, before I had well finished,
All suddenly mount
And scatter wheeling in great broken rings
Upon their clamorous wings.

But now they drift on the still water
Mysterious, beautiful;
Among what rushes will they build;
By what lake's edge or pool
Delight men's eyes when I awake some day
To find they have flown away?

I have looked upon these brilliant creatures

And now my heart is sore.
All's changed since I, hearing at twilight
The first time on this shore
The bell-beat of their wings above my head,
Trod with a lighter tread.

Unwearied still, lover by lover,
They paddle in the cold
Companionable streams or climb the air;
Their hearts have not grown old,
Attend upon them still.
Passion or conquest, wander where they will,

October, 1916.

PRESENCES

This night has been so strange that it seemed
As if the hair stood up on my head.
From going down of the sun I have dreamed
That women laughing, or timid or wild,
In rustle of lace or silken stuff,
Climbed up my creaking stair. They had read
All I have rhymed of that monstrous thing
Returned and yet unrequited love.
They stood in the door and stood between
My great wood lectern and the fire
Till I could hear their hearts beating:
One is a harlot, and one a child
That never looked upon man with desire,
And one, it may be, a queen.

November, 1915.

In this first number under Pound's direction, Wyndham Lewis made his appearance in a series of "Imaginary Letters." They were written to his wife (Lewis was in the war) and we continued to publish them for over a year. Their length prevents me from giving them all. I have edited down to essentials, on the basis of their ideas —as an example of Lewis' "leaping mind."

Imaginary Letters

(Six Letters of William Bland Burn to his Wife)

WYNDHAM LEWIS

I

Petrograd, January 7, 1917

DEAR Lydia,

. . . I am glad you ask me those questions. "Why not be happy?" The chief use of a wife, after love, is to disgust you with your weaknesses, and to watch them constantly returning, by all sorts of bye-ways, to the attack. Or rather they seem to regard a wife as ideal "cover," and a first-rate avenue of return. You kick one out one day, and you find him the next skulking beneath your wife's petticoat waiting his chance. The conjugal skirt is a trap from which, any day you feel like hunting, you can return with a full bag.

"Why not be happy?" That is, why not abandon the plane of exasperation and restlessness, and be content with the approximations and self-deceptions of the majority? Well, of course happiness of that sort is not within my grasp, if I wished it. But why expect from *you* a perpetual discipline? That discipline is however, at least as easy for you as for me, if you think of it. The serenity and ease with which you accomplish the most gruesome self-restraints at first surprised me—until I remembered that you did not take them seriously, like me, or suffer from their necessity. Not having a sense of values (very roughly a masculine corner) but only the complacency of an obedient mummer, you cover the harshest ground with Spartan face. It is only when you are left alone that you complain or question seriously. You forget a little the intricacies of our ceremonial dance, and find that worrying. Don't be offended at what I have been saying. You need not be ashamed of being calmly hypnotic. Yorke was older than you when he was born. We should all be mad if our mothers did not invigorate us with the airs of a twinkling, early and sweet world, and feed us with a remote "happiness."

You want more "happiness," though, for your child. Why? I would not be anything but what I am (unless I could find something "unhappier") and why should *he*, in the future, wish to be anything but what I think he will become? There is an intoxication in the vistas of effort and self-castigation which cannot be bought with "happiness." Again you might say, "*Why* be so hard on this person or on that, and not accept him as a "good fellow," or take him at the valuation of the world, and derive amusement and sentimental satisfaction from him, Richards, Hepburn, Tom, Mrs. Fisher Wake, etc., etc. They have all been "quarrelled with." That is, I have not

111

been civil, and we do not see them. But I have left you a Menu of equally amusing birds to while away life with. You would have quarrelled with the first lot in time and in due course on unreasonable grounds, if I had not forestalled you. I have merely done the job cleanly and reasonably. *Clean* is not the word, you argue, for this cold-blooded process. It is not veiled in the forms and frenzies of life, but indecently done before people shocked into attention. The intellect is cruel and repugnant. Dirty, that is. (Everything loathsome is related to dirt).

I am attributing a line of argument to you, and a tone, which your questions do not warrant. But I am taking them to their ultimate development. I must always do this, c'est mon mal et ma gloire.

Thousands of beautiful women have spent their lives in cloisters; there are millions of old maids. When I am with you I show a full, if not excessive, appreciation of your sex. You have a child. With a sort of lofty cunning you dote on my cleverness and improve your own. You would not be with me if you required anything much different from what you get. But still you deplore some of my notions and habits. I suspect my friend Villerant of having smiled at my naivete, and also suggested that in some things I was cracked and difficult.

I will follow the line of argument that your questions imply: "Why not ease off a little?" You would say, "You will admit that it is *uncomfortable* to be at loggerheads with *anybody*. You flatter a person by taking so much notice of him as to turn your back."

(At this point I interject: "It is nevertheless more *comfortable* for me, in the long run, to be rude than to be polite. It is a physical discomfort not to show, after a time, my feelings.")

You continue: "Being so easily disgusted with people suggests a naive idealism. We are all ridiculous, looked at properly, by means of our little forked bodies. We are disgusting physically (except a few in their fluffy and velvety youth). So why carp, and glare, and sheer off? Take life, in the English-civilized way, as a joke; our funny bodies and their peculiar needs, our ambitions, greeds, as comic stunts of an evidently gentleman-creator, who is most unquestionably 'a sport.' "

At this point, my dear lady, I am going to stop you, and bring in the counter-flux; release the over-mounting objections.

First. I feel that we are obviously in the position of Ulysses' companions; and there is nothing I resent more than people settling down to become what is sensible for a swine. I will still stalk about with my stumpy legs, and hold my snout high, however absurd it may be. We must get through this enchantment without too many memories of abasement. We most need, in the inner fact, *changing back into men again!* And I don't want the "happiness" of the swill-pail, but a perpetual restlessness until the magic is over! I set out somewhere on a legendary expedition= I do not date from Nineteen Two.= I do not feel like sniggering over our plight. I am *permanently* in a bad temper!=(I am not "a sport.")

So! So! So!

Society, most people, have their little bit of beauty and energy which is a small compartment of life. The rest is the gentleman-animal, which ambles along, the end-in-itself= oh yes!

I do not like the gentleman-animal. He is a poor beast. His glory is to belong to a distinguished herd. He prefers to himself a Human Cliché of manners, catch-phrases, fashionable slang, herd-voice (when he Baas the well-instructed can instantly tell that he comes from a *very* distinguished herd; or from a quite good herd; or from a respectable herd, as the case may be). When he hears a similar Baa he pricks his ears up, and Baas more loudly and lispingly himself, to show his label and that he is there, he prefers a code which is, most of it, imbecile in its inductions, impracticable, and not holding water. Human weakness, human *need*—is the worse for a gloss. You do not agree? I have that feeling very strongly.

But I have amplified too much, and will return to what I wished immediately to say.=The best that most people can see is the amiable-comic, the comfortable, the advantages of the gentleman-animal. I, who see beauty and energy so much that they bulk and outweigh a thousand times these cowardly contentments and *pis-allers,* why should you expect me to admit society as anything but an organized poltroonery and forgetfulness? The gentleman-animal has his points. And it is just when he is successful that we should dislike him most. For he is the most cunning effort of society to close its eyes and clog its ears. He is the great sham reconciliation and justifying of ease.

In glancing through what I have written in this letter, I find things that, were I writing for any but a familiar ear, would require restating. There is an implication, for instance, that enthusiastic herd-man could, if he would, produce some excellent ego in place of his social self, and that it is this immoral waste of fine material

that I object to= whereas of course he is radically boring and ob-
noxious. He is a *perfect metis,* the gentleman-animal, having crossed
consummately his human and inhuman qualities. I like to see things
side by side, perfectly dual and unmixed. Neither side of a man is
responsible for the other.

Kiss Yorke for me. All love to yourself.

Yours, William Burn.

II

Petrograd, February, 1917.

My dear Lydia:

Once more to the charge= I will take two things and answer
them.=First, you object to my treatment of the Gentleman, because
you sharply maintain, more or less, that I by no means object to
being a gentleman myself.=On that point, my dear girl, you have
not got me. For many purposes, on occasion I should not hesitate
to emphasize the fact that I was not born in the gutter. If, for instance, I was applying for a post where such a qualification was
necessary, Harrow would not be forgotten. The Gutter generally
spoils a man's complexion in childhood. He grows up with sores
around his mouth and a constantly dirty skin. His eyes, unless he
has them well in hand, become wolfish and hard, etc. Who would not
be better pleased that he was born on the sunny side of the wall?
All that has nothing to do with my argument. Those things are in
themselves nothing to linger round, although the opposite, squalor
and meanness, it is more excusable to remember and lament.

But in your last letter you reveal an idea that seems chiefly to
have struck you, and which is at the bottom of your present obstinacy. I will give you my opinion on it in the form of a criticism of
an article I read yesterday in an English paper (one of those you
sent me).

A Russian war-novel is discussed. The writer of the article "does
not care much for Russian books," he finds that "the Englishman
begins where the Russian leaves off." The Russian book seems to
deal with the inner conflict of a Russian grocer on the outbreak of
War. The Russian grocer is confused and annoyed. He asks what
all this bloody trouble has to do with *him*—the small grocer. He
cogitates on the causes of such upheavals, and is not convinced that
there is anything in them calling for his participation. But eventually
he realizes that there is a great and moving abstraction called Russia

=the *old* abstraction in fact, the old Pied Piper whistling his mournful airs, and waving towards a snow-bound horizon. And—*le voilà* in khaki=or the Russian equivalent. At this point he becomes "noble," and of interest to the writer of the article—But there, alas, the book ends,= Now, (of course the writer of the article continues) *we* in England do not do things in that way. We do not portray the boring and hardly respectable conflict. No Englishman (all Englishmen having the instincts of gentlemen) admits the possibility of such a conflict. *We* are *accomplished* beings, *des hommes, ou plutôt des gentlemen faits!* We should begin with the English grocer already in khaki, quite calm, (he would probably be described as a little "grim" withal) in the midst of his military training on Salisbury Plain. A Kiplingesque picture of that: Revetting would come in, and bomb-throwing at night. He next would be in the trenches. The writer would show, without the cunning, hardly respectable, disguise of any art, how the Balham grocer of to-day was the same soldier, really, that won at Waterloo= You would not get a person or a fact, but a piece of patriotic propaganda (the writer of course being meanwhile a shrewd fellow, highly approved and well-paid).

Now glance at Tolstoi for a moment, that arch Russian bore, and at his book of Sebastopol sketches. He was an hereditary noble, and it is rather difficult to say that an hereditary noble is not a gentleman. But can the English journalist in his *"fort interieur"* admit that Tolstoi was a gentleman, all things considered? These foreign "nobles" are a funny sort of gentlemen, anyway. For let us see how Tolstoi writes of the Russians at Sebastopol.= He arrives at the town of Sebastopol. He has read in the Moscow newspapers of the "heroic defenders of Sebastopol." His first impression is one of astonishment and disappointment of a sort. For there is nothing noticeably heroic about the demeanour of the soldiers working at the quays or walking in the streets. They are not even heroic by reason of the ineffable "cheeriness" of the British Tommy—(No journalist would be tolerated for a moment who did not, once in every twenty lines, remark on this ineffable national heroism of humour.)=Tolstoi, that is, does not *want* to see heroes, but men under given conditions and, that is, sure enough, what he sees. He also, being an hereditary noble and so on, does not want to make his living. One more opportunity of truth and clearness! Next, when Tolstoi gets up to the bastions, he again sees no heroes with any ineffable national cachet. The "heroes" of his sketches and tales, in fact, stoop and scurry along behind parapets in lonely sectors, and when they see another man coming straighten themselves out, and clank their spurs. They kill people in nightmares, and pray pessimistically to their God. You cannot at the end apply *any* labels to them. Tolstoi's account of their sensations and genuine exploits would not strike terror in the heart of future enemies of the Russian race; it is not an advertisement, or the ordinary mawkish bluff thrown over a reality. He had the sense to see human beings and not Russians. And *Russians* are chiefly redoubtable, and admirable, because of this capacity of impersonal seeing and feeling. Where they are least Russian in fact.

The discriminating enemy in reading these sketches would fear that more than he would any unreal or interested gush.

There always remains the question as to whether, by gush and bluff and painting a pretty picture of a man, you cannot make him *become* that picture= and whether, politically, it may not be desirable to manufacture illusions of that description. But what have we got to do with politicians?

Again, I am not saying that Russians have not a national gush. Tolstoi himself indulges in it. Everybody indulges in such things. It is a question only of the scale of such indulgence; of the absence per head in a population of the reverse.

So then, what the paper-writer's point amounted to was that only *gentlemen* (or, sententiously, *men*) were worth writing about= or only at the moment when a man becomes a "gentleman" is he interesting, worth noticing, or suitable for portrayal. We all, however, know the simple rules and manifestations of this ideal figure. There is not much left to say on the subject. Ah yes, but there is such and such a one's ineffable *way* of being a gentleman!—

In London you will meet few educated people who really are willing or able to give Russian books their due. Dostoevsky is a sort of epileptic bore, Tolstoi a wrong-headed old altruistic bore, Gorky a Tramp-stunt bore, Turgenev, even, although in another category, in some way disappointing. —All Russian writers insist on discovering America, opening discussions on matters that our institutions, our position in society, our Franco-English intelligence preclude any consideration of. There is something permanently transcendental and disconcerting about the Slav infant, and he pours his words out and argues interminably, and is such an inveterate drunkard,—as though his natural powers of indecorum and earnestness were not already enough.

What really could be said of the Russian is this=Shakespeare is evidently better than any Russian novelist, or more permanently valuable. But the little Russian Grocer could rival Hamlet in vacillation; or any Russian, Shakespeare, in his portrayal of the *machinery* of the mind. Dostoevsky is not more dark and furious than Shakespeare's pessimistic figures, Lear, Macbeth, etc. *But we are not Englishmen of Shakespeare's days.*

We are very pleased that in the time of Elizabeth such a national ornament existed. But Shakespeare would be an anachronism to-day.

Dostoevsky and Co. were anachronisms as contemporaries of Tennyson and Napoleon III. *Had they been embedded two centuries back in Sixteenth Century Russia,* they would not be read, but would not cause annoyance and be called epileptic bores. Epilepsy would have been all right in those distances.—There is nothing dévoué about epilepsy to-day, any more than there is about a King!

I think I have been lucid, if rather long-winded=

How I look on these Christian Demi-Gods of the Steppes you know. I like them immensely. For a single brandyish whiff from one of Dostoevsky's mouths, at some vivid angle of turpitude I would give all English literature back to Shelley's songs. Turgenev's *Sportsman's Sketches* enchant me. They are so sober, delicate and nonchalant; I can think of nothing like them. Gogol's Tchichikoff is back with Cervantes, Sterne and the others who have not any peers in these days.

Today= the requirements of the little man, especially of this day, are a similar thing to the *Russian,* the *Englishman,* etc. We must disembarrass ourselves of this fetish or gush, as of that other.— I want to live with Shakespeare and Cervantes=and I have gone to war for good with all things that would oppose a return to those realities.

I feel you, in my absence, becoming enmeshed in environing respectability and its amiable notions. I feel that this letter may require another fervour to drive home, or excuse, its own=A *coup de poing* is the best method of enforcing an idea (or a shell)= the mouth is similarly a more satisfactory aperture than the ear for introducing a philosophy into another body. Yorke is the embodiment of my philosophy. I love Yorke in exactly the way that I love a character in Molière or Turgenev. Yorke is the only living thing *except yourself,* that I know or find alive to the same extent.

I am looking forward to your next letter. Much love.

W. B. Burn.

III

Dear Lydd,

I am glad you decree that the debate shall continue. You seem to desire a debate to the death.

I don't know why my coming to Russia should have provoked this stubborn battle in your brain; this kind of revolution against Russia! I suppose you are pretty jealous of this immense land, and you perhaps feel that my liaison with it is hardly intellectually respectable. Russia is *too* elementary! However, to approach your latest objections. Mine is not really a case of "national engouement" as you would persuade me (only engouement for Russian things instead of those of my own country). All Russian books of the last twenty years that I have read are disappointing. "Sanine" is certainly not as good as Bernard Shaw. Gorky was the best figure—and writer. Living here, you can get a better sense of the books of the Russian writers of the last century, but it is not like living among their books. Nor are the people around you as prepossessing as the fictitious nation. But where would art be if they were? The Russian novelists have given an almost unexampled illusion of a living people. Their Christianity, good sense and the method of realism each contributed to this.

Not only are most Russians not Dostoevskys, they are not even Volchaninovs or Pavel Pavlovitches. Raskolnikoffs and Golyadkins mope and trot about in certain members, but they badly need the presence of their creator. When they were looked at by their great brother he entered into them as he looked and they ran mad at once, eventually exploding with energy.

There are masses of the cheaply-energetic Oriental (non-Jew) and of the unsatisfactory-Teutonic. The springs of Dostoevsky's imagination I have chiefly found in thick, pungent, suddenly discovered Oases; in families, restaurants or moods of the town. But it is only the books that matter. And the Russian novels were made with this material, condensed, vividly exploited. They are better books than any Englishman or Frenchman wrote at the same period, not because genius varies, but because the material was richer and realler. When an Englishman was given a similar chance, we threw up Shakespeare.

William Blake pushed on into the unimmanent atmosphere of spooks and of legend and produced a powerful group of phantoms. He vituperated his enemies—enemies are always real and interesting —and plagiarised children and Elizabethans. In that way, with a queer and clever engineering of his own, he climbed up where Shakespeare and all successful genius resides; he established himself there as a matter of course; with a proselytizing lack of self-consciousness he took up his abode in that simple and exclusive heaven—first having enthusiastically removed all his clothes!

Now, we can admit that a nation is not necessary for a fine book. If the human material should be found faulty, you can turn to scorpions and beetles, or, like Blake, you can affect the heavily historied bogey; awaken the man who built the Pyramids and pretend that it was *he* who awakened *you*.

And there is the scholar's book, which is merely embarrassed by a handy matter, which naturally thrives on the remote, not brought to new life, matter, but left where it is, with its academic perspectives, or whose only interest or use for immediate things is dispassionate and critical and whose success is a structure of delicate adjustments, not the belief of an incurable love. All the full and tragic artists partake of the destiny of the popular hero; thousands of people contribute to their success only in this case without meaning to; each man or woman hands in his or her fraction of vitality; wherever they go, there is a great crowd with them. Their brain is the record of their sympathies, people pour in and are piled up, with a persistent classification, until giant-like and permanent images, the "types" of drama or fiction are produced: Raskolnikoffs, Golyadkins and Alioshas. It is the sense of power bestowed by this throng that enables them to create so hotly, and with so unreasonable a faith.

You remember my remarks about Colossi in a former letter. You can only get Colossi by sticking two or more men together. The perfected unamalgamated man recedes from any semblance of human or material power. As he refines he loses in stamina and scale, carried to its farthest limit it is the gnat's song, a sigh, a shadow. These things are in different categories, not, as is popularly assumed, a big and a little of the same species. One thing is not *better* than the other. You pay your money and take your choice.

But when twenty men are conglomerated into a giant, it is not, in the case of genius, simply an addition sum. The fine fellow is the head of the Colossus. But we must admit that he never succeeds in quite actively canalizing the mass. There is always the slovenly character of all giants about the organism. His superb megaphone is not so successful as the attenuated voice of the whittled-down human reed. Dostoevsky was a peculiarly untidy and undependable freak of vastness, addicted to interminable nervous seizures (do you know of a single story of his in which there is not an epileptic?), drunken to a fault; but a true god. And every Russian I meet I know to be a posthumous fragment of my favourite Deity. So there you are. It is useless your talking about "national engouements"; it is idle your hinting that my caprice for Colossi (and such dirty, uncouth and childish ones at that—not nice clean Greek ones!) is unintelligent and compromising. You stick to the gentlemanly silver buzzing of the French critical perfection. I wish to live in the sanguine, unsavoury fairy-land where the Giants consort and where the Man-Child wanders. I hope this will not divide us. For I like the fastidious things as well; as much as you do.

I now am going to break the ice and refer to something that so far, in my shyness, I have avoided. You, for your part, have pretended also not to have been conscious of it. So we have discussed nearly everything except this. I think it is unfortunate that we have not had it out, before, and gazed at it in mutual horror.

I refer to my ugliness.

The horrible thought steals over me as I write this that you may have thought I considered myself handsome—or at least unique! And I even seem to remember occasions on which you looked quizzingly and pityingly at me when I was speaking of beauty; as though you considered that I would not have spoken in that way had I not imagined that I had my share of looks. Also I do not, let me say for your instruction, consider myself *tall*. Unlike most little men, I know that I am short and stunted.

And as to my looks, there is no blotch or puff in my face with which I am not bitterly acquainted. I know that my lower lip protrudes ill-temperedly. My hands are a Palagial nightmare, ou plutôt abyssal. The horrible straight thick thatch of hair does not seem to me a silken chevelure. My stumpy muscular limbs, my objectionable buttocks that protrude, the back of my head that also protrudes, preventing me from ever getting a hat to fit me properly, I have all these details noted and oh! hated and deplored. My small and staring eyes, with the pockets underneath, I know do not redeem, as eyes are said frequently to do, the disgusting mask in which they are set. I have the face of a blind man, sunk in a dark and filthy stupor; my raised triangular eyebrows and jutting lip give this impression. I am physically, I know, one of the most ungainly blighted and repulsive of God's creatures. Why, then, was I filled so full of this will to Beauty, of these convulsions towards realization of power? Why was I given the wisdom to hate myself? Is the body I was given such a botched and valueless thing, because Nature regarded a fine body as wasted in my case, seeing I should live in and through other people, and never, in that sense, be *at home?*

"Here, you haven't much use for a showy thing of this sort, Mr. Burn. With a nobby brain like that you won't have much use for these trifles. Take this poor devil's, Mr. Burn, you need a fine coat less than he does. The World is at your feet. *I* know Mr. Burn!"

This was chucked over to me! There is probably an imbecile somewhere with the head of a god, and a bearing that would be appropriate to me. Neither he nor I are selling matches. But when I approach the world with my books, they think I am vending laces and never quite get over the notion.

I can console myself, however. I can say, "You can enter into his form and possess it more than he ever will do himself. What is your imagination for?"

A sort of burglar's consolation, although damned real.

So this plague of mine is probably a sacrifice, I am relieving someone of this winsome, glad, alluring carcase.

Alas!

But you will see in all this, I expect, nothing but an attempt to extenuate my ugliness and put it in a more favourable light, a rather romantic light, even. But I am not doing that. I know that there is no getting away from or forgiveness for such preposterous and hate-producing plainness. For it is a sort of uncomeliness that arouses one's worst feelings; is it not?

With such a physique, I should never have married, I am aware. Thank God, Yorke, by a miracle (the miracle of your beauty, I suppose) appears to have escaped the contamination of my flesh or to have sailed over it in some way.

But how horrible it must be for you, my dear girl! A score of times I have said to myself that I would not come back to you, but release you from such a repulsive little satyr.

All cats are grey in the dark, we know. But how that ugly bumpy little body, and big head, with its rough red puffy skin must disgust you when I take you in my arms—*you,* who have a dower of bodily perfection and whom I smirch even at this distance in think· ing of you. And the abominable lechery that the sight of you awakens in me. What a gruesome beast I must be!

Can you stand me? Tell me the truth!

We have not got on quite so well lately. Your letters are curi- ous. You seem to be becoming unduly critical of my mind, a ten- dency you have not formerly displayed. Are you accusing my mind of what you would really say of my body? Is it because you have never been harsh enough to curse and comment upon my distress- ing person, that you now attack my mind? *Must* you abuse and at last complain of *something?*

Perhaps this letter may deflect your criticism into its natural channel. Or do you consider my mental enthusiasms part and parcel of my ugliness? Do you see my twisted and thwarted body with a wave of exasperation, in my enthusiasm for the epileptic pages of the unfortunate Feodor?

One truth, however, I have tested enough for it to be no more experimental. I am fixed on that. The body does not matter the smallest fraction where the mind is concerned. I can imagine beauty as fluently and fully as if I had the head of Apollo. The smallness of my eyes does not contract the surging and spreading of my understanding. The twists in a body can only impress them- selves on a spirit that dwells constantly therein. Mine comes back to its disgraceful bed, and lies cramped and ill in it. But it was nurtured straight before it ever lay there. A fine and comely ap- pearance is useful for repose only. Goethe's god-like person gave him plenty of calm sleep. If I said *too much* you would sneer and think that the grapes were sour! ! If my body were weakly and sick and my mind were one of those that had the power to go here and there and break into other minds, that body would not prevent me from imagining physical heroism. Or rather, I could imagine it no better if my mind had been originally installed in a sinewy carcase, like Hackenscidt's. I am debarred from nothing in *my* world: only from *you*.

I know I have not got you as I otherwise should. I know it was madness to choose such a beauty.

Schopenhauer's wretched phrase "Women consider that *they* supply the beauty" had stuck in my head. And yet why abuse him? It is true, up to a point, women *do* reply for the beauty. But!— Obviously there is a limit beyond which they are likely to regard their proverbial fairness as inadequate! My face, I am aware, is far the other side of that limit!

You know how physical beauty knocks me over. The "beautiful young man" species holds me as tongue-tied and gets me in the same way that social eminence does the humble or inexperienced. I simply stand gaping at a handsome young man. Each of his gestures or smiles is balm to me. My face, like some belching ocean plant spread towards the light, seems to expand in front of his comeliness in the idiotic hope of a cure. Such boys are as soothing as rain to a man with a fever. And after passing some time with one of these dazzling pictures, I feel less ugly myself, instead of, as you would suppose, uglier by contrast. Women do not affect me in the same way. I do not feel that their beauty is so hard or so deep; therefore that the same divine properties of healing do not go with it.

Young Adrian Mitchell, Willie Plant, Menzies, Peele: willowy, well dressed, bland perfection! They could do nothing wrong in my eyes.

Women must feel cheap beside a really beautiful young man.

But beauty of any sort takes my breath away and routs all my unbattled bag of tricks—dreams, values, prejudices.

And so in this way, too, my ugliness is a bad weakness, and is an element of unreliability in my life. It is, from another standpoint, of serious worldly disadvantage to me. Women simply will not stand it or overlook it. But men also do not consider my peculiar ill-looks as consonant with what my books claim; with what I know my writing *is*.

I enter a room—there stands before the assembled company a walking lampoon of Mankind; for those of penetration a sort of lewd drunken and preposterous version of William Blake, his bottom and the back of his head sticking waggishly out, an idiotic grin on his face! What a reincarnation! If I could only have my posterior shaved down a bit!

I think I must have convinced you that my silence has not hidden complacency. Possibly that huge mass of humility at the rear of my cranium should not be so despised, although nothing can compensate me for those horrible cushions that prop me up like a child when I sit down.

The choice of such an extremely good-looking woman as yourself for my wife was the result of all that I have just been explaining to you. Beauty was all I wanted to begin with, not children, flea hunter, gooseberry or canned meat.

It was only when I married you and duly found you undressed at night, that the dull old Nature-hack woke up and gave a snort. He became an institution. Familiarity bred contempt. I produced Yorke! I was mildly surprised to find myself on such intimate terms with anything so beautiful. No beautiful man could stand as much ugliness as you have.

For a long time I have felt that I had your secret, that you were not really *of* the Beautiful, but in reality ugly, like me, and that your passions put you on my side. But when one says that you are a woman, ça dit tout.

Let us see what your next letter will be!

W. Bland Burn.

IV

Petrograd, 9th March 1917.

Dear Lydia:

Your letter was short and preternaturally unsweet. You drop the discussion entirely; I at least succeeded in making you loosen your hold on that.

My photograph of myself meets with a very cold reception. In fact, your undemonstrativeness, amounting to disdain, has hurt me very much! Cheerless and unprepossessing as it is, you might have paid a little more attention to it. After all, it is *me*: Bland, your husband!— need I add, Yorke's father?

Your letter I find wounding, there, in two ways. First, you ill-naturedly drop our little controversy. That was disagreeably meant. And secondly, the first photograph that a husband sends to his loving wife is ignored and persiflage opened to a flank.

In exchange for my aunt sallies you send me a very disagreeable object. Was it necessary? Am I expected to call you "my Gothic husband?" I am not going to. Your vanity finds strange paths and means to satisfy itself.

I suppose I shall be accused of "obtuseness" in your next letter if I do not rave over the abortion you sent me and say how much *character* and *genius* there is in your lip and—the other items.

Decidedly, times have changed! A charming wife! Are you too fastidious to refer to parts of my anatomy more distinctly than—"other items"? Are they to be relegated with dignity to the distant plane of an item? And they are *not* items! Ah, no certainly not *items,* whatever else they may be! As to my lip, it may not contain any genius, but you have frequently placed your two lips on either side of it and given a throaty trill of a laugh, provoking it to libidinous misdemeanour you would prefer to forget. You would prefer to forget?—And our frolics have borne fruit! You are after all, my dear lady, only a reproductive machine, painted up in order not to be too unappetising. But you are a machine that has two legs which enable you at any time to run away if you feel inclined. Any time in the last five years you could have done so. The first inclination that you have shown to use your legs in that way has been in the last few months. I therefore must suppose that you have some adulterous plans, in which, I do not, however, take the faintest interest. You can burn my letters and photographs, and pawn the jewels and other pledges of my unhappy love! Now go to Hell.
—Yours, W. B. Burn.

V

Petrograd, 28th April 1917.

My dear old Grecian cockshy,

All right, the certain acerbity of tone that has marked our correspondence lately shall cease. But I am much too rough a person ever to settle quite down again. You have really done something unpardonable. You have taken no notice of my most particular protégé. Had you spat on him it would have been less wounding than the exact reception you gave him. In fact, I am not sure that that would not have been the treatment that would have pleased me best.

The motives of your present letter I do not pretend to understand. You say "were quite aware how offensive I could be, just as you were not oblivious to the fact that I was no beauty." Are you trying to get some of your own back? You continue, "It is also quite unnecessary to underline your good points—I am aware of them, too; that is why I married you." When you say, "I rather like your eyes" am I to take that as an insolent thrust, or do you really mean it? I think they are most God-forsaken orbs, but there is no accounting for taste. Perhaps you see points in my horrible "items"? You refer to yourself, my clever spouse, as "the reproductrice of Yorke" and assert that as you are not my wife, then there is nothing to be readjusted. You say that Peele is really my wife. Now what may you mean by that? Greek Peele, (a Greek like you) the immaculate nut, the very high-well-born nickel nib of perfection, is the only object I should die for in this world. His blue eyes are violent mirthful fountains that splash out their delicate exaltation. When his eyes are turned into mine, and I look into his, I am nearly suffocated as though water were dashed into my mouth. His red lips make words so beautiful that if I could use the words made by them I could smash the sonnets in an instant: leave gentle Shakespeare far behind. His nostrils are little cups from which he sips the air, over delicate crystal. His body is a shining flexible wand, with a million magic properties. But my dear girl, I am not even his friend! If you suggest anything gross, even in fancy, it is a non-sense. Grossness only occurs where—it must. All my grossness is for you, believe me. *All* for you! You are *truly* my wife, my dear.

You, as you say, are the Reproductrice of Yorke—an extremely intelligent Reproductrice; you give one some rude slaps, like a good punching ball.

Now, it is very interesting; I can hardly conceive how we can live together after the horrible quarrel that has suddenly sprung up in the post. If you do not say things, you are not able, properly, to think them. You had said several unacceptable things and although you may never say them again, you will now be able to think them. Up till this time we have both displayed such exceptional delicacy that our relationship has really been very pampered. So I doubt if it can stand the resounding whacks that we have both dealt it. It is at present tottering and squinting at me very like Charlie Chaplin when his opponent gets him on the forehead with a brick. Still, there may be a Chaplinesque recovery!

You're a clever old witch! You sit there calmly with the talkative Yorke and receive my epistles like a volcanic diplomat. The most you do is to dribble a little lava down the otherwise self-possessed pages of your letters. Meantime, I have had no explanation of the genesis of this correspondence. You have always displayed wholesome respect for what I had to say and never certainly have taken the trouble to meddle with the affairs of my mind until I came here. I know that you had the strongest objection to my making this trip. But you never gave me any reason. As soon as I got here you wrote me a careful letter in a different spirit to anything that you had previously shown. Other careful letters followed, all of them aggressive. I just jawed ahead to you in answer to them. Our traditional shyness prevented me from asking you too plainly what had happened.

But when I forced your hand and smashed our shyness for good, you answered with a tongue I had had no previous indication that you were ripe to use.

So we'd better have a little more light on the subject before again building up the necessary wall of reserve.

The Revolution here is on a par with all other contemporary events. I am afraid it will make the War more interminable than ever. All the Jews are mobilized. They march about in huge tribes with banners. They have formed themselves into a sort of Parliament, getting elected all over the place or electing themselves. Someone has published all their real names—a horrible list, calculated to make a pious Ally cross himself. Then a Jew called Lenin has arrived, whose real name is Rosenbauer. He prances all over the place and causes a great deal of confusion. Meantime the Russians come out with their families and watch in astonishment the proceedings of the Jews.

As a matter of fact, there are a good many Russians spouting and flinging themselves about too. But the Jews have easily most of the place in the sun. Now, Jews are a most attractive race. But they are consumed with such an antipathy for this country and show such a strange predilection for Germany in all things and in all places that their spirited intervention is, at this particular moment, unfortunate. Will Russia make a separate peace?—the great question, no doubt, everywhere at present!

I, on the spot, can give no sort of answer. If there were nothing but Russians in Russia, Russia would not.

Things really are in rather a fine state here at present. It is a sort of sociable wilderness. But the bourgeois is bustling. Hard, significant American money is pouring in, rapidly filling up every empty but respectable little pocket. The Jews would never let things stop like *this,* anyway. What will be the upshot of it all here and in other countries? A change for the worse, naturally. Only *more* hypocrisy, confusion and vulgarity. After this war, and the "democratisation" of all countries, no man will ever say what he means, yes, seldomer even than at present. *The thing that is not* will reign in the lands.

So my opinion of this precious revolution is that it will give the War a year or two more life and accelerate, after the war, the cheapening and decay of the earth.

I therefore sally forth daily and watch the manoeuvres of my long-nosed friends with displeasure. A band of big clear-faced child-like soldiers, led by an active little bourgeois officer, counter-mark, and make a Slingsby baby of the genuine Yorke. You conclude your letter: "Cannot you think of *anyone else* with a large bottom?"—I cannot—that you would commit adultery with. So I presume you are fooling. I believe you are still in London.

Yours, Bland Burn.

The Hippopotamus

T. S. ELIOT

The broad backed hippopotamus
Rests on his belly in the mud;
Although he seems so firm to us
Yet he is merely flesh and blood.

Flesh-and-blood is weak and frail,
Susceptible to nervous shock;
While the True Church can never fail
For it is based upon a rock.

The hippo's feeble steps may err
In compassing material ends,
While the True Church need never stir
To gather in its dividends.

The potamus can never reach
The mango on the mango-tree;
But fruits of pomegranate and peach
Refresh the Church from over sea.

At mating time the hippo's voice
Betrays inflexions hoarse and odd,

But every week we hear rejoice
The Church, at being one with God.

The hippopotamus's day
Is past in sleep; at night he hunts;
God works in a mysterious way—
The Church can sleep and feed at once.

I saw the potamus take wing
Ascending from the damp savannas,
And quiring angels round him sing
The praise of God, in loud hosannas.

Blood of the Lamb shall wash him clean
And him shall heavenly arms enfold,
Among the saints he shall be seen
Performing on a harp of gold.

He shall be washed as white as snow,
By all the martyr'd virgins kist,
While the True Church remains below
Wrapt in the old miasmal mist.

Before we received the manuscript of Joyce's Ulysses, *his* Portrait
of the Artist *had been published in this country by B. W. Huebsch.
I hailed it as "the most beautiful piece of writing and the most creative piece of prose" to be found anywhere in the world at the moment, and devoted several pages to quotations from it, so that* Little
Review *readers would be sure to greet the "miracle."*
Jane wrote about Joyce's critics:

James Joyce
JANE HEAP

I SUPPOSE Mr. Joyce had some idea in mind when he gave his book
the title of A Portrait of the *Artist* as a Young Man. But the critics
seem to want it their own way and say, "Mr. Joyce paints the Irishman as he really is." . . . Irishman, doctor, lawyer, merchant, chief,
I suppose. Francis Hackett says it "reveals the inevitable malaise of
serious youth." Why then doesn't this inevitable malaise of all our
serious youth end inevitably like this: the call "to create proudly
out of the freedom and power of his soul, a living thing, new and
soaring, and beautiful, impalpable, imperishable."

H. G. Wells assures us that the youth of his country need not suffer such tortures of adolescence because of England's more commonsense treatment of the sex question. And all the time Mr. Joyce was talking about the artist of any land, not the youth of England or any other country. In this country there is only God to thank that the young artist does not go entirely mad over one and all of its institutions. In our country the young artists could suffer tortures far beyond anything suffered by Stephen, over the utter emptiness of the place. But he will always suffer. He will always be "a naked runner lost in a storm of spears."

There is too much geography of the body in this education of ours. You can talk about or write about or paint or sculpt some parts of the body but others must be treated like the Bad Lands. You can write about what you see that you don't like, what you touch, taste, or hear; but you can't write about what you smell; if you do you are accused of using nasty words. I could say a lot more about the geography of the body, and how its influence goes all the way through until the censor makes a geography for your mind and soul. But I want to talk about nasty words. The result of this education is that we have all the nasty words in the world in our language. How often a European or an Oriental will say: "Oh, to us it is something very nice—beautiful; but to you it would not be nice; it is much different in English." When they told James Joyce he had words like that in his book he must have been as surprised as a painter would be if he were told that some of his colors were immoral.

His story is told the way a person in a sick room sharply remembers all the over-felt impressions and experiences of a time of fever; until the story itself catches the fever and becomes a thing of more definite, closer-known, keener-felt consciousness—and of a restless oblivion of self-consciousness.

The whole comment of the reviewers has been on the background for the portrait: "the social, political, and religious life of Ireland today," etc. But there is the portrait itself—bearing a slight resemblance to the Playboy, a strong sensitive romancer; and the painting of the portrait—spontaneous, masterly, free: the color like this: "The spell of arms and voices: the white arms of roads, their promise of close embraces and the black arms of tall ships that stand against the moon, their tale of distant nations."

Ezra wrote of the "Portrait's" critical reception on the continent:

A Portrait of the Artist as a Young Man was so well reviewed in the April number of this paper that I have indeed little to add, but I would reaffirm all that I have yet said or written of the book, begining in *The Egoist,* continuing in *The Drama,* etc. Joyce is the best prose writer of my decade. Wyndham Lewis's *Tarr* is the only contemporary novel that can compare with *A Portrait; Tarr* being more inventive, more volcanic, and "not so well written." And that last comparison is perhaps vicious. It would be ridiculous to measure Dostoevsky with the T-Square of Flaubert. Equally with Joyce and Lewis, the two men are so different, the two methods are so different that it is rash to attempt comparisons. Neither can I attempt to predict which will find the greater number of readers; all the readers who matter will certainly read both of the books.

As for Joyce, perhaps Jean de Bosschère will pardon me if I quote from a post card which he wrote me on beginning *A Portrait.* It was, naturally, not intended for publication, but is interesting to see how a fine piece of English first strikes the critic from the continent.

"Charles Louis Philippe n'a pas fait mieux. Joyce le dépasse par le style qui n'est plus *le* style. Cette nudité de tout ornement rhétorique, de toute forme idiomatique (malgré la plus stricte sévérité contre le détour ou l'esthétique) et beaucoup d'autres qualités fondamentales font de ce livre la plus sérieuse oeuvre anglaise que j'aie lue. Les soixante premières pages sont incomparables. . . ."

The "most serious," or to translate it more colloquially: "It matters more than any other English book I have read."

. . . Joyce has had a remarkable "press," but back of that and much more important is the fact that the critics have praised with conviction, a personal and vital conviction.

Certain Noble Plays of Japan. Cuala Press, Dublin
Noh, or Accomplishment. Knopf, New York. Macmillan, London

EZRA POUND

THE earlier and limited edition of this work of Ernest Fenollosa contains four plays, with an introduction by W. B. Yeats. The larger edition contains fifteen plays and abridgements and all of Fenollosa's notes concerning the Japanese stage that I have yet been able to prepare for publication. This Japanese stuff has not the solidity, the body, of Rihaku (Li Po). It is not so important as the Chinese work left by Fenollosa, but on the other hand it is infinitely better than Tagore and the back-wash from India. Motokiyo and the fourteenth-century Japanese poets are worth more than Kabir. Fenollosa has given us more than Tagore has. Japan is not a Chinese decadence. Japan "went on with things" after China had quit. And China "quit" fairly early: T'ang is the best of her poetry, and after Sung her art grows steadily weaker.

It would be hard to prove that the Japanese does not attempt (in his art, that is) to die in aromatic pain of the cherry blossom; but his delicacy is not always a weakness. His preoccupation with nuances may set one against him. Where a Chinese poet shows a sort of rugged endurance, the Japanese dramatist presents a fine point of punctilio. He is "romanticist" against the "classical" *and* poetic matter-of-factness of the Chinese writer. The sense of punctilio is, so far as I can make out, a Japanese characteristic, and a differentiating characteristic, and from it the Japanese poetry obtains a quality of its own.

The poetic sense, almost the sole thing which one can postulate as underlying all great poetry and indispensible to it, is simply the sense of overwhelming emotional values. (For those who must have definitions: Poetry is a verbal statement of emotional values. A poem is an emotional value verbally stated.) In the face of this sense of emotional values there are no national borders. One can not consider Rihaku as a foreigner, one can only consider him human. One can not consider Odysseus, or Hamlet, or Kagekiyo as foreigners, one can only consider them human.

At one point in the Noh plays, namely in the climax of *Kagekiyo* we find a truly Homeric laughter, and I do not think the final passages of this play will greatly suffer by any comparison the reader will be able to make. If I had found nothing else in Fenollosa's notes I should have been well paid for the three years I have spent on them.

If I dispraise Tagore now I can only say that I was among the first to praise him before he became a popular fad. The decadence of Tagore may be measured. His first translations were revised by W. B. Yeats; later translations by Evelyn Underhill, facilis et perfacilis descensus, and now they say he has taken to writing in English, a language for which he has no special talent. If his first drafts contained such clichés as "sunshine in my soul," he was at least conscious at that time of his defects. Praise was rightly given to his first poems because it was demonstrated and demonstrable that they were well done in Bengali, i.e., that they were written in a precise and objective language, and in a metric full of interest and variety. The popular megaphone took up phrases made to define the originals and applied them to the translations. Imagine a criticism of Herrick and Campion applied to a French or German prose translation of these poets, however excellent as a translation in prose! As the vulgarizer hates any form of literary excellence, he was well content with obscuring the real grounds for praise. The unimportant element, that which has made Tagore the prey of religiose nincompoops, might easily have passed without comment. However, it has proved the bacillus of decay. Sir Rabindranath having been raised in a country where the author need not defend himself against blandishment. . . . I mean the force of the babu press is scarcely enough to turn anyone's head or his judgement. . . . Sir Rabindranath is not particularly culpable. His disciples may bear the blame as best they may; along with his publishers. But no old established publishing house cares a damn about literature; and once Tagore had become a commercial property, they could scarcely be expected to care for his literary integrity.

He might still wash and be clean; that is to say there is still time for him to suppress about three-fourths of the stuff he has published in English, and retain some sort of literary position.

Another man who stands in peril is Edgar Masters. He did a good job in *The Spoon River Anthology*. What is good in it is good in common with like things in the Greek anthology, Villon and Crabbe: plus Masters' sense of real people. The work as a whole needs rewriting. The difference between a fine poem and a mediocre one is often only the fact that the good poet could force himself to rewrite. "No appearance of labor?" No, there need be no appearance of labor. I have seen too many early drafts of known and accepted poems not to know the difference between a draft and the final work. Masters must go back and take the gobbetts of magazine cliché out of his later work; he must spend more time on *Spoon River* if he wants his stuff to last as Crabbe's *Borough* has lasted. There is a great gulph between a "successful" book and a book that endures; that endures even a couple of centuries.

I would not at any cost minimize what Edgar Masters has done, but his fight is not yet over.

We printed seven very beautiful poems by Yeats—"Upon a Dying Lady"—in our August 1917 number. Since I cannot reproduce them —except at a prohibitive price—I offer a letter about them instead.

The Reader Critic

Yeats's "Upon a Dying Lady"

I wonder how many of your readers know that the Seven Poems by William Butler Yeats in the August number of *The Little Review* were inspired by and written about Miss Mabel Beardsley, the sister of Aubrey Beardsley? I remember when Yeats was writing them. She was dying of a lingering illness. She was a Catholic, and it is of course well known that Aubrey Beardsley became a Catholic before he died. Artists, poets and writers like Charles Shannon and Charles Ricketts, W. B. Yeats, and other old friends of her brother and herself, used to take turns in visiting her. Some of them made points of collecting their best and in some cases most improper stories for her. I hope that she kept a diary and entered some of the stories in it. W. B. Yeats was tremendously moved by her fine spirit and gaiety. The Seven Poems were the result.

The story is one that Meredith would have loved. And she was a joyous creature that Meredith would have loved had he known her. There was no wearing of black there, no making a luxury of her grief, no flaunting it in the faces of others, even though they might sympathize with or share her feelings. It was all quite French, what a spirited French woman would do. She would have enjoyed the story published in the Letters of Meredith that an old Cornish woman told him:

"A hunting Squire in her neighborhood had a very handsome wife, whom he valued less than the fox's tail. One of the Vivians eyed her, admired, condoled, desired and carried her off. Some days after, she was taken with compunction or compassion, and about midnight the forsaken squire, sitting in his library, heard three knocks at the window. 'That's Bess,' he said, and let her in. She was for weeping and protesting repentance, but he kissed her, taking the blame on himself, rightly, and the house was quiet. Old Lady Vivian, like many old ladies, had outgrown her notions of masculine sentiment in these matters; she said to my friend: 'What are the man's family making such a fuss about! My son only had her a fortnight!' "

—*J., New York*

Advice to a Young Poet

EZRA POUND

THE opening sentence of your note shows a lamentable unfamiliarity with the work of Homer, Villon and Catullus . . . not to mention such lesser lights as Dante, Gautier, Cavalcanti, Li Po, Omar, Corbière, or even Shakespeare (to cite a familiar example). You are evidently ignorant as Ham of both prose and poetry. You appear to have read next to nothing. Stendhal, Fielding, Flaubert, Brantôme,— what have you read or studied anyhow?

How do you expect to make yourself interesting to men who have hammered their minds hard against this sort of thing?

And as for what is called "knowledge of the human heart"? It needs intellect as well as intuition.

If you knew more of what had been done, you wouldn't expect to make people fall before you in adoration of what you take to be "new and colourful combinations," but which people of wider reading find rather worn and unexciting.

You began with a certain gift, a sort of emotionée decorativeness, vide small boy by brick wall, impressions of scenes, etc. That's all very well, and very nice, but what the hell do you know or feel that we haven't known and felt already? On what basis do you propose to interest us?

There's plenty of this decoration in Spenser and Tasso, etc., etc., in French of the last half century, 1850-1900, etc. AND one is fed up with it.

If you could persuade yourself to read something, if you could persuade yourself really to find out a little about the art you dab at . . . you might at the end of five years send me something interesting.

The fact that you like pretty things does not distinguish you from 500,000 other people, young impressionist painters still doing not-quite-Monet, etc., etc.

Lewis, Joyce, Eliot all give me something I shouldn't have noticed for myself.

You won't better your art by refusing to recognize that at twenty-four you haven't knocked the world flat with admiration of your talents. You simply haven't begun the process by which the young person of temperament hammers itself into an artist (or into nothing, depending on the capacity for being self-hammered inherent in the personal substance).

You might begin on Aristotle's *Poetics,* Longinus on the Sublime,

Dante's *De Vulgari Eloquio*. Scattered remarks of Coleridge and De Quincey, and the early Elizabethan critics would do you no harm. You also need to educate yourself, as said above, in both prose and poetry.

Because the native American has nearly always been too lazy to take these preliminary steps, we have had next to no native writing worth anything.

Mastering an art does not consist in trying to bluff people. Work shows; there is no substitute for it; holding one theory or another doesn't in the least get a man over the difficulty, etc., etc.

Poetry has run off into Gongorism, concetti, etc., at various times, odd words, strained metaphors and comparisons, etc., etc. We know perfectly well all about that. At twenty I emitted the same kind of asinine generalities regarding Christianity and its beauties that you now let off about poetry.

A Boy, Chicago:

I am a boy sixteen years old, and one could not expect me to know much about poetry—especially free verse. But I have heard of your magazine as a magazine that was ready to print what all kinds of people thought. So I have written a little verse—it is not a poem— telling you something about what is going on inside my mind, for these matters trouble every boy's mind, although you may think that we are light-minded at my age.

BLINDNESS

I suppose I must be blind.
People say continually that the world is a wicked place;
I hear them talking about it all the time.
They say our city streets reek
With sin and sorrow
And all manner of misery and filth,
And yet I do not see any of it.
I go up and down these streets every day
And I see that they are ugly and that many people
Are deformed and sick and hungry;
But I close my eyes to it.
I suppose somebody will call me cowardly, but what shall I do?
I have no money to give the poor, and perhaps

That is not getting at their real trouble anyway.
I cannot heal the sick and deformed.
I cannot make the streets cleaner.
So I just think of other things.
Of my books at home, or the tennis courts in the park,
Or my pretty sister or anything.
There is nothing wrong in my own world.
I am happy. I like my school well enough.
I have my boy friends, and they are healthy athletic boys.
All the girls I know are good girls,
With charming and high minds.
And yet it is true that many boys lie and steal,
And girls run away and are dragged into lives of shame.
Why do I not see it? Why do I not do anything?
Why am I so helpless, if I have any duty to others?

*In the October 1917 number we published a story by Wyndham
Lewis which was promptly suppressed by Anthony Comstock:*

Cantelman's Spring-Mate

WYNDHAM LEWIS

CANTELMAN walked in the strenuous fields, steam rising from them
as though from an exertion, dissecting the daisies specked in the
small wood, the primroses on the banks, the marshy lakes, and all
God's creatures. The heat of a heavy premature Summer was cooking the little narrow belt of earth-air, causing everything innocently
to burst its skin, bask abjectly and profoundly. Everything was enchanted with itself and with everything else. The horses considered
the mares immensely appetising masses of quivering shiny flesh: was
there not something of "je ne sais quoi" about a mare, that no other
beast's better half possessed? The birds with their little gnarled feet,
and beaks made for fishing worms out of the mould, or the river,
would have considered Shelley's references to the skylark—or any
other poet's paeans to their species—as lamentably inadequate to describe the beauty of birds! The female bird, for her particular part,
reflected that, in spite of the ineptitude of her sweetheart's latest
song, which he insisted on deafening her with, never seemed to tire
of, and was so persuaded that she liked as much as he did himself,
and although outwardly she remained strictly critical and vicious:
that all the same and nevertheless, chock, chock, peep, peep, he was a
fluffy object from which certain satisfaction could be derived! And

both the male and the female reflected together as they stood a foot or so apart looking at each other with one eye, and at the landscape with the other, that of all nourishment the red earthworm was the juiciest and sweetest! The sow, as she watched her hog, with his splenetic energy, and guttural articulation, a sound between content and complaint, not noticing the untidy habits of both of them, gave a sharp grunt of sex-hunger, and jerked rapidly towards him. The only jarring note in this vast mutual admiration society was the fact that many of its members showed their fondness for their neighbour in an embarrassing way: that is they killed and ate them. But the weaker were so used to dying violent deaths and being eaten that they worried very little about it.—The West was gushing up a harmless volcano of fire, obviously intended as an immense dreamy nightcap.

Cantelman in the midst of his cogitation on surrounding life, surprised his faithless and unfriendly brain in the act of turning over an object which humiliated his meditation. He found that he was wondering whether at his return through the village lying between him and the Camp, he would see the girl he had passed there three hours before. At that time he had not begun his philosophizing, and without interference from conscience, he had noticed the redness of her cheeks, the animal fulness of the child-bearing hips, with an eye as innocent as the bird or the beast. He laughed without shame or pleasure, lit his pipe and turned back towards the village.=His field-boots were covered with dust: his head was wet with perspiration and he carried his cap, in unmilitary fashion, in his hand. In a week he was leaving for the Front, for the first time. So his thoughts and sensations all had, as a philosophic background, the prospect of death. The Infantry, and his commission, implied death or mutilation unless he were very lucky. He had not a high opinion of his luck. He was pretty miserable at the thought, in a deliberate, unemotional way. But as he realised this he again laughed, a similar sound to that that the girl had caused.=For what was he unhappy about? He wanted to remain amongst his fellow insects and beasts, which were so beautiful, did he then: Well well! On the other hand, who was it that told him to do anything else? After all, supposing the values they attached to each other of "beautiful," "interesting," "divine," were unjustified in many cases on cooler observation:— nevertheless birds *were* more beautiful than pigs: and if pigs were absurd and ugly, rather than handsome, and possibly chivalrous, as

138

they imagined themselves; then equally the odour of the violet was pleasant, and there was nothing offensive about most trees. The newspapers were the things that stank most on earth, and human beings anywhere were the most ugly and offensive of the brutes because of the confusion caused by their consciousness. Had it not been for that unmaterial gift that some bungling or wild hand had bestowed, our sisters and brothers would be no worse than dogs and sheep. That they could not reconcile their little meagre stream of sublimity with the needs of animal life should not be railed at. Well then, should not the sad human amalgam, all it did, all it willed, all it demanded, be thrown over, for the fake and confusion that it was, and should not such as possessed a greater quantity of that wine of reason, retire, metaphorically, to the wilderness, and sit forever in a formal and gentle elation, refusing to be disturbed?—Should such allow himself to be disturbed by the quarrels of jews, the desperate perplexities, resulting in desperate dice throws, of politicians, the crack-jaw and unreasoning tumult?

On the other hand, Cantelman had a little more human, as well as a little more divine, than those usually on his left and right, and he had had, not so long ago, conspicuous hopes that such a conjuncture might produce a new human chemistry. But he must repudiate the human entirely, if that were to be brought off. His present occupation, the trampling boots upon his feet, the belt that crossed his back and breast, was his sacrifice, his compliment to, the animal.

He then began dissecting his laugh, comparing it to the pig's grunt and the bird's cough. He laughed again several times in order to listen to it.

At the village he met the girl, this time with a second girl. He stared at her "in such a funny way" that she laughed. He once more laughed, the same sound as before, and bid her good evening. She immediately became civil. Enquiries about the village, and the best way back to camp across the marsh, put in as nimble and at the same time rustic a form as he could contrive, lay the first tentative brick of what might become the dwelling of a friend, a sweetheart, a ghost, anything in the absurd world! He asked her to come and show him a short cut she had indicated.

"I *couldn't!* My mother's waiting for me!" in a rush of expostulation and semi-affected alarm. However, she concluded, in a minute or two, that she could.

He wished that she had been some Anne Garland, the lady whose lips were always flying open like a door with a defective latch. He had made Anne's acquaintance under distressing circumstances.

On his arrival at Gideon brook, the mighty brand-new camp on the edge of the marsh, he found that his colleague in charge of the advance party had got him a bed-space in a room with four officers of another regiment. It had seemed impossible that there were any duller men than those in the mess of his particular battalion: but it was a dullness he had become accustomed to.

He saw his four new companions with a sinking of the heart, and steady gnawing anger at such concentration of furious foolishness.

Cantelman did not know their names, and he hated them in order as follows:

A. he hated because he found him a sturdy, shortish young man with a bull-like stoop and energetic rush in his walk, with flat feet spread out to left to right, and slightly bowed legs. This physique was enhanced by his leggings: and not improved, though hidden, in his slacks. He had a swarthy and vivacious face, with a sort of semitic cunning and insolence painted on it. His cheeks had a broad carmine flush on general sallowness. The mind painted on this face for the perusal of whoever had the art of such lettering, was as vulgar stuff, in Cantelman's judgement, as could be found. To *see* this face constantly was like *hearing* perpetually a cheap and foolish music. A. was an officer, but naturally not a gentleman.

B. he disliked, because, being lean and fresh-coloured, with glasses, he stank, to Cantelman's peculiar nose, of Jack London, Summer Numbers of magazines, bad flabby Suburban Tennis, flabby clerkship in inert, though still prosperous, city offices. He brought a demoralizing dullness into the room with him, with a brisk punctiliousness, several inches higher from the ground than A.

C. he resented for the sullen stupidity with which he moved about, the fat having settled at the bottom of his cheeks, and pulled the corners of his mouth down, from sheer stagnation. His accent dragged the listener through the larger slums of Scotland, harrowing him with the bestial cheerlessness of morose religion and poverty. The man was certainly, from every point of view, social prestige, character, intelligence, far less suited to hold a commission than most of the privates in his platoon.

D. reproduced the characteristics of the other three, in different quantities: his only personal contribution being a senile sing-song

140

voice, from the North, and a blond beam, or partially toothless grin, for a face.

This was the society into the midst of which Cantelman had been dropped on his arrival at Gideon brook, ten days previous to this. They had all looked up, (for it was always *all*, they having the inseparability of their kind) with friendly welcome, as brother officers should. He avoided their eyes, and sat amongst them for a few days, reading the *Trumpet-Major*, belonging to B. He had even seemed to snatch Hardy away from B. as though B. had no business to possess such books. Then they avoided his eye as though an animal disguised as an officer and gentleman like themselves had got into their room, for whom, therein, the *Trumpet-Major* and nothing else exercised fascination. He came among them suddenly, and not appearing to see them, settled down into a morbid intercourse with a romantic abstraction. The *Trumpet-Major*, it is true, was a soldier, that is why he was there. But he was an imaginary one, and imbedded in the passionate affairs of the village of a mock-county, and distant time. Cantelman bit the flesh at the side of his thumbs, as he surveyed the Yeomanry Cavalry revelling in the absent farmer's house, and the infantile Farnese Hercules, with the boastfulness of the Red, explaining to his military companions the condescensions of his infatuation. Anne Garland stood in the moonlight, and Loveday hesitated to reveal his rival, weighing a rough chivalry against self-interest.

Cantelman eventually decamped with the *Trumpet-Major*, taking him across to Havre, and B. never saw his book again. Cantelman had also tried to take a book away from A. (a book incompatible with A's vulgar physique). But A. had snatched it back, and mounted guard surlily and cunningly over it.

In his present rustic encounter, then, he was influenced in his feelings towards his first shepherdess by memories of Wessex heroines, and the something more that being the daughter of a landscape-painter would give. Anne, imbued with the delicacy of the Mill, filled his mind to the injury of this crude marsh-plant. But he had his programme. Since he was forced back, by his logic and body, among the madness of natural things, he would live up to his part.

The young woman had, or had given herself, the unlikely name of Stella. In the narrow road where they got away from the village, Cantelman put his arm around Stella's waist and immediately experienced all the sensations that he had been divining in the creatures around him; the horse, the bird and the pig. The way in which Stella's hips stood out, the solid blood-heated expanse on which his hand lay, had the amplitude and flatness of a mare. Her lips had at once no practical significance, but only the aesthetic blandishment of a bull-like flower. With the gesture of a fabulous Faust he drew her against him, and kissed her with a crafty gentleness.

Cantelman turned up that evening in his quarters in a state of baffling good-humour. He took up the *Trumpet-Major* and was soon surrounded by the breathing and scratching of his roommates, reading and writing. He chuckled somewhere where Hardy was funny. At this human noise the others fixed their eyes on him in sour alarm. He gave another, this time gratuitous, chuckle. They returned with disgust at his habits, his peculiarity, to what he considered their maid-servant's fiction and correspondence. Oh Christ, what abysms! Oh Christ, what abysms! Cantelman shook noisily in the wicker chair like a dog or a fly-blown old gentleman.

Once more on the following evening he was out in the fields, and once more his thoughts were engaged in recapitulations.=The miraculous camouflage of Nature did not deceive this observer. He saw everywhere the gun-pits and the "nests of death." Each puff of green leaves he knew was in some way as harmful as the burst of a shell. Decay and ruins, it is true, were soon covered up, but there was yet that parallel, and the sight of things smashed and corruption. In the factory town ten miles away to the right, whose smoke could be seen, life was just as dangerous for the poor, and as uncomfortable, as for the soldier in his trench. The hypocrisy of Nature and the hypocrisy of War were the same. The only safety in life was for the man with the soft job. But that fellow was not conforming to life's conditions. He was life's paid man, and had the mark of the sneak. He was making too much of life, and too much out of it. He, Cantelman, did not want to owe anything to life, or enter into league or understanding with her! The thing was either to go out of existence: or, failing that, remain in it unreconciled, indifferent to Nature's threat, consorting openly with her enemies, making a war within her war upon her servants. In short, the spectacle of the handsome English spring produced nothing but ideas of defiance in Cantelman's mind.

As to Stella, she was a sort of Whizbang. With a treachery worthy of a Hun, Nature tempted him towards her. He was drugged with delicious appetites. Very well! He would hoist the unseen power with his own petard. He would throw back Stella where she was discharged from (if it were allowable, now, to change her into a bomb), first having relieved himself of this humiliating gnawing and yearning in his blood.

As to Stella, considered as an unconscious agent, all women were contaminated with Nature's hostile power and might be treated as spies or enemies. The only time they could be trusted, or were likely to stand up to Nature and show their teeth, was as mothers. So he approached Stella with as much falsity as he could master.

At their third meeting he brought her a ring. Her melting gratitude was immediately ligotted with long arms, full of the contradictory and offending fire of the spring. On the warm earth consent flowed up into her body from all the veins of the landscape. The nightingale sang ceaselessly in the small wood at the top of the field where they lay. He grinned up towards it, and once more turned to the devouring of his mate. He felt that he was raiding the bowels of Nature: not fecundating the Aspasias of our flimsy flesh, or assuaging, or competing with, the nightingale. Cantelman was proud that he could remain deliberate and aloof, and gaze bravely, like a minute insect, up at the immense and melancholy night, with all its mad nightingales, piously folded small brown wings in a million nests, night-working stars, and misty useless watchmen. They got up at last: she went furtively back to her home. Cantelman on his way to camp had a smile of severe satisfaction on his face. It did not occur to him that his action might be supremely unimportant as far as Stella was concerned. He had not even asked himself if, had he not been there that night, someone else might or might not have been there in his place. He was also convinced that the laurels were his, and that Nature had come off badly. He was still convinced of this when he received six weeks afterwards, in France, a long appeal from Stella, telling him that she was going to have a child. She received no answer to that nor any subsequent letter. They came to Cantelman with great regularity in the trenches; he read them all through from beginning to end, without comment of any sort. And when he beat a German's brains out, it was with the same impartial malignity that he had displayed in the English night with his Springmate. Only he considered there too that he was in some way outwitting Nature; he had no adequate realization of the extent to which, evidently, the death of a Hun was to the advantage of the animal world.

A Song

WILLIAM BUTLER YEATS

I thought no more was needed
Youth to prolong
Than dumb-bell and foil
To keep the body young.
Oh who could have foretold
That the heart grows old?

Though I have many words
What woman's satisfied?
I am no longer faint
Because at her side.
Oh who could have foretold
That the heart grows old?

I have not lost desire
But the heart that I had,
I thought 'twould burn my body
Laid on the death bed.
But who could have foretold
That the heart grows old?

Poems of Po Chu-I

(772-846 a. d.)

TRANSLATED BY ARTHUR WALEY

THE HARPER OF CHAO

The singers have hushed their notes of clear song;
The red sleeves of the dancers are motionless.
Hugging his lute, the old harper of Chao
Rocks and sways as he touches the five chords.
The loud notes swell and scatter abroad:
"Sa, sa," like wind blowing the rain.
The soft notes dying almost to nothing:
"Ch'ieh, ch'ieh," like the voice of ghosts talking.
Now as glad as the magpie's lucky song:
Again bitter as the gibbon's ominous cry.
His ten fingers have no fixed note;
Up and down—"*kung*," "*chih*" and "*yu*."*
And those who sit and listen to the tune he plays

* Notes of the scale.

Of soul and body lose the mastery.
And those who pass that way as he plays the tune
Suddenly stop and cannot raise their feet.
Alas, alas that the ears of common men
Should love the modern and not love the old!
Thus it is that the harp in the green window
Day by day is covered deeper with dust.

ON THE WAY TO HANGCHOW:
ANCHORED ON THE RIVER AT NIGHT

Little sleeping and much grieving, the traveller
Rises at midnight and looks back toward home.
The sands are bright with moonlight that joins the shores;
The sail is white with dew that has covered the boat.
Nearing the sea, the river grows broader and broader:
    Approaching autumn, the nights longer and longer;
Thirty times we have slept amid mists and waves,
And still we have not reached Hangchow!

Summary
EZRA POUND

The Little Review is now the first effort to do comparatively what *The English Review* did during its first year and a half: that is, to maintain the rights and position of literature, I do not say in contempt of the public, but in spite of the curious system of trade and traders which has grown up with the purpose or result of interposing itself between literature and the public.

We act in spite of the public's utter impotence to get good literature for itself, and in despite of the efforts of the "trade" to satiate the public with a substitute, to still their appetite for literature by providing them, at a cheaper rate and more conveniently, with a swallowable substitute.

Whereanent a very successful journalist has said to me: We, i. e. we journalists, are like mediums. People go to a spiritist séance and hear what they want to hear. It is the same with a leading article: we write so that the reader will find what he wants to find.

That is the root of the matter; there is good journalism and bad journalism, and journalism that "looks" like "literature" and literature, etc . . . .

But the root of the difference is that in journalism the reader finds what he is looking for, what he, the reader, wants; whereas in literature he must find at least a part of what the author intended.

That is why "the first impression of a work of genius" is "nearly always disagreeable," at least to the "average man." The public loathe the violence done to their self-conceit whenever an author conveys to them an idea that is his, not their own.

This difference is lasting and profound. Even in the vaguest of poetry, or the vaguest music, where in a sense the receiver may, or must, make half the beauty he is to receive, there is always something of the author or composer which must be transmitted.

In journalism, or the "bad art" which is but journalism thinly disguised, there is no such strain on the public.

The Reader Critic

Letters from Ezra Pound

Chère Editeuse:

May I be permitted to reply in the correspondence columns to several other writers of letters?

A. R. S. Cher Monsieur: There is one section of our magazine devoted (DEEvoted) to "interpretation"; it is, if you have not divined it, The Reader Critic. It is, so far as I know, the only publication that ever has "interpreted" our native country. Never before has the intelligent foreigner been able to learn "what the American artist is up against."

V. H., (Maine). Chère Madam: Could Lewis but hear you, through his gas-mask, gazing at the ruins of one of the gun parapets of his battery, I think he would smile with the delicate and contented smile that I have at moments seen "lighting his countenance." There was once a man who began an article: "WE MUST KILL JOHN BULL, we must kill him with Art." These words smote the astonished eyes of the British public. No other Englishman had ever before so blasphemed the effete national symbol. Neither had any one else very much objected to the ladies in nightgowns which distinguished Punch's caricatures. The writer was, needless to say, Wyndham Lewis. He will probably have died for his country before they find out what he meant.

L. P. Cher Monsieur: You ask "What sympathy can the majority of readers feel for the foreign editor, Ezra Pound, with his contemptuous invective against the vulgus"? Are the majority of the readers "vulgus"? We had hoped the few choice spirits were gathered. Perhaps they have only migrated to this side of the ocean.

There was also a lady or mother who wrote to me (personally) from New Jersey, asking me to stop the magazine as Lewis's writings were "bad for her milk." (I am afraid there is no way of softening her phrase for our readers). Madame, what you need is lactol and not literature; you should apply to a druggist.

And there is the person who says all my stuff is "in a way propaganda. If not," what am I "trying to do," etc. Cher Monsieur: My propaganda is the propaganda of all realist and almost all fine unrealist literature; if I seek to "do" anything it is only to stimulate a certain awareness. It would not distress me if the reader should suddenly look upon his surroundings and upon his own consciousness and try to see both for himself, in his own terms, not in my terms, nor in the terms of President Wilson, or W. D. Howells, or *Scribner's,* or any other patent cut-size machine, or home-mould or town-mould, or year-mould. Voilà toute ma petite propagande. It is so little propaganda that I am quite content if it has no such effects, and if two or three pleasant people are enabled to get through a dull evening more easily with the aid of my sketches; or those of the writers whom I have brought to this magazine. There are some people who are not entertained by *Success,* the *Saturday Evening Post, The Seven Arts, The Dial* and all that contingent. "Matter," as Lewis has written, "which does not contain enough intelligence to permeate it, grows, as you know, rotten and gangrenous." It is not everyone who enjoys the aroma of a dormant and elderly corporis litterarum, nor the stertorous wheeze of its breathing.

If I were propaganding I should exhort you to get a decent international copyright law—though as my own income will presumably never equal that of a plumber, or stir the cupidity of the most class-hating, millionaire-cursing socialist, I have very little interest in this matter.

I should exhort you to enliven your universities. I should, whatever your nationality, exhort you to understand that art is exceeding slow in the making, that a good poet can scarcely write more than twenty good pages a year, and that even less than this, if it be good, should earn him his livelihood. (This problem with good augury I shall of course attempt to solve with this magazine.) I should, if you are American, exhort you, for your own good, to try not to drive all your best artists out of the country. (Not that I object to living in

London, North Italy, Paris, or that my name need be dragged into the matter). I would ask you to try to understand WHY American literature from 1870 to 1910 is summed up in the sentence: "Henry James stayed in Paris reading Flaubert and Turgenev. Mr. William Dean Howells returned to America and read the writings of Henry James." And WHY Whistler stayed in Europe, although Chase went back to the Philadelphia Fine Arts Academy. These are simple questions which the serious reader will not try to shirk answering.

However these matters do not belong to the body of the magazine, which will at best, as the clubman complains, be devoted to "invention" if there is enough invention to fill it; and at worst to active cerebration.

Votre bien dévoué,

Ezra Pound.

Jane Heap wrote her first creative piece . . . which, with its "zones of pain where one may rest," still has emotional importance. . . .

Sketches—jh.

WHITE

I.

Sharp, empty air. . . . Out of the black mouths of engines white smoke rises on thin stems into white ghosts of ancient trees; together they rise into ghosts of ancient forests, sway and surge and are gone again a million years.

II.

The hot air of the day stays in the city until night. The long slope of my roof presses the heat down upon me. Soon it will rain. But there is no rest in me: my heart is wandering too far. My friends may still be in the city, but I do not seek them. I go to the animals in the park. Within their enclosures black shadows of camels lie in the darkness. A great white camel broods in the moonlight, apart from the rest. His lonely eyes are closed and he moves his head slowly from side to side on his long neck, swaying in pain, searching in a dream for his lost world. I have seen a Norwegian ship carrying its carved head through the waters of a fjord with such a movement. . . .

Now the high clouds cover the moon. Out on the lake a wind assails the layers of heat. A white peacock sits in a tree, aloof, elegant, incorruptible . . . A light green spirit . . . Across the first thunder he lifts his long white laugh at us like a maniac.

VOID

I cannot live long in your city: it has no zones of pain for me where I may rest, no places where old joys dwell and I may suffer. It is as empty for me as the honeycomb cliff cities of the Southwest. For I shall not know love again in this or any place.

. . . and Hart Crane, who had already shown us several poems which we rejected, brought in one that we liked. With its resemblance to Eliot, I still like it better than certain of his later poems too marked by the Rimbaud influence.

In Shadow
HART CRANE

Out in the late amber afternoon,
Confused among chrysanthemums,
Her parasol, a pale balloon,
Like a waiting moon, in shadow swims.

Her furtive lace and misty hair
Over the garden dial distill
The sunlight,—then withdrawing, wear
Again the shadows at her will.

Gently yet suddenly, the sheen
Of stars inwraps her parasol.
She hears my step behind the green
Twilight, stiller than shadows, fall.

"Come, it is too late,—too late
To risk alone the light's decline:
Nor has the evening long to wait,"—
But her own words are night's and mine.

In January 1918 Ezra sent us, for serial publication, **Women and Men** *by Ford Madox Ford (who was then known as Ford Madox Hueffer). Most of it is so uninteresting, as I reread it, that I will include only episodes V and VI, under the sub-title of "Average People."*

Women and Men

FORD MADOX HUEFFER

V.

AVERAGE PEOPLE

I HAVE a friend whom I will call T. T went to Rugby and Oxford. He ate his dinners at the Middle Temple. He was called to the bar and he at once had a brief for a mining company of which one of his uncles was the chairman of directors. Just after this—when T was twenty-five—he came in for six thousand a year. From that day to this he has never done anything. Nothing. Nothing at all. I meet him from time to time at my club and for some reason or other I like him very well and he likes me. He tells me a good deal about racing. And this is the mode of his regular life.

He is forty-one—and a bachelor. He has an immense house in Palace Gardens, Kensington. The house contains thirty rooms and T has six servants. The house is an inheritance from his uncle which T has never taken the trouble to get rid of. The six servants are needed in order to keep it tidy. The only one of them that T ever sees is his "man." He rises from his bed every morning at 8:30. Over his bath and his dressing he spends exactly an hour—breakfasting at 9:30. Over his breakfast and the *Morning Post* he spends exactly an hour, finishing at 10:30. Half an hour he spends with his "man," discussing what he will have for dinner, what tie he will put on with what suit; or, if he wants any new clothes, which he does very frequently, he discusses what is being worn by various gentlemen whom his "man" has seen. At 11 he puts on the suit and the tie that his "man" has sanctioned and laid out in his dressing room. At 11:30 he walks across Kensington Gardens and into the Row where he strolls, leans on the railings and talks to various riders or sits upon a penny chair. This lasts him until a quarter to one. A quarter of an hour takes him to his club in the neighbourhood of King Street, St. James's. At his club he sits for half an hour in a deep arm chair reposing both his soul and his body. This is for the good of his digestion for he knows that it is unhealthy to eat immediately after having taken exercise. After lunch, which consists of a soup, a meat and cheese or apple tart, washed down with either barley water or very weak whisky and vichy—which is excellent against the gout,—after lunch he sits until 3:30 in the same deep arm chair. At 3:30 he strolls a little farther eastward where he finds an institution which keeps one's health in order by means of various exercises with dumb bells. Here he exercises himself for an hour, wearing practically no clothes and standing before the open window for the benefit of the fresh air. Dressing himself occupies him for half an hour. At five o'clock he takes a cup of tea and one slice of buttered toast. At half past five he walks to the Bath Club. Here he takes a Turkish bath with a plunge afterwards into the swimming bath. This occupies one hour and a half. At seven o'clock he takes a taxi cab and goes home, arriving there at 7:15. Three quarters of an hour he devotes to dressing for dinner. At eight o'clock he dines, always alone because conversation is unhealthy during serious meals. By nine o'clock he has finished dinner. From nine until ten he takes a nap, being awakened as the hour strikes by his "man." From ten to eleven he reads the evening papers. At eleven o'clock he goes to bed. And he tells me that he falls asleep the moment his head touches the pillow and that he sleeps the dreamless sleep of infants and of the pure in heart, until eight o'clock when his "man" wakes him up with a cup of tea and the first post. So the ideal day of this ideal average man runs its appointed course. And it is a positive fact that my friend once uttered these words. He said:

"My dear chap. How could you pass your day better? Tell me how? I once read a hymn and it struck me so much that I copied it out." And Mr. T produced a little note book from which amazingly he read out the words:

> "Sweet day so cool, so calm, so bright
> The bridal of the earth and sky.
> The dews shall weep thy fall to-night
> For thou, with all thy sweets, must die" . . . .

"That," Mr. T said, "exactly reminds me of my days. Of course I shall die one day and if it isn't wrong to say so I hope to go to Heaven for I have never done any harm in my life. I behave always I hope like an English gentleman and I look carefully after my health which is cherishing the image of Himself that God has given me." Mr. T was speaking in a tone of the deepest seriousness. And indeed he really had cherished in himself the image of his Maker. His gentle walks, his sobriety in both eating and drinking, his careful avoidance of all disturbing emotions, his daily health exercises, his naps and his Turkish baths—all these things really had made him a perfect man of forty-one in the very pink of health. The flesh of his cheeks was vivid and firm, his eyes were clear and blue, his hair crisp, blond and in excellent condition. His walk was springy, his back erect and he was beautifully and unobtrusively dressed. So perhaps this is the average man. . . . Let us now turn to the average woman.

About fifteen years ago I wanted some mushroom catsup. It was in a scattered, little-populated village of the South of England. The village stood on what had formerly been common land, running all down the side of a range of hills. But this common had been long since squatted on, so that it was a maze of little hawthorn hedges surrounding little closes. Each close had a few old apple or cherry trees, a patch of potato ground, a cabbage patch, a few rows of scarlet runners, a few plants of monthly roses, a few plants of marjoram, fennel, borage or thyme. And in each little patch there stood a small dwelling. Mostly these were the original squatters' huts built of mud, whitewashed outside and crowned with old thatched roofs on which there grew grasses, house-leeks or even irises. There were a great many of these little houses beneath the September sunshine and it was all a maze of the small green hedges.

I had been up to the shop in search of my catsup, but though they sold everything from boots and straw hats to darning needles, bacon, haricot beans, oatmeal and British wines they had no catsup. I was wandering desultorily homewards among the small hedges down hill, looking at the distant sea, seven miles away over the marsh. Just beyond a little hedge I saw a woman digging potatoes in the dry hot ground. She looked up as I passed and said:

"Hullo, Measter!"

I answered: "Hullo, Missus!" and I was passing on when it occurred to me to ask her whether she knew anyone who sold catsup. She answered:

"Naw! Aw doan't knaw no one!"

I walked on a little farther and then sat down on a stile for half an hour or so, enjoying the pleasant weather and taking a read in the country paper which I had bought in the shop. Then I saw the large, stalwart old woman coming along the stony path carrying two great trugs of the potatoes that she had dug up. I had to get down from the stile to let her pass. And then seeing that she was going my way, that she was evidently oldish and was probably tired, I took the potato trugs from her and carried them. She strode along in front of me between the hedges. She wore an immense pair of men's hobnailed boots that dragged along the stones of the causeway with metallic sounds. She wore an immense shawl of wool that had been beaten by the weather until it was of a dull liver colour, an immense skirt that had once been of lilac cotton print, but was now a rusty brown, and an immense straw hat that had been given to her by some one as being worn out and that had cost two pence when it was new. Her face was as large, as round and as much the same colour as a copper warming pan. Her mouth was immense and quite toothless except for one large fang and as she smiled cheerfully all the time, her great gums were always to be seen. Her shoulders were immense and moved with the roll and heave of those of a great bullock. This was the wisest and upon the whole the most estimable human being that I ever knew at all well. Her hands were enormous and stained a deep blackish green over their original copper colour by the hops that it was her profession to tie.

As we walked along she told me that she was exactly the same age as our Queen who was then just seventy. She told me also that she wasn't of those parts but was a Paddock Wood woman by birth, which meant that she came from the true hop country. She told me also that her husband had died fifteen years before of the sting of a viper, that his poor old leg went all like green jelly up to his thigh before he died and that he had been the best basket maker in all Kent. She also told me that we can't all have everything and that the only thing to do is to "keep all on gooing."

I delivered up her trugs to her at her garden gate and she said to me with a cheerful nod:

"Well I'll do the same for you, mate, when you come to be my age," and, with this witticism she shambled over the rough stone of her garden path and into her dark door beneath the low thatch, that was two yards thick. Her cottage was more dilapidated than any that I have ever seen in my life. It stood in a very long narrow triangle of ground, so that the hedge that I walked along must have been at least eighty yards in length, while at its broadest part the potato patch could not have measured twenty spade breadths. But before I was come to the end of the hedge her voice was calling out after me:

"Measter! Dun yo really want ketchup?"

I replied that I really did.

She said:

"Old Meary Spratt up by Hungry Hall wheer ye see me diggin'—she makes ketchup."

I asked her why she had not told me before and she answered:

"Well, ye see the Quality do be asking foolish questions. I thought ye didn't really want to know."

But indeed, as I learnt afterwards, it wasn't only the dislike of being asked foolish questions. In Meary Walker's long, wise life she had experienced one thing—that no man with a collar and a tie is to be trusted. She had had it vaguely in her mind that, when I asked the question, I might be some sort of excise officer trying to find out where illicit distilling was carried on. She didn't know that the making of catsup was not illegal. She had heard that many of her poor neighbours had been fined heavily for selling bottles of home-made sloe-gin or mead. She had refused to answer, out of a sense of automatic caution for fear she should get poor old Meary Spratt into trouble.

But next morning she turned up at my cottage carrying two bottles of Meary Spratt's catsup in an old basket covered with a cloth. And after that, seeing her rather often at the shop on Saturday nights when all the world came to buy its Sunday provisions and, because she came in to heat the bake oven with faggots once a week, and to do the washing—in that isolated neighbourhood, among the deep woods of the Weald, I got to know her as well as I ever knew anybody. This is her biography:

VI

She was the daughter of a day labourer among the hopfields of Paddock Wood. When she had been born, the youngest of five, her own mother had died. Her father had brought a stepmother into the house. I never discovered that the step-mother was notably cruel to Meary. But those were the Hungry Forties. The children never had enough to eat. Once, Meary cut off one of her big toes. She had jumped down into a ditch after a piece of turnip peel. She had of course had no shoes or stockings and there had been a broken bottle in the ditch.

So her childhood had been a matter of hunger, thirst and frequent chastisements with the end of a leather strap that her father wore round his waist. When she was fourteen she was sent to service in a great house where all the maids slept together under the roof. Here they told each other legends at night—odd legends that exactly resembled the fairy tales of Grimm—legends of princes and princesses, of castles, or of travelling companions on the road. A great many of these stories seemed to hinge upon the price of salt which at one time was extravagantly dear in the popular memory, so that one princess offered to have her heart cut out in order to purchase a pound of salt that should restore her father to health.

From this house Meary Walker ran away with a gipsy—or at least he was what in that part of the world was called a "pikey"—a user of the turnpike road. So, for many years they led a wandering existence, until at last they settled down in this village. Until the date of that settlement Meary had not troubled to marry her Walker. But then a parson insisted on it, but it did not trouble her much either way.

Walker had always been a man of weak health. To put it shortly, he had what is called the artistic temperament—a small, dark, delicate man whose one enthusiasm was his art of making baskets. In that he certainly excelled. But he was lazy and all the work of their support fell on Meary. She tied hops—and this is rather skilled work, —she picked them in the autumn; she helped the neighbours with baking and brewing. She cleaned up the church once a week. She planted the potatoes and cropped them. She was the first cottager in East Kent to keep poultry for profit. In her biography, which I have related at greater length in another book, you could find traces of great benevolence and of considerable heroism. Thus, one hard winter, she supported not only herself and her husband, but her old friend Meary Spratt, at that time a widow with six children. Meary Spratt was in bed with pneumonia and its after effects from December to March. Meary Walker nursed her, washed and tended the children and made the livings of all of them.

Then there came the time when she broke her leg and had to be taken against her will to the hospital which was seven miles away. She did not want to be in the hospital; she was anxious to be with Walker who was then dying of gangrene of the leg. She was anxious too about a sitting hen; one of her neighbours had promised her half a crown for a clutch of chickens. She used to lie in hospital, patting her broken knee under the bed clothes and exclaiming:

"Get well, get well, oh do get well quickly!" And even twenty years afterwards when she rehearsed these scenes and these words there would remain in the repetition a whole world of passionate wistfulness. But indeed, she translated her passion into words. One night, driven beyond endurance by the want of news of Walker and of her sitting hen, she escaped from the hospital window and crawled on her hands and knees the whole seven miles from the hospital to her home. She found when she arrived in the dawn that Walker was in his coffin. The chickens however were a healthy brood. Her admiration for Walker, the weak and lazy artist in basket making, never decreased. She treasured his best baskets to the end of her life as you and I might treasure Rembrandts. Once, ten years after, she sat for a whole day on his grave. The old sexton growing confused with years had made a mistake and was going to inter another man's wife on top of Walker. Meary stopped that.

For the last twenty-six years or so of her life she lived in the mud hut which I had first seen her enter. She went on as before, tying hops, heating ovens, picking up stones, keeping a hen or two. She looked after, fed and nursed—for the love of God—a particularly disagreeable old man called Purdey who had been a London cab driver. He sat all day in a grandfather's chair, grumbling and swearing at Meary whenever she came in. He was eighty-two. He had no claim whatever upon her and he never paid her a penny of money. She could not have told you why she did it, but no doubt it was just the mothering instinct.

So she kept on going all through life. She was always cheerful: she had always on her tongue some fragment of peasant wisdom. Once, coming back from market, she sat down outside a public house and a soldier treated her to a pot of beer. Presently there rode up the Duke of Cambridge in his field marshal's uniform and beside him there was the Shah of Persia. They were watching a sham fight in the neighbourhood. Meary raised her pot of beer towards these Royal personages and wished them health. They nodded in return.

"Well," Meary called out to the Duke, "you're only your mother's son like the rest of us." Once, the Portuguese ambassador amiably telling her that, in his language, bread was *"pom"* she expressed surprise but then she added—

"Oh well poor dear, when you're hungry you've got to eat it, like the rest of us, whatever you call it."

She was sorry for him because he had to call bread by such an outlandish name. She could not think how he remembered the word. Yet she knew that *Brot* was the German for bread and *Apfel* for apples because, during the Napoleonic Wars of her youth, the Hanoverian Legion had garrisoned that part of the country. One of what she called the jarman legions had murdered a friend of her mother's who had been his sweetheart and when he was hung for it at Canterbury he asked for *Brot* and *Apfel* on the scaffold. She saw him hung, a pleasant fair boy, and when she looked down at her hands she said they were as white as lard.

So she worked on until she was seventy-eight. One day she discovered a swelling under her left breast. It gave her no pain but she wanted to know what it was. So she put a hot brick to it. She knew that if it was cancer that was a bad thing to do, but she wanted to get it settled. The swelling became worse. So she walked to the hospital—the same hospital that she had crawled away from. They operated on her next morning—and she was dead by noon. Her last words were:

"Who's going to look after old Purdey?"

She was buried in the workhouse cemetery. The number of her grave is 1642. Mr. Purdey was taken to the Union that night. And there he still is, aged ninety-seven, a disagreeable old man.

And so we come back to the question of the average woman. Was Meary Walker this person? I wonder. If so the average among women is fairly high. Yet, in her own village nobody thought very much of Meary. She was popular with many people and hated by a few. Yet, as far as I can say, her life, in each of its days, was as perfect as that of my friend Mr. T. She never had a penny from me that she had not worked for, or never so much as a pair of old boots from anyone else. Was she then the average woman? I should not like to say that she was not. For, in spite of all our modernity, still the widest of all classes of employment is given by the land. There are more peasants in the world than there are anything else. And Meary was just a peasant woman, attracting no particular notice from her fellows. On the other hand there was Meary Spratt her bosom friend.

Meary Spratt was much more like the average woman of fiction. She was decidedly emotional, she was certainly not truthful: she begged, and when she begged she would scream and howl and yell in the highest of keys, pulling her gnarled, rheumatic fingers into repulsive shapes and screaming like a locomotive to show how much they pained her, or sobbing with the most dramatic emphasis when she related how Meary Walker had saved her six little children from starvation. On the other hand she would relate, with a proper female virtue, the fact—I fancy it may have been true—that, at some portion of her career Meary Walker had a daughter by somebody who was not Walker and that the daughter was in service in Folkestone. She would also say that Meary Walker was an arrant miser who had saved up a large fortune in bank notes which were quilted into her stays. She said she had heard the stays crackle.

Meary Spratt had never had a child by anyone but a husband. But then she had had four husbands as well as nineteen children, all of whom had lived. She is quite a small woman with an appallingly shrill voice and no doubt she is feminine in that her tongue never stops. In the early morning among the dews you will hear her voice. She will be picking what she calls mushrooms for her catsup. You will hear her all the while like this screaming quite loudly while you listen from your bedroom window, she being in the field beyond the hedge and it being four o'clock of a very dewy morning.

"He! He! He!" she will scream, "here is a nice little one! A little pinky one! Now I'm going to pick you! Up you come, my little darling! Ah, doesn't it hurt!" And then she will give a shrill yell to show the pain that the mushroom feels when it is being picked. And then she will continue: "Oh, oh Lord! Oh my poor shoulders! Oh! my poor legs! They do fairly terrify me with rhumatiz! Oh, oh, Lord!"

And you will hear her voice seeming to get shriller as it gets fainter and she goes over the marshy grass, into the mist, until she comes on another little pink one. She is seventy-six and it is cold out on the marshes in that October weather.

Yes, she is decidedly feminine. She has only been married three years to Mr. Spratford—so she gets called Meary Spratt. Mr. Spratford was eighty-two when they married. Between them they have had thirty-one children. And they lived in a little brick cottage not much larger than a dog kennel. When you ask Mr. Spratford why he married—Mr. Spratford was a most venerable looking peasant, like a Biblical patriarch, with very white hair curling round a fine bald head and with noble faded blue eyes; and when he spoke he always gesticulated nobly with one hand and uttered the most edifying moral sentiments. He was extremely dishonest and had three times been to prison for robbing poor old women. Indeed, when I first made his acquaintance he did a week's work for me, charged me double prices and begged me not to tell anybody that I had paid him at all because he was on his club—and this is about the meanest crime that any peasant can commit. It was an offence so mean that even Meary Spratford—who you will observe was a woman and who would have had no scruple at all about pilfering from any member of the quality—even Meary Spratford was outraged and made him pay back his club money for that week. She could not bear to think of the members of the club being defrauded, because they were quite poor people. It is true that she came to me afterwards, and, groaning and sobbing, she tried to get the money out of me to make up for her noble act—but when you asked Mr. Spratford why he married he answered:

"Well, you see, sir, in a manner of speaking us do be very poor people and us bean't able to afford more than one blanket apiece, and one small fire for each of us, coals do be so dear." (He got all his coals for nothing from the poor old parson and so did Mrs. Spratt.) "So if we do marry we do have two blankets atop of us at night and we have one big fire and sit on either side of it."

So said Mr. Spratford. But when it came to his wife she would scream out:

"Why did us marry? Why I like to have a man about the house and a woman looks better like among her neebours if she do have a husband." So that no doubt Mrs. Spratt was feminine enough, just as Mr. Spratford was undoubtedly masculine. He died raving on the mud floor of his hut. His wife had not the strength to lift him into bed and the four men who had held him down during the night had had to go to work in the morning. He tore his bald head to ribbons with his nails and Mrs. Spratt for years afterwards could make anybody sick with her dramatic rehearsals of how he died. When she was really worked up over this narration she would even scratch her own forehead until it bled. So perhaps she was really a more womanly woman than Mrs. Walker. She kept on going just the same: she is still keeping on going. But she made much more noise about it. That, I believe, is what is demanded of man's weaker vessels.

But even in the village, Meary Spratt was regarded as unusually loquacious whereas Meary Walker attracted, as I have said, no attention at all. It was as if Meary Walker was just a woman whereas Meary Spratt was at least a super-woman, or as if she were a woman endowed with the lungs of a locomotive whistle. Indeed, I am certain that anyone there would have told you that Meary Walker was just an average woman.

Villon's Epitaph*

WITTER BYNNER

I who have lived and have not thought

* From the French of Francois Villon.

But gone with nature as I ought,
　　Letting good things occur,
Am now amazed and cannot see
Why death should care so much for me.
　　I never cared for her.

Scarron's Epitaph*

He who now lies here asleep
None would envy, few would weep:
A man whom death had mortified
A thousand times before he died.

Peaceful be the step you take,
You who pass him—lest he wake.
For his first good night is due.
Let poor Scarron sleep it through.

Although William Carlos Williams had already made his debut in the Little Review, *I choose for reprinting his sketches in the January 1918 number.*

Improvisations
WILLIAM CARLOS WILLIAMS

I.

1

So far away　August　green as it yet is. They say the sun still comes up o'mornings and it's harvest moon now. Always one leaf at the peak-twig swirling, swirling and apples rotting in the ditch.

2

My wife's uncle went to school with Amundsen. After he　Amundsen　returned from the South Pole there was a Scandinavian dinner, which bored him　Amundsen　like a boyhood friend. There was a young woman at his table, silent and aloof from the rest. She left early and he　restless at some impalpable delay　apologised suddenly and went off with two friends, his great, lean bulk twitching agilely. One knew why the poles attracted him. Then my wife's mother told us the same old thing, of how a girl in their village jilted him　years back. But the girl at the supper! Ah—that comes later　when we are wiser　and older!

* From the French of Francois Villon.

160

3

What can it mean to you that a child wears pretty clothes and speaks three languages or that its mother goes to the best shops? It means: July has good need of his blazing sun. But if you pick one berry from the ash tree I'd not know it again for the same no matter how the rain washed. Make my bed of witch-hazel twigs, said the old man, since they bloom on the brink of winter.

II.

2

How smoothly the car runs. And these rows of celery, how they bitter the air—winter's authentic fore-taste. Here among these farms how the year has aged, yet here's last year and the year before and all years. One might rest here time without end, watch out his stretch and see no other bending than spring to autumn, winter to summer and earth turning into leaves and leaves into earth and—how restful these long beet rows,—the caress of the low clouds,—the river lapping at the reeds. Was it ever so high as this, so full? How quickly we've come this far. Which way is north now? North now? why that way I think. Ah here's the house at last, here's April, but—the blinds are down! It's all dark here. Scratch a hurried note. Slip it over the sill. Well, some other time.

How smoothly the car runs. This must be the road. Queer how a road juts in. How the dark catches among those trees! How the light clings to the canal! Yes there's one table taken, we'll not be alone. This place has possibilities. Will you bring her here? Perhaps—and when we meet on the stair, shall we speak, say it is some acquaintance —or pass silent? Well, a jest's a jest but   how poor this tea is. Think of a life in this place, here in these hills by these truck-farms. Whose life? Why there, back of you. If a woman laughs a little loudly one always thinks that way of her. But how she bedizens the country-side. Quite an old-world glamour. If it were not for—but one cannot have everything. What poor tea it was. How cold it's grown. Cheering, a light is   that way   among the trees. That heavy laugh! how it will rattle these branches in six weeks' time.

3

The frontispiece is her portrait and further on,—the obituary sermon: she held the school upon her shoulders. Did she. Well—turn in here then:—we found money in the blood and some in the room and on the stairs. My God I never knew a man had so much blood in his head!—and thirteen empty whisky bottles. I am sorry but those who come this way meet strange company. This is you see death's canticle.

V.

1

It is still warm enough to slip from weeds into the lake's edge, your clothes blushing in the grass and three small boys grinning behind the derelict hearth's side. But summer is up among the huckleberries near the path's end and snake's eggs lie curling in the sun on the lonely summit. But—well—let's wish it were higher   after all these years staring at it   deplore the paunched clouds   glimpse the sky's thin counter crest and plunge into the gulch. Sticky cobwebs tell of feverish midnights. Crack a rock (what's a thousand years!) and send it crashing among the oaks! Wind a pine tree in a grey-worm's net and play it for a trout; oh—but it's the moon does that! No, summer has gone down the other side of the mountain. Carry home what we can. What have you brought off? Ah here are thimble berries.

2

The little Polish Father of Kingsland does not understand, he cannot understand. These are exquisite differences never to be resolved. He comes at mid-night through mid-winter slush to baptise a dying newborn; he smiles suavely and shrugs his shoulders: a clear middle A touched by a master—but he cannot understand. And Benny, Sharon, Henrietta and Josephine, what is it to them? Yet jointly they come more into the way of the music. And white haired Miss Ball! The empty school is humming to her little melody played with one finger at the noon hour   but   it is beyond them all. There is much heavy breathing, many tight shut lips, a smothered laugh whiles, two laughs cracking together,—three together sometimes and then   a burst of wind lifting the dust again.

3

What I like best's the long unbroken line of the hills there. Yes, it's a good view. Come, let's visit the orchard. Here's peaches twenty years on the branch. Not ripe yet!? Why—! Those hills! Those hills! But you'ld be young again! Well, fourteen's a hard year for boy or girl, let alone one older driving the pricks in, but though there's more in a song than the notes of it and a smile's a pretty baby when you've none other—let's not turn backward. Mumble the words, you understand, call them four brothers, strain to catch the sense but

162

have to admit it's in a language they've not taught you, a flaw somewhere,—and for answer: well, that long unbroken line of the hills there.

Coda

Squalor and filth with a sweet cur nestling in the grimy blankets of your bed and on the better roads striplings dreaming of wealth and happiness. Country life in America! The crackling grackle that dartled at the hill's bottom have joined their flock and swing with the rest over a broken roof toward Dixie.

VI.

1

Some fifteen years   we'll say   I served this friend,   was his valet, nurse, physician, fool and master: nothing too menial—to say the least. Enough of that: so.

Stand aside while they pass. This is what they found in the rock when it was cracked open: this finger nail. Hide your face among the lower leaves, here's a meeting should have led to better things but—it is only one branch out of the forest and night pressing you for an answer! Velvet night weighing upon your eye-balls with gentle insistence; calling you away,—Come with me, now, tonight! Come with me!   now   tonight.

2

You speak of the enormity of her disease, of her poverty. Bah, these are the fiddle she makes tunes on   and it's tunes bring the world dancing to your house door, even on this swamp side. You speak of the helpless waiting, waiting till the thing squeeze her windpipe shut. Oh, that's best of all, that's romance—with the devil himself a hero. No my boy. You speak of her man's callous stinginess. Yes, my God, how can he refuse to buy milk when it's alone milk that she can swallow now? But   how is it she picks market beans for him day in day out, in the sun, in the frost? You understand? You speak of so many things, you blame me for my indifference. Well, this is you see my sister and death, great death, is robbing her of life. It dwarfs most things.

3

Hercules is in Hackettstown doing farm labor. Look at his hands if you'll not believe me. And what do I care if yellow and red are Spain's riches and Spain's good blood, here yellow and red mean simply autumn! The odor of the poor farmer's fried supper is mixing with the smell of the hemlocks, mist is in the valley hugging the ground and over Parsippany—where an oldish man leans talking to a young woman—the moon is swinging from its star.

In February 1918 Ezra did a study of modern French poets. His critical comment is more interesting than the poems he chose, so I give the gist of it:

A Study in French Poets

EZRA POUND

1.

THE time when the intellectual affairs of America could be conducted on a monolingual basis is over. It has been irksome for long. We offer no apology for printing most of this number in French. The intellectual life of London is dependent on people who understand this language about as well as their own. America's part in contemporary culture is based chiefly upon two men familiar with Paris: Whistler and Henry James. It is something in the nature of a national disgrace that a New Zealand paper, *The Triad,* should be more alert to, and have better regular criticism of, contemporary French publications than any American periodical has yet had.

. . . Certain delicate wines will not travel; they are not always the best wines. Foreign criticism may sometimes correct the criticism *du cru.* I do not pretend to give the reader a summary of contemporary French opinion, even were such a summary of opinion available. Certain French poets have qualities strong enough to be perceptible to me, that is, to at least one alien reader.

I have written long since that certain things are translatable from one language to another, i. e., that, generally speaking, a man's tale or his image will "translate," his music will, practically, never translate. In the same way, if his work be taken abroad in the original tongue, certain properties seem to become less apparent, or less important. It is impossible for me to take much interest in the problem of the mute "e" in French verse; fancy styles, questions of local "taste" lose importance. Even though I know the overwhelming importance of technique, technicalities in a foreign tongue can not have for me the importance they have to a man writing in that tongue. Or, . . . almost the only technique perceptible to a foreigner is the technique which consists in the artist's presenting his content as free as possible from the clutteration of dead technicali-

164

ties, fustian à la Louis XV; and from timidities of workmanship. And this is perhaps the only technique that ever matters, the only *maestria*.

The writings of critics who merely try to gauge current opinion, who try to say the thing advisable at the moment, are and have always been, and will be always dung. In defense of my throwing over current French opinion I urge that foreign opinion has at times been a corrective. England has never accepted the continental opinion of Byron, the right estimate lies perhaps between the two. Heine is better read outside Germany than within. The continent has never accepted the idiotic British adulation of Milton, on the other hand the idiotic neglect of Landor has never been rectified by the continent.

2

I can not in this sketch "aim at completeness." I believe in a general way that the American reader has heard of Baudelaire and Verlaine and Mallarmé; that Mallarmé, perhaps unread, is apt to be slightly overestimated; that Gautier's reputation, despite its greatness, is not yet as great as it should be. At any rate he seems to me the back bone of French nineteenth-century poetry.

After a man has lived a reasonable time with the two volumes of Gautier's poetry, he might pleasantly venture upon the authors whom I indicate in this essay; and he might have, I think, a fair chance of seeing them in proper perspective. I omit nebulous mushifiers, because I think their work bad; I omit the Parnassiens, Samain and Heredia, firstly because their work seems to me to show little that was not already implicit in Gautier; secondly because America has had enough Parnassianism—perhaps second rate, but still enough. . . .

I aim at a sort of qualitative analysis. If the reader familiarizes himself with the work of Gautier, Baudelaire, Verlaine, Mallarmé, Samain, Heredia, and of the authors I quote here, I think he will have a pretty fair idea of the sort of poetry that has been written in France during the last half century, or at least the last forty years, and, for what my opinion is worth, he will know most of the best,— and a certain amount of the half-good. He may also purchase Van Bever and Léautaud's anthology and find samples of some forty or fifty more poets.

After Gautier, France produced, as nearly as I can understand, three chief and admirable poets: Tristan Corbière, perhaps the most poignant writer since Villon; Rimbaud, a vivid and indubitable genius; and Laforgue,—a slighter but in some ways a finer "artist," than either of the others. I don't mean that he "writes better" than Rimbaud; and Eliot has pointed out the wrongness of Symons's phrase "Laforgue the eternal adult, Rimbaud the eternal child." I wrote five years ago that some of Rimbaud's effects seemed to come as the beauty of certain silver crystals produced by a chemical means the name of which I have since forgotten; Laforgue always knows what he is at; Rimbaud, the "genius" in the narrowest and deepest sense of the term, the "most modern," seems, almost without knowing it, to hit on the various ways in which the best writers were to follow him, slowly. There is no use gassing about these differences; the reader can see the thing itself in the poems. In another stumbling formulation I might say "Laforgue is the last word; he, out of infinite knowledge of all the ways of saying a thing, finds the right one. Rimbaud, when right, does the thing right because he simply can't be bothered to do it anyhow else."

Jules Laforgue

(1860-'87)

I begin with Laforgue because he is, in a way, the end of a period; he summed up and summarized and dismissed nineteenth-century French literature, its foibles and fashions, as Flaubert in *Bouvard and Pécuchet* summed up nineteenth-century general civilization. He, Laforgue, satirized inimitably Flaubert's heavy "Salammbo" manner. But he manages to be more than a critic, for in the process of this ironic summary he conveys himself, *il raconte lui-même en racontant son âge et ses moeurs,* he conveys the subtle moods and delicate passion of an exquisite and rare personality: "point ce 'gaillard-là' ni le Superbe . . . mais au fond distinguée et franche comme une herbe."

I am well aware that this sort of thing will drive most of our bull-moose readers to the perilous borders of apoplexy. It may give pleasure to those who believe that man is incomplete without a certain amount of mentality. Laforgue is an angel whom our modern poetic Jacob must struggle with. . . .

Tristan Corbiere

(1841-1875)

Corbière seems to me the greatest poet of the period. "La Rapsode Foraine et le Pardon de Sainte Anne" is, to my mind, beyond all comment. He first published in '73, remained practically unknown until Verlaine's essay in '84, and was hardly known to the "public" until the Messein edition of his work in '91.

People, at least some of them, think more highly of his Breton subjects than of the Parisian, but I can not see that he loses force on leaving the sea-board; for example his "Frère et Soeur Jumeaux" seems to me "by the same hand" and rather better than his "Roscoff." His language does not need any particular subject matter, or prefer one to another. "Mannequin idéal, tête-de-turc du leurre," "Fille de marbe, en rut!," "Je voudrais être chien à une fille publique" are all, with a constant emission of equally vigorous phrases, to be found in the city poems. At his weakest he is touched with the style of his time, i. e., he falls into a phrase *à la Hugo*,—but seldom. And he is conscious of the will to break from this manner, and is the first, I think, to satirize it, or at least the first to hurl anything as apt and violent as "garde nationale épique" or "inventeur de la larme écrite" at the Romantico-rhetorico and the sentimento-romantico of Hugo and Lamartine. His nearest kinships in our period are to Gautier and Laforgue, though it is Villon whom most by life and temperament he must be said to resemble.

Laforgue was, for four or five years, "reader" to the present Kaiser's mama (what an existence); he escaped and died of *la misère*.

Arthur Rimbaud

(1854-1891)

Rimbaud's first book appeared in '73. His complete poems with a preface by Verlaine in '95. Laforgue conveys his content by comment, Corbière by ejaculation, as if the words were wrenched and knocked out of him by fatality; by the violence of his feeling, Rimbaud presents. A thick suave colour, firm, even.

. . . Rimbaud does not endanger his intensity by a chuckle. He is serious as Cézanne is serious. Comparisons across an art are always vague and inexact, and there are no real parallels; still it is possible to think of Corbière a little as one thinks of Goya, without Goya's Spanish, with infinite differences, but with a macabre intensity, and

167

a modernity that we have not yet surpassed. There are possible grounds for comparisons of like sort between Rimbaud and Cézanne.

Tailhade and Rimbaud were both born in '54; there is not a question of priority in date, I do not know who hit first on the form, but Rimbaud's "Chercheuses" is a very good example of a mould not unlike that into which Tailhade has cast his best poems.

Remy de Gourmont
(1858-1915)

As in prose Remy de Gourmont found his own form, so also in poetry, influenced presumably by the mediaeval sequaires and particularly by that Goddeschalk quoted in his (De Gourmont's) work on "Le Latin Mystique," he recreated the "litanies." It is one of the great gifts of "symbolisme," of the doctrine that one should "suggest" not "present"; it is, in his hand, an effective indirectness. The procession of all beautiful women moves before one in the "Litanies de la Rose"; and the rhythm is incomparable.* It is not a poem to lie on the page, it must come to life in audition, or in the finer audition which one may have in imagining sound. One must "hear" it, in one way or another, and out of that intoxication comes beauty. One does no injustice to De Gourmont by giving this poem alone. The "Litany of the Trees" is of equal or almost equal beauty. The Sonnets in prose are different; they rise out of natural speech, out of conversation. Paul Fort perhaps began or rebegan the use of conversational speech in rhyming prose paragraphs, at times charmingly.

De Regnier
(Born 1864)

De Régnier is counted a successor to the Parnassiens, and has indeed written much of gods and of marble fountains, as much perhaps of the marble decor as have other contemporaries of late renaissance and of more modern house furniture. His "J'ai feint que les dieux m'aient parlé" opens charmingly. He has in the "Odelettes" made two darts into vers libre which are perhaps worth many more orderly pages, and show lyric sweetness.

Here we have the modern tone in De Régnier. My own feeling at the moment is that his hellenics, his verse on classical and ancient subjects, is likely to be overshadowed by that of Samain and Heredia.

* "Fleur hypocrite, Fleur du silence. . . ."

I have doubts whether his books will hold against the Cléopatra sonnets, or if he has equalled, in this vein, the poem beginning "Mon âme est une enfante en robe de parade." But in the lyrics odelette, and in this last given poem in particular we find him leading perhaps onward toward Vildrac, and toward a style which might be the basis for a certain style F. M. Hueffer has used in English vers libre, rather than remembering the Parnassiens.

Emile Verhaeren

Verhaeren has been so well introduced to America by his recent obituary notices that one can hardly represent him better than by the well-known "Les Pauvres". . . .

Viele-Griffin

Two men, Vielé-Griffin and Stuart Merril, who are half Americans, have won for themselves places among the recent French poets. Vielé-Griffin's poem for the death of Mallarmé is among his better known works. . . .

Stuart Merril

I know that I have seen somewhere a beautiful and effective ballad of Merril's. His "Chambre D'Amour" would be more interesting if Samain had not written "L'Infante," but Merril's painting is perhaps interesting as comparison.

There is a great mass of this poetry full of highly cultured house furnishing; I think Catulle Mendès also wrote it. Merril's "Nocturne" illustrates a mode of symboliste writing which has been since played out and parodied. . . .

Laurent Tailhade
(Born 1854)

Tailhade's satires seem rough if one come upon them straight from reading Laforgue, and Laforgue will seem, and is presumably, the greatly finer artist; but the reader must not fail to note certain definite differences. Laforgue is criticizing, and conveying a mood. He is more or less literary, playing with words. Tailhade is painting contemporary Paris, with verve. His eye is on the thing itself. He has, au fond, not very much in common with Laforgue. He was born six years before Laforgue and in the same year as Rimbaud. Their tem-

peraments are by no means identical. I do not know whether Tailhade wrote "Hydrotherapie" before Rimbaud had done "Les
Chercheuses." Rimbaud in that poem identifies himself more or less
with the child and its feeling. Tailhade is detached. I do not say
this as praise of either one or the other. I am only trying to keep
things distinct.

From this beneficent treatment of the amiable burgess; from this
perfectly poetic inclusion of modernity, this unrhetorical inclusion
of the factories in the vicinity of Grenelle (inclusion quite different
from the allegorical presentation of workmen's trousers in sculpture,
and the grandiloquent theorizing about the socialistic up-lift or
down-pull of smoke and machinery), Tailhade can move to personal
satire, a personal satire impersonalized by its glaze and its finish.

But perhaps the most characteristic phase of Tailhade is in his
pictures of the bourgeoisie. Here is one depicted with all Tailhadian
serenity. Note also the opulence of his vocables: ("Diner Cham-
pêtre). . . . Landor and Swinburne have I think forestalled Tailhade's hellenic poems in our affections. There are also his ballades
to be considered.

Francis Jammes

(Born 1868)

The bulk of Jammes' unsparable poetry is perhaps larger than
that of any man still living in France. The three first books of poems,
and "Le Triumphe de la Vie" containing "Existences," the more
than "Spoon River" of France, must contain about six hundred pages
worth reading. "Existences" can not be rendered in snippets. It is
not a series of poems but the canvas of an whole small town or half
city, unique, inimitable and "to the life," full of verve. Only those
who have read it and "L'Angelus de l'Aube," can appreciate the full
tragedy of Jammes' debacle. Paul Fort had what his friends boasted
as "tone," and he has diluted himself with topicalities; in Jammes'
case it is more charitable to suppose some organic malady, some definite softening of the brain, for he seems perfectly simple and naive
in his deliquescence. It may be, in both cases, that the organisms
have broken beneath the strain of modern existence. But the artist
has no business to break.

The fault is the fault, or danger, which Dante has labeled "mulie-
bria"; of its excess Jammes has since perished. But the poem to the

donkey can, in certain moods, please one. In other moods the play-ful simplicity, at least in excess, is almost infuriating. He runs so close to sentimentalizing—when he does not fall into that puddle—that there are numerous excuses for those who refuse him altogether. "J'allai à Lourdes" has pathos. Compare it with Corbière's "St. Anne" and the decadence is apparent; it is indeed a sort of half-way house between the barbaric Breton religion and the ultimate deli-quescence of French Catholicism in Claudel, who (as I think it is James Stephens has said) "is merely lying on his back kicking his heels in it."

Jammes goes to pieces on such adjectives as "pauvre" and "petite," just as De Regnier slips on "cher," "aimée" and "tiède"; and in their train flock the herd whose adjectival centre appears to waver from "nue" to "frémissante." And there is, in many French poets, a fatal proclivity to fuss, just a little, too much over their subjects. Jammes has also the furniture tendency, and to it we owe several of his quite charming poems. However the strongest impression I get today, read-ing his work in inverse order, (i. e. "Jean de Noarrieu" before these earlier poems) is of the very great stylistic advance made in that poem over his earlier work.

. . . If I at all rightly understand the words "vouloir chasser les choses que nous savons" they are an excellent warning; and their pose, that of simplicity over-done, has been the end of Maeterlinck, and of how many other poets whose poetic machinery consists in so great part of pretending to know less than they do?

Jammes' poems are well represented in Miss Lowell's book on *Six French Poets,* especially by the well-known "Amsterdam" and "Madame de Warens," which are also in Van Bever and Léautaud. He reaches, as I have said, his greatest verve in "Existences" in the volume "Le Triomphe de la Vie."

I do not wish to speak in superlatives, but "Existences," if not Jammes' best work, and if not the most important single volume by any living French poet, either of which it well may be, is at any rate indispensable. It is one of the first half dozen books that a man want-ing to know contemporary French work, must indulge in.

Moreas

It must not be thought that these very "modern" poets owe their modernity merely to some magic chemical present in the Parisian milieu. Moréas was born in 1856, the year after Verhæren, but his Madeline-aux-serpents might be William Morris on Rapunzel. . . .

A difference with Morris might have arisen, of course, over the now long-discussed question of vers-libre, but who are we to dig up that Babylon. The school-boys' papers of Toulouse had learnt all about it before the old gentlemen of *The Century* and *Harpers* had discovered that such things exist.

One will not have understood the French poetry of the last half-century unless one makes allowance for what they call the gothic as well as the roman or classic influence. We should probably call it (their "gothic") "mediaevalism," its tone is that of their XIII century poets, Crestien de Troies, Marie de France, or perhaps even D'Orléans (as we noticed in the quotation from Vielé-Griffin). Tail-hade in his "Hymne Antique" displays what we would call Swinburnism (greekish).

. . . I believe Moréas was a real poet.

Spire

André Spire is well represented in this collection by his "Dames Anciennes." The contents of his volumes are of very uneven value: Zionist propaganda, addresses, and a certain number of well-written poems.

Vildrac

Vildrac's "Gloire" is in a way commentary on Romains' Ode to the Crowd; a critique of part, at least, of unanimism. Vildrac's two best-known poems are "Une Auberge" and "Visite"; the first a forlorn scene, not too unlike Van Gogh, though not done with Van Gogh's vigour.

The story or incident in "Visite" is that of a man stirring himself out of his evening comfort to visit some pathetic dull friends. . . . The relation of Vildrac's verse narratives to the short-story form is most interesting.

Jules Romains

The reader who has gone through Spire, Romains, and Vildrac, will have a fair idea of the poetry written by this group of men. Romains has always seemed to me, and is I think generally recognized as, the nerve-centre, the dynamic centre of the group.

. . . The fact of the matter is that we are regaining for cities a little of what savage man has for the forest. We live by instinct; receive news by instinct; have conquered machinery as primitive man conquered the jungle. Romains feels this, though his phrases may not be ours. Wyndham Lewis on giants is nearer Romains than anything else in English, but vorticism is, in the realm of biology, the hypothesis of the dominant cell. Lewis on giants comes perhaps nearer Romains than did the original talks about the Vortex. There is in inferior minds a passion for unity, that is for a confusion and melting together of things which a good mind will want kept distinct. Absolutely uninformed English criticism has treated Unanimism as if it were a vague general propaganda, and this criticism has cited some of our worst and stupidest versifiers as a corresponding manifestation in England. One can only account for such error by the very plausible hypothesis that the erring critics have not read "Puissances de Paris."

Romains has felt this general replunge of mind into instinct, or this development of instinct to cope with a metropolis; in so far as he has expressed the emotions of this consciousness he is poet; he has, aside from that, tried to formulate this new consciousness, and in so far as such formulation is dogmatic, debatable, intellectual, hypothetical, he is open to argument and dispute; that is to say he is philosopher, and his philosophy is definite and defined. He has made a new kind of poetry. . . .

Lines like Romains', so well packed with thought, so careful that you will get the idea, can not be poured out by the bushel like those of contemporary rhetoricians, like those of Claudel and Fort. . . . His work is perhaps the fullest statement of the poetic consciousness of our time, or the scope of that consciousness. I am not saying he is the most poignant poet; simply that in him we have the fullest poetic exposition.

His style is not a "model," it has the freshness of grass, not of new furniture polish. In his work many nouns meet their verbs for the first time. . . .

The limitation of Romains' work, as of a deal of Browning's, is that, having once understood it, one may not need or care to reread it. This restriction applies also, in a wholly different way to "Endymion"; having once filled the mind with Keats' colour, or the beauty of things described, one gets no new thrill from the re-reading of them in not very well-written verse. This limitation applies to all poetry that is not implicit in its own medium, that is, which is not indissolubly bound in with the actual words, word music, the fineness and firmness of the actual writing, as in Villon, or in "Collis O Heliconii."

My general conclusions, redoing and reviewing this period of French poetry, are (after my paw-over of some sixty new volumes as mentioned, and after re-reading most of what I had read before) 1., as stated in my opening, that mediocre poetry is about the same in all countries; that France has as much drivel, gas, mush, etc., poured into verse, as has any other nation.

2. That it is impossible "to make a silk purse out of a sow's ear," or poetry out of nothing; that all attempts to "expand" a subject into poetry are futile, fundamentally; that the subject matter must be coterminous with the expression. Tasso, Spenser, Ariosto, prose-poems, diffuse forms of all sorts are all a preciosity, a parlour-game, and dilutations go to the scrap heap.

3. That Corbière, Rimbaud, Laforgue are permanent; that probably some of De Gourmont's and Tailhade's poems are permanent, or at least reasonably durable; that Romains is indispensable, for the present at any rate; that people who say they "don't like French poetry" are possibly matoids, and certainly ignorant of the scope and variety of French work. In the same way people are ignorant of the qualities of French people; ignorant that if they do not feel at home in Amiens (as I do not), there are other races in France; in the Charente if you walk across country you meet people exactly like the nicest people you can meet in the American country and *they are not "foreign."*

All France is not to be found in Paris. The adjective "French" is current in America with a dozen erroneous or stupid connotations. If it means, as it did in the mouth of my contemporary, "talcum powder" and surface neatness, the selection of poems I have given here would almost show the need of, or at least a reason for French Parnassianism; for it shows the French poets violent, whether with the violent words of Corbière, or the quiet violence of the irony in Laforgue, the sudden annihilations of his "turn-back" on the subject. People forget that the incision of Voltaire is no more all of French Literature than is the *robustezza* of Brantôme. (Burton of the "Anatomy" is our only writer who can match him.) They forget the two distinct finenesses of the latin French and of the French "gothic," that is of the eighteenth century, of Bernard (if one take a writer of no great importance to illustrate a definite quality), or of D'Orleans and of Froissart in verse. From this delicacy, if they can not be doing with it, they may turn easily to Villon or Basselin. Only a general distaste for literature can be operative against all of these writers.

(To me, what price scholarship? Ezra freely uses the adjective "permanent" for poets who have no permanency because they are not concerned with the affirmed permanent emotions of mankind. And in all the poems he quotes there is no single one that will compare with Apollinaire's permanent, poignant lines in "Adieu"):

> J'ai cueilli ce brin de bruyère
> L'automne est morte, souviens t'en
> Nous ne nous verrons plus sur terre
> Odeur du temps, brin de bruyère
> Et souviens-toi que je t'attends.*

In March 1918 we began the serialization of Joyce's "Ulysses." I announced it in this fashion:

James Joyce in "The Little Review"

I have just received the first three instalments of James Joyce's new novel which is to run serially in the *Little Review*, beginning with the March number.

It is called "Ulysses."

It carries on the story of Stephan Dedalus, the central figure in "A Portrait of the Artist as a Young Man."

It is, I believe, even better than the "Portrait."

So far it has been read by only one critic of international reputation. He says: "It is certainly worth running a magazine if one can get stuff like this to put in it. Compression, intensity. It looks to me rather better than Flaubert."

This announcement means that we are about to publish a prose masterpiece.

The critic of international importance was, of course, Ezra, who had asked Joyce to let us see the manuscript. I considered it not "rather better" than Flaubert, but entirely better. I remember the

* *From "Alcools—Poèms 1898-1913," by Guillaume Apollinaire. Published by the Nouvelle Revue Francaise, Paris.*

morning, in our West Eighth Street studio, when I opened the
manuscript and read straight through to Episode III which begins:
"Ineluctable modality of the visible: at least that if no more, thought
through my eyes. Signatures of all things I am here to read, seaspawn
and seawrack, the nearing tide . . ." I remember calling out to
Jane, "This is the most beautiful thing we'll ever have to publish."
Today I have no feeling that Ulysses *is better than the* Portrait—
larger, yes; but they have the same value: the same man.

We continued the serialization of Ulysses *until, in October 1920,*
we were arrested for publishing "obscene literature" by the Society
for the Suppression of Vice.

Broken Necks

BEN HECHT

I STOOD on the corner that day adjusting certain important adjectives
in my life. I had seen two men hanged and it was Spring. How the
wine ran through the little greedy half-dead swarming in the streets.
Yes, those endless, bobbing faces almost looked at each other, almost
smiled into each other's eyes—insufferable and inhuman breach of
democracy. But there was something immoral about the day. The
music of dreams tugged at the endless shuffling feet. The music of
desires—little starved and fearful things come out for a moment in
the sun and wind—piped vainly for dancers. There was something
vague and bewildered about the buildings and the people as if there
was a great undying shout in the streets. What a panic this monotonous return of Spring breeds among the little half-dead as they
shuffle and bob along with a tingle in their heels and a blindness
come suddenly into their eyes. For it is through the mists of greedy
complacencies that the little half-dead are able to pick their steps
with certainty and precision. Now comes this wine and this music
and this disturbance as of a great undying shout sweeping the
bristling shafts of stone, and the mists vanish for a moment. In the
blindness which falls upon them is an undertow tugging at their feet.

I stood on the corner that day observing how in the spring the
bodies of women were like the bodies of long, lithe animals prowling
under orange and lavender, green and turquoise dresses and how
the men with their coats dangling across their arms were like hot
beetles that had removed their shells. But as I watched the endless
faces filled with half-startled and half-placid confusion, and as I
noted what the poets call the gayety of spring in the hearts of men,

there came to me out of the swarm and roar of the day the mockery which it is the duty of philosophers to hear. For I had seen two men hanged and had most properly come away a philosopher.

Where was he who might have been crawling along the treadmill of time lighted today for another instant by the spring? The creature who had spat at the cross on the scaffold, whose perfect tusks had grinned out of the gloom above our heads an hour ago? Laughing in Hell, if death makes men wise. For Hell is a place of wise laughter. And the other one, who had died vomiting terror?

There was a group of us waiting patiently for the tall steel doors of the jail to open. Righteous men we were with stern cold faces come to transact with proper dignity certain grave business in the interest of the little greedy half-dead who even here shuffled through the streets with the lie of Spring in their heels. And after we had been admitted and our credentials cunningly examined, we were marched through barred corridors and told to enter a door and make ourselves comfortable inside. Within this door stretched the room which was to witness the hangings. It was a long and narrow room with towering walls. It could have been built only for one purpose, as a room in which to hang men. The grey plaster of its walls was unrelieved by any humanizing design. They formed, these walls, a geometrical monotone unbroken by windows or doors except the one through which we had entered. The floor was of stone.

Forty long benches such as picnickers use in groves, had been introduced into this vault of a room. They seemed puny wooden toys under the sweep and stretch of the towering, slot-like walls. We came walking slowly into the room. We were doctors, public officials, jail attendants and newspaper men. We sat down on the benches and faced the gallows.

The timber of the gallows reached from the stone floor to the dark, forgotten ceiling. Fifteen feet above the floor was a platform. On this platform the men who were to be hanged were to stand until a part of its floor which was on hinges swung back and dropped them. Then they would be left dangling from the ropes. These ropes hung now from a cross beam fifteen feet above the floor of the platform. They were two bright yellow manila ropes. Each ended in a noose the size of a man's head. We on the benches stared with uncomfortable eyes at these ropes. In the gloom our faces floated like little pale discs above the benches. The ends of cigars and cigarettes made tiny red spots in the darkness and above our heads little grey and violet

parasols of smoke opened and vanished. They were eager and efficient ropes and they had personality. They became, when we had
scrutinized them for a long space, the strange and attenuated furniture entirely suited to this room. About their slim and elegant
stretch there was something monstrous suggested. Things which are
sometimes seen in a fever assume the grotesque dimensions of these
ropes.

People do not think in these places. They sit with their mouths
somewhat parted and smoke cigars and nod politely to each other as
they talk. They stare about them as do children in a strange house,
noting this and observing that. Indeed, it was not till an hour later
that I became a philosopher and found it necessary to adjust
adjectives.

There were two men on the scaffold platform. One was a stout
man with snow-colored hair. He was well dressed but we noticed
with grave smiles that he seemed unduly conscious of his freshly
shined patent leather shoes. He kept moving them about and we
watched them closely as so many cats in the dark might watch two
bewildered mice. At length achieving a comparative equanimity under our gaze, he thrust his hands behind him and stood stiffly facing
the ropes. There was nothing left to think of about him other than
that he was fat. The other man was a jail guard.

Then we noticed simultaneously a little box-like shack which
stood against the plaster wall at the rear of the gallows' platform.
It was just large enough to accommodate a man. We remarked in
stern sophisticated whispers to each other that the man who sprung
the trap under the feet of the men about to hang was hidden in this
enclosure. For a space we stared at a small circular window in the
gallows shack, diverted by banal speculation. How did this man feel
who actually did the thing which killed two men? As we stared a
face, vague and dark, appeared in the little window and then vanished. We were content, and here and there in the gloom, matches
were struck and the faces of men lighting cigars remained in glowing
prints upon the dark air.

Suddenly, as if greatly ahead of time, men started entering the
room from the single door at the side of the gallows. Three public
officials walked first. Behind them walked two priests in white and
purple surplices. Between the two priests was a young man with a
colorless face. He was in his shirt sleeves and without a collar. He
looked as if he had been interrupted washing dishes. Following these

were several jail guards. We did not count their number. Behind the guards walked two priests in white and purple surplices. Between them walked the second man. For the first man without a collar who walked between the two priests we had no eyes. There was about him a lack of something which made him akin to us on the benches. He stopped and wobbled and his head rolled and from his lips issued a moan.

"Oh my Lord Jesus Christ," he said.

His lips as he walked were peeled back in the manner of a man suffering from nausea. We did not look long at him. But the other —we stared and watched and forgot to puff on our cigars. He was a man with gaunt features and the face of an unbarbered Caesar, lined and hollowed like the wing of a bat. He had a lean and muscular neck and he walked high shouldered like an Egyptian. To the drooping lines of his mouth and chin clung a dark curling covering of hair like the beard on the paintings of the adolescent Christ. He walked with his jaw thrust forward, lean and hollow jaws like the jaws of a starving monk. His eyes, round and black, nestled deep in his head, black and burning like the eyes of a voodoo priest.

We watched this man and moved about on our benches. We knew his name and the deeds he had done in the world. He had moved among the little greedy half-dead with altogether curious inspirations. At night he had flattened himself against dark alley walls and waited with a gun in his hand for men to approach him, and he had gone prowling after them like a stoical coyote crept into the city out of the darkness beyond. Thus he had grown rich and careless and taken to darting through the streets by day as he had done by night. In the sun there came into his heart a joyous hate which had misguided him. It caused him finally to stand upon a street corner shouting and shooting into the swarm of things about him until the street grew lonely and strangely rid of all sounds but the whoop of his voice and the little bark of his gun. It was very sad, for the little heaped figures that lay strewn in the emptied street might have been our wives and our mothers. Eventually a tall red-faced man bristling with gold buttons, pounced upon him from the rear and held him as he continued to shout and wave a useless gun toward the high roofs of the crowded buildings.

Here he was walking up the slim wooden stairs that led to the gallows platform, and here he was standing under the looped rope that dangled at his ear and beside another man who continued to moan,

"My Lord Jesus Christ, forgive me. Forgive us all." But we did not look at this one. The platform was now crowded with men but we did not look at them. They came forward with long black straps and proceeded to bind the man who was moaning. Then a priest came forward and stood beside the man who was moaning and rested an ivory crucifix upon his lips and opened a book under his rolling eyes. But our eyes, held as by some vast thing about to happen, that will any minute happen, remained upon the gaunt, unbarbered face with its Christ-like beard, with the mystic snarl in its eyes, of the man who stood under the other rope. An inexplicable fascination held our eyes upon him. And under our unblinking stares he grew and grew and became lopsided and out of focus and the features of his face swam apart into the grimace of a man laughing.

Then our eyes cleared and we saw that his arms were strapped flat against his sides and his legs strapped tightly together at the ankles and the knees, and that a priest in a white and purple surplice with a startled face was offering an ivory crucifix for him to kiss. We watched him look at the crucifix, his eyes becoming filled with yellow lights; and watched his lips peel back and the teeth, exaggerated in their nakedness, shine in a grin. Suddenly he closed his mouth and spat at the crucifix. Beside him the man under the rope was moaning "Oh my Creator. Let me see. Let me see." And his head wabbled toward the opened book the priest in front of him held to his eyes.

Of this we were conscious in an uninterested way. For a man had spat upon a crucifix and there was that in us which made us lower our heads and tremble and move uneasily. Other men stepped forward on the gallows platform and hung long white robes upon the two under the ropes. The robes fastened in a pucker about their necks and fell to the floor and were fastened in another pucker about their ankles. Then a man with unbelievable gestures slipped the rope over the head of the moaning one and drew the noose tight with unbelievable little jerks so that the knot fell under the man's ear.

"Oh Lord Jesus Christ, my Jesus Christ, fogive me. Forgive us all" moaned the man, his face almost vanishing in the gloom.

About the neck of the other whom we were watching, as men watching something about to explode, the second rope was fixed and jerked into place. And then a voice shot from the platform. It came from the blur and flurry of men grouped behind the ropes.

"Have you anything to say?" it inquired.

A cry answered from the one who was moaning. His words blurred and buzzing filled the room. "Oh my Creator, my Creator," he sang. "I am going to my Creator."

And the man with the face that was lined and hollowed like the wing of a bat remained silent, gazing with his glowing eyes down upon our heads. In his puckered white robe he loomed out of the gloom like some grotesque and stoical sage in masquerade, except for his teeth which were bared and swimming in saliva. The faces above the ropes remained visible for several instants. Two men bearing white masks then approached them. The one who moaned was rolling his eyes up and down the towering gloomy walls as if in frantic, helpless search. The other was staring down upon us in a strange, disinterested manner, his lips peeling back, his jaws thrusting forward. He drew a long breath and then vanished behind the white mask with a secret in his eyes.

Both men had disappeared. There were to be seen only two long white bundles curiously shapeless. We were silent. The moaning of the man who had kissed the crucifix suddenly resumed. It filled the room. It came louder and louder from the depths of the long white bundle, crawling over us and along the towering walls that had no windows. From the other white bundle came silence. The feet under it stared at us without movement. The moaning burst into words— "Oh My Creator"—and was lost in a crash. The trap had banged down.

A great swaying howl rolled into the vault-like room. It swept like a curtain between us and the two white bundles that had shot through the trap. The two men were hanging. The howling came from the prisoners in the cells beyond in the jail, howling like the sustained cry of an army out of a wilderness. The two white bundles that were hanging, stirred. One of them turned slightly, with a certain idleness. The other began to expand and contract. A curious animation gradually took possession of it. Several minutes passed and the white bundles continued to bob and twitch. The one to the left which contained the man who had moaned began now to throb and quiver like a plucked and vibrating violin string. The rope above it hummed, filling the room with the whang of its monotone. The other bundle remained turning idly. A large group of men had risen from the benches in front. Several of them held black stethoscopes in their hands. They waited.

The rest of us stood to our feet. There was silence and the moments passed with our eyes unwavering. The two bundles seemed mysteriously wound up as if they would go on turning idly forever. Then they began to act as if someone were trying to blow them up from inside. Between the masks and the puckered tops of the white robes the necks of the two men hanging within the bundles became visible. Suddenly the turning ceased and the two bundles began to behave as if someone were jerking with an amazing violence on the ropes which supported them in mid air. They executed a frenzied and staccato jig.

The bundles hung motionless at the ends of the two ropes, limp dead banners out of which the wind had died. A physician removing the stethoscope from his ears said something that ended with the words, "twelve minutes." A second physician repeated what he had said.

We crowded forward from the benches, gathering about the two figures which had dropped their white robes. They were no longer interesting. A certain fascination had gone out of them, out of the ropes, out of the tall spectral timbers of the gallows. We passed them a few minutes later on our way out of the door. They were lying on two wheel cots. Their masks had been removed and their faces colored like stained glass watched us with mouths opened.

I had forgotten my hat. We had moved into the lobby of the jail and I hurried back after my hat. I stood for a moment gazing at the towering grey walls, the wood structure, the two strands of rope that dropped from the beam. They had been cut. There was no one in the room. I seized my hat which was on a bench and ran awkwardly after the men who had gone. Outside a man with a sharp beard said to me, shaking his head, "Well, that boy died game, didn't he?"

The man was drawing deep breaths and looked about him bewilderedly in the sunny street.

I walked on until I came to the corner where the necessity of adjusting certain important adjectives in my life caused me to stop. Up and down the street swarmed the endless faces of the little greedy half-dead, lighted for a moment by the great sun. And having completed my philosophy, and because it was on this corner the gaunt and hollow-faced one had once stood, his heart filled with a joyous hate shouting at the buildings, I laughed and spat and eyed a woman whose body was like the body of a long lithe animal prowling under a lavender and turquoise dress.

Three Illuminations of Rimbaud

(Translated by Helen Rootham)

VAGABONDS

Pitiful brother! What atrocious vigils I owe to him. "I did not take this enterprise in hand seriously. I made sport of his infirmity. It would be my fault if we returned into exile and slavery." He attributed a strange bad luck and a strange innocence to me, and added disquieting reasons. I replied jeeringly to this satanic doctor, and finished by escaping through the window. Far beyond this country (swept by wandering melodies), I created phantoms of a nocturnal luxury to come.

After this distraction—partly hygienic—I stretched myself on a straw mattress. And nearly every night, as soon as he was asleep my poor brother rose, his mouth all leprous-stained, his eyes torn out, —for so he dreamed himself to be!—and drew me into the room howling out his idiot nightmare.

In all sincerity I had promised to restore him to his primitive state of "Child of the Sun,"—and so we wander (drinking Palermian wine and eating tramp's biscuits), I in haste to find the necessary spot and the necessary formula.

TOILERS

It is a hot February morning. An inopportune south wind raises memories of our absurd indigence, our youthful poverty.—Henrika was wearing a brown and white check cotton dress in the fashion of last century, a bonnet trimmed with ribbons, and a silk handkerchief round her neck. It was more sombre than mourning. We were taking a walk in the suburbs; the weather was oppressive, and the south wind disturbed all the evil odours of the ravaged gardens and the dried-up fields.

Evidently all this did not tire my wife as it tired me. The floods of the preceding month had left a shallow pool behind them near the path up which we were climbing, and my wife called my attention to some tiny fish swimming in it.

The town, with its smoke and the noises of its factories, seemed to follow us far along the roads. O, where is that other world, that habitation blessed by heaven? Where are those gentle shades? The south wind recalled the miserable incidents of my childhood, my despair in summer, the horrible amount of strength and knowledge that fate has always put out of my reach. No, we will not spend the summer in this niggardly country where we shall never be anything but two betrothed orphans. This muscular arm shall no longer drag about a loved image.

The skies are like grey crystal. I see a strange design of bridges,—some straight, some curved, others descending slantingly on to the first. They multiply themselves in the smooth windings of the canal, but are so long and light that the canal banks, covered with domes, seem to sink and grow less. Some of these bridges are still encumbered with hovels; on others are masts, signals and frail parapets. Stringed instruments are heard on the hills, and minor chords cross each other and disappear; a red coat can be seen,—perhaps other costumes and musical instruments. Are they playing popular airs, odds and ends from courtly concerts, or snatches of public hymns?

The water is grey and blue, and as wide as an arm of the sea.

A white ray of sunshine falling from heaven destroys the illusion.

SOIR HISTORIQUE

One evening a naive tourist (retired from our economic horrors) hears the hand of a master touching the harpsichord of the meadows. Cards are being played at the bottom of the lake, that mirror which evokes images of queens and of passing loves. There where the sun is setting, saints and nuns can be seen, threads of harmony and legendary scales can be heard.

The passing of huntsmen and of bands of people makes him tremble. Comedy distills itself on the grassy trestles. The poor and the feeble overcrowd these senseless plans.

Before his slave's vision Germany seems to pile herself up towards the moon; the tartar deserts grow light; ancient seditions stir and mutter in the heart of the Celestial Empire. Ascending rocky staircases and seated in chairs of stone, the little pale, flat-faced peoples of Africa and the west are improving their minds. There are sea-ballets, and ballets of the night, and impossible melodies.

There is the same bourgeois magic at every place where the magic carpet sets us down. The most elementary physician feels that it is no longer possible to submit to this atmosphere of egoism—haze of a physical remorse—the existence of which it is painful even to acknowledge. No, it is the time of steaming vapours, of heaving seas, of subterranean conflagrations, of planets swept away and subsequent exterminations:—certainties not very cleverly hinted at in the Bible and by the Nornes, and which it will be given to some serious-minded person to watch over.

Nevertheless there will be no legendary effect!

Cooperation

(A Note on the Volume Completed)

EZRA POUND

I SEE no reason for diffidence regarding the fourth volume of the *Little Review*, and the first volume of the present effort.

We have published some of Mr. Yeats' best poems, poems as obviously destined for perpetuity as are those in his "Wind Among the Reeds"; we have begun publishing Hueffer and Joyce; if we have not published "Tarr" it is only because "Tarr" was already in process, and we have published whatever else of Wyndham Lewis's work has been ready. We have published the small bulk of Mr. Eliot's poetry that has been written during the current year. And we have brought out a French number which may serve as a paradigm for the rest of America's periodicals.

The response has been oligarchic. The plain man in his gum overshoes, with his touching belief in W. J. Bryan, Eddie Bok, etc., is not with us. There are apparently a few dozen people who want, with vigour, a magazine which can be read by men of some education and of some mental alertness; there are a few hundred more people who want this thing with less vigour; or who have at their disposal fewer "resources."

My net value to the concern appears to be about $2350; of which over $2000 does not "accrue" to the protagonist. It might be argued with some subtlety that I make the limited public an annual present of that sum, for the privilege of giving them what they do not much want, and for, let us say, forcing upon them a certain amount of literature, and a certain amount of enlightened criticism.

This donation I have willingly made, and will as willingly repeat, *but* I can not be expected to keep it up for an indefinite period.

"Et les vers cherchent le repos."

I have done my French number, I find it necessary to do most of the Henry James number myself; I will willingly do a Remy De-Gourmont number, and even a Spanish number if the available material proves worth the trouble, but I can not indefinitely do the work that is performed on the *Mercure* by a whole staff of rubricists. (A condensation of this sort of hundred-eyed labour is no saving of energy for the condenser).

Creation is a very slow process. It is possible, by doing a certain amount of well-paid but unimportant work, for me to buy leisure sufficient for whatever creative processes are possible to me. It is not possible for me to add to that dual existence a third function. Leaving polysyllables, either the editing of the foreign section of the *Little Review* has got to pay my board and rent, etc., and leave me sufficient leisure for my own compositions, or I have got to spend my half time on something more lucrative.

It is bad economy for me to spend a morning tying up stray copies of the *Little Review* for posting, or in answering queries as to why last month's number hasn't arrived. This function could be carried on by a deputy, almost by an infant.

It is not that I desire to "get" such a lot of it (£s.d) as that I decline to have my own work (such as it is) smothered by executive functions. And unless said functions can relieve me of the necessity of writing ephemeral stuff for other papers I shall be compelled to "relinquish them."

Or, still more baldly, I can not write six sorts of journalism four days a week, edit the *Little Review* three days a week, and continue my career as an author.

There are plenty of voices ready with the quite obvious reply that: nobody wants me to continue my hideous career as either author, editor, or journalist. I can, in imagination, hear the poluploisbious twitter of rural requests for my silence and extinction. This rumble is however exaggerated, there are several score, perhaps even several hundred (certainly not a full thousand, but perhaps several hundred) people who would rather I wrote a few good poems than a great fatras of newspaper or periodic comment, and these few score or few hundred are (with my own feelings included) the only people for whom I care three-fourths of a tinker's curse.

(Add to the verse, perhaps, a little prose, perhaps imaginative, which I might regard as literature, not merely as disputation, didacticism, higher instruction, postgraduate lecturing, acting as battistrada for new artists and writers, etc.)

So that, roughly speaking, either the *Little Review* will have to provide me with the necessities of life and a reasonable amount of leisure, by May 1st, 1919, or I shall have to apply my energies elsewhere.

Marianne Moore gave us a poem which I didn't, and don't, care for:

186

You Say You Said

MARIANNE MOORE

"Few words are best."
    Not here. Discretion has been abandoned in this part of the
    world too lately
    For it to be admired. Disgust for it is like the
Equinox—all things in

One. Disgust is
    No psychologist and has not opportunity to be a hypocrite.
    It says to the saw-toothed bayonet and to the cue
Of blood behind the sub-

Marine—to the
    Poisoned comb, to the Kaiser of Germany and to the intolerant
    gateman at the exit from the eastbound express; "I hate
You less than you must hate

Yourselves: You have
    Accoutred me. 'Without enemies one's courage flags'.
    Your error has been timed
    To aid me, I am in debt to you for you have primed
Me against subterfuge."

*Ezra and I disagreed about this poet. This is how I would express
my disagreement today:*

*It is almost impossible for me to express, with moderation, my
dislike of intellectual poetry. It is an anomaly. I can't read it without impatience. It can enrage me.*

My position needs no defense—the simplest statement defends it:
INTELLECTUAL POETRY IS NOT POETRY.

*Poetry is not made from, nor read with, the mind. It arises in an-
other center of man. You shouldn't have to* THINK *when you read a
poem. Instead, "un monde vous frappe dans la poitrine et abolit
tout ce qui n'est pas lui."*

*There is no idea in intellectual poetry that cannot be better ex-
pressed in prose. There is no emotion in intellectual poetry that
springs from the affirmed permanent emotions of mankind.*

*Eliot is a poet—he uses his mind to reveal the life of his emotions.
Marianne Moore is an intellectual—she uses the life of her mind as
her subject-matter. Some subject-matters are proper to poetry; some*

are not. The difference is always between the verbal and the formal.

The Marianne Moores live in, and write from, the phenomenal world. Poets live in, and write from, the noumenal world.

One would think that by the twentieth century such distinctions would have become a part of common knowledge. They haven't. Intellectuals don't yet know the hierarchies in art. But there are so many essential things they don't know. They don't yet know the hierarchies in humanity.

These are the distinctions the Little Review *knew. Such information gave it its quality, its vitality, its essentiality. Permanent material.*

Marianne Moore and Mina Loy
EZRA POUND

IN the verse of Marianne Moore I detect traces of emotion; in that of Mina Loy I detect no emotion whatever. Both of these women are, possibly in unconsciousness, among the followers of Jules Laforgue (whose work shows a great deal of emotion). It is possible, as I have written, or intended to write elsewhere, to divide poetry into three sorts; (1.) melopoeia, to wit, poetry which moves by its music, whether it be a music in the words or an aptitude for, or suggestion of, accompanying music; (2.) imagism, or poetry wherein the feelings of painting and sculpture are predominant (certain men move in phantasmagoria; the images of their gods, whole countrysides, stretches of hill land and forest, travel with them); and there is, thirdly, logopoeia or poetry that is akin to nothing but language, which is a dance of the intelligence among words and ideas and modification of ideas and characters. Pope and the eighteenth-century writers had in this medium a certain limited range. The intelligence of Laforgue ran through the whole gamut of his time. T. S. Eliot has gone on with it. Browning wrote a condensed form of drama, full of things of the senses, scarcely ever pure logopoeia.

One wonders what the devil anyone will make of this sort of thing who has not in his wit all the clues. It has none of the stupidity beloved of the "lyric" enthusiast and the writer and reader who take refuge in scenery description of nature, because they are unable to cope with the human. These two contributors to the "Others" Anthology write logopoeia. It is, in their case, the utterance of clever people in despair, or hovering upon the brink of that precipice. It is of those who have acceded with Renan "La bêtise humaine est la seule chose qui donne une idée de l'infini." It is a mind cry, more than a heart cry. "Take the world if thou wilt but leave me an asylum for my affection" is not their lamentation, but rather "In the midst of this desolation, give me at least one intelligence to converse with."

The arid clarity, not without its own beauty, of le tempérament de l'Americaine, is in the poems of these two writers. . . .

The point of my praise, for I intend this as praise, even if I do not burst into the phrases of Victor Hugo, is that without any pretences and without clamors about nationality, these girls have written a distinctly national product, they have written something which could not have come out of any other country, and (while I have before now seen a deal of rubbish by both of them) they are interesting and readable (by me, that is).

Jane and I had other ideas about poetry. In My Thirty Years' War *I wrote about the appearance upon our scene of the extraordinary Baroness von Freytag von Loringhoven (pages 177–183). The first poem she gave us was "Mustir," dedicated to Marcel Duchamps who painted the "Nude Descending the Staircase." Many of our readers protested, but we kept on publishing the Baroness and in the end, I think, vindicated her—as I hope to prove later on.*

Mefk Maru Mustir Daas

ELSE VON FREYTAG VON LORINGHOVEN

The sweet corners of thine tired mouth   Mustir
So world-old   tired to nobility
To more   to shame   to hatred of thineself
So world-old tired   tired to nobility
Thine body is the prey of mice

And every day the corners of thine tired mouth   Mustir
Grow sweeter helpless   sneer the more despair
And bloody pale-red poison foams from them
At every noble thing   to kill thine soul
Because thine body is the prey of mice
And dies so slowly

So noble is thine tired soul   Mustir
She cannot help to mourn out of thine eyes
Thine eyelids   nostrils   pallor of thine cheek

To mourn upon the curving of thine lip
Upon the crystal of thine pallid ear
To beg forgiveness with flashing smile
Like amber-coloured honey

The sweet corners of thine tired mouth   Mustir
Undo thine sin.   Thine pain is killed in play
Thine body's torture stimulates in play
And silly little bells of perfect tune
Ring in thine throat
Thou art a country devasted   bare   Mustir
Exhausted soil with sandy trembling hills
No food   no water   and ashamed of it
Thou shiver   and an amber-yellow sun
Goes down the horizon
Thou art desert with mirages which drive the mind insane
To walk   and die   a-starving.—

The Chinese Written Character as a Medium for Poetry
(Abridged)

BY ERNEST FENOLLOSA AND EZRA POUND

My subject is poetry, not language, yet the roots of poetry are in language. In the study of a language so alien in form to ours as is Chinese in its written character, it is necessary to inquire how those universal elements of form which constitute poetics can derive appropriate nutriment.

In what sense can verse, written in terms of visible hieroglyphics, be reckoned true poetry? It might seem that poetry, which like music is a *time art*, weaving its unities out of successive impressions of sound, could with difficulty assimilate a verbal medium consisting largely of semi-pictorial appeals to the eye.

Contrast, for example, Gray's line:

The curfew tolls the knell of parting day.

with the Chinese line:

Moon   rays   like   pure   snow

Unless the sound of the latter be given, what have they in common?

It is not enough to adduce that each contains a certain body of prosaic meaning; for the question is, how can the Chinese line imply, *as form,* the very element that distinguishes poetry from prose?

On second glance, it is seen that the Chinese words, though visible, occur in just as necessary an order as the phonetic symbols of Gray. All that poetic form requires is a regular and flexible sequence, as plastic as thought itself. The characters may be seen and read, silently by the eye, one after the other:

Moon rays like pure snow.

Perhaps we do not always sufficiently consider that thought is successive, not through some accident or weakness of our subjective operations but because the operations of nature are successive. The transferences of force from agent to agent, which constitute natural phenomena, occupy time. Therefore, a reproduction of them in imagination requires the same temporal order.*

Suppose that we look out of a window and watch a man. Suddenly he turns his head and actively fixes his attention upon something. We look ourselves and see that his vision has been focussed upon a horse. We saw, first, the man before he acted; second, while he acted; third, the object toward which his action was directed. In speech we split up the rapid continuity of this action and of its picture into its three essential parts or joints in the right order, and say:

Man sees horse.

It is clear that these three joints, or words, are only three phonetic symbols, which stand for the three terms of a natural process. But we could quite as easily denote these three stages of our thought by symbols equally arbitrary, *which had no basis in sound;* for example, by three Chinese characters

If we all knew *what division* of this mental horse picture each of these signs stood for, we could communicate continuous thought to one another as easily by drawing them as by speaking words. We habitually employ the visible language of gesture in much this same manner.

* [*Style, that is to say, limpidity, as opposed to rhetoric.*—E. P.]

But Chinese notation is something much more than arbitrary symbols. It is based upon a vivid shorthand picture of the operations of nature. In the algebraic figure and in the spoken word there is no natural connection between thing and sign: all depends upon sheer convention. But the Chinese method follows natural suggestion. First stands the man on his two legs. Second, his eye moves through space: a bold figure represented by running legs under an eye, a modified picture of an eye, a modified picture of running legs but unforgettable once you have seen it. Third stands the horse on his four legs.

The thought picture is not only called up by these signs as well as by words but far more vividly and concretely. Legs belong to all three characters: they are *alive*. The group holds something of the quality of a continuous moving picture.

The untruth of a painting or a photograph is that, in spite of its concreteness, it drops the element of natural succession.

Contrast the Laocoon statue with Browning's lines:

"I sprang to the saddle, and Jorris, and he

. . . . . .

And into the midnight we galloped abreast."

One superiority of verbal poetry as an art rests in its getting back to the fundamental reality of *time*. Chinese poetry has the unique advantage of combining both elements. It speaks at once with the vividness of painting, and with the mobility of sounds. It is, in some sense, more objective than either, more dramatic. In reading Chinese we do not seem to be juggling mental counters, but to be watching *things* work out their own fate.

Leaving for a moment the form of the sentence, let us look more closely at this quality of vividness in the structure of detached Chinese words. The earlier forms of these characters were pictorial, and their hold upon the imagination is little shaken, even in later conventional modifications. It is not so well known, perhaps, that the great number of these ideographic roots carry in them a *verbal idea of action*. It might be thought that a picture is naturally the picture of a *thing*, and that therefore the root ideas of Chinese are what grammar calls nouns.

But examination shows that a large number of the primitive Chinese characters, even the so-called radicals, are shorthand pictures of actions or processes.

For example, the ideograph meaning "to speak" is a mouth with two words and a flame coming out of it. The sign meaning "to grow up with difficulty" is grass with a twisted root. But this concrete *verb* quality, both in nature and in the Chinese signs, becomes far more striking and poetic when we pass from such simple, original pictures to compounds. In this process of compounding, two things added together do not produce a third thing but suggest some fundamental relation between them. For example, the ideograph for a "messmate" is a man and a fire.

A true noun, an isolated thing, does not exist in nature. Things are only the terminal points, or rather the meeting points of actions, cross-sections cut through actions, snap-shots. Neither can a pure verb, an abstract motion, be possible in nature. The eye sees noun and verb as one: things in motion, motion in things, and so the Chinese conception tends to represent them.

The sun underlying the bursting forth of plants = spring.

The sun tangled in the branches of the tree sign = east.

"Rice-field" plus "struggle" = male.

"Boat" plus "water" = boat-water, a ripple.

Let us return to the form of the sentence and see what power it adds to the verbal units from which it builds. I wonder how many people have asked themselves why the sentence form exists at all, why it seems so universally necessary *in all languages?* Why *must* all possess it, and what is the normal type of it? If it be so universal it ought to correspond to some primary law of nature.

I fancy the professional grammarians have given but a lame response to this inquiry. Their definitions fall into two types: one, that a sentence expresses a "complete thought"; the other, that in it we bring about a union of subject and predicate.

The former has the advantage of trying for some natural objective standard, since it is evident that a thought can not be the test of its own completeness. But in nature there is *no* completeness. On the other hand, practical completeness may be expressed by a mere interjection, as "Hi! there!," or "Scat," or even by shaking one's fist. No sentence is needed to make one's meaning clear. On the other hand, no full sentence really completes a thought. The man who sees and the horse which is seen will not stand still. The man was planning a ride before he looked. The horse kicked when the man tried to catch him. The truth is that acts are successive, even continuous; one causes or passes into another. And though we may string ever so many clauses into a single compound sentence, motion leaks every-where, like electricity from an exposed wire. All processes in nature are inter-related; and thus there could be no complete sentence (according to this definition) save one which it would take all time to pronounce.

In the second definition of the sentence, as "uniting a subject and a predicate," the grammarian falls back on pure subjectivity. *We* do it all; it is a little private juggling between our right and left hands. The subject is that about which *I* am going to talk; the predicate is that which *I* am going to say about it. The sentence according to this definition is not an attribute of nature but an accident of man as a conversational animal.

If it were really so, then there could be no possible test of the truth of a sentence. Falsehood would be as specious as verity. Speech would carry no conviction.

Of course this view of the grammarians springs from the dis-credited, or rather the useless, logic of the middle ages. According to this logic, thought deals with abstractions, concepts drawn out of things by a sifting process. These logicians never inquired how the "qualities" which they pulled out of things came to be there. The truth of all their little checker-board juggling depended upon the natural order by which these powers or properties or qualities were folded in concrete things, yet they despised the "thing" as a mere "particular," or pawn. It was as if Botany should reason from the leafpatterns woven into our table-cloths. Valid scientific thought consists in following as closely as may be the actual and entangled lines of forces as they pulse through things. Thought deals with no bloodless concepts but watches *things move* under its microscope.

The sentence form was forced upon primitive men by nature itself. It was not we who made it; it was a reflection of the temporal order in causation. All truth has to be expressed in sentences because all truth is the *transference of power*. The type of sentence in nature is a flash of lightning. It passes between two terms, a cloud and the earth. No unit of natural process can be less than this. All natural processes are, in their units, as much as this. Light, heat, gravity, chemical affinity, human will have this in common, that they re-distribute force. Their unit of process can be represented as:

term from which	transference of force	term to which

194

If we regard this transference as the conscious or unconscious act of an agent we can translate the diagram into:

agent   act   object

In this the act is the very substance of the fact denoted. The agent and the object are only limiting terms.

It seems to me that the normal and typical sentence in English as well as in Chinese expresses just this unit of natural process. It consists of three necessary words; the first denoting the agent or subject from which the act starts; the second embodying the very stroke of the act; the third pointing to the object, the receiver of the impact. The form of the Chinese transitive sentence, and of the English (omitting particles) exactly corresponds to this universal form of action in nature. This brings language close to *things,* and in its strong reliance upon verbs it erects all speech into a kind of dramatic poetry.

A different sentence order is frequent in inflected languages like Latin, German or Japanese. This is because they are inflected, i.e., they have little tags and word-endings, or labels to show which is the agent, the object, etc. In uninflected languages, like English and Chinese, there is nothing but the order of the words to distinguish their functions. And this order would be no sufficient indication, were it not the *natural order*—that is, the order of cause and effect.

It is true that there are, in language, intransitive and passive forms, sentences built out of the verb "to be," and finally negative forms. To grammarians and logicians these have seemed more primitive than the transitive, or at least exceptions to the transitive. I had long suspected that these apparently exceptional forms had grown from the transitive or worn away from it by alteration or modification. This view is confirmed by Chinese examples, wherein it is still possible to watch the transformation going on.

The intransitive form derives from the transitive by dropping a generalized, customary, reflexive or cognate object. "He runs (a race)." "The sky reddens (itself)." "We breathe (air)." Thus we get weak and incomplete sentences which suspend the picture and lead us to think of some verbs as denoting states rather than acts. Outside grammar the word "state" would hardly be recognized as scientific. Who can doubt that when we say, "The wall shines," we mean that it actively reflects light to our eye?

The beauty of Chinese verbs is that they are all transitive or intransitive at pleasure. There is no such thing as a naturally intransitive verb. The passive form is evidently a correlative sentence, which turns about and makes the object into a subject. That the object is not in itself passive, but contributes some positive force of its own to the action, is in harmony both with scientific law and with ordinary experience. The English passive voice with "is" seemed at first an obstacle to this hypothesis, but one suspected that the true form was a generalized transitive verb meaning something like "receive," which had degenerated into an auxiliary. It was a delight to find this the case in Chinese.

In nature there are no negations, no possible transfers of negative force. The presence of negative sentences in language would seem to corroborate the logicians' view that assertion is an arbitrary subjective act. *We* can assert a negation, though nature can not. But here again science comes to our aid against the logician: all apparently negative or disruptive movements bring into play other positive forces. It requires great effort to annihilate. Therefore we should suspect that, if we could follow back the history of all negative particles, we should find that they also are sprung from transitive verbs. It is too late to demonstrate such derivations in the Aryan languages, the clue has been lost, but in Chinese we can still watch positive verbal conceptions passing over into so-called negatives. Thus in Chinese the sign meaning "to be lost in the forest" relates to a state of non-existence. English "not" = the Sanskrit *na*, which may come from the root *na*, to be lost, to perish.

Lastly comes the infinitive which substitutes for a specific colored verb the universal copula "is," followed by a noun or an adjective. We do not say a tree "greens itself," but "the tree is green;" not that "monkeys bring forth live young," but that "the monkey is a mammal." This is an ultimate weakness of language. It has come from generalizing all intransitive words into one. As "live," "see," "walk," "breathe," are generalized into states by dropping their objects, so these weak verbs are in turn reduced to the abstractest state of all, namely, bare existence.

There is in reality no such verb as a pure copula, no such original conception, our very word *exist* means "to stand forth," to show oneself by a definite act. "Is" comes from the Aryan root *as*, to breathe. "Be" is from *bhu*, to grow.

In Chinese the chief verb for "is" not only means actively "to have" but shows by its derivation that it expresses something even more concrete, namely, "to snatch from the moon with the hand." Here the baldest symbol of prosaic analysis is transformed by magic into a splendid flash of concrete poetry.

I shall not have entered vainly into this long analysis of the sentence if I have succeeded in showing how poetical is the Chinese form and how close to nature. In translating Chinese, verse especially, we must hold as closely as possible to the concrete force of the original, eschewing adjectives, nouns and intransitive forms wherever we can, and seeking instead strong and individual verbs.

Lastly we notice that the likeness of form between Chinese and English sentences renders translation from one to the other exceptionally easy. The genius of the two is much the same. Frequently it is possible by omitting English particles to make a literal word-for-word translation which will be not only intelligible in English, but even the strongest and most poetical English. Here, however, one must follow closely what is said, not merely what is abstractly meant.

Let us go back from the Chinese sentence to the individual written word. How are such words to be classified? Are some of them nouns by nature, some verbs and some adjectives? Are there pronouns and prepositions and conjunctions in Chinese as in good Christian languages?

One is led to suspect from an analysis of the Aryan languages that such differences are not natural, and that they have been unfortunately invented by grammarians to confuse the simple poetic outlook on life. All nations have written their strongest and most vivid literature before they invented a grammar. Moreover, all Aryan etymology points back to roots which are the equivalents of simple Sanskrit verbs, such as we find tabulated at the back of our Skeat. Nature herself has no grammar.*

Fancy picking up a man and telling him that he is a noun, a dead thing rather than a bundle of functions. A "part of speech" is only *what it does*. Frequently our lines of cleavage fail, one part of speech acts for another. They *act for* one another because they were originally one and the same.

* [*Even Latin, (living Latin) had not the network they foist upon unfortunate school-children. These are borrowed sometimes from Greek grammarians, even as I have seen English grammars borrowing oblique cases from Latin grammars. Sometimes they sprang from the grammatizing or categorizing passion of pedants. Living Latin had only the feel of the cases. The ablative and dative eotion.—* E. P.]

197

Few of us realize that in our own language these very differences once grew up in living articulation; that they still retain life. It is only when the difficulty of placing some odd term arises or when we are forced to translate into some very different language, that we attain for a moment the inner heat of thought, a heat which melts down the parts of speech to recast them at will.

One of the most interesting facts about the Chinese language is that in it we can see, not only the forms of sentences, but literally the parts of speech growing up, budding forth one from another. Like nature, the Chinese words are alive and plastic, because *thing* and *action* are not formally separated. The Chinese language naturally knows no grammar. It is only lately that foreigners, European and Japanese, have begun to torture this vital speech by forcing it to fit the bed of their definitions. We import into our reading of Chinese all the weakness of our own formalisms. This is especially sad in poetry, because the one necessity, even in our own poetry, is to keep words as flexible as possible, as full of the sap of nature.

Let us go further with our example. In English we call "to shine" a *verb in the infinitive*, because it gives the abstract meaning of the verb without conditions. If we want a corresponding adjective we take a different word, "bright." If we need a noun we say "luminosity," which is abstract, being derived from an adjective.* To get a tolerably concrete noun, we have to leave behind the verb and adjective roots, and light upon a thing arbitrarily cut off from its power of action, say "the sun" or "the moon." Of course there is nothing in nature so cut off, and therefore this nounizing is itself an abstraction. Even if we did have a common word underlying at once the verb "shine," the adjective "bright," and the noun "sun," we should probably call it an "infinitive of the infinitive." According to our ideas, it should be something extremely abstract, too intangible for use.

The Chinese have one word, *ming*, or *mei*. Its ideograph is the sign of the sun together with the sign of the moon. It serves as verb, noun, adjective. Thus you write literally, "the sun and moon of the cup" for "the cup's brightness." Placed as a verb, you write "the cup sun-and-moons," actually "cup sun-and-moon," or in a weakened

* [*A good writer would use "shine" (i. e., to shine), shining, and "the shine" or "sheen," possibly thinking of the German "shöne" and "Schönheit"; but this does not invalidate Prof. Fenollosa's next contention.*—E. P.]

198

thought, "is like sun," i. e., shines. "Sun-and-moon-cup" is naturally a bright cup. There is no possible confusion of the real meaning, though a stupid scholar may spend a week trying to decide what "part of speech" he should use in translating a very simple and direct thought from Chinese to English.

The fact is that almost every written Chinese word is properly just such an underlying word, and yet it is *not* abstract. It is not exclusive of parts of speech, but comprehensive; not something which is neither a noun, verb, or adjective, but something which is all of them at once and at all times. Usage may incline the full meaning now a little more to one side, now to another, according to the point of view, but through all cases the poet is free to deal with it richly and concretely, as does nature.

In the derivation of nouns from verbs, the Chinese language is forestalled by the Aryan. Almost all the Sanskrit roots, which seem to underlie European languages, are primitive verbs, which express characteristic actions of visible nature. The verb must be the primary fact of nature, since motion and change are all that we can recognize in her. In the primitive transitive sentence, such as "Farmer pounds rice," the agent and the object are nouns only in so far as they limit a unit of action. "Farmer" and "rice" are mere hard terms which define the extremes of the pounding. But in themselves, apart from this sentence-function, they are naturally verbs. The farmer is one who tills the ground, and the rice is a plant which grows in a special way. This is indicated in the Chinese characters. And this probably exemplifies the ordinary derivation of nouns from verbs. In all languages, Chinese included, a noun is originally "that which does something," that which performs the verbal action. Thus the moon comes from the root *ma,* and means "the measurer." The sun means that which begets.

The derivation of adjectives from the verb need hardly be exemplified. Even with us, to-day, we can still watch participles passing over into adjectives. In Japanese the adjective is frankly part of the inflection of the verb, a special mood, so that every verb is also an adjective. This brings us close to nature, because everywhere the quality is only a power of action regarded as having an abstract inherence. Green is only a certain rapidity of vibration, hardness a degree of tenseness in cohering. In Chinese the adjective always retains a substratum of verbal meaning. We should try to render this in translation, not be content with some bloodless adjectival abstraction plus "is."

Still more interesting are the Chinese "prepositions," they are often post-positions. Prepositions are so important, so pivotal in European speech only because we have weakly yielded up the force of our intransitive verbs. We have to add small supernumerary words to bring back the original power. We still say "I see a horse," but with the weak verb "look," we have to add the directive particle "at" before we can restore the natural transitiveness.*

Prepositions represent a few simple ways in which incomplete verbs complete themselves. Pointing toward nouns as a limit they bring force to bear upon them. That is to say, they are naturally verbs, of generalized or condensed use. In Aryan languages it is often difficult to trace the verbal origins of simple prepositions. Only in "off" do we see a fragment of the thought "to throw off." In Chinese the preposition is frankly a verb, specially used in a generalized sense. These verbs are often used in their specially verbal sense, and it greatly weakens an English translation if they are systematically rendered by colorless prepositions.

Thus in Chinese: By=to cause; to=to fall toward; in=to remain, to dwell; from=to follow; and so on.

Conjunctions are similarly derivative, they usually serve to mediate actions between verbs, and therefore they are necessarily themselves actions. Thus in Chinese: Because=to use; and=to be included under one; another form of "and"=to be parallel; or=to partake; if=to let one do, to permit. The same is true of a host of other particles, no longer traceable in the Aryan tongues.

Pronouns appear a thorn in our evolution theory, since they have been taken as unanalyzable expressions of personality. In Chinese even they yield up their striking secrets of verbal metaphor. They are a constant source of weakness if colorlessly translated. Take, for example, the five forms of "I." There is the sign of a "spear in the hand"=a very emphatic I; five and a mouth=a weak and defensive I, holding off a crowd by speaking; to conceal=a selfish and private I; self (the cocoon sign) and a mouth=an egoistic I, one who takes

* [*This is a bad example. We can say "I look a fool," "look," transitive, now means resemble. The main contention is however correct. We tend to abandon specific words like "resemble" and substitute, for them, vague verbs with prepositional directors, or riders.—E. P.*]

200

pleasure in his own speaking; the self presented is used only when one is speaking to one's self.

I trust that this digression concerning parts of speech may have justified itself. It proves, first, the enormous interest of the Chinese language in throwing light upon our forgotten mental processes, and thus furnishes a new chapter in the philosophy of language. Secondly, it is indispensable for understanding the poetical raw material which the Chinese language affords. Poetry differs from prose in the concrete colors of its diction. It is not enough for it to furnish a meaning to philosophers. It must appeal to emotions with the charm of direct impression, flashing through regions where the intellect can only grope.* Poetry must render what is said, not what is merely meant. Abstract meaning gives little vividness, and fullness of imagination gives all. Chinese poetry demands that we abandon our narrow grammatical categories, that we follow the original text with a wealth of concrete verbs.

But this is only the beginning of the matter. So far we have exhibited the Chinese characters and the Chinese sentence chiefly as vivid shorthand pictures of actions and processes in nature. These embody true poetry as far as they go. Such actions are *seen*, but Chinese would be a poor language and Chinese poetry but a narrow art, could they not go on to represent also what is unseen. The best poetry deals not only with natural images but with lofty thoughts, spiritual suggestions and obscure relations. The greater part of natural truth is hidden in processes too minute for vision and in harmonies too large, in vibrations, cohesions and in affinities. The Chinese compass these also, and with great power and beauty.

You will ask, how could the Chinese have built up a great intellectual fabric from mere picture writing? To the ordinary western mind, which believes that thought is concerned with logical categories and which rather condemns the faculty of direct imagination, this feat seems quite impossible. Yet the Chinese language with its peculiar material has passed over from the seen to the unseen by exactly the same process which all ancient races employed. The process is metaphor, the use of material images to suggest immaterial relations.†

The whole delicate substance of speech is built upon substrata of metaphor. Abstract terms, pressed by etymology, reveal their ancient

* [Cf. *principle of Primary apparition, "Spirit of Romance."*—E. P.]
† [Compare *Aristotle's Poetics.*—E. P.]

201

roots still embedded in direct action. But the primitive metaphors do not spring from arbitrary subjective processes. They are possible only because they follow objective lines of relations in nature herself. Relations are more real and more important than the things which they relate. The forces which produce the branch-angles of an oak lay potent in the acorn. Similar lines of resistance, half curbing the out-pressing vitalities, govern the branching of rivers and of nations. Thus a nerve, a wire, a roadway, and a clearing-house are only varying channels which communication forces for itself. This is more than analogy, it is identity of structure. Nature furnishes her own clues. Had the world not been full of homologies, sympathies, and identities, thought would have been starved and language chained to the obvious. There would have been no bridge whereby to cross from the minor truth of the seen to the major truth of the unseen. Not more than a few hundred roots out of our large vocabularies could have dealt directly with physical processes. These we can fairly well identify in primitive Sanskrit. They are, almost without exception, vivid verbs. The wealth of European speech grew, following slowly the intricate maze of nature's suggestions and affinities. Metaphor was piled upon metaphor in quasigeological strata.

Metaphor, the revealer of nature, is the very substance of poetry. The known interprets the obscure, the universe is alive with myth. The beauty and freedom of the observed world furnish a model, and life is pregnant with art. It is a mistake to suppose, with some philosophers of aesthetics, that art and poetry aim to deal with the general and the abstract. This misconception has been foisted upon us by mediaeval logic. Art and poetry deal with the concrete of nature, not with rows of separate "particulars," for such rows do not exist. Poetry is finer than prose because it gives us more concrete truth in the same compass of words. Metaphor, its chief device, is at once the substance of nature and of language. Poetry only does consciously* what the primitive races did unconsciously. The chief work of literary men in dealing with language, and of poets especially, lies in feeling back along the ancient lines of advance.†

* [*Vide also an article on "Vorticism" in the Fortnightly Review for September, 1914. "The language of exploration."*—E. P.]

† [*I would submit in all humility that this applies in the rendering of ancient texts. The poet in dealing with his own time, must also see to it that language does not petrify on his hands. He must prepare for new advances along the lines of true metaphor that is interpretive metaphor, or image, as diametrically opposed to untrue, or ornamental, metaphor.*—E. P.]

He must do this so that he may keep his words enriched by all their subtle undertones of meaning. The original metaphors stand as a kind of luminous background, giving color and vitality, forcing them closer to the concreteness of natural processes. Shakespeare everywhere teems with examples. For these reasons poetry was the earliest of the world arts; poetry, language and the care of myth grew up together.

I have alleged all this because it enables me to show clearly why I believe that the Chinese written language has not only absorbed the poetic substance of nature and built with it a second world of metaphor, but has, through its very pictorial visibility, been able to retain its original creative poetry with far more vigor and vividness than any phonetic tongue. Let us first see how near it is to the heart of nature in its metaphors. We can watch it passing from the seen to the unseen, as we saw it passing from verb to pronoun. It retains the primitive sap, it is not cut and dried like a walking-stick. We have been told that these people are cold, practical, mechanical, literal, and without a trace of imaginative genius. That is nonsense.

Our ancestors built the accumulations of metaphor into structures of language and into systems of thought. Languages to-day are thin and cold because we think less and less into them. We are forced, for the sake of quickness and sharpness, to file down each word to its narrowest edge of meaning. Nature would seem to have become less like a paradise and more and more like a factory. We are content to accept the vulgar misuse of the moment. A late stage of decay is arrested and embalmed in the dictionary. Only scholars and poets feel painfully back along the thread of our etymologies and piece together our diction, as best they may, from forgotten fragments. This anemia of modern speech is only too well encouraged by the feeble cohesive force of our phonetic symbols. There is little or nothing in a phonetic word to exhibit the embryonic stages of its growth. It does not bear its metaphor on its face. We forget that personality once meant, not the soul, but the soul's mask. This is the sort of thing one can not possibly forget in using the Chinese symbols.

In this Chinese shows its advantage. Its etymology is constantly visible. It retains the creative impulse and process, visible and at work. After thousands of years the lines of metaphoric advance are still shown, and in many cases actually retained in the meaning. Thus a word, instead of growing gradually poorer and poorer as with us, becomes richer and still more rich from age to age, almost consciously luminous. Its uses in national philosophy and history, in biography and in poetry, throw about it a nimbus of meanings. These center about the graphic symbol. The memory can hold them and use them. The very soil of Chinese life seems entangled in the roots of its speech. The manifold illustrations which crowd its annals of personal experience, the lines of tendency which converge upon a tragic climax, moral character as the very core of the principle—all these are flashed at once on the mind as reinforcing values with an accumulation of meaning which a phonetic language can hardly hope to attain. Their ideographs are like blood-stained battle flags to an old campaigner. With us, the poet is the only one for whom the accumulated treasures of the race-words are real and active. Poetic language is always vibrant with fold on fold of overtones, and with natural affinities, but in Chinese the visibility of the metaphor tends to raise this quality to its intensest power.

I have mentioned the tyranny of mediæval logic. According to this European logic thought is a kind of brickyard. It is baked into little hard units or concepts. These are piled in rows according to size and then labeled with words for future use. This use consists in picking out a few bricks, each by its convenient label, and sticking them together into a sort of wall called a sentence by the use either of white mortar for the positive copula "is," or black mortar for the negative copula "is not." In this way we produce such admirable propositions as "A ring-tailed baboon is not a constitutional assembly."

Let us consider a row of cherry trees. From each of these in turn we proceed to take an "abstract," as the phrase is, a certain common lump of qualities which we may express together by the name cherry or cherryness. Next we place in a second table several such characteristic concepts: cherry, rose, sunset, iron-rust, flamingo. From these we abstract some further common quality, dilutation or mediocrity, and label it "red" or "redness." It is evident that this process of abstraction may be carried on indefinitely and with all sorts of material. We may go on forever building pyramids of attenuated concept until we reach the apex "being."

But we have done enough to illustrate the characteristic process. At the base of the pyramid lie *things,* but stunned, as it were. They can never know themselves for things until they pass up and down among the layers of the pyramids. The way of passing up and down the pyramid may be exemplified as follows: We take a concept of lower attenuation, such as "cherry"; we see that it is contained under one higher, such as "redness." Then we are permitted to say in sentence form, "Cherryness is contained under redness," or for short, "(the) cherry is red." If, on the other hand, we do not find our chosen subject under a given predicate we use the black copula and say, for example, " (The) cherry is not liquid."

From this point we might go on to the theory of the syllogism, but we refrain. It is enough to note that the practised logician finds it convenient to store his mind with long lists of nouns and adjectives, for these are naturally the names of classes. Most text-books on language begin with such lists. The study of verbs is meager, for in such a system there is only one real working verb, to-wit, the quasi-verb "is." All other verbs can be transformed into participles and gerunds. For example, "to run" practically becomes a case of "running." Instead of thinking directly, "The man runs," our logician makes two subjective equations, namely: The individual in question is contained under the class "man"; and the class "man" is contained under the class of "running things."

The sheer loss and weakness of this method is apparent and flagrant. Even in its own sphere it can not think half of what to think. It has no way of bringing together any two concepts which do not happen to stand one under the other and in the same pyramid. It is impossible to represent change in this system or any kind of growth. This is probably why the conception of evolution came so late in Europe. *It could not make way until it was prepared to destroy the inveterate logic of classification.*

Far worse than this, such logic can not deal with any kind of interaction or with any multiplicity of function. According to it, the function of my muscles is as isolated from the function of my nerves, as from an earthquake in the moon. For it the poor neglected things at the bases of the pyramids are only so many particulars or pawns.

Science fought till she got at the things. All her work has been done from the base of the pyramids, not from the apex. She has discovered how functions cohere in things. She expresses her results in grouped sentences which embody no nouns or adjectives but verbs of special character. The true formula for thought is: The cherry tree is all that it does. Its correlated verbs compose it. At bottom these verbs are transitive. Such verbs may be almost infinite in number.

In diction and in grammatical form science is utterly opposed to logic. Primitive men who created language agreed with science and not with logic. Logic has abused the language which they left to her mercy. Poetry agrees with science and not with logic.

Poems

EZRA POUND

HOMAGE A LA LANGUE d'OC

Alba

When the nightingale to his mate
Sings day-long and night late
My love and I keep state
    In bower,
    In flower,
    'Till the watchman on the tower
Cry:
      "Up! Thou rascal, Rise,
     I see the white
        Light
       And the night
          Flies"

I

Compleynt of a gentleman who has been waiting outside for some time.

"O Plasmatour and true celestial light,
Lord powerful, engirdléd all with might,
Give my good-fellow aid in fools' despite
Who stirs not forth this night,
       And day comes on.

Sst! my good fellow, art awake or sleeping?
Sleep thou no more. I see the star upleaping
That hath the dawn in keeping,
       And day comes on!
Hi! Harry, hear me, for I sing aright
Sleep not thou now, I hear the bird in flight
That plaineth of the going of the night,
       And day comes on!

Come now! Old swenkin! Rise up from thy bed,
I see the signs upon the welkin spread,

If thou come not, the cost be on thy head.
        And day comes on!!

And here I am since going down of sun,
And pray to God that is St. Mary's son,
To bring thee safe back, my companion.
        And day comes on.

And thou out here beneath the porch of stone
Bade me to see that a good watch was done,
And now Thou'lt none of me, and wilt have none
Of song of mine.
        And day comes on."
        Bass voice from within.
"Wait, my good fellow. For such joy I take
With her venust and noblest to my make
To hold embracèd and will not her forsake
For yammer of the cuckold,
        Though day break."
        (*Girart Bornello*)

II

Avril

When the springtime is sweet
And the birds repeat
Their new song in the leaves,
'Tis meet
A man go where he will.

But from where my heart is set
No message I get;
My heart all wakes and grieves;
Defeat
Or luck, I must have my fill.

Our love comes out
Like the branch that turns about
On the top of the hawthorne,
With frost and hail at night
Suffers despite
'Till I have my hand 'neath her cloak.

I remember the young day

When we set strife away,
And she gave me such gesning,
Her love and her ring:,
God grant I die not by any man's stroke
'Till I have my hand 'neath her cloak.

I care not for their clamour
Who have come between me and my charmer,
For I know how words run loose,
Big talk and little use.
Spoilers of pleasure,
We take their measure.

(Guilhem de Peitieu)

III

Descant on a Theme by Cerclamon
When the sweet air goes bitter,
And the cold birds twitter
Where the leaf falls from the twig,
I sough and sing
        that Love goes out
          Leaving me no power to hold him.

Of love I have naught
Save troubles and sad thought,
And nothing is grievous
        as I desirous,
Wanting only what
No man can get or has got.

With the noblest that stands in men's sight,
If all the world be in despite
        I care not a glove.
Where my love is, there is a glitter of sun;
God give me life, and let my course run
        'Till I have her I love
          To lie with and prove.

I do not live, nor cure me,
Nor feel my ache—great as it is,
For love will give
        me no respite,
Nor do I know when I turn left or right

nor when I go out.
For in her is all my delight
And all that can save me.

I shake and burn and quiver
From love, awake and in swevyn,
Such fear I have she deliver
        me not from pain,
        Who know not how to ask her;
        Who can not.
Two years, three years I seek
And though I fear to speak out,
        Still she must know it.
If she won't have me now, Death is my portion
        Would I had died that day
        I came into her sway.
God! How softly this kills!
When her love-look steals on me.
Killed me she has, I know not how it was,
        For I would not look on a woman.

Joy I have none, if she make me not mad
        Or set me quiet, or bid me chatter.
Good is it to me if she flout
        Or turn me inside out, and about.
        My ill doth she turn sweet.
        How swift it is. Pleasure is 'neath her feet.

        For I am traist and loose,
        I am true, or a liar,
        All vile, or all gentle,
        Or shaking between,
            as she desire,
I, Cerclamon, sorry and glad,
        The man whom love had
            and has ever;
        Alas! whoe'er it please or pain,
        She can me retain.

I am gone from one joy,
From one I loved never so much,
        She by one touch
        Reft me away; .

So doth bewilder me
I can not say my say
          nor my desire,
And when she looks on me
It seems to me
          I lose all wit and sense.
The noblest girls men love
'Gainst her I prize not as a glove
Worn and old.
Though the whole world run rack
And go dark with cloud,
Light is
Where she stands,
And a clamour loud
          in my ears.

Vergier

In orchard under the hawthorne
She has her lover till morn'
Till the traist man cry out to warn
Them. God how swift the night,
        And day comes on.

O Plasmatour, that thou end not the night,
Nor take my belovèd from my sight,
Nor I, nor tower-man, look on daylight,
'Fore God, How swift the night,
        And day comes on.

"Lovely thou art, to hold me close and kisst,
Now cry the birds out, in the meadow mist,
Despite the cuckold, do thou as thou list,
So swiftly goes the night
        And day comes on.

"My pretty boy, make we our play again
Here in the orchard where the birds complain,
'Till the traist watcher his song unrein,
Ah God! How swift the night
        And day comes on."

"Out of the wind that blows from her,
That dancing and gentle is and pleasanter,

Have I drunk a draught, sweeter than scent of myrrh.
Ah God! How swift the night.
        And day comes on."

Venust the lady, and none lovelier,
For her great beauty, many men look on her,
Out of my love will her heart not stir.
By God, how swift the night.
        And day comes on.

The Reader Critic

EZRA POUND'S CRITICS

A Letter:

The *Little Review* is flourishing only decadent blunderings under the magical wand of the grand dervish, Mr. Ezra Pound. The fact is that most of the writings are lacking aesthetically, poetically, and philosophically. From the psychological point of view, one sees in the articles the sad picture, which runs like red thread on white cloth, of the miserable personalities of their authors. Too much they mention themselves. For instance, Mr. Ezra Pound, who likes also to show how many languages he knows, speaks in his poem as follows: "—and said, 'Mr. Pound is shocked at my levity.'" This visiting card is no manifestation of high poetic power. Many times he pictures as facts the aberrations of his fancy, as when he rhapsodizes over a nightingale. To beautify his rhyme he thinks he must mention the sweetest of all songsters. But in so doing he over-compliments the little bird when he states:
        "When the nightingale to his mate
        Sings day-long and night late."
If Ezra Pound had ever with his own ears heard a nightingale, he would have to admit that the bird sings to his mate only at night during the short mating period. Whether he mistook an English sparrow for a nightingale I know not; the fact remains that the poet does not know when the nightingale sings.

[I have heard the most literal-minded, undifferentiated men say "I lived a whole life-time in those few minutes."

"The fact remains that the poet does not know when the nightingale sings." It is neither necessary nor interesting for a poet to know these facts. The glory of reason is limited by the possibilities of the human mechanism. Emotion—art emotion—creates its own realities. —*jh.*]

Leonard Cline:

. . . It is a tremendous shock to be hurtled into the company of devil-begotten Ezra Pound, put up between yellow boards by Alfred A. Knopf, under the nomenclature of "Lustra." This word "lustra" means one of two things, either expiatory sacrifices or morasses. Ezra Pound is too absolutely degraded to offer sacrifices, much less expiatory ones; therefore we must be content to consider the book a collection of morasses, quicksands.

Bogs the poems certainly are. There is an enormous charm about some of them, and one is in jeopardy of being lured to tread out upon them, and only when the hungry mud sucks a shoe off and one gets a stocking slimy, realize one's delusion. They have the appearance of poetry; the lines are all split up; and now and again there is a really delightful metaphor, to give the devil his due. This it is which has induced people out upon them, and has given Ezra's corrupting influence a wide scope. As a rule these poems are not poems; beauty is never flippant. . . .

[Who is this man in Detroit who thinks he can limit beauty? If it's a sin to "make beauty flippant," isn't it a minor sin compared to limiting beauty? Mr. Cline is akin to all that brood who have lines inside of which beauty must move—the range of their vision. Beauty for them must be pleasing, pretty, decorous, obvious, and "clean." I remember a similar criticism in another Michigan paper some time ago. When the Chicago Little Theatre Company played *The Medea* in one of its cities a critic wrote: "The Little Theatre gave a beautiful performance of *The Medea,* if tragedy can ever be called beautiful."—*jh.*]

New York Reader:

. . . I am sorry about one thing,—you don't seem to be able to get rid of the propaganda. All the things Pound sends you are in a way propaganda. If not, what are they trying to do; just shock people?

[I am with you on the propaganda. Extermination seems simple and direct and lasting and the only solution to me. Shocking people

212

I believe is a fever of extreme youth which cools very soon,—as soon as caught almost. If one could only shock them to the foundations there might be some interest, but they are never shocked beyond where they are always trembling anyway. Eliot is quite outside that kind of interest.]

Marsden Hartley:

Our Americans abroad are certainly formidable in their intelligence. I am wanting to think however that erudition is one thing, the dictionary another, and poetry different from either of them. I suffer for "Little lamb who made thee, dost thou know who made thee" in the presence of the Pound-Eliot phraseology. Poetry may be the place for private excursions into the oddities of language, little journies into the lairs of little known animals, but it does not seem to me the place for the rattling of so much tin. Bronze is still good enough for the common ear.

Pound has stated himself clearly further over in the issue on the value of savantism and literacy. Critics should of necessity know more because they have more to profess. I congratulate E. P. on knowing a genuine lot. There is a something outside of books so engaging however, that many haven't time for the life of the printed page, enticing as it is. Life is such a game, that there are many who can't get down to culture.

From Chicago:

The June *Little Review* has just arrived. Never have I seen such drawings as Szukalski's. My heart actually began to beat faster when I saw them. Frankly, the rest of the magazine should have been blank. Everything else in it appears pallid beside those furious sketches. Da Vinci come to life. The lines are full of energy, they move across the page: they make channels for themselves on the paper. Magnificent! Wonderful!

["Never have I seen such drawings" and then "Da Vinci come to life." I suppose this has meaning? Another reader writes "Here is a new Beardsley." Loose thinking and loose comparisons of this kind damn what they intend to praise and show up an ignorance of both sides.

A line in drawing is the path of an emotion, not the boundary of an object. In this sense Szukalski has no line: neither is he concerned with line as design. His drawings are the energetic illustration of ideas, not the expression of emotions.—*jh*.]

[Sometimes I grow a bit weary of the kindergarten questions by people who have failed to read before asking. My remarks were about the artist and his creation, not about economics: the man and his bread. All I can say to people insisting on the great audience idea is to try this "to-have-great-poets-we-must-have-great-audiences" test on other forms of creation,—physical creation, for instance.

To have great audiences an art magazine must have a great sales department. The *Little Review* has no sales department—yet?—*jh*.]

An Old Reader:

. . . For a long time the *Little Review* was my religion; it converted me to faith in New America, it inspired me to dreams and creative work. It was my first American sweetheart, and as long as it remained such it aroused in me the whole gamut of love emotions, from passionate admiration to passionate hatred.

. . . But surely the spirit of the old *Little Review* is dead. You seem to be proud of your evolution, of the graves of your old gods that loom in your eyes like stepping-stones to those heights where you bask in the wisdom of the Ezras. The beauty of the old *Little Review*, the secret of its magnetism and appeal to Young America, lay in its youthfulness, its spontaneity, in its puerility, if you wish. For puerility mates with originality. The Ezras know too much. Their minds are black, scarcely smouldering logs. They are yogis; you remember how Galsworthy hoped that you would escape the danger of becoming yogis?

An Ezraized *Little Review* will have no appeal to Young America. Shall I tell you that in my summer class I had students from various western states to the University of California because they saw my name in the catalogue, and they associated my name with the old *Little Review*? These worshippers are cold to the recent issues. And I sympathize with them. The new *Little Review* is gargoylitic, monotonously so. We can still enjoy a passage in Wyndham Lewis, although Remy de Gourmont has said the same things more beautifully and less flippantly. We are still grateful for such a jewel as Maxwell Bodenheim's "Poet's Heart"; Bodenheim does not suffer from self-consciousness, from too-much-knowing. But it is Ezra who sprawls all over the *Little Review* and bedecks it with gargoyles. Mr. Pound is digestible only in the early miniatures:

"Oh fan of white silk, clear as frost on the grass-blade." . . .

I hope that you will soon tire of your over-sophisticated associates and drive them out of the sanctuary. After all you are a rock . . . you are still persisting at the impossible and the miraculous. I am looking forward to the next stage in your evolution. And I send you my hearty greeting, over the gargoylitic heads of your wiseacres, for the next fresh, spontaneous *Little Review*.

[This letter I think will find an echo in the minds of many of our first subscribers. I have several faults to find with its point of view, but one especially: I cannot see why personal qualities such as freshness, spontaneity, enthusiasm, etc., are in any way a guarantee for an interesting or important magazine. Being temperamentally spontaneous, my actions will always be characterized by impulsiveness, etc. But I know that spontaneity will never help me to write an immortal poem. You must keep things in their proper correspondences.—*M. C. A.*]

Temple Inscriptions (In China)

BY WITTER BYNNER

> Half-way up the hill
> And into the light.
>
> Where the heart is,
> There is Buddha.
> How can the hills of the spirit
> Be only in the Western Quarter?
>
> The distant water,
> The near hills,
> The deep blue of the clearing sky.
>
> What is sacred is universal.
> The three religions have for their soul
> One principle.
>
> The pure wind,
> The bright moon,
> The clear and thoughtful heart.

"Exiles"

BY JAMES JOYCE

James Joyce's play, "Exiles," was brought out in New York by B. W. Huebsch in 1919. There was a good deal of disagreement

*about its meaning and we published a symposium of interpretation.
John Rodker, English writer and critic, Israel Solon, American
writer, Dr. Samuel A. Tannenbaum, New York psychologist, and
Jane Heap presented their different theories. Jane's article affords
a perfect example of what I most wanted from her mind; what I
most wanted for the* Little Review—*a "special illumination about
life"* . . . *true psychology or, in other words, creative imagination.
Her analysis of Joyce's characters—especially of the hero, Richard—
shows the kind of imaginative understanding that one finds almost
nowhere; certainly nothing that comes from the analytical offices or
writings of contemporary psychiatrists can touch the illumination
of Jane's thought.*

*The discussion about "Exiles" went on for years, until Jane's
final summing-up of the drama in our Spring 1925 number. There
she classified it under the "conflict of quality."*

*The three other analysts are too uninteresting, and too wrong, to
quote in full.*

I. By John Rodker:

Joyce exploits that part of mind merging on the subconscious. The
drama is one of will versus instinct . . . the particular psychological triangle is one of barely comprehended instincts, desires for freedom (equally undefined), emotions that hardly crystallize before
fading out. Inter-action of thought and will is carried so close to this
borderline that the reader fears continually lest he miss any implication. Analysis digs continually deeper. At a certain moment it
is lost. Mind will go no further. [*Really! Rodker has said precisely
nothing. M. C. A.*]

II. By Israel Solon

I was most painfully disappointed with Joyce's "Exiles" . . . because of what he might have achieved and came near achieving but
failed to achieve. With his theme, the author of the "Portrait" and
"Ulysses" should have achieved nothing short of the sublime. No
poet since Sophocles has had so dramatic a vehicle. Indeed, I think
Joyce's the more dramatic.

Sophocles took for his theme the fate of a man incompletely born
and who was therefore bound to rejoin his mother. Sophocles held
that man strictly to his inheritance. And so vividly did he present
his argument that to this day those of us who are doomed to love

our mothers are forced to accept his terrible but valid judgment
. . . Joyce in "Exiles" has taken for his dramatic vehicle the fate
of two men who are in love with each other and who are at the
same time bound by the letter of conventional morality more completely than most men; the disguises winked at by organized society
and therefore made available to most men are not available to these
two. They will have nothing they may not have openly. Drawn to
each other from within and held back from without, these two men
are doomed to keep within sight of each other but beyond the reach
of each other. Here is matter worthy of the very best that Joyce has
within him. Why, then, does he fail to achieve the measure of greatness we have every right to expect of him and the theme he has
chosen?

I believe it is because he has failed to make his characters conscious of what fate has in store for them. Had he made them fully
aware, had he, furthermore, made them struggle valiantly against
it, then if they had won in the end we should have had great comedy,
and if they had lost we should have had sublime tragedy. Consciousness would have made of them such responsible human beings as
would have engaged our sympathies to the utmost; whereas unconsciousness has left them feeble victims blindly wallowing to no purpose. And since it is unthinkable to me that the author of the "Portrait" and "Ulysses" could be lacking in moral courage, I am forced
to the conclusion that James Joyce was not himself aware of the
matter of his play. [*To which I can only say "Bosh."—M. C. A.*]

III. By Samuel A. Tannenbaum, M.D.

. . . To the psychologist trained in psychoanalysis the book will
be welcome as an inspired contribution from the depths of an artist's soul to one of the most tabooed and falsified motives of human
conduct—we mean homosexuality . . . Richard Rowan's, the protagonist's, homopsychism is never once referred to in the story but
is clearly to be deduced from his character and conduct. He has no
love for his dead mother and several times refers bitterly to her
hardness of heart, at the same time crediting her with having been
a remarkable woman; of his "handsome father," on the contrary,
he always speaks with great affection. He is utterly incapable of
making love to a woman or of loving anyone unless she is or has
been in love with a man to whom he is attached. [*Ditto, as above.*
—M. C. A.]

IV. by jh.

I find it difficult to put any of my thoughts on *Exiles* into words. They are not used to words: they die. I feel that Joyce's play has died in words. I do not mean because of the words literally—all Art is linguistic. But even Art must fail many times before it conquers those things whose nature it is to keep themselves a secret from us forever.

On the surface the play gives itself up to many interpretations. Propagandists declare it is a play on the freedom of the individual. Other reviewers talk of triangles and Ibsen and neurotics. All these things are easy and semi-intelligent things to say. But when it is unanimously agreed that Joyce hasn't "put over his idea clearly" or that he hasn't known just what he was trying to put over, I grow a bit nervous and wonder why it doesn't appear to them that perhaps Joyce couldn't reach their darkness. I also wonder why not read *Exiles* with Joyce in mind. The man who wrote *A Portrait of the Artist* and *Ulysses*, a highly-conscious, over-sensitized artist living at the vortex* of modern psychology, would scarcely go back to dealing with material in a pre-Nietzsche manner. Joyce is not Galsworthy; on the other hand he is not D. H. Lawrence. And to discuss courage in connection with Joyce is ridiculous. Joyce outlived courage in some other incarnation.

There are people, a few, always the artist I should say, who inspire such strong love in all who know them that these in turn become inspired by love for one another. The truth of the matter is that such a person is neither loved nor lover but in some way seems to be an incarnation of love, possessing an eternal element and because of it a languor, a brooding, a clairvoyance of life and a disdain. In other people he breeds a longing akin to the longing for immortality. They do not love him: they become him. Richard is one of these.

There is much talk of freedom in the play. Everyone wanting everyone else to be free, it is shown that there is at no time any freedom for anyone. The discussion of the wife's decision when she went away with Richard—unasked by him—proves she had no freedom to make a decision. She may have been in love with Robert, but she had no choice: she was Richard. Robert is in love with Richard, has always been; but he is an unthinking, natural man.

* *Zurich.*

218

He follows nature with his brain and thinks he is in love with Richard's wife, a woman being the conventional symbol for a man's love. But when he has a meeting with her and they are left alone by Richard in perfect freedom they are foiled, they are both Richard, both trying to reach Richard, not each other. Richard's old conflict with his mother (just indicated) was based on her refusal to become him. The wife sees the child going the way of all of them.

There is nowhere in the world for Richard to turn for love. Sex as other men know it can be for him only a boring, distasteful need of the body. Love strikes back at him from every source. His becomes a Midas tragedy.

He is tormented by the commonplace "beaten path" love-making of Robert and his wife. He asks her infinite questions; he directs the love-making to save his sensibilities. He says to Robert: "Not like this—this is not for people like us." Yet he wishes darkly that they had dishonoured him in a common, sneaking way. Not that he cares for either of them, not that he cares for honour or for conventions, but then he might have been free of them. They would have acted for once without his spirit having been the moving force.

We see Richard wearily contemplating his despair. There is much of the child in Richard. He has a need to create some hold on life, some connection with the experiences of other men. He chooses the least uncomplimentary to himself of those in the play as the symbol through which he can make his connection with love. He sees himself less handicapped intellectually in the music teacher, so he loves love through her. When they taunt him with her he answers "No, not even she would understand." He writes all night endless pages at this image of himself, and in the morning walks on the beach maddened by emptiness and despair. At the last curtain he falls on to a couch, worn and helpless, in need only of a "great sweet mother"; but he must be forever on the wheel: his wife kneels beside him babbling of her love.

Later on, Dr. Albert C. Barnes, the well-known art-collector of Philadelphia, wrote to Jane as follows:

Dear jh:—I like your psychology better than the—evident—professional psychoanalyst's. But I think you miss what is an obvious situation:—Richard, an old philanderer, wants Bertha to fall into his fault because thereby Richard would attain the feeling of satisfaction that comes from his hurt self-regarding sentiment being re-established on a parity with his esteem for Bertha. The poignancy is due to frustration long continued. I mean that he hasn't been true to Bertha (and incidentally to Robert), so if she falls from his respect for conventional standards he squares himself with himself. You'll see what I'm trying to say stated clearly in McDougall's *Social Psychology* in his analyses of the self-regarding sentiment, and of the sentiments of reproach—it's a sort of subjective, inverted, vicarious reproach. Dostoevsky plays this whole gamut beautifully in *The Eternal Husband*. Of course I'm taking only an element in the analysis;—with the rest I agree with you in the main.

. . . to which Jane replied:

I think where you miss is to take a second premise for a first and call it an obvious thing. You call Richard an old philanderer, but I am letting that go by and trying to show *why* he is a philanderer, though the common usage of this word can have no concern with Richard.

In his effort to make some so-called normal connection with life he may have been conventionally untrue to Bertha and Robert, but it is his unfaithfulness to himself in these episodes that makes his suffering so great. Normal sex, any sex is not for him: a law of nature which he did not vote, as he said. He repudiates the truth of his participation in any of this philandering. Nothing that Bertha or Robert could ever think of him, no matter how deeply they could fall into his fault,—nothing could affect his self-regarding sentiment. His self-regarding sentiment is as absolute as his sex position, and is affected only seemingly. He comes home late in the night after a debauch and kneels beside Bertha's bed and confesses all his wanderings. She has, through her love, become Richard—as I pointed out in my previous article. She lives apart from all sex life; she is to him a pure manifestation of himself. By these confessions he puts away the loathsome experiences,—puts them on this physically pure self and can again be free and reestablished in his true psychic position.

If I were Remy de Gourmont I might be able to tell you all I think about the problem of this Love that seeks a completion in scarcely definable psychic contacts never intimated nor sought by that blind reproductive force called love.—*jh*.]

In 1925 we published the last of the "Exiles" discussion. Jane wrote:

At last Joyce's *Exiles* has been produced. The Neighborhood

Playhouse has won a leaf or two of laurel. When *Ulysses* began to appear in the *Little Review* we began to get letters from the intellectual theatres in the large cities asking us about Rights and if we knew, etc., about *Exiles* production? Earnest persons came to us and asked—"didn't we think that the 'Theatre Guild,' if it really wanted to do something, should give *Exiles*"? Ida Rauh tried several times to get it put on at the Provincetown Playhouse, but John Quinn, who represented Mr. Joyce, was afraid of the Provincetown properties and wanted a decently furnished living-room, guaranteed, before he would talk rights. Now it has been produced and . . . the living-room was all right.

We once had a symposium on *Exiles* in the *Little Review* . . . I was in the symposium and after knowing more Joyce and after seeing the play, I do not change what I tried to say at that time: the conflict is the conflict of quality. This quality, as I am using the word, can best be compared to fine and coarse-mesh nets. A person equipped with a fine-mesh net catches impressions, emotions, realizations, whole worlds that easily slip through the mesh of coarser nets. Richard, the husband, is one of these with the fine-mesh net, his wife and his friend have the coarse-mesh nets of the rest of the world. Naturally, one builds up his world and understands life from the things he finds in his net. Where this difference in quality exists, people are literally "worlds apart," there is no communication possible: Exiles. The wife and the friend do not understand Richard's words, his suffering, his motives, his personal aristocracy. Richard understands that they are alike, he does not suffer because they are about to betray him, he suffers because he cannot put upon them his special illumination about life and love, he wants them to act as they could not act, perhaps, in a succession of lives.

For the August 1918 Little Review *Ezra composed his famous Henry James number. It is impossible to give space to all the critical notes and annotations which made the number so complete a critique of James. I have chosen the most readable passages of three of the articles.*

Henry James

(As seen from the "Yellow Book")

ETHEL COBURN MAYNE

MR. POUND has asked me to say what we of the *Yellow Book* and the

Savoy found specially stimulating in Henry James. "The things you saw clearest," he suggests, "we may have missed."

I am not versed in our younger writers' view of Henry James's work. This is probably a good thing. I may point out as "ours" the very lustres that they also hail; should I do this, it will reinforce my faith (and surely theirs) in both epochs. For we must, despite our differences, be at one in believing that artists at all times are after the same thing essentially; and therefore that real lustres do not fade, nor even turn rococo and amusing, like the lustres on the chimney-pieces.

Shortly, then, what we found stimulating in Henry James was the new world he took us to. No one had been there before him. His style was of course his own; he could not have been *chef d'école* without a personal style. We took that, in that sense, for granted; but the style, too, was the air of that new world in which we moved with fellow-creatures round us. It was like landing on the Moon or Mars, and finding the familiar turned into the strange, yet recognisable by the familiar and the strange within ourselves. That is to say, he was a master; this is the mark of all the masters.

But the newness had to die, for newness bears its death about with it. Here comes the test for permanence. If the younger writers, landing on the Jacobean planet, find that they can breathe its air, get food and drink, enjoy themselves, go forth from it refreshed to make new planets of their own—then all is well, and Henry James is great, and we, who could be dazzled by the newness, need not blush because we blinked.

The finest air of that planet was the magic of his earlier—not his earliest—manner. We read him at that hour of his career as much to see how he would say it as to see what he would say. "I don't care what he does if he will go on doing it like that," we used to cry; and he went on doing it like that in *Washington Square, The Portrait of a Lady, The Aspern Papers,* in the many tales which had for theme that question—which it is? and which is which?—of the blessing or the bans of "success" or "failure" in the artist's life; in the great ghost-stories. All these were to us the source of joys as actual and exquisite as the joy of sunlight. The day we had a new Henry James to read could have no utterly bad moment, for there was always the volume or the story to come back to or go on to. We found—let us state it boldly—everything we wanted in them. There was the pure fable, whatever it might be, and we never found it, in those middle-period pieces, wanting in the fable-quality. His themes were intimately thrilling; then there was the method, subtle yet not over-subtle, lucid yet profound, still waters really running deep, the preparation and the involution, the return upon itself; and for "showing" of all this, there were the diction and the manner, beautiful and lustrous—pages that shone and shimmered and sparkled, that spread and spilt and built before our eyes the grass and flowers and trees, the streams and brooks, the old grey churches and old rose-red houses making up the English landscape that for Henry James was an elysian "description." The world is like a knell that very seldom summons us to heaven; but he did not describe. You found yourself in the enchanted place and never knew how you got there. Was it better than the "real" place? You often thought it was, and people told you you were decadent, that that was decadence—to find the words about it better than the thing itself. You said you didn't care; if this were decadence you were glad to be a decadent. It was a time, believe me, worth the living in, when Henry James was in his middle period.

This was the best time, for at both ends of his career he fell into extremes. At the beginning his ease threatened to, or actually did sometimes, turn into slickness. The blithe accomplishment would look like little more than that; you occasionally "wished he wouldn't." He soon felt this himself and—didn't. Then began the middle period; and it was for us what I have said. But it developed; there came the hesitation and retreat, the infinite circumlocution. At first, it was delightful (*The Awkward Age; the Wings of a Dove*); but even already, the reading of a Henry James became like the playing of a difficult piece of music. You knew you wouldn't be able to play it the first time; you must practise, you must finger and pedal. His aspect had always better answered to the *volte-face* in this method of expression than to the facile early style. In the portrait of him as a little boy which fronts the first autobiographical book, you catch already the apprehension, humourous and mournful, of all that he could "see." I never beheld, for my part, any creature who struck me as to his degree assailed by the perceptions. The great, heavy-lidded eyes, upon my word, were more alarmed than piercing. They *were* piercing, but it was as if he wished they weren't, for dear life's sake.

All this was faithfully reflected in the latest literary manner— in no example more distressfully than in that critical essay on the

Younger Novelists which for us who had adored him was the sad surprise of his career. He selected for that essay writers to whom he certainly did no great honour save in noticing them at all, but that he should notice them at all was our amazement and our grief. And that he dismissed with a contemptuous word the only one he rightly noticed—Mr. D. H. Lawrence—was a "turn of the screw" which still we groan to think of.

That fell mistake came out of the alarm with which he saw the onset of the new age, with its new orientation. The great eyes shut, and with them shut, he chose his prophets. He rushed, thus blind, into the wrong temple—rather, into none at all, not even a young lions' den, but a mere plaster meeting-house. Nothing that he ever wrote is difficult as this to read, and when it is read, you are poorer than before. True, that the bouquets thus bestowed are meagre to invisibility, but that he should have deigned to offer even those . . .!

We saw where Henry James went wrong in all these matters; yet earlier than the fatal essay, earlier even than the *volte-face* which became a running-away, we had perceived another question coming to assail devotion. Here again that shyness of his answers it. This man of the world was what we must call shy, because there is a deeper meaning in the word than the most commonly accepted one. He was shy as a race-horse is shy—all stares and starts, and for the same reason that the race-horse is. He was too highly specialised. A man of the world: as I wrote that, I saw that I was face to face with the question which transcends the other questions about Henry James. "The world": was he concerned with any world but one, that of the drawing-rooms? And, being concerned with that alone, with what about it? He saw no aspect of it but "relations"; at any rate, reacted to no other. The younger generation has abandoned that aspect. "Relations" are not the young writers' game (as Henry James would certainly have said, with his delight in gentle slang). It is a new orientation; we Jacobeans find the path a trifle stony. Our own was briery, not stony; tentacles were, so to speak, our tools and tentacles are useless against stones!

Nevertheless, we had seen, so far as it was given to us to see, the "feet upon the fender" note in him. He was always drinking tea in the drawing-room, we said. He made the drawing-room a working-model of the universe; and *was* it? To-day the question has been answered: it is not.

Here, of course, we tread upon the sacred ground of "subject."

224

The writer's choice of subject is not matter for discussion; with treatment only is criticism concerned. The dogma, like all dogmas, may be pushed too far. At some hour in the judgment-day of writers the question will be put: "In how many directions could he see?" . . . This number of *The Little Review* is (as I hope) a proof that Henry James survives; yet I know one or two young writers of the serious sort who never read a word of him. That would not have been conceivable in our day, in those who really "meant it." Something must have happened and I hope Mr. Pound will tell us what it is.

Probably the drawing-room is at the bottom of it; but there is also what one of these who have not read a word of Henry James describes as the "bull-in-the-china-shop stunt." This young person does that stunt, and brilliantly; I who had called it, more respectfully the "square touch," cried out: "We were Aeolian harps, confound it!"—and the air of an orange, black-and-white and blue-and-purple studio became foul with shameful words. "Sensitive"; "sentimental"; "tremulous": the hideous sounds swept the full-gamut of the damned Aeolian harp; but even to say damned was vain; I ought to have said bloody.

I think that is what has happened. The bull in the china shop has smashed up the Aeolian harp (it must have been a curiosity-shop); and what in Henry James was only "harp" will go, and what was not, will stay. Again, I leave to Mr. Pound the task of disentanglement.

In Explanation

EZRA POUND

I.

IT IS suitable that our discussion should be opened by one of Henry James's fellow contributors to the *Yellow Book*, by a representative of the decade of brilliancy and nuances. My own essay is a dull grind of an affair, a Baedecker to the continent. I have not answered Miss Mayne's questions very well. James, to the wildest and most vigorous "bull" of my generation, was "an extraordinary old woman but one of the few doing anything decent." That, I think, is as brief an expression of the "serious" attitude of the younger and demi-ainé serious writers as can be compass'd.

Mr. Hueffer in his volume on James, has made a vigorous answer to the drawing-room or not-going-down-town question.

. . . I set out, in my own essay, to explain, not why Henry James is less read than formerly—I do not know that he is. I tried to set down a few reasons why he ought to be, or at least might be, more read. . . .

Some may say that his work was over, well over, finely completed, and heaven knows there is a mass—a monument of that work, heavy for one man's shoulders to have borne up, labour enough for two life-times; still we would have had a few more years of his writing. Perhaps the grasp was relaxing, perhaps we should have had no strongly-planned book; but we should have had paragraphs cropping up here and there. Or we should have had, at least, conversation, wonderful conversation; and even if we did not hear it ourselves, we should have known that it was going on somewhere. The massive head, the slow uplift of the hand, *gli occhi onesti e tardi*, the long sentences piling themselves up in elaborate phrase after phrase, the lightning incision, the pauses, the slightly shaking admonitory gesture with its "wu-w-wait a little, wait a little, something will come," blague and benignity and the weight of so many years' careful, incessant labour of minute observation always there to enrich the talk. I had heard it but seldom, yet it was all unforgettable.

The man had this curious power of founding affection in those who had scarcely seen him and even in many who had not, who but knew him at second hand.

No man who has not lived on both sides of the Atlantic can well appraise Henry James; his death marks the end of a period. The *Times* says: "The Americans will understand his changing his nationality," or something of that sort. The "Americans" will understand nothing whatsoever about it. They have understood nothing about it. They do not even know what they lost. They have not stopped for eight minutes to consider the meaning of his last public act. After a year of ceaseless labour, of letter writing, of argument, of striving in every way to bring in America on the side of civilization, he died of apoplexy. On the side of civilization—civilization against barbarism, civilization, not Utopia, not a country or countries where the right always prevails in six weeks! After a life-time spent in trying to make two continents understand each other, in trying, and only his thoughtful readers can have any conception of how he had tried, to make three nations intelligible one to another. I am tired of hearing pettiness talked about Henry James's style. The subject has been discussed enough in all conscience, along with the minor James.

226

What I have not heard is any word of the major James, of the hater of tyranny; book after early book against oppression, against all the sordid petty personal crushing oppression, the domination of modern life, not worked out in the diagrams of Greek tragedy, not labelled "epos" or "Aeschylus." The outbursts in *The Tragic Muse,* the whole of *The Turn of the Screw,* human liberty, personal liberty, the rights of the individual against all sorts of intangible bondage! The passion of it, the continual passion of it in this man who, fools said, didn't "feel." I have never yet found a man of emotion against whom idiots didn't raise this cry.

And the great labour, this labour of translation, of making America intelligible, of making it possible for individuals to meet across national borders. I think half the American idiom is recorded in Henry James's writing, and whole decades of American life that otherwise would have been utterly lost, wasted, rotting in the unhermetic jars of bad writing, of inaccurate writing. No English reader will ever know how good are his New York and his New England; no one who does not see his grandmother's friends in the pages of the American books. The whole great assaying and weighing, the research for the significance of nationality, French, English, American. No one seems to talk of these things.

. . . America has not yet realized that never in history has one of her great men abandoned his citizenship out of shame. It was the last act—the last thing left. He had worked all his life for the nation and for a year he had laboured for the national honour. No other American was of sufficient importance for his change of allegiance to have constituted an international act; no other American would have been welcome in the same public manner.

. . . Henry James's perception came thirty years before Armageddon. That is all I wish to point out. Flaubert said of the war of 1870: "If they had read my *Education Sentimentale,* this sort of thing wouldn't have happened." Artists are the antennae of the race, but the bullet-headed many will never learn to trust their great artists. If it is the business of the artist to make humanity aware of itself; here the thing was done, the pages of diagnosis.

. . . Two things I claim. First, that there was emotional greatness in Henry James's hatred of tyranny; secondly, that there was titanic volume, weight, in the masses he sets in opposition within his work. He uses forces no whit less specifically powerful than the proverbial "doom of the house,"—Destiny, *Deus ex machina,*—of great traditional art. His art was great art as opposed to over-elaborate or over-refined art by virtue of the major conflicts he portrays. In his books he showed race against race, immutable; the essential Americanness, or Englishness or Frenchness—in *The American,* the difference between one nation and another; not flag-waving and treaties, not the machinery of government, but "why" there is always misunderstanding, why men of different race are not the same.

. . . Peace comes of communication. No man of our time has so laboured to create means of communication as did the late Henry James. The whole of great art is a struggle for communication. . . .

Henry James was aware of the spherical form of the planet, and susceptible to a given situation, and to the tone and tonality of persons as perhaps no other author in all literature. The victim and the votary of the "scene," he had no very great narrative sense, or at the least, he attained the narrative faculty but *per aspera,* through very great striving.

It is impossible to speak accurately of "his style" for he passed through several styles which differ greatly from one another; but in his last, his most complicated and elaborate, he is capable of great concision; and if, in it, the single sentence is apt to turn and perform evolutions for almost pages at a time, he nevertheless manages to say on one page more than many a more "direct" author would convey only in the course of a chapter.

His plots and incidents are often but adumbrations or symbols of the quality of his "people," illustrations invented, contrived, often fictitiously and almost transparently, to show what acts, what situations, what contingencies would befit or display certain characters. We are hardly asked to accept them as happening.

He did not begin his career with any theory of art for art's sake, and a lack of this theory may have damaged his earlier work.

. . . I take it as the supreme reward for an artist; the supreme return that his artistic conscience can make him after years spent in its service, that the momentum of his art, the sheer bulk of his processes, the (si licet) size of his flywheel, should heave him out of himself, out of his personal limitations, out of the tangles of heredity and of environment, out of the bias of early training, of early predilections, whether of Florence, A.D. 1300, or of Back Bay of 1872, and leave him simply the great true recorder.

228

And this reward came to Henry James in the ripeness of his talents; even further perhaps, it entered his life and his conversation. The stages of his emergence (out of the unfortunate cobwebs) are marked quite clearly in his work. He displays himself in *French Poets and Novelists,* constantly balancing over the question of whether or no the characters presented in their works are, or are not, fit persons to be received in the James family back-parlour.

. . . To lay all his faults on the table, we may begin with his self-confessed limitation, that "he never went down town." He displayed in fact a passion for high life comparable only to that supposed to inhere in the readers of a magazine called "Forget-me-not."

. . . Balzac gains what force his crude writing permits him by representing his people under the ἀνάγκη of modernity, cash necessity; James, by leaving cash necessity nearly always out of the story, sacrifices, or rather fails to attain, certain intensities.

He never manages the classic, I mean as Flaubert gives us in each main character: *Everyman.* One may conceivably be bored by certain pages in Flaubert, but one takes from him a solid and concrete memory, a property. Emma Bovary and Frederic and M. Arnoux are respectively every woman and every man of their period. Maupassant's *Bel Ami* is not. Neither are Henry James's people. They are always or nearly always the bibelots.

But he does, nevertheless, treat of major issues, forces, even of epic forces, and in a way all his own. If Balzac tried to give a whole civilization, a whole humanity, James was not content with a rough sketch of one country. . . . We may rest our claim for his greatness in the magnitude of his protagonists, in the magnitude of the forces he analyzed and portrayed. This is not the bare matter of a number of titled people, a few duchesses and a few butlers.

. . . He has written history of a personal sort, social history well documented and complete, and he has put America on the map both in memoir and fiction, giving to her a reality such as is attained only by scenes recorded in the arts and in the writing of masters. Mr. Eliot has written . . . that, whatever anyone else thinks of Henry James, no one but an American can ever know, really know, how good he is at bottom, how good his "America" is.

(There follow some thirty pages of documentation by Ezra, two articles by Eliot, one by John Rodker, one by Theodora Bosanquet, one by Orage:

Henry James and the Ghostly

A. R. ORAGE

I HAVE seen it written that Henry James was a greater psychologist than his brother William, and I have seen it denied with indignation. The dispute might have been saved by the true statement that, as psychologists, the two brothers were equally accomplished but in different fields. The field of William James was in the main the field of normal and of abnormal conscious psychology; the field of Henry James was the field of the sub-conscious, both normal and abnormal. The difference to those who know what the terms mean, is not only considerable; but it accounts entirely for the difference of method employed by the two brothers and even, to a great extent, for the difference in their modes of life. The conscious can be studied by the scientist in the laboratory; the material is, moreover, largely under his control; and all the ordinary rules of scientific research apply to it. But the sub-conscious is a shyer creature altogether. It is not susceptible of direct observation; it cannot be conjured up or laid at will; it must be watched, attended upon, and delicately, oh most delicately, observed; it entails a discipline of the imagination and of the senses, and a discipline of the mind of the observer who must beware of even so much as breathing in the presence of the subconscious subject; in a word, its study is much more an art than a science.

I am not suggesting that Henry James arrived by his method at any conclusions likely to be of value to the science of psychology.

Conclusions were not what he aimed at; he aimed, like every author, at representation. Nor, again, am I suggesting that Henry James held intellectually any theories on the sub-conscious. He was, as it were, professionally inclusive and professionally open-minded. At the same time, it would be possible, I hold, to discover in the solution of his works quite definite conclusions and quite definite theories which the intellect might precipitate into the crystallized dust of formal definitions. But why attempt it if Henry James himself did not? Why translate into terms of science a work of art? Why substitute for representation mere definitions? Only, if it be done, to convince his readers that they are really in the current of the most recent and the deepest thought of our day.

For the surprising thing about Henry James's novels is that one approaches them as stories and leaves them having assisted at a piece of life. One begins to read him as a diversion and finds at the end of him that one has had real experiences. He is, in fact, the magician of psychology, who not only describes—who, indeed does not describe, but portrays,—but reveals. He takes his readers through a new world. This marvellous magical gift, moreover, is exercised, like all true magic, by the simplest of means. For the most part Henry James's characters cannot be said to be selected for their extraordinariness; nor had he the accessories of the stage-magician for his properties. Quite ordinary people in quite ordinary surroundings are sufficient for his purpose—which is to show us, not the conscious, but the subconscious, in man. "There," he seems to say,—having placed his reader at a point of vantage for observation,—"just observe and listen and hold your mind in readiness to catch the smallest gesture and the lightest tone. These persons, you will notice, are not at the first glance anything out of the common, nor are they up to anything very unusual. Nevertheless, watch them and try to see and to feel what they are doing!" And as his readers look at the figures through Henry James's eyes, they are aware of a strange transformation in the ordinary people before them. While still remaining ordinary, extraordinary manifestations begin to be visible among them. They arouse wonder, they arouse pity, they arouse admiration, they arouse horror or fear. There are few emotions they are not capable of producing under the wand of Henry James. Yet, all the time—I must insist upon it—these people remain ordinary.

Such an art of second-sight as this was not likely to be confined to the merely incarnated. If Henry James drew our attention to the sub-conscious "double" or psychic penumbra of living figures, he was almost certain in the end to present his figures as doubles without a body, in a word, as ghosts. And I was among the critics who, long before Henry James had written his *Two Magics,* prophesied that he would shortly be writing of shadows directly. No student of his works can fail to observe how imperceptibly his method of dealing with real persons shades into his dealing with ghosts. There is a little more quietness, a little more mystery, a little more holding of the breath in the process of observation; but fundamentally the method is the same. His stories of the unembodied are, I think, the flower of his art. In these Henry James rose to the perfection of his observation. In them he examined the sub-conscious, as it were, face to face.

I have remarked on another occasion that Henry James would be happy among the dead, for he understood them while he was still living. But let me supplement the remark here by the observation that Henry James did not commune with the disembodied alone, but aloud and in the hearing and in the experience of all his intended readers. His mission (if I may use the word and grieve for it) was to act as a kind of Charon to ferry the understanding over the dark passage of the Styx and to show us that we are such stuff as ghosts are made of.

In Memory
T. S. ELIOT

JAMES's critical genius comes out most tellingly in his mastery over, his baffling escape from, Ideas; a mastery and an escape which are perhaps the last test of a superior intelligence. He had a mind so fine that no idea could violate it. . . . In England ideas run wild and pasture on the emotions; instead of thinking with our feelings (a very different thing), we corrupt our feelings with ideas; we produce the political, the emotional idea, evading sensation and thought.

The James number illustrates, at least to my satisfaction, why I usually preferred Pound as critic to Pound as creator . . . with the exception of poems like the following:

Phanopoiea
EZRA POUND

φ α ν ο π ο ε ι α

I.

ROSE WHITE, YELLOW, SILVER

The swirl of light follows me through the square,
The smoke of incense
Mounts from the four horns of my bed-posts,
The water-jet of gold light bears us up through the ceilings,
Lapped in the gold-coloured flame I descend through the aether.
The silver ball forms in my hand,
It falls and rolls at your feet.

232

II.

SALTUS

The swirling sphere has opened
    and you are caught up to the skies,
You are englobed in my sapphire.
                Io! Io!

You have perceived the blades of the flame
The flutter of sharp-edged sandals

The folding and lapping brightness
Has held in the air before you.

You have perceived the leaves of the flame.

III.

CONCAVA VALLIS

The wire-like bands of colour involute
    mount from my fingers,
I have wrapped the wind round your shoulders
And the molten metal of your shoulders
    bends into the turn of the wind,

AOI!
The whirling tissue of light
    is woven and grows solid beneath us;
The sea-clear sapphire of air, the sea-dark clarity,
    stretches both sea-cliff and ocean.

The Valet
BY DJUNA BARNES

THE fields about Louis-Georges' house grew green in early spring,

233

leaving the surrounding country in melancholy gray, for Louis-Georges was the only man who sowed his ground to rye.

Louis-Georges was of small stature. His face was oblong, too pale. A dry mouth lay crookedly beneath a nose ending in a slight bulb. His long animal-like arms swung half a rhythm ahead of his legs.

He prided himself on his farming, though he knew nothing about it. He surveyed the tender coming green with kindly good nature, his acres were always a month ahead of his neighbors in their debut.

Sometimes standing in the doorway, breathing through the thick hair in his nostrils, stretching his gloves, he would look at the low-lying sheds and the stables and the dull brown patches of ploughed earth, and mutter "Splendid, splendid!"

Finally he would stroll in among the cattle where, in dizzy circles, large colored flies swayed, emitting a soft insistent drone like taffeta rubbed against taffeta.

He liked to think that he knew a great deal about horses. He would look solemnly at the trainer and discuss length of neck, thinness and shape of flank by the hour, stroking the hocks of his pet racer. Sometimes he would say to Vera Sovna: "There's more real breeding in the rump of a mare than in all the crowned heads of England."

Sometimes he and Vera Sovna would play in the hay, and about the grain bins. She in her long flounces, leaping in and out, screaming and laughing, stamping her high heels, setting up a great commotion among her ruffles.

Once Louis-George caught a rat, bare handed, and with such skill that it could not bite. He disguised his pride in showing it to her by pretending that he had done so to inform her of the rodent menace to winter grain.

Vera Sovna was a tall creature with thin shoulders; she was always shrugging them as if her shoulder-blades were heavy. She dressed in black and laughed a good deal in a very high key.

She had been a great friend of Louis-Georges' mother, but since her death she had fallen into disrepute. It was hinted that she was "something" to Louis-Georges; and when the townsfolk and neighboring landholders saw her enter the house they would not content themselves until they saw her leave it.

If she came out holding her skirts crookedly above her thin ankles, they would find the roofs of their mouths in sudden disapproval, while if she walked slowly, dragging her dress, they would say: "See

234

what a dust Vera Sovna brings up in the driveway; she stamps as if she were a mare."

If she knew anything of this feeling, she never showed it. She would drive through the town and turn neither to right or left until she passed the markets with their bright yellow gourds and squashes, their rosy apples and their splendid tomatoes, exhaling an odor of decaying sunlight. On the rare occasions when Louis-Georges accompanied her she would cross her legs at the knee, leaning forward pointing a finger at him, shaking her head, laughing.

Sometimes she would go into the maids' quarters to play with Leah's child, a little creature with weak legs and neck, who always thrust out his stomach for her to pat.

The maids, Berthe and Leah, were well-built complacent women with serene blue eyes, quite far apart, and good mouths in which fine teeth grew gratefully and upon whom round ample busts flourished like plants. They went about their work singing or chewing long green salad leaves.

In her youth Leah had done something for which she prayed at intervals. Her memory was always taking her hastily away to kneel before the gaudy wax Christ that hung on a beam in the barn. Resting her head against the boards she would lift her work-worn hands, bosom high, sighing, praying, murmuring.

Or she would help Berthe with the milking, throwing her thick ankles under the cow's udders, bringing down a sudden fury of milk, shining and splashing over her big clean knuckles, saying quietly, evenly:

"I think we will have rain before dawn."

And her sister would answer: "Yes, before dawn."

Leah would spend hours in the garden, her little one crawling after her, leaving childish smears on the dusty leaves of the growing corn, digging his hands into the vegetable tops, falling and pretending to have fallen on purpose; grinning up at the sun foolishly until his eyes watered.

These two women and Louis-Georges' valet, Vanka, made up the household, saving occasional visits from Louis-Georges' aunts, Myra and Ella.

This man Vanka was a mixture of Russian and Jew. He bit his nails, talked of the revolution, moved clumsily.

His clothes fitted him badly, he pomaded his hair, which was reddish yellow, pulled out the short hairs that tormented his throat, and from beneath his white brows distributed a kindly intelligent look. The most painful thing about him was his attempt to seem alert, his effort to keep pace with his master.

Louis-Georges would say "Well, now, Vanka, what did they do to you in Russia when you were a boy?"

"They shot my brother for a red," Vanka would answer, pulling the hairs. "They threw him into prison, and my sister took him his food. One day our father was also arrested, then she took two dinner pails instead of one. And once she heard a noise, it sounded like a shot, and our father returned her one of the pails. They say he looked up at her like a man who is gazed at over the shoulder." He had told the tale often, adding: "My sister became almost bald later on, yet she was a handsome woman; the students used to come to her chambers to hear her talk."

At such times Louis-Georges would excuse himself and shut himself up to write, in a large and scrawling hand, letters to his aunts with some of Vanka's phrases in them.

Sometimes Vera Sovna would come in to watch him, lifting her ruffles, raising her brows. Too, she would turn and look for a long time at Vanka who returned her look with cold persistence, the way of a man who is afraid, who does not approve, and yet who likes.

She would stand with her back to the fireplace, her high heels a little apart, tapping the stretched silk of her skirt, saying:

"You will ruin your eyes," adding: "Vanka, won't you stop him."

She seldom got answers to her remarks. Louis-Georges would continue, grunting at her, to be sure, and smiling, but never lifting his eyes: and as for Vanka he would stand there, catching the sheets of paper as they were finished.

Finally Louis-Georges would push back his chair, saying: "Come, we will have tea."

In the end he fell into a slow illness. It attacked his limbs, he was forced to walk with a cane. He complained of his heart, but he persisted in going out to look at the horses, to the barn to amuse Vera Sovna, swaying a little as he watched the slow circling flies, sniffing the pleasant odors of cow's milk and dung.

He still had plans for the haying season, for his crops, but he gave them over to his farm hands, who, left to themselves, wandered aimlessly home at odd hours.

About six months later he took to his bed.

His aunts came, testing with their withered noses the smell of decaying wood and paregoric, whispering that "he never used to get like this."

Raising their ample shoulders to ease the little black velvet straps that sank into their flesh, they sat on either side of his bed.

They looked at each other in a pitifully surprised way. They had never seen illness, and death but once—a suicide, and this they understood: one has impulses, but not maladies.

They were afraid of meeting Vera Sovna. Their position was a difficult one: having been on friendly terms while Louis-Georges' mother lived, they had nevertheless to maintain a certain dignity and reserve when the very townsfolk had turned against her. Therefore they left her an hour in the evening to herself. She would come creeping in saying:

"Oh my dear," telling him long unheard stories about a week she had spent in London. A curious week full of near adventure, with amusing tales of hotel keepers, nobility. And sometimes leaning close to him, that he might hear, he saw that she was weeping.

But in spite of this and of his illness and the new quality in the air, Vera Sovna was strangely gay.

During this illness the two girls served as nurses, changing the sheets, turning him over, rubbing him with alcohol, bringing him his soup, crossing themselves.

Vanka stood long hours by the bedside coughing. Sometimes he would fall off into sleep, at others he would try to talk of the revolution.

Vera Sovna had taken to dining in the kitchen, a long bare room that pleased her. From the window one could see the orchards and the pump and the long slope down to the edge of the meadow. And the room was pleasant to look upon. The table, like the earth itself, was simple and abundant. It might have been a meadow that Leah and Berthe browsed in, red-cheeked, gaining health, strength.

Great hams, smoked fowl with oddly taut legs hung from the beams, and under these the girls moved as if there were some bond between them.

They accepted Vera Sovna's company cheerfully, uncomplainingly, and when she went away they cleared up her crumbs, thinking and talking of other things, forgetting.

Nothing suffered on account of his illness. The household matters went smoothly, the crops ripened, the haying season passed, and the sod in the orchards sounded with the thud of ripe falling fruit.

Louis-Georges suffered alone, detached, as if he had never been. Even about Vera Sovna there was a strange quiet brilliancy, the brilliancy of one who is about to receive something. She caressed the medicine bottles, tended the flowers.

Leah and Berthe were unperturbed, except from overwork; the face of Vanka alone changed.

He bore the expression at once of a man in pain and of a man who is about to come into peace. The flickering light in Louis-Georges' face cast its shadow on that of his valet.

Myra and Ella became gradually excited. They kept brushing imaginary specks of dust from their shoulders and bodices, sending each other in to observe him. They comforted themselves looking at him, pretending each to the other that he was quite improved. It was not so much that they were sorry to have him die, as it was that they were not prepared to have him die.

When the doctor arrived they shifted their burden of worry. They bought medicine with great relish, hurriedly. Finally to lessen the torment they closed their eyes as they sat on either side of his bed, picturing him already dead, laid out, hands crossed, that they might gain comfort upon opening them, to find him still alive.

When they knew that he was really dying they could not keep from touching him. They tried to cover him up in those parts that exposed too plainly his illness: the thin throat, the damp pulsing spot in the neck. They fondled his hands, driving doctor and nurse into a passion.

At last, in desperation, Myra knelt by his bed, touched his face, stroked his cheeks, trying to break the monotonous calm of approaching death.

Death did not seem to be anywhere in him saving in his face, it seemed to Myra that to drive it from his eyes would mean life. And it was then that she and her sister were locked out, to wander up and down the hall, afraid to speak, afraid to weep, unless by that much they might hasten his death.

When he finally died, they had the problem of Vera Sovna.

But they soon forgot her trying to follow the orders left by the dead man. Louis-Georges had been very careful to see to it that things should go on growing, he had given many orders, planned new seasons, talked of "next year," knowing that he would not be there.

The hens cackled with splendid performances, the stables resounded with the good spirits of the horses, the fields were all but shedding their very life on the earth as Vanka moved noiselessly about, folding the dead man's clothes.

When the undertaker arrived Vanka would not let them touch the body. He washed and dressed it to suit himself. It was he who laid Louis-Georges in the shiny coffin, it was he who arranged the flowers, and he finally left the room on the flat of his whole noisy feet for the first time in years. He went to his own room overlooking the garden.

He paced the room. It seemed to him that he had left something undone. He had loved service and order; he did not know that he also loved Louis-Georges, who made service necessary and order desirable.

This distressed him, he rubbed his hands, holding them close to his mouth, as if by the sound of one hand passing over the other he might learn some secret in the stoppage of sound.

Leah had made a scene, he thought of that. A small enough scene, considering. She had brought her baby in, dropping him beside the body, giving the flat voiced: "Now you can play with him a minute."

He had not interfered, the child had been too frightened to disturb the cold excellence of Louis-Georges' arrangement, and Leah had gone out soon enough in stolid silence. He could hear them descending the steps, her heavy slow tread followed by the quick uneven movements of the child.

Vanka could hear the rustling of the trees in the garden, the call of an owl from the barn; one of the mares whinnied and, stamping, fell off into silence again.

He opened the window. He thought he caught the sound of feet on the pebbles that bordered the hydrangea bushes; a faint perfume such as the flounces of Vera Sovna exhaled came to him. Irritated, he turned away when he heard her calling.

"Vanka, come, my foot is caught in the vine."

Her face, with wide hanging lips, came above the sill, and the same moment she jumped into the room.

They stood looking at each other. They had never been alone together before. He did not know what to do.

She was a little disheveled, twigs from the shrubbery clung to the black flounces of her gown. She raised her thin shoulders once, twice, and sighed.

She reached out her arm, whispering:

"Vanka."

He moved away from her, staring at her.

"Vanka," she repeated and came close, leaning a little on him.

In a voice of command, she said simply. "You must tell me something."

"I will tell you," he answered automatically.

"See, look at your hands—" she kissed them suddenly, dropping her wet lips into the middle of the palms, making him start and shiver.

"Look at these eyes—ah fortunate man," she continued, "most fortunate Vanka; he would let you touch him, close, near the heart, the skin. You could know what he looked like, how he stood, how his ankle went into his foot." He ceased to hear her.

"And his shoulders, how they set. You dressed and undressed him, knew him, all of him, for many years,—you see, you understand? Tell me, tell me what he was like!"

He turned to her. "I will tell you," he said, "if you are still, if you will sit down, if you are quiet."

She sat down with another sigh, with a touch of her old gaiety; she raised her eyes, watching him.

"His arms were too long, you could tell that—but beautiful, and his back was thin, tapering—full of breeding—"

Three Professional Studies
WILLIAM CARLOS WILLIAMS
THE DOCTOR

IT IS idle to talk to me of cowardice. . . .

Once I came near drowning. I dived from a row-boat during a storm to recover my oars which I had lost, having "caught a crab." I had light clothes on. I am not a very strong swimmer. I recovered one of the oars but the wind carried my boat away faster than I could follow. The waves were high. I swam as hard as I could until out of breath. My clothes began to drag. I tried to remove my shoes. I couldn't. I swallowed some water. I thought I was done for when there crossed my mind these sentences: So this is the end? What a waste of life to die so stupidly.

The thought was singularly emotionless, simply a clear vision of the situation. So much was this so that I was instantly sobered. My action taking on at once the quality of the thought, tucking the one oar under my left arm I swam quietly along hoping someone would

240

see the empty boat and come out for me, which a man did. My courage, if you will, turned upon the color of my thought.

I ask no more than the surface of a leaf for my feet and you can take the rest. I have nothing for my feet. There is nothing to stand on. I receive nothing for my work. There is always nothing, nothing —everywhere. I am I: that is all I know and that is nothing.

My intelligence will not permit itself to be insulted. All or nothing and since I cannot accept all,—except by proxy,—nothing. I stand still. I practice medicine in a small town. I reserve myself for myself. I indulge my intelligence, preferring that whisky to another. I read Dora Marsden's practical philosophy and smile; it calls to my mind an image of J. P. Morgan.

I am a young man, I am in perfect health, I am agile, good-looking. I do not smoke since it drugs the intelligence; I want all my reactions. I do not drink except for the taste; I despise the lurid vapors of alcohol. I do not care much for illicit relations with women. I am married and have two children.

When my father died last week I saw that the funeral was decently done. I was affected by the burial service. I felt warm toward my mother. I felt grateful to my wife and others for their solicitous behavior. I was touched by the letters of sympathy. There was not a cruel or bitter thought in my body. I felt soft, gently inclined to all for their kind words and attentions. I shook hands with the pall bearers. I saw all details carried out and what—? Joyce's talk of the funeral ride was in my head as I journeyed to the graveyard behind my poor father's dead body. Joyce's technique seemed to me childish—Victrola.

It seems incredible but my father is gone. I cannot believe it no matter how I try. But my intelligence tells me that and nothing else.

I am now wearing my father's black coat which is warmer than my grey one. My mother's mental and financial status is much simpler and more satisfactory now than it was a fortnight ago and beyond that—nothing.

I will write a poem. I will call it *Tetelestai*. It shall be a setting up of the meanest against the great. It shall be the most ironic, the bitterest mockery of the human heart I can think of. It shall pretend to raise a distinction where none exists for there is—nothing. No. I will not. I will not draw such a picture. I will not so demean myself. I will be myself in my poem. I will pretend distinction for neither great nor mean. King or the meanest of us all: I am a third. I neither guard my heart nor do I bang it on difficulties whose solutions have been proven time and time again to be simply—nothing. I write poems but they have nothing to do with courage or the lack of it or with the attendant qualities.

King, yes, but it is not lack of courage that keeps me from the attack. The meanest of us all, yes, but not from an excess of courage like a martyr. It is not lack of gifts that keeps me from the attack. In my freshman year of college although I was youngest in the class of one hundred and twenty-six I was rated sixth at the finish of the year. Next year I would be first! My interest vanished at that instant.

It is not that I do not dare, it is that it is meaningless to be either one man or another: this or that: it means always and forever—nothing. "Winds have roared and kissed me" = nothing = tobacco. All things have sensual qualities. Qui est spectateur de la lumiere? chanted Rodin. I smell, I taste, I mix colors. I will soon die.

Why then do I write? Why then do I serve my neighbors? Why not be an inversion of the martyrs and instead of dying for ALL—let me die for NOTHING.

But why die at all? Why not live and write? Why not do what I want to? I want to write. It does not drug my senses, it sharpens them. It is the holy ghost of that trinity: The Senses, Action, Composition. I am damned only when I cannot write. I have proved it under all sorts of conditions. It is so.

I go in one house and out of another practicing my illicit trade of smelling, seeing, hearing, touching, tasting, weighing. I use my intelligence for the mutual benefit of my patients and myself. I have no other profession. I do not always get on well in this town. I am more than likely to turn out a bankrupt any day. I will move away then. I see no other reason for moving. I especially cannot compete with other doctors. I refuse to join church, Elks, Royal Arcanum, club, Masons.—It amused me to learn from the reading of the masonic ritual over my father's body that the "lamb skin" apron stands for purity!—I do not see the sense of operating on people myself when they can get a better man to do it cheaper in New York. I know I cannot safely lance every bulging ear-drum and that it costs my patients twenty-five dollars every time I call Dr. Demerest. Yet I figure it to be worth my while and worth the expense to call him.

I find a doctor in this community to have a special function. He is primarily an outpost. He should be keen at diagnosis, of the patient's ills as of his own limitations. He should be flexible in judgment and

242

ready always to act quickly in every emergency not often by the lucrative performances of his own hands but most often by directing the patient elsewhere, his own hands idle.

People pay for the edged caress of the knife, the most obviously intimate of personal attentions. There is money in surgery. I am interested in babies because their processes are not yet affected by calification and because diagnosis rests almost wholly upon a perception of the objective signs. Courage seems singularly out of place in my life.

MRS. M—

Mrs. M, whom I have never seen or heard of, summons me to her house: Come tomorrow morning at ten.

Vinie Johnson opens the door for me. I attended her old-time nigger mother in childbirth when I began practice here. Vinie in neat black dress, high, white housemaid's apron.

Over Vinie's left shoulder a life-size plaster head on imitation bronze and onyx pedestal: Ethiopian princess. Vinie. The same race.

A little clean boy with upstanding, orange-red hair moves out from behind the maid to see me. Rather pale. I've seen him in school. Has a bad heart I think. Ornate furnishings. Nothing special. About 2500 a year.

Mrs. M says to go right up.

Mrs. M is in her room on the bed. Young, heavy flesh, orange-red hair. Pink silk morning wrapper, boudoir cap, quilt over her body, arms resting out straight at her sides. Face flushed, eyes clear, slight hyper-animation. Doesn't look very sick. Nice girl. She smiles and introduces herself: Mrs. N recommended you. I sit side-saddle at foot of bed at her feet and look. We talk. I study her face and listen intently to what she is saying, trying to guess why I have been called.

She talks. A simple expansive manner. Nothing out of the way. By the position in bed I had expected some necessity for an internal examination. We talk. I am stimulated.

She got out of bed this morning and could hardly stand she was so dizzy. Fell against the door jamb of bath room. Weak in the knees, had to go back to bed.

Hm. Another case of grippe.—Temperature slightly subnormal. No headache, no backache, no pains anywhere. Hm.

One month ago awoke with a terrific pain in lower abdomen. Thought she would have to scream out. Woke husband. Was nauseated. Went to bathroom and fainted. If it hadn't been for that and her husband's urging she would not have called me this time.

Pulse regular, soft—a little too soft. I wish I had brought my sphygmomanometer. Rate a trifle rapid.

She has been doing canteen work in New York.

Has had three children. Was in bed 5 to 7 months after each. Appendicitis after first, puerperal fever next, then abcess of the breast. Has never nursed a baby. The second one is dead.

Matured early—at nine. Due to that and frequent intermission of menses combined with heat flashes a "specialist" thought she might be having change of life. Not likely at 33.

The unmentionable details. Sign of weakened blood tissue, natural effort of the body to conserve blood. I used to think I was in a delicate condition every month or two.

Try pulse again. Wave-like accelerations of the beat. Skin of arms cold, mottled bluish. Always has cold feet. Often cold clear to the hips. No pain anywhere. Just dizzy and weak. You said that before; probably blood does not get to brain. Especially likely to happen in early morning.

Best time of day is evening but has to get up before six a. m. to see that husband gets off with a good breakfast. Lips full but palish. Transparent skin. Cheeks high colored but blotchy. Clear, grey eyes. Habitual smile. Straightforward manner full of engaging sweetness. Good forehead.—I am never quiet, never sick with little things. When I get anything I try to stay on my feet for I know that if ever I get down it will be long before I get up again. Two meals a day. Not much appetite. Has lost 15 pounds since moving to this town. War times. Young husband. The draft.

I want to examine your heart. She opens the silk wrapper. Can't listen through ironed corset cover. Untie the tape. Thin chemise. Better pull that down too. Cheeks flush a little. After all I am a strange man.

Percuss heart. Not enlarged. The left breast held up, under palm of my left hand. Look for apex beat. Palpate. Can't find it. Auscultation. No adventitious murmurs. Very slight accentuation of second sound. Heart now beating more rapidly than before. Excitement of the examination. Strange man.

Liver not tender. Spleen not palpable. No distention of stomach. Lungs clear. No history of edema of ankles. No cough.

Hm. Recapitulate.

What sort of an attack was it you had a month ago. Tell me in detail.—I lay in bed. I awoke with a pain low down in my stomach. Very low down. Over the womb it seemed. I waited and waited for it to pass but it became worse. I gripped the side of the bed and held on as long as I could so as not to wake my husband. When I saw I couldn't stand it much longer I tried to get up. In doing so I woke him. He helped me to the bathroom. He said my face got the most peculiar color he ever saw. Green. I thought I was going to die. I have been very ill but I never thought I was going to die. But that time I did. Sweat broke out all over me. I fainted. But after a while I woke up, ate a good breakfast, went to the city, stayed in all day shopping and felt fine. It wasn't wise I know. That's what worried me this time.

I had a cold about that time too. Oh! Tell me about that. Did you have any other pains then? Yes, in the legs and back. Headache? Yes. I was working at the canteen. One of the naval surgeons came in and noticed how hoarse I was. Oh! He said I was sick. Oh! But it was such a bad night he said I should not go home. He said to keep quiet and to keep my circulation up. It was cold and rainy. I worked all night, emptied sixty trays, that was my job. By morning I felt fine. My voice came back and I really felt splendid. Good. Yes, the work acted like whisky—only it was better.

Oh, and night before last, new year's eve, I danced till 4 A.M.

Have you any relatives in the war? No, but my husband was called just as the armistice was signed.

You realize, Mrs. M, that you are suffering from an acute heart strain due to dancing too long last Tuesday night, a strain superimposed on a heart just recovering from the grippe and overwork, a heart muscle already weakened by infections following childbirth and always perhaps rather flabby by inheritance. If you had rested—

Yes but my husband is one of those men who can't stay home. He says the traffic on this corner kills him. Ha, ha! He no more than gets into the house on Saturday than he wants to go somewhere always. Holidays the same.

He is a few years younger than you is he not? Well, the dizziness and weakness you understand are due to faulty circulation. The blood does not get to your brain quickly enough or in sufficient quantity to supply the needs.

Yes, I feel as if something is shutting up in there sometimes.

Remain in bed today. Rest for an hour after lunch every day when you are able. Medicine—well, we'll see. You will with care largely overcome this setback. My advice is simply—you understand—DO NOTHING.

Tingling with hidden rapture I descend and enter the street.

SOMETHING

Stuiso. Morse Avenue. Right away. Something in her throat—come quick. I go. It's the woman herself. She has been ill a week. Damn these people. One look. Peritonsilar abcess, right side.

Do something for her doctor. She can't eat, she can't drink, she can't sleep—nothing. Do something to help her. I'll pay you.

Put some water on to boil. Bring that chair here. Turn it around —here by the window. Come here, Mrs. Sit down. Get a basin for her to spit in. We'll have to wait for the water to boil.

Kitchen. Table. Dirty white oil-cloth, three soup plates on it full of yellow cornmeal mush, paler yellow scrapings of cheese over it. Large dish full of stuff in center of table. A pail of it half full on the range. Three children, faces reflecting cornmeal mush, take large silverplated spoons and begin to eat, standing up. An old woman sits in the corner with premature baby of the dead mother. Baby doing well. What are you feeding it? Condens' milk. Alright. The mother of feeding children dashes back and forth, in and out of front room, after basin, children, dinner, water, towel, a glass, everything. Face wearing mild expression of torture. She is watched half fearfully, half defiantly by children who want to eat mush at once and not wait. Father of children wearing sheepish smile gets chair and takes charge of the sick woman. She stolid, willing but apprehensive, trying not to swallow spittle. Allows self to be pushed about and turned at will. Her husband—seems so at any rate—almost impossible to tell relationships in these families—walks up and down, hands in pockets, smiles disdainfully, says: Go on, doc, cut her throat. Smiles supercilious smile. Talks in Italian patois. Derogatory look at me. Probably expressing his opinion. I am defended by the younger man.

The children dig into the mush and chew it off the spoons. The largest boy age 8 glances sidewise, sees mother is not looking, shovels out a spoonful from brother's dish. My God do they like it? Haven't they enough? Screams. Mother rushes at him, slaps his face. The children do not even know I am in the room.

Water is boiling. Drop in the gag. So. Wait for it to cool. Alright

246

now. She sits in the chair. I insert the gag, pinch the handles to-gether, the ratchet works. Her mouth is pried open. Oh. Agh. Ah—Hold this. Hold her head. She subsides into bovine passivity. Trembles a little like a cow about to be slaughtered. Gurgles of indifferent nature from uninterested children.

I look in. Force down the tongue. I plunge knife into abcess. No struggle. What is this woman? Blood. I cut deeper, forcing the scalpel down. Ah, there it comes I pull out the gag. Patient grasps basin. Spits into it five times. A little pus and blood.

Torrent of words from man with the cap on. Disgust. The smiling fellow interprets. He says: Not enough. Should fill the bowl full!

You damned fool what do you want me to do, cut her whole neck open?

Mon dieu, mon dieu, que la chirurgie soi beni!

They used to say in the French Hospital that I was a natural surgeon. I had a wonderfully steady and gentle hand. Had good luck with cases. I had observed that the men who handled the cut tissues gently were usually repaid by no infection and good healing.

Three dollars. Multiplied. The way to get rich. Rich surgeons. My God how many bad surgeons there are. Who knows better than I?

I walk out of the back door. I lift my nose. I smell the wind.

Oh well, if you cannot succeed in this town go to some city. Initia-tive, courage. Newburg-on-the-Hudson.

I want to write, to write, to write. My meat is hard to find.

What if I have not the courage?

Poems

WALLACE STEVENS

NUANCES OF A THEME BY WILLIAMS

It's a strange courage
you give me, ancient star:

Shine alone in the sunrise
toward which you lend no part!

I

Shine alone, shine nakedly, shine like bronze,
that reflects neither my face nor any inner part
of my being, shine like fire, that mirrors nothing.

Lend no part to any humanity that suffuses
you in its own light.
Be not chimera of morning,
Half-man, half-star.
Be not an intelligence,
Like a widow's bird
Or an old horse.

ANECDOTE OF CANNA

Huge are the canna in the dreams of
X, the mighty thought, the mighty man.
They fill the terrace of his capitol.

His thought sleeps not. Yet thought that wakes
In sleep may never meet another thought
Or thing . . . Now day-break comes . . .

X promenades the dewy stones,
Observes the canna with a clinging eye,
Observes and then continues to observe.

Prohibition and Art of Conversation
BY JOHN BUTLER YEATS*

How is it that every American whether man or woman, here in his
own country or abroad in Europe, possesses the genius of acquaintanceship; and why is it that the English possess so little of this delightful quality that it is hardly an exaggeration to say that there
are in England old married couples who, living in absolute loyalty,
are not and never will be real acquaintances, neither of them knowing or caring what the other thinks? The answer is that class is an
English institution and has the character of the people, and that it
has never been adopted in this country. In an American train if
two people like each other's looks they follow the natural impulse
and become acquainted. In England we examine each other, under
such circumstances, with suspicious criticism, because notwithstand-
ing appearance, we might not be of the same class. Every Englishman is of class, down to the cat's meal man; and classes do not asso-
ciate. The inferior class would indeed fraternize readily enough with

* William Butler Yeats's father, who had lived in this country for years and ate
(and talked) daily at Petipas, a famous old French restaurant on West 29th Street.

the higher class, but to that the other would not consent. The social atmosphere in England is dark and chilly as its November skies. And this November weather penetrates everywhere, not merely keeping men apart, because of different class, but encouraging strangeness and aloofness as a habit and social law, so that every Englishman remains solitary, with his friends, even with his wife.

Coming to this country some ten years ago, I, being of friendly and social kind and a portrait painter interested in physiognomy, nothing delighted me so much as my sudden escape from class restriction. I found that everywhere I went I could speak to the man whose face attracted me. He would not rebuff me. He had neither the sulkiness of my inferior nor the haughtiness of my superior, and, doing our best to be mutually agreeable, good manners flourished and often in the train there was good conversation, without which life would be unendurable.

Yet, these last few weeks, it has been borne in on me that class, even the rigid unbending class of England, has its advantages, for it is only too evident that this country is in its social and moral relations cyclonic; while England enjoys a peaceful mental and moral climate: the skies undisturbed, except for an occasional breeze, a mere zephyr, only enough to ruffle the anglican seas of stagnation and dullness. Because of class Englishmen do not think alike and are resolved to resist as long as possible every attempt to make them do so. A family named Smith will not hold the same opinion as a family called Brown, if they're of different class: one being in the retail trade and the other in the wholesale. And then there is the enduring distinction between the people who are in business and those who are outside it; and so it is everywhere. Before any opinion can get possession of the national mind it has to knock at so many doors and explain itself so often and meet this and that objection that the process is long and tedious and the result a compromise, but one from which every kind of violence and extreme is purged in the original proposition. In America it is different. Here the aim of every American is to think as his neighbors do. The Englishman thinks as his class does, and he likes to remember that the aim of his class is to divide itself in forced hostility from every other class. Hence, it comes about that America, in its politics, in its manners, in what it reads and thinks is cyclonic, and England anticyclonic. There is plenty of gun powder in England but the grains are so widely separated that a general conflagration is more than difficult.

Therefore, I say, sadly, that if you will have democracy, democracy must guard itself against its own failings by establishing in its midst the institution of class. That Americans should be condemned to put away their good manners and easy charm and virile friendliness, and adopt in their place the churlishness and sulky hostility of English bad manners, is a dreadful thought. Yet, what other remedy is there against the ever-recurring democratic cyclone?

We are now in the midst of a great cyclone and perhaps a succession of them, for I am told prohibition is to be followed by a movement against tobacco. It is a genuine cyclone with all the characteristics. It has come from nowhere, and it came swiftly, and it is so violent that it destroys what is good as well as what is bad. The innocent suffering with the guilty. The innocent who are innumerable and the guilty who are comparatively few in number, and, as the years go by, growing fewer every day that passes. And this is not all, for there are good and prudent men who, with their families, people of the highest characters, as good citizens, must also suffer. For is not their property to be destroyed? Vast sums anxiously put into what seemed good investments. I said just now this cyclonic movement has come from nowhere. Yet beyond a doubt, its birth has been in the feminine mind. The woman has no sense of property, she has not the feeling because we have never allowed her to own anything. If among children you give anything to a little girl at once she is ready to give it away; give it to a boy, if he be normal he will carry it away where he can lock it up in selfish security. He has the sense of property which she is without. Again, the missionary spirit, which is one of the curses of America, and of every society and every household into which it enters, and of poetry itself which we are told must be uplifting. This desire to improve your neighbor by making him adopt all your ideas and be as like yourself as possible, reaches its most aggravating form in the female mind. There is also such a thing as feminine vengeance. It is a fact that through all the past and everywhere except in the highest aristocratic circles of Europe, woman has been a subject race. Humiliated and crushed by husbands and fathers and brothers. She has at last asserted herself and, being as it is a servile war, vengeance is one of its objects. Of course, she does not say so.

Bold frankness and sincerity are not feminine characteristics. All the same, all over America in every home, in the big house and in the little cottages, the women are triumphant and vengeance smiles in their eyes. We men are now in our turn to have a case of subjection. First goes the drink, and then tobacco. It is our consolation, however, to know that they won't abolish themselves. Perhaps indeed they calculate that, every other temptation being removed, they themselves will remain the one sovereign temptation; and be sure they will not start any sumptuary laws. To the last they will paint, they will trick themselves out and make themselves amorously delightful. Nor shall we object; on this matter, at any rate, there will be on our part no resentment. They can never be too charming, too tempting. We both can say "Let temptation flourish"; which brings me to another great distinction of man or woman. We men believe in temptation and would walk surrounded and wooed by it in our hearts; we think of temptation as invitation, which any man, according to his knowledge and discretion, may accept or refuse. Woman on the other hand would clear life of every temptation, making it as bare as a barrackyard or a prison dormitory. And for that matter I have sometimes met a woman who, if she had the power, would abolish every other woman except herself. Such an egotism lurks in the soul of the seductive sex. We men believe that we are here to be tempted, that temptations are the richness and value of life and that we should be free to choose among our temptations,—which we should yield to and which refuse. And there are cases where we would make some compromise. For in this wise do men gather experience and learn to know themselves and find out the will of God, growing in stature and in strength, and every poet will tell you that if temptations were not numerous and powerful there would be no songs to sing. The whole movement is a female origin. It has the birthmark.

I have said that women are without the feeling of property. Let me add that they have no feeling for conversation. They do not know what it means. For one thing they lack the impartial intellect. Woman is a contradictory being. She is devoted in self-sacrifice and yet remains a hardened egotist. For many years I belonged to a conversation society in London where, sometimes, an uxorious member would bring his wife. As long as she remained in the room there was no real conversation. We thought only of pleasing her. It is what she asked of us. The woman's idea of conversation is a something inspired by herself. To conversation that is inspired by women I prefer that which is inspired by wine. Woman-made conversation is mere gallantry, the talk of courts and royal circles, whereas wine, according to the old proverb, is the very spirit of truth. No less is it the spirit of friendliness. I have often dined in teetotaled houses, and though everything was there that taste and wealth could provide, the one thing without which nothing mattered was absent. There was no conversation. It did not even begin. We looked at each other, admired each other, and the ice water circled and I was glad when it was all over. In contrast with this, I remember the first evening I dined out in New York: I was only a few days in the country and at the house to which I was invited I met a company all strange to me and, I fancied, to each other: when, as we sat together, in embarrassed silence and constrained attitudes, a footman entered, with a salver on which were cocktails: to me at that time, a novelty. How gladly all of us, men and women, drank these, and with what good will an intelligent acquaintanceship began and talk sprang up. I observed afterwards that most of the guests contented themselves with their one cocktail, yet all talked with animation. The blessed effect of a few cocktails handed to each of us, by the kind-hearted footman. For I am sure he had a kind heart.

Years ago I belonged to a well-known conversation club in Ireland. We were a numerous company and we met every Saturday evening. It was an important club, for we discussed current events and at that time current events were momentous (when are they not so in Ireland?); yet, although we met early in the evening, conversation invariably started so late that it finished late, I myself seldom getting home till four in the morning. Why this tedious delay and these unseemly hours? Because the club was teetotaled. Had there been a round of drinks, we should have started and finished our discussion in time for every decent man to have got home and to bed by twelve o'clock. That club was a fascination and I remember it with gratitude. You heard the latest news and divined political secrets and, to crown all, the police suspected us: but it spoiled my Saturday night's sleep and, by the fatigue that resulted, all my Sunday; and all because of its damned teetotalism. A little drink is to conversation what a little petroleum is in the lighting of a fire. I am told conversation can be started without drink, exactly as, if you had the patience, you might light a fire by rubbing together two sticks. But they must be dry sticks. Conversation among shy strangers, without the kindly touch of generous wine, is just as impossible. Drink is one of the conveniences of social life as petroleum is of the kitchen.

Have you ever observed the teetotaler among a company who took their wine? Was not the good man invariably a trouble and a kill-joy? Drink quiets the critical facilities. It cuts away the ligatures that bind the wings of the imagination. That is its high function for which we thank it. For a space it frees the soul from black care and we are free as the birds in the sky. The teetotaler is all criticism, and it is destructive criticism. Constructive criticism is with us who taste the ruby grape and we like paradox, for we do historically know that every great movement of thought and speculation has made its first appearance as paradox; and besides, while it challenges constructive logic to do its best, it baffles the other sort. The man of cold water hates paradox and loves himself and, rejoicing in his diabolical lawyer-like faculty of destruction, proceeds to destroy what he cannot possibly understand. Paradox embodies desire and of desire he has none, except for his own egotistical glory. The French general who overcame the Germans at Verdun was asked how he did it. "The Germans," he said, "thought two and two made four, whereas we knew they made five. That is why we conquered the Germans." It was a famous man of genius who remarked that "a glass of port wine ripened thought." Take away wine from human converse, and you hand it over to the pedants and—the women.

Among the enemies of conversation, as of life itself, I count the drunkards, as well as the teetotalers; and had I my way I would put them all into some large prison that they might torment each other: the drunkards, because they have no drink, and the teetotalers, because they have no one to scold, no one on whom to exercise their missionary gift. I hate the drunkard because he insults my dignity as a man, and puts me to shame. For the same reason I detest the prohibitionist, who would turn our cities into prison reformatories. But what do women care? What have they ever cared for the dignity of human nature? That is a Roman thought, quite beyond their scope. Alas! we have only ourselves to blame and cannot wonder if, educated as slaves, they manifest the faults of slaves.

Behind all movements of this kind we invariably find the idle rich, and particularly their women. These people leading empty lives would fain persuade themselves that they are not as useless as they seem to themselves and others. There is besides, to minds so constituted, the irresistible attraction of a movement which because of its alleged importance offers them absolution for every kind of misdeed in carrying it out. It is only by struggling with life that people discover the importance of scruple and the moral life; and these people lead lives in which there is no sort of struggle. There is the irresponsible street boy who will break a window merely because he finds a stone; equally irresponsible are the idle rich and their womenkind. This whole movement is branded with the whimsies and caprices and hysterical nonsense of the rich women, of whom some are very mature in years. Now finding their charms vanished they would try and recover a lost ascendancy. Beauty and youth gone forever, women are still interesting because of increase in goodness and wisdom. These withered women have nothing except their money and their frenzied partizanship. It is lamentable and it is piteous. Anger is drowned in pity.

Turgenieff said of George Sand in her old age that she was "such a good comrade." These matured women of the idle rich are not good comrades. For charm they have only their money and their hard-eyed partizanship. They are new without being loved. This womanhood is wretched.

Snow Scene: Puppet Booth
MARK TURBYFILL

The better to put you in mood for the lady,
Conceive your mind an arched proscenium;
Gather full the night-drop,
The night-blue black—unplumbed.
Shake the sound of snow-bells,
And float down the gesture of five white lines
Adorned with little glittering note-heads.
For she is the lady painted against a thin China saucer,
Her gown a broad silken petal,
And, as a phrase slowly spoken,
Three cloth-sewn flowerets at the hem.
She raises her brow to the point of perplexity:
". . . . The *murmuring* snow? the snow *murmuring?*"
She reasons: "The *falling* snow,—yes. But I have never
        heard the snow murmur. No."

Yet in the cold, white night,
(For all the doubts of the lovely lady)
I have heard them sprinkling down—
The little white snow-notes, murmuring,
With a faint, silvery sound,
Or like the murmur of her silken gown
As she turned away.

From our De Gourmont number (February-March, 1919) I shall quote a few paragraphs of Ezra's introduction and lift from the text those aphorisms of De Gourmont's that have always most appealed to me.

De Gourmont: A Distinction

(Followed by Notes)

EZRA POUND

I

THE mind of Rémy de Gourmont was less like the mind of Henry James than any contemporary mind I can think of. . . . On no occasion would any man of my generation have broached an intimate idea to H. J., or to Thomas Hardy, O. M., or, years since, to Swinburne, or even to Mr. Yeats with any feeling that the said idea was likely to be received, grasped, comprehended. However much one may have admired Yeats' poetry, however much one may have been admonished by Henry James' prose works, one has never thought of agreeing with either.

You could, on the other hand, have said to De Gourmont anything that came into your head; you could have sent him anything you had written with a reasonable assurance that he would have known what you were driving at. If this distinction is purely my own, and subjective, and even if it be wholly untrue, one will be very hard pressed to find any other man born in the "fifties" of whom it is even suggestible.

II

De Gourmont was an intelligence almost more than an artist; when he portrays, he is concerned with hardly more than the permanent human elements. His people are only by accident *of* any particular era. He is poet, more by possessing a certain quality of mind than by virtue of having written fine poems; you could scarcely contend that he was a novelist.

He was intensely aware of the differences of emotional timbre; and as a man's message is precisely his façon de voir, his modality of apperception, this particular awareness was his "message" . . .

Emotions to Henry James were more or less things that other people had and that one didn't go into. . . . De Gourmont is interested in hardly anything save emotions, and the ideas that will go into them.

One reads *Les Chevaux de Diomède* (1897) as one would have listened to incense in the old Imperial court. There are many spirits incapable. De Gourmont calls it a "romance of possible adventures"; it might be called equally an aroma, the fragrance of roses and poplars, the savour of wisdoms, not part of the canon of literature, a book like "Daphnis and Chloe" or like Marcel Schwob's "Livre de Monelle"; not a solidarity like Flaubert; but an osmosis, a pervasion.

"My true life is in the unspoken words of my body."

. . . I do not think it possible to overemphasize Gourmont's sense of beauty. The mist clings to the lacquer. His spirit was the spirit of Omakitsu; his *pays natal* was near to the peach-blossom-fountain of the untranslatable poem.

De Gourmont's wisdom is not wholly unlike the wisdom which those ignorant of Latin may, if the gods favour their understanding, derive from Golding's *Metamorphoses*.

Needless to say, Gourmont's essays are of uneven value as the necessary subject-matter is of uneven value. Taken together, proportionately placed in his work, they are a portrait of the civilized mind. I incline to think them the best portrait available, the best record, that is, of the civilized mind from 1885-1915.

There are plenty of people who do not know what the civilized mind is like, just as there are plenty of mules in England who did not read Landor contemporaneously, or who did not in his day read Montaigne. Civilisation is individual.

Gourmont arouses the senses of the imagination, preparing the mind for receptivities. His wisdom, if not of the senses, is at any rate via the senses. We base our "science" on perceptions, our ethics have not yet attained this palpable basis. . . . E.P.

"La vraie terre natale est celle où on a eu sa première émotion forte."

"Je veux bien que l'on me protège contre des ennemis inconnus, l'escarpe ou le cambrioleur,—mais contre moi-même, vices ou passions, non."—*Madame Boulton.*

"Tout ce qui se passe dans la vie, c'est de la mauvaise littérature."

"Apprendre pour apprendre est peut-être aussi grossier que manger pour manger."

"La maternité, c'est beau tant qu'on n'y fait pas attention. C'est vulgaire dès qu'on admire."

"Etre impersonnel c'est être personnel selon un mode particulier: Voyez Flaubert. On dirait en jargon: l'objectif est une des formes du subjectif."

"Or l'art ne joue pas; il est grave, même quand il rit, même quand il danse. Il faut encore comprendre qu'en art tout ce qui n'est pas nécessaire est inutile; et tout ce qui est inutile est mauvais."—*Jehan Rictus.*

"Avec de la patience, on atteint quelquefois l'exactitude, et avec de la conscience, la véracité; ce sont les qualités fondamentales de l'histoire."

"C'est singulier en littérature, quand la forme n'est pas nouvelle, le fond ne l'est pas non plus."

"Sa vocation était de paraître malheureuse, de passer dans la vie comme une ombre gémissante, d'inspirer de la pitié, du doute et de l'inquiétude. Elle avait toujours l'air de porter des fleurs vers une tombe abandonée."—*La Femme en Noir.*

"Dieu aime la mélodie grégorienne, mais avec modératon. Il a soin de varier le programme quotidien des concerts célestes, dont le fond reste le plain-chant lithurgique, par des auditions de Bach, Mozart, Handel, Hayden, 'et même Gounod.' Dieu ignore Wagner, mais il aime la variété."—*Le Dieu des Belges.*

"Si le cosmopolitisme littéraire gagnait encore et qu'il réussît à éteindre ce que les différences de race ont allumé de haine, de sang, parmi les hommes, j'y verrais un gain pour la civilisation et pour l'humanité tout entière."—*Cosmopolitisme.*

Those interested in the subject will take *Le Problème du Style*, 1902, entire; the general position may perhaps be indicated very vaguely by the following quotations—E.P.:

"Quant à la peur de se gâter le style, c'est bon pour un Bembo, qui use d'une langue factice. Le style peut se fatiguer comme l'homme même; il vieillira de même que l'intelligence et la sensibilité dont il est le signe; mais pas plus que l'individu, il ne changera de personalité, à moins d'un cataclysme psychologique. Le régime alimentaire, le séjour à la campagne ou à Paris, les occupations sentimentales et leurs suites, les maladies ont bien plus d'influence sur un style vrai que les mauvaises lectures. Le style est un produit physiologique, et l'une des plus constants; quoique dans la dépendance des diverses fonctions vitales."

" 'Le style est l'homme même' est un propos de naturaliste, qui sait que le chant des oiseaux est déterminé par la forme de leur bec, l'attache de leur langue, le diamêtre de leur gorge, la capacité de leurs poumons."

"Le style, c'est de sentir, de voir, de penser, et rien plus."

"Le style est une spécialisation de la sensibilité."

"Une idée n'est qu'une sensation défraichie, une image éffacée."

"La vie est un dèpouillement. Le but de l'activité propre d'un homme est de nettoyer sa personnalité, de la laver de toutes les souillures qu'y déposa l'éducation, de la dégager de toutes les empreintes qu'y laissèrent nos admirations adolescentes."

"Depuis un siècle et demi, les connaissances scientifiques ont augmenté énormément; l'esprit scientifique a rétrogardé; il n'y a plus de contact immédiat entre ceux qui créent la science, et (je cite pour la seconde fois la réflexion capitale de Buffon): 'On n'acquiert aucune connaissance transmissible qu'en voyant par soi-même: Les ouvrages de seconde main amusent l'intelligence et ne stimulent pas son activite.' "

"Rien ne pousse à la concision comme l'abondance des idées."— *Le Probléme du Style*, 1902.

Poem

ELSE VON FREYTAG-LORINGHOVEN

APPALLING HEART
City stir—wind on eardrum—
dancewind: herbstained—
flowerstained—silken—rustling—
tripping—swishing—frolicking—
courtesing—careening—brushing—
flowing—lying down—bending—
teasing—kissing: treearms—grass—
limbs—lips.
City stir on eardrum—.
In night lonely
peers—:

moon—riding!
pale—with beauty aghast—
too exalted to share!
in space blue—rides she away from mine chest—
illumined strangely—
appalling sister!

Herbstained—flowerstained—
shellscented—seafaring—
foresthunting—junglewise—
desert gazing—
rides heart from chest—
lashing with beauty—
afleet—
across chimney—
tinfoil river
to meet
another's dark heart!

As I have already said, Jane had once written: "There are no un-known geniuses, there is no artist anywhere unknown to other artists . . . this is one of the simplest axioms about the nature of the artist." Certainly the Little Review *never discovered any un-known talents from all the manuscripts that came in, with the excep-tion of Sade Iverson's poem, "The Milliner," which we published in our first year, and the poems of "the Baroness." Then one day, from an unknown source, came a simple little poem which I published immediately. It is strange that I can still repeat it after all these years:*

> Only the thought of you
> Lives in me yet.
> Face of you, form of you,
> These I forget.
> All the sweet pain of you,
> Hopeless and keen,
> This I retain of you,
> All else has been
> Like a sweet dream of you
> Mistily seen.

Finally in 1920, there arrived a story from a boy in Detroit which we liked enough to print at once. I have never heard since of this writer.

Landscape with Trees, and Colored Twilight with Music Past the End of the City

CARLOS A. V. KRAL

THERE is a wide land that is low and flat and has sheets of blue gray water over its outer edges far from its interior, and often in the great light and heat that come down upon it this land seems bright and shimmering; but it is a gloomy land like all the others, and some of its parts are more gloomy than others. At a certain time in one place in the land a poor city had been made, and there upon the heavy silent grass among wild trees it seemed lonely and pitiful, as if the trees and grass were but waiting to creep in nearer and rot it and replace forever its poor dustiness and ferocity.

The city had been placed near a small heavy green marsh, a little below the fields, that lay in abundant water with a narrow stream going through it; and over the stream from one part of a road to another was an old dust-muffled white wooden bridge with a row of shabby gray willows like bunches of worn ostrich plumes at one side. In the wild fields amid some poor gardens a few dirty houses stood, with people who were hangers-on of the city living in them.

This place I saw one hot summer morning. In the city I had thought the gloomy sky was gray, but having come out I found it bright, with small vague white clouds. Approaching the place I saw it as from above and far away, before a sky bleached by hot sunlight, and bleaching all that was before and beneath it: an expanse of rough pale fields covered with shaggy grass that was dotted by the black shrubs of thorn-apple. Some delicate rectangles of blue forest oak lay in a few places, dark lone oaks and elms stood in the white-green fields, and along narrow white dusty roads were short rows of black poplar trees. At the foot of a slope the marsh waved gently like a grainfield, with the heat and light making it at times almost invisible.

And in this powerful soft and white hot light I strolled, examining the bunches of pale green apples on the apple shrubs, plucking dried brown tops of clover . . . I strolled and frequently looked back and about to see all: the lighted hot silver sky; the grass, most lacking in strength of all the green, for it was already in seed and full of mustard in profuse yellow bloom; the gray little willows and pale marsh; the lone trees; the dark forest squares; and the black, black poplars.

And the poplars made one watch them carefully; small trees on that great lighted plain, but twenty meters tall close by; thick high trees, the branches growing low on the straight trunks, the grass and weeds high about, and the wind constantly turning up the light under-sides of the tough round little leaves, or opening places in the dark mass to let the strangely lighted sky shine through. The trees seemed to sparkle. And with their surface leaves a-flutter and their heavy interiors still they were strong and buoyant; and they made the light about and beneath them green and green-white; and the noise of them up in the free airs was loud and authoritative.

So the place on a hot summer morning with birds chattering in the woods and marsh and all scents faint in the dry heat and light. But on a chilly damp evening I saw that place again, and it was strong, coloured, and even vast and sublime.

I moved that night on roads laid as about a triangle, through, across, and back from that region, and twice over its stream, by the white bridge and another distant one. First, in the silence the light was fading. The sky of afternoon became strange, unreal, and soft; pale, paler, pale blue, milky green, and the white clouds, of which it held many, were drawn out into shreds or fluted; one round cloud was like the head of a Greek statue of a man, a pure white cloud lighted at the top with gold. It grew darker. Then the great sky above and in the west beyond the clouds became dark clear pink, almost purple, the clouds soft rosy pink; in the north the sky remained clear green and the clouds there were long faint streaks of brown and amber. The dark green and purpling world beneath contracted and grew strong, and yet was vaster, vaster; all objects were of new, surprising, dense substance; the darkened east and the whole air became deep purple, like the purple of grapes, and denser and more fragrant; it seemed as if the whole air, heavy with scent, was composed of masses of particles of liquid or glass that reflected the differently colored lights, pink, and green, and deepening purple from the sky and the darkening earth. Great round purple and green earth under the vast purple and pink and greenish curve of the sky! The grass, full of red, pink and white clover, besides the mustard, the poor tall milkweed, burdock, and pink and purple thistles, gave perfume that was wellnigh overpowering; and I smelled the strong odor out of a little cowstable. And all was strange. Off in the purple and pink gloom where were the gardens and the cabbage-fields, some poor people still worked; far back across the fields some small birds flew off somberly in a low line. The little woods had become so dense, blue and black, that they surprised and seemed to menace; the poplars were heavy and black, no light went through them now; and on a willow bough that had been broken down the fine dead gray leaves were rustling as I crossed the bridge. Among the wretched houses that stood upon the fields was a narrow ugly cottage painted drab and become almost black through neglect. A front corner whereat was a porch had sunk down into the ground, and high rank grass, dandelions, and other weeds grew close about the low building, rotting it. The house stood close, beneath one row of the high dark poplar branches. Away, but the only one at all near, was a much larger, taller, and even more gloomy house, with shuttered windows, in a wide yard with old lilac trees full of sprouts and some grass through which dirty chickens walked silently; and the yard was enclosed by palings of broken lath.

A family once lived in the cottage: a silent man, past thirty, with a dark skin, a heavy soft body, and a limp thick mustache that hung down; when he was about his home the man wore a faint shamefaced leer, and he was thoroughly indifferent to everything there, though he could beat a child long and cruelly; a man of only those few poor qualities and desires which fools like him considered to be for men. The woman was tall, thin, younger somewhat than he, with faded yellow hair, thin tough gray skin, and cheeks much narrower than her forehead, with a slight flush high on them. She liked idleness and comfort, and being dallied with by men; when she had been younger her slenderness, and a certain slowness and awkwardness she had, roused some desire; but she was of a poor spirit, dared to do only what was customary, and she had not much used herself: now that she was older she had become only procrastinative and given to dull meditation and occasionally to sharp irritation. She even exhibited an interest in the few objects and persons about her and the few acts possible to her, an interest which was acquired but which resembled the garrulous interest of other women who lived as she. She was uncouth and repulsive, but even yet enough of a woman. And though she did not know how to work well and could not learn, she worked constantly. Of the two children born of her one was still not a year old, a helpless, drooling, noseless infant; the other was three years old, a dark sneaking, whining boy with short dark hair all over his head, clothed in a dress of red cotton plaid and white drawers and body garment beneath. This boy could wander back across the weedy fields and play in the litter of the brook, beside the bridge in the green light under the willows. According to the style of the time the woman herself wore ugly cotton gowns with yokes, straps, and flounces; more cotton cloth beneath; high stained gray corsets round her pale stooped body; and heavy leather shoes fastened with buttons. Her weak hair was in a large loose ball at the top of her forehead and in a knot behind.

And what a people! What a time! Theirs was a race dim, cold, and tenuous of feeling, yet at times pervaded by a curious bright light; a race of great passionless strength, and a wild indestructible faith, or fixity of will; a race that loves a little, curiously, with shame; and that is indifferent to all but certain elemental things. It was a time when that race was far in the rear, but had, perhaps in defence, a vanity and self-admiration gigantic. With their hearts protected against all that they had not yet attained, as their bodies were concealed in clothes; mercilessly hostile to all that they did not understand, they were a people to dread. But such as these in the cottage on the fields one could love, for they were of the poor, the weak, the outcast, and the oppressed of the others.

In the morning very early, as he had returned silent and sour with sweat late in the night before, in the morning when it was light, but when the colours, the grays and greens, were repulsive and the air foggy and cold, the man with food in a newspaper wrapper went quickly and silently away toward the city; and he seemed very tiny as he moved over the foggy fields sucking the smoke from a cigar. Under his jacket he wore tight on his softish body a faded black cotton shirt, and on his head a serge cap with a shining forepiece like a naval officer's.

The woman began at once to work. Near the rotten wooden steps at the back of the cottage in the cold fog she began to wash clothes in tubs on an unfolded trestle. A cloth bag of wooden clips, a swab with stiff dirty cloths, and a broom hung on the outer house wall. In gray smoking soapy water she washed the clothes, rubbing them on a board ridged with zinc, washed the filthy clothes, her calico, the shirts and drawers, narrow stockings, sheets from the beds, the clouts of the baby. She pumped the water and carried it herself, silently, bending her tall thin body, straining and working it past all reserve, it and her thin arms with sharp yellow elbows. She hung the clothes on blackened ropes stretched between some old sheds, outhouses, and slanted posts; she too was tiny there on the great dim fields. At first she wet her feet in the sop-like grass, wet almost to the knee her cotton skirts and her long ugly white legs in loose cotton stockings gartered above the knee with shoe-latch; and she shuddered with the cold. Then as the sun rose higher and it became hot she sweated and panted. In the first of the morning the light was golden on the green fields and marsh; but it became ever more silver.

Two hours after she had begun to work her oldest child appeared to her in the kitchen doorway in its old sleeping dress, whining and sniffling with the morning chill and the confusion of being just awake, and twisting and rubbing on the side of the door-frame for its fear at interrupting her. She looked at it with no sort of kindness or welcome, and with impatience warned it not to wake the other. Then she continued her work. But on his snuffling plaintively that he was cold, she finished and wrung the cloth she held, and half drying her hands and arms on the sodden apron over her front she went, bent from the rubbing, up the steps and in at the door guiding and pushing the child back into the kitchen before her. Handling him partly as if he were another grown person and partly as if he were some wooden instrument with which she had not had practice and in whose use she felt little interest, she got him into clothes. She sat in a low-bottomed chair and held and turned him before her. She washed his face with a rag that smelled as if it were rotten and combed his hair with a comb full of head grease that smelled bitter. While being dressed the child wept and snivelled in fear and uncertainty; she sometimes ignored him, sometimes scolded him, sometimes berated him as if he were an adult enemy; but sometimes she looked upon him as if in consternation and dread. Then at the table she fed him coffee with milk and sugar and with wafers soaked in it. While this child was taking its food she walked guardedly into the bedroom to look at the other, and having found it awake, apparently to her annoyance, she uncovered it in her awkward hasty irritated way, took it up, dressed it in a blue shift and diaper, and then gave it one of her limp livid breasts. To this child's dress she added a boiled bonnet and a shawl, and she fastened it into a small woven chair with a hole in the seat and a rimmed shelf before and bore it out beside the washing-tubs. She had now to take the first child, importuning, to the outhouse, already buzzing with flies. She too sat down. Then she began to work again, and she continued until all the clothes were washed and hung on the lines. It was then not much short of noon. There on the great shaggy empty fields under the sunlit and sun-washed sky, to the noise of the black poplars and the air over the fields she lived and worked. She would have been perplexed at being watched or thought of; that would have been incomprehensible, distasteful, coldly and cruelly resented and despised.

She prepared to eat. The heat was making the small rooms suffocating even where there was a draught. She sat at the side of the weak oval wooden table in the kitchen, between it and the wall, the baby at her left in a high chair, the other child far around at the right out of her reach, sitting forward on its chair, which was too far from the table, half drinking, half spooning its food into its mouth, seriously absorbed with the food and pleased with it, but watchful and afraid of her. She herself ate much in a careless, smearing way. She ate a heap of chopped boiled potatoes reheated but not browned, dead white, some thick greasy meat sauce warmed, and some stewed rhubarb that she had saved in a dish, and she drank much coffee with milk listlessly out of a large white cup. Sprawling sidewise in her chair she watched the children carelessly; once she got up to jerk the older child closer to the table, and once she leaned forward to pull his food away when in repletion he complained of it. The bedroom, beside the room in front of the kitchen, was stifling, odoured of the tumbled bed-clothes, almost intolerable when she went in there to arrange the beds.

Having again taken the older child to the outhouse and having replaced the soaked and yellowed clouts of the baby laid upon her knees with its bent legs in the air, and again given it her breast, she put aside the dishes from which they had eaten and the frying pan and coffee pot, and dragged out from a dark place under a shelf a deep basket of red berries covered with a carpet, and began to pinch off the stems, take out the many that were decayed, and to wash, sugar, cook, and seal the rest into cylindrical flawed glass jars for preservation till winter. In the stifling bare rotting kitchen with a fire of wood going hotly in the stove to boil the fruit she did this work, sitting for long periods that made the back ache over the stemming, wiping away from her face, with the backs of stained hands, flies and the long antennae of her hair. She chopped the wood for the stove. The infant slept upon an old divan drawn with its face to the wall in the forward room, sweating in its clothes and giving off the odour of a baby.

The other child, sidling, whining, and surreptitious, stole a glass jar, and with it got back through the fields and down the path to the brook. It played there in the water in the softened light under the willows, broke the jar upon a stone among the gray litter, and cut the inside of the lower part of its thumb on an edge of the heavy glass. The pale greenish glass was dark clear green along the broken edge. Back came the child up the bank, along the road, and across the fields crying in perplexity and fear in the heat, and smearing itself with the startling welling dark blood. Confused, impotent, and terrified lest the blame be upon her, the woman received the child; then she became fierce and wrathful; but her excitement quickly subsided and was replaced by nervous weakness; she did not even finish fastening the bandage well, but wound it carelessly round the hand and told the child to go. With the clumsy bandage the child was fretful. Weakened and quieter, becoming more weary, the woman worked through the afternoon which was passing from the earth, boiled the fruit, went here and there, changed the baby's clouts, suckled it, wiped its spittle. As she wearied, she would sometimes stop aimlessly before the infant when it cried, and remain standing with her poor weakened and sweated body sagging forward at the waist, her high corsets thrusting up before and behind as if to plane off her head and leave it but a plug upon her shoulders, and partly looking away she would follow the baby's attempt to put something into its mouth. If it seemed about to fail she would put out her hand to assist, but she would drop the hand at once if the baby succeeded alone. When she had finished with the fruit the washed clothes were dry; these she took down, dragged in in a broken basket, dampened carelessly, and folded. She no longer spoke.

The hours passed. The little lonely cottage under the vast bright sky endured for those hours. The gloomy earth with its green trees endured. The poplars clattered their thick leather leaves in the wind; the marsh and the willows rustled. All endured. Nothing went past on the poor road. The light weakened slowly. At last it began to be that twilight of the wide pale green sky with white clouds lighted with gold. Finally it became the twilight of vastness, pink and purple, dense air, and heavy scents.

Silently, stiffly, and slowly the mother fed her children for the last time that day, ate something herself aimlessly and languidly, arranged for the man's stronger food later, and then prepared the children for the bed, washing the larger child's stained dusty feet and wrapping again the cut hand. Carrying the night-dressed infant on one arm over her sagging shoulder and pushing the other by the head, which pressed back against her legs, she took them through the darkening room before the kitchen, into the bedroom, through whose window the sunset could now be seen above the grass, the marsh, and the lands across it. The room had some old faded stained paper pasted on the walls, a small bed for the child, a large high wooden one for the rest, a stand of drawers, a poor glass, and on the wooden floor lay a bit of ragged carpet; and the beds, for the hot weather, were almost without anything but the dirty hard red mattresses and sheets. She placed the infant, already asleep, on the large bed; the other child in its torn sleeping dress she put into its own bed; and she went out to the other room. The cut child was feverish because of its wound, but it began to sleep after rolling about for a little.

The larger room where the woman now sat was bare also, the floor was dirty and entirely uncovered; the broken torn divan stood against the wall, there was a table, also against the wall, two rocking chairs and another chair, a shelf with a stopped black clock upon it and a stack of newspapers about to slip down, some crooked dusty curtains at the windows; there was little else. At the left of the front wall was a double door frame through which to go into the darkening front room with the crooked window and the colored glasses. This room was perfectly empty. The woman sat by a double window at the right near an outer door to the porch; the door was open and had a sagging screen of wood and rusted metal. Here there was air, and above and about the porch were the thick darkening gloomy poplar branches. It was almost as if one were in the branches. She had sunk down into a sort of child's woven chair that had once been painted white, and she sat stiffly with her chin upon her hand, sidewise in the chair. She sat in the green and gray of the coming gloom. Beside her on the floor was a broken paper box containing clothes to mend, and she bent down, drew up one of the man's black shirts by a corner, glanced at it, then let it fall listlessly: once more she sat still, sat in the poor dirty room full of twilight subdued, and coloured still more than without, by the heavy green trees.

And to her this land, the city not far off, the house, herself, her clothes, her few absurd, cloudy but hard thoughts, beliefs, and purposes were not strange; nor was there in all things, in the world and sky, in that of herself which was fellow to all human beings of all times, anything strange or appalling, moving even. For in herself was little to create, or to see, these qualities. She was so weary that her body was weak and numb and extremely sensitive; she felt distinctly her head, breasts against the corsets, back, aching legs, and feet; this, and but little else, was all that she felt.

So she sat, and it grew darker and gloomier; and she remained there without moving.

At last, when it was much later, all at once, as has happened how many times, someone in that other house away upon the darkened fields started music, faint for the distance, from a piano perhaps, or some mechanical device; weird music, with high chords; and it was music which in that strange place, in the deepening gloom, with the trees rustling, was strangely firm and had authority and strength; and over the dew-wet grass and the weeds of the fields and through the pink and deep purple light and the quivering green trees it came into that room as if destined so to come. It seemed that it came through the dense dark but coloured and wet air in great slowly made curves and bows that were almost circles, and that each note had power to go down deep into the heart, the breast, and to find there large decayed round spots and to draw from those spots slow terrible powerful notes of sympathy to mingle with the others. This music continued.

Leaning forward of a sudden, both elbows on her knees, which were close together, toes turned in, and her open hands covering her face, the woman began to weep. She made great sobs with long pauses between. She sobbed slowly and somewhat as if without feeling, and yet there was something like the violent retching of one poisoned in those sobs. She sobbed a long time. Then she became quieter and quieter, and at last began to have done.

The heavy poplar trees rattled in the gloomy dark. There began to be greater cold. What dim light had been left in the room gave place to complete cold heavy darkness. There was darkness over the world.

The arms, the hands still over the face, dropped forward, the head with its limp weak hair sank down, the face sliding along the bare thin arms, first on the underside, then as the arms turned

268

over, on the back; and then, arms out, hands hanging limply at the wrists, she slept, bent almost double. In the chilly black empty room of that cottage out upon the wide terrible fields, among the trees, by the heavy high poplar trees that were always moving, she slept with haggard cheeks. The children lay on the beds in the other dark chamber, the larger breathing and turning uneasily for its wound and for the cold so that it could be heard. The cold increased.

The music continued for a time, then ceased; the dark seemed to become more murky; the poor leaves rustled in the winds that came and went out of and into the unlighted sky.

Affectionate
ELSA VON FREYTAG-LORINGHOVEN

> Wheels are growing on rose-bushes
> gray and affectionate
> O Jonathan—Jonathan—dear
> Did some swallow Prendergast's silverheels—
> be drunk forever and more
> —with lemon appendicitis?

Breviora
EZRA POUND

POETRY is the statement of overwhelming emotional values; all the rest is an affair of cuisine, of art.

On n'émeut que par la clarté. Stendhal is right in that clause. He was right in his argument for prose, but Poetry also aims at giving a feeling precisely evaluated.

Satire is the expression of disgust with false evaluations.

A passage is "poetic" or "unpoetic" in two respects:

    (a) the degree in which the emotional element inheres.

    (b) the justness of the evaluation.

It is good or bad poetry according to the quality of the expression.

Sentimentality, sob-stuff: false statement of values.

Good art is expression of emotional values which do not give way to the intellect. Bad art is merely an assertion of emotion, which intellect, common-sense, knocks into a cocked hat.

Wordsworth, emotion almost null, emotional element scarcely present, and evaluation largely humbug.

Milton, baroque.

Dante: Era già l'ora che volge il desio.

Victorians, Tennyson, Browning, Swinburne, all given to "laying it on" in one way or another; not but what there are sound things in both Swinburne and Browning. Kipling, a mere exaggerration of Victoriania, banjo rendering of the Browno-Swinburnian compost.

The better tradition of English:

"Seafarer," lines in the "Wanderer," parts of Layaman, Chaucer, Gavin Douglas, Golding, Marlowe (translations as well as original work), William Shakespeare (as certain other critics have noted), Ballads and Elizabethan songs (rigorously selected), Wyatt, Donne, Waller, Herrick, later a few catches of Dorset and Rochester, Crabbe, Landor (selected and sifted).

In Latin:

Catullus, of the most poignant poets.

Horace, complicated proposition, to be dealt with elsewhere.

Ovid, particularization, sense of the Gods, very great poet, underestimated during the last 150 or 200 years, perhaps underestimated ever since the renaissance.

Propertius, quality (more anon).

Gallus, too little honoured.

Martial, valuable for his opposition to the rhetoricians. This importance not understood until one realizes that he *was* in such opposition; similiar situation now, literati vs. journalism. "The rhetoricians ruined the empire."

The rhetoricians amylowellized Cicero.

When one mentions simple facts of this sort [the stupidity of public and critics] idiots say that you are "embittered"; and when you call a block-head a block-head he can not believe you, he usually says that you are clever but insincere. Indeed I find it harder to convince a man that you really think him an ass, no matter how obvious his inanity, than to convince him of any other proposition whatsoever. Et pourtant there are people whom one does quite quietly and sincerely and placidly believe to be thoroughly stupid, inane and insipid.

The Classics

The most pernicious symptom of democracy is the growing clamour for the universal distribution of ignorance. Mr. Solon does not join in this clamour, but he rather implies that I have insisted on all authors knowing the classics. At least his readers might easily mistake him to mean that I had said this; that I had "insisted."

I have merely said that young men hoping to leave permanent works are rather stupid not to enlighten themselves.

The masters have seldom been illiterates. Shakespeare's "woodnotes" are a fiction of that pompous ass Milton. Shakespeare had his Ovid from Golding (excellent medium), he had his antiquity from North's "Plutarch," he had great erudition from Florio's "Montaigne." With these three books on his shelf no man need be lacking in "literacy."

Dante was a savant. Chaucer, likewise. Villon had escaped from the university of Paris and made a constant parade of his tags. Catullus presumably knew more Greek (or knew what he knew with greater intensity) than any Roman of his time. Heine is perhaps the least savant, yet he had happened on Bertrans de Born at a time when troubadours were less known than at present.

But I have never said that all authors should be savants, or that they should all read the classics.

A critic however is less likely to be taken in by literary and artistic shell-games if he have his mind decently stored with masterwork which will serve him for comparison. The more of it he has in his head the quicker his eye and perception; the more speedily will he see the germ of corruption, the ineluctable signs of impermanence.

And again what have we to do with Romain Rolland, or other Bloomsbury fads six years late?

The current-events-clubs are always getting these crazes. Nothing but some sort of habit of close comparison, of close inspection of the actual text of authors themselves in contradistinction to diluted reviews, will be any use in these matters.

Barbusse is Catulle Mendès' son-in-law. He won the prize of "concours de poesie de l'Echo de Paris" in 1893; at the age of nineteen. (One should not treasure this up against him.) He edited "Je sais tout." He published a volume of poems, "Pleureuses," in 1895. In "Le Feu" he is more topical and therefore more widely known. *As writing* it does not improve on

LA LETTRE
Je t'écris et la lampe écoute.
L'horloge attend à petits coups;
Je vais fermer les yeux sans doute
Et je vais m'endormir de nous . . . . .

La lampe est douce et j'ai la fièvre;
On n'entend que ta voix, ta voix . . .
J'ai ton nom qui rit sur ma lèvre
Et ta caresse est dans mes doigts.
J'ai de la douceur de naguère;
Ton pauvre coeur sanglote en moi;
Et mi-rêvenant, je sais guère
Si c'est moi qui t'écris, ou toi . . . .
                    (from "Pleureuses," 1895.)

He has very considerable depiction in his prose.

The Reader Critic

Pounding Ezra

ih

JUDGING from reverberations a great many people suffer loudly and continually over Mr. Pound.

Harriet Monroe is not the first to tell us that the *Little Review* is under the dictatorship of Pound. Our idea of having a foreign editor is not to sit in our New York office and mess up, censor, or throw out work sent to us by an editor in London. We have let Ezra Pound be our foreign editor in the only way we see it. We have let him be as foreign as he likes: foreign to taste, foreign to courtesy, foreign to our standards of Art. All because we believe in the fundamental idea back of our connection with Mr. Pound: the interest and value of an intellectual communication between Europe and America. If anyone can tell us of a more untiring, efficient, better-equipped poet to take over the foreign office let us hear from him.

I have had countless letters from Jews, Letts, Greeks, Finns, Irish, etc., protesting against Mr. Pound's ignorance and indiscrimination. I have answered that this is always true of mushroom nations: this fixed imperception of the qualities and culture of all other nations. And then there are some of us who come from races of ancient culture to whom Mr. Pound's ravings sound but the torturings of an inferiority complex.

. . . and all this has nothing to do with editing a magazine. Criticism, praise, contempt, commiseration,—there is not enough resistance in the whole country for one grown human being. As long as Mr. Pound sends us work by Yeats, Joyce, Eliot, de Bosschere,—

work bearing the stamp of originality and permanence—we have no complaint of him as an editor. If we are slightly jarred by his manner of asking for alms, or by any other personal manifestation, we can take care of that outside the magazine. We need no commiseration for our connection with Mr. Pound. We are not blind deficient children. All this again I say has nothing to do with editing a magazine of the arts. It is all very much only the outermost vibrations of discussions and replies.

I think I really started to write this because I scented an implied criticism of Chicago in Mr. Jepson's article. Every one gets jumpy over criticism for one cause or another: if not from mental timidity, from sentimentality. I reject all criticism of Chicago, sentimentally. I have seen some of the great cities of the world and many of the finer ones. I know Chicago to the skin and bone. And Chicago has a thrall.

I know it has an Art Institute which advertises Art and Commerce. It has electric-lighted statues in its parks and will be ruined forever by a "city beautiful" plan designed by some of its aunts of art. I know its "artistic" life is segregated to a few blocks on the Boulevard and can be easily avoided. Its artists live like refugees or work on newspapers. I know its blatancies, its swaggers, its displays, its timidities of approaching adolescence. Its people: infantile. I know all the other obvious, chronic things.

I know its glamour.

Ezra's Mind

LOLA RIDGE

MAY all the ancient and non-plebeian gods praise you for that letter in the November number. You can't continue to let any one rock the *Little Review*. And E. P. has for some time needed just such a cool and unperturbed hand to press him back into his seat. It isn't his knocking—that waste of creative (and destructive) energy is *his* look-out; America's so-easily abraded and so-quickly healing skin needs all it can get—of whip-cuts, not of mud and rotten eggs. And there's something about Pound's vituperations that savors of none too remote gutters—and rival stalls and tongues akimbo and herrings obvious in a rising temperature.

I've sometimes felt like saying something like this out loud but —*I'm* frugal! and then he's done lovely things and I admire his cold shining thin-glass mind through which so many colors pass leaving no stain—and then—my stone-arm balks at swinging in rhythm with the mob's.

Note from an Article by May Sinclair in the "English Review"

If the *Little Review* had never printed anything but what came to it through its foreign editor it might by this time have ranked as an important international concern; unfortunately it printed many things for which Mr. Pound was not responsible, and when it trespassed its iniquities were laid on him.

Business

DEAR LITTLE REVIEW: Do you ever read the advertisements of the other magazines? *Broom* has a blurb like this in its February number: "Four years have passed since the death of Apollinaire . . . and none of his writings have yet been presented to the American public." The *Dial's* Christmas cards described it as the only journal devoted to art and letters in America. Such deliberate dishonesty! Why doesn't jh go after them?

[These magazines are business concerns. They use the advertising methods of certain grades of business. They place themselves. The *Little Review* is for and by the artist, we have no interest in confusing the public or in directing it to buy only from us. Buying and selling isn't our fun. *jh*.]

"The Public Taste"

MARY WIDNEY

I HAVE BEEN puzzled by that explanatory "making no compromise with the public taste" which appears relentlessly upon the *Little Review* covers. It seems singularly obtuse for so perspicacious a magazine. The whole spirit of the work between its covers belies the obvious interpretation: that you are capitalizing your agnosticism—not too delicately angling for the dilettante iconoclast. If you are sincerely regardless of the public taste why be so blatant about it? A true contempt is impersonal—a true disregard cannot be cognizant of the thing disregarded. The small boy whistling in the graveyard—and the *Little Review* slapping the face of public taste. Some way it lacks dignity, and, what is more serious, casts aspersions on the worthiness of the movement it espouses. I may be misunderstanding grossly, but as I have said, I am puzzled. Won't you explain?

[I should like to write you a long heart-felt letter about that slogan. It has been one of my compromises for the past three years. It came to us, among many other precious things, from Ezra Pound.

Taste in Art is a thing that could never get my attention; and so, anything as casual as that taste made by the newspapers, lecture bureaus, the fashion-art magazines, and Mr. Mencken could never lead me to endorse the slogan.

I believe in peace and silence for and from the "masses"—a happy undisturbed people. I don't know how this can be brought about. —jh.]

We heard of Emanuel Carnevali from Poetry, *as I remember, and were glad to present his tortured tales of an immigrant's life in America.*

Tales of a Hurried Man
EMANUEL CARNEVALI

TALE III

1.

Home, sweet home!

THE way to my house begins half a mile away from it. It begins at the corner where the grey-purple sweating Hartford Lunch is. From Broadway into the street the air becomes denser, the façades are more resolutely drab, a sagging of the Broadway mood makes my heart faint in an indefinite sorrow. This little tragedy happens everyday, each time I am on the way to my house. . . .

I turn at the corner where the necessary wooden-faced saloon is. And there is West End Avenue. Whitish and greenish the houses, the colors of the wives of the poor wops. Here is a valley formed by two smooth asphalt hillsides. And here is my house. The door of it is as dirty and drivelling as the mouth of a very old man, who chews tobacco.

Way upstairs are my rooms.

I enter, I open the windows . . . "Damn it, why does she close them?" She says that they might get in from the fire-escape. I would like to meet the desperado who'd be so desperate as to come around these quarters to steal! A wave of dank smell has lapped

me around. I have taken a chair and sat down. Now I'm in my
own home!

2.

Let's begin from the roof, it is nearer the sky. Let's begin from
the roof, I breathe better up here than in my room or in the street.

It is sunset time. If I were good my mind would fill slowly with
darkness and there would be a play of silent shadows in my mind,—
that and that only. Life is a beautiful thing, if my lungs are good.
But I stretch my arms and my crooked fingers would grasp something more than air. No one knows how young I am. Do they want
me to become a cheat? There are lots of cheats that want to force
you to acknowledge their youth, their beauty, their vigor. I am
young and alone. If I were old I would be satisfied being alone and I
would sit still and let the darkness swaddle me. Night, and the
friends who think and do not think of me, frighten me. The friends
are afraid to dabble into me, as though they saw me as a pond of
treacherous green water. My face is often green, that's why.

I don't want to go down to my rooms any more. I don't want to
see her anymore. I want the Earth to stop running around like a
damn fool, and I want him to listen to a thing I have to say. I want
the Earth to stop going and I want him to watch me die. I could
touch this intangible air if I sent my body whirling through it, in a
spider's dance, to break over the flagstones. I would give a hundred
persons at least the thrill of their lives. I want the setting sun to
steal my eyes and carry them along with him, under the earth.

But I reckon I shall walk down again to my apartment. And
every day that cranes its grey face toward me will have my offering
of a few words. I reckon I shall walk down to my apartment and
open the door with a yale key, just like everybody. And they will
not say that I have gone away from them to find the truth. They
will not say I did not love them and they will admit that I am the
most American of the Americans. I might at least force them to see
my hatred. To see that I hate them more than their husbands do,
more than their wives, more than they who feed them and than they
who gather their leaving, more than the waiters and the doctors.
Always my great sadness looms beyond my world and theirs, just as
the sun lies beyond all weathers. Words do not make me glad, and
I am not an artist. Frightful words uttered by a thousand in a
thousand ways are all comprehensible to me, as my own word is more

frightful than any. The word that was first and that shall be the last when they shall join my two eyelashes in their last kiss and my two hands shall touch in their last caress; a word that you might mistake for the word Death.

I am an emigrant and I have left my home, I am homeless and I want a home. You look at me with evil eyes, with squinting eyes, you don't look at me, you sneer at me. I am emigrant, waiting, I know millions that are like me.

3.

Come, friends! We shall find one another again with the words of my confession! Don't insult me calling me "writer" and I won't call you butcher, grocer, waiter, doctor, business man, thief and murderer. Listen a while, if you please. Beside a few scandalous items, such as: the wife works oftener than I, in fact, she works all the time, and I only now and then . . . I am all right. And don't worry, I have them all on my conscience, the days of loafing and writing! (But, god! still heavier on my conscience are the days lost working in a restaurant or in a factory).

We'll get along. Let God congratulate himself for the simple things he turns out of the ground which go, dressed in humility's colors, to bring a modest happiness into every house: potatoes, rhubarb, beans, lettuce and radishes.

The wife is working and I am not, so I do the things around the house. . . .

Alone with my wife, I have meals that are feasts. Anti-puritan meals. To the eternal glory of the magnificent eaters of my old land, Lorenzo de' Medici, Alessandro Borgia, Leone X, and Cornaro before he had got tired. Crunching a plant of dandelion under my teeth and devouring with my eyes the small space of my wife's breasts that she lets me see; eating a bleeding beefsteak . . . god! we are in a cage but we are lions and monkeys yet! And if, in ten years, people will only chew foodstuff instead of eating, what the hell! we eat and laugh now, we eat and weep together, eh girl! And no one knows we have a real home, by Jesus Christ, so they'll leave us alone.

4.

I go into the kitchen, nibble at a piece of cheese and a loaf of bread, walk up and down, wash my face to chill the headache, walk all through the house, stop in front of each mirror to see whether my face has assumed at last a less vague aspect, whether there is yet on it the beginning of something that these weary hands and legs may follow.

The wind falters and gasps like a furnished-room-house landlady coming up the stairs. The wind comes, breast forward, into the space between that high wall and my window and puffs up my curtains. I sit by the window and the curtains touch my face again and again, doting lovelessly. . . . "Sex" is tormenting me, that kind of unhappy lust of a weary mind. The decay of a room is in its things and all the wind brings is some more dust and the thick stench of boiling laundry from the floor below. That awful wall! to determine all the sloppings, blotches, cracks and scars over its stupid nudity! I went to look at the letter-box downstairs about ten times today. All they send is words, anyway, and I know all about words, I am a writer.

I have heard old men half blind and half deaf blabber of home-sweet-home, and an immense lady teacher (more than 250 pounds), long time ago in my childhood, taught me the song:

> Casa mia, casa mia,
> benché piccola tu sia . . .

(House of mine, house of mine—however small thou art . . .) I have read all the big books, Jean-Christophe size, books which contain the bulk of a house, THE HOUSE. But my house is one of today and she is like a modern girl: with whom you have to be careful if you want to keep her; and the moment she jilts you, or you see a better one, everything is ended and nothing remains in the heart of you, or anywhere else; maybe a twisted smile remains. We have become used to tragedy.

5.

We shall take a walk along the Drive. . . .

How good the home is to those who come back from a walk. These things that know you know me too. . . .

Lunchtime, lunchtime! Oh, the dear little tree of parsley, in the glass, by the sink! Last night all the carpets were swollen with dust, now they are clean, naked. The bed is so well made—it is like a new book yet unopened. Black-stained bananas, what perfume your skin holds! Skin them and delight! The smell of cooking food is incense for the gods that will never die, and the color of the salad you are making is the flag of mine own soul!

At night, the lights alongside the river kindle many diamonds everywhere—glints of ripples, rails and window-panes. The fires of the city in the night are the fire-place by which tragic old gods sit to forget how intricate is the world they made. In the moonlit night the frayed profile of the Palisades is deep black. Spring air, which you had forgotten, never thought would come again, is here, holding aloof in her kind hands our weary hearts.

The wife moves about, working, and from her childish hands come cleanliness, order and good smell to the home—and caresses for me. If I have done my work well I have kept sadness away. Despair always comes from outside. The trouble is, one can't keep the place shut well enough.

But in the night the gaslight is a sun of a diseased world and the table, the chairs, the bookshelf, are sapless and silent and sad, like lepers. The book-shelf. Take a book. Any book. The first line of the first book pulls along all the lines of all the books; I have them all in my blood, these little black microbes—once you read one you're infected and chronic. And they shout too loud! It's a shame to let people print such things! Aren't you afraid? And we, the readers, pass before the gaping graves of these books, before these bodies torn asunder, we look at a man stretch an arm out of his grave and shake his bloody heart at us . . . and we say, "I like . . . I like . . . I don't like. . . ."

I burn with restlessness, I smoulder without fire, and my bed-sheets smell with my yesterdays—I can't sleep. There are many persons here, bothering me. All uninvited guests, crowding around my bed, shamelessly curious—I can't dismiss them. I can't touch them, I can't grasp a hand and feel it like a realization in my fingers—these are real ghosts! They ask all sorts of impossible questions. And each of them has a naked soul to show me that nauseates me! You come into my home, at night, to exhibit your shames, damn little beggars, you! Those eyes I saw today that seemed to acknowledge me so naïvely, now they want to know too much. To them all I can't be anything else but a man who is in bed and can't sleep. And these people are the same whom I said I loved, whom I caressed, whom I even kissed, during this same day, in the daylight. The daylight is a liar! I must run away from these people who do not love me enough.

I go into the other room where she sleeps. I go there to get from her all the strength my heart needs to beat to its next beat. If she knew how many things I want she'd be so desperate, she'd scream and die. But as it is she gives back the kiss, and a drowsy arm comes out and binds me to her warm face. Thus I take much, very much, and I steal back into my room afraid that even the silence might know of my theft. . . .

I get up, and go into the kitchen. To survey the pans and dishes a little. An aluminum pan shines like a baldhead in a darkened theatre and some sauce-pans are holes of deeper darkness in the darkness. A chair is sitting quietly in the shadow. From my room a shocking streak of light is a sunlit road of some fantastic midnight. A sinister shadow binds the legs of the table. The fire escape is a skeleton peeping in.

In my room the typewriter hides under its cover. The white-glaring bed shrieks. The brushes and mirrors have died of the sickness of uncleanliness and dust. The scars and blotches on the wall make strange faces at me. Outside the trains puff and blow fiercely, they want to rip the universe! They are throbbings of the physical pain of the Earth. The locomotive driver, the damn fool who makes that noise, who thinks it's good for him or for anybody to make that noise, who thinks it is good for him not to consider me, not to consider that I can't stand that noise . . . that I can't stand it . . . I can't, I can't!

6.

Memories weep or mourn, all memories do. I have left the home and her. I could have painted the walls half blue and half pink, and could have drawn a heavy-headed, sad-headed sunflower in the middle. I could have drawn my nightmares on the walls of my bedroom, and laughed at them, having exalted them by art. I could have wrung wreaths of oak leaves and maple leaves—from the Palisades— all around and I could have strewn the floor with sand and pebbles and my bedroom with ashes. I could have bought silk handkerchiefs and hung them from the windows—different ones every day. I could have planted beans, parsley and morning-glories in a box full of dirt out on the fire escape where it's forbidden to "place any encumbrance." And I could have written a tremendously happy treatise to show why the wops break one and every law of the United States. But they don't—and it wouldn't have sufficed—and reform is reform and I chose revolution—I quit.

I quit. I am a vagabond again. I am a roomer. In a furnished-room house. One of the homes of the homeless, of the orphans, the whores, the pimps, the poor spinsters, the poor bachelors, the homosexuals, the young stenogs who won't make good, waiters and doormen, the homes of the useless and the strangers. The typical American Home, the Furnished-room. The New World is tired of the Family. The New World damns the european shackles of the Family and has a new institution—a transitory institution in the transitory New World, the furnished room welcomes with miserable arms the hopeless rebels of the earth. I am the typical American,—see? Unacknowledged. Nobody knows me and, for a compensation, everybody knows me—so I talk crudely and democratically to everyone alike, for I love no one in especial. In the furnished-room one drops regularly the filth of the body and of the brain—never the wind comes in to take them away—the room is the composite of my spiritual and material offals—it knows all that's wrong with me as the horrible corpse of a man who died of disease knows exactly all that was wrong with the man. It knows nothing of what is good in me. So it can't acknowledge me, and I can't be a hero here. I must be the abject fool its eyes make of me.

Old houses, where the old families may live, are colour of the earth, arisen from the earth like trees—in this Spring they have their blossoms, in the Summer their fruits. The true American home is the furnished-room. The rich, the middle-class! Don't let them fool you about that—their houses are imitations—unreal and ugly—and there are hotels. Hotels and furnished-rooms. And concubines, pimps, middlemen and purveyors to these, THE LUNCH-ROOM and the RESTAURANT. If you can eat in a restaurant all your life then you can sleep in a furnished-room or a hotel all your life. A few maybe—or maybe many—for what do I know? isn't my misery blinding me?—oh, Christ, I am crying—if I don't see well it's because there are tears before my eyes! I tell you—I have known too many who know nothing about the old negro songs and nothing about New England and the pies that were or are made there, which are the tradition of the country—and many do not know how tremendously, and maybe successfully, sacrilegious skyscrapers are. These are the homeless, and I am one of them. They don't eat like men, they don't sleep like men, they don't see any colours. Why have you taken the colours away from your cities? They will soon become blind. Aren't colours the sustenance of your eyesight, do they not determine, define our eyesight—you—the chemists, the doctors, the engineers of America, you have made this country grey. Why do you handle grey things only, why does everything turn grey in your

hands? Do you want us all to lose our eyesight? A scientist says there
is romance in machines—who the hell wants romance! We're talking
of colours, colours, and taste and smell. Why do you take the joy out
of oranges and peaches—kill fruits? And you want to choke us—
with that smoke—is it you, the scientists? Or who is it? It can't be the
scientists, only. Is it a passage? Is it for the children? I am not a fool!
You'd want me to make a better, more specific complaint, wouldn't
you? But this is my own, and a million Greeks—oh, have you seen
the beautiful greeks that work in kitchens and restaurants—and have
you heard them? They are still singing the songs of the mountains
—and a million Italians—have you seen them go home from work,
loaded over with two jackets and a sweater and with immense mit-
tens to fight the cold, with the skin of their necks like bark—well,
they say "L'America, donne senza colore e frutta senza sapore"—
America, women without colour and fruits without taste. And
maybe they are right. Don't you see the millions of girls, almost all
the poor little working girls, rouged and powdered, looking like
thanksgiving masks or funny deadfaces. I will say it better, sometime—I think there is some use for such a complaint—but now I have
no time, I'm going, I'm going along, I am going along, I am going
along. Furnished-rooms—they got me again. They took me back.
There is always a brothel for a prostitute and always a sick lust in
some one for her, no matter how old and sick she is—so the furnished-room took me back. I make great signs to the sky, in front
of my windows, at night. I say: say, it's better not to go on this way,
you'd better stop—send a message to the young men "that the fight
is for nothing and the only good mood is that which requires suicide
at its end." I make a petition for them that are in my same plight—
the roomers, the hotel customers, the movies' patrons. I don't think
of revolution. When men would go out to kill, I shut myself in my
room and sit down and sometimes I want to die and sometimes I
weep. Memories come to visit me—only memories, no friends.
Friends are like apples gathered from the appletree of one's own
orchard—no orchard, no appletree, no friend. Someone suffers too,
who knows me, and he says "I am your friend." But no one knows
that I do not only suffer, that I am also going along, going along,
going along. I cry tears that are diamonds and drops of silver and
sapphires when the moonshine smites them: so there is beauty beyond my sorrow and I am going there. I am a vagabond, and I shriek
amongst my wrecks of memories and my failures like a crazy child
among old toys that are always new to him. I don't fake you, I never

told you that I am talking to God. And I am not talking to you, either, so leave me alone. I never understand who or what God is —sometimes he is a sentimental symbol. I am a vagabond. God, for all that, means home, it means family, father, mother, wife, sisters and brothers. No such things here. I have come in to the country where there are only vagabonds and liars and ghosts. The liars laugh and say they have a family and mother and sisters and they swagger around talking of "our country." I know that they're liars because they talk of their "old glory," and "the good old days"—and this is a New World. The ghosts flutter around taunting us with japanese and chinese silks and with european shrouds. I know a few: one is a fat woman who smokes cigars, one is a man who has whiskers like D'Artagnan, one is a toothless sleepy-eyed stinker who gets sore with everybody and then bows to them saying "I am so sad!," one is a lady's man, one is a business man who is tired of his face.

I have left, in a real old country, an old house. There was too much tragedy in it. And no outlet, because everybody was too wise. The house was tired of standing on its walls and hearing the howls of the dying old people inside. If ever the great wind that I, a vagabond, am acquainted with, will come over that house, it will slash it into strips and shrivel it and scatter it. I came where there are no houses. I haven't seen any. Maybe, down South, out West . . . or up North—but not where I have been. I have been around and have looked around and I have eyes, and I am no statistician and then. . . . I talk to no one in particular. And I got married and had a home. That was a mistake.

Now, I am again a vagabond, spilling words from a hole in my pocket, knowing only other vagabonds like me and urging them to wander around. To wander and go, hurriedly, like myself. When we are tired, we meet and sing old, very old songs that no one understands except us, and we call one another "brother" and "artist"— and we often weep together—it is when we realize that there cannot be brothers without there being a family, or artists without there being a home . . . when we realize that we are liars too.

The Reader Critic

The Real Question

HART CRANE

I RATHER enjoy these little "fusses," and almost all arguments when removed from the time-honoured realms of morality. The trouble with you is that you have had to fight against the mere taboo element so long (and nobly!) that you are apt to become merely personal in your answers to other arraignments. You do this brilliantly, but when it comes to the real question in hand you are apt to miss fire.

[You take me too seriously. I may have spoken about this "taboo element," and a lot of other things, but I have never fought anything.

I make quite an effort to miss the "real question."

When I was little I could never see a strange cat without shying a stone at it with hoots of challenge. I like cats, I never tried to hit one; I have rescued and even wept over cats, but I like to see them run. There is something in their nature that calls for the stone. Many people call for the stone. . . . Yes, you may call us personal. We try to address our remarks to the person we have in mind rather than, as is the convention, to the (or a) literary state.—*jh*.]

On Sherwood Anderson

jh

IF I were an easy writer I should like some time to write my impression of Sherwood. The evidence about everyone is always wrong—I mean the evidence that we give about ourselves in words and acts and appearance to him who runs. The artist can prove no alibi once he has produced. The critics protest that Sherwood "writes of the soul of the American people." Since that soul as advertised is made up of Desire for Greatness, Money-Getting, Conformity, and Sanity I fail to see Sherwood as its laureate. Sherwood is more inevitable than conscious. He is apropos his material. He is pre-natal and he writes about a pre-natal America. He writes about people who are for the first time struggling with other problems and impulses than those of "gettin' on."

On the other hand those who froth at his "inarticulate prosiness" or his "bad English" miss him entirely. We printed a story of his in the *Little Review* with this as a first sentence: "There was a woman come to Chicago once." We got so much jeering that we were almost tempted to explain that we liked it. The *Little Review* is a record of the creative energy of this period: absolute achievement, experiments and existences. There is the evidence in Sherwood Anderson's writing of an existence that is important and great.

284

Great grammar or great existence?—what is a great writer?

A Visit

(From the French of Charles Vildrac)

WITTER BYNNER

Seated by his table,
His dreams delicately enclosed
In the domain of his lamp,
He heard against his window
The soft assault of the snow.

Then he thought abruptly
Of a man he knew
And had not seen for a long time.
And he felt in his throat
An oppressive something,
Something made of sadness
and a little shame.
He knew that the man was humble
Both in heart and in word,
With no ways of charming,
And that he lived like those trees
You see alone on a bleak plain;

He knew that for months
Many a time he had promised
This man to go and see him
And that for each of the promises
The man had thanked him gently,
Pretending to believe them.

He knew besides that the man loved him.

This was what filled his reverie,
Filled his room with whispers,
Which he did not try to turn away.
Then an inner command
Made him instantly alert:
His throat was eased
And his eyes glad and laughing:

He dressed himself quickly,
He went outdoors

And started through the snow
For the man's house.

       . . . . .

After the first words,
When he was seated in the light
Between the man and his wife
Both of them surprised and eager,
He realized that they were directing at him
Those silences that ask questions
And make the sort of blank one leaves
Purposely in one's writing;
He noted on the two faces
A sort of secret anxiety.
He wondered and all at once he understood;

These folk, alas, did not believe
That he had come of a sudden
At so late an hour, from so far and through the snow,
Only for his gladness and theirs,
Only to keep a promise;

And they waited, both of them,
For him to reveal abruptly and in a breath
The solemn reason of his coming,
They were anxious to know
What good luck might be happening to them,
What service might be expected of them!

He would at once have spoken
The words to undeceive them,
But they weighed his words,
They anticipated the moment
When he would tell them his reason.
He felt as bewildered and clumsy
As a man accused.
And so he was separated from them
Till the very last minute
When he rose to go.

Then something unbent;
Then they dared understand:
He had come only for them!

Somebody had wished to see them,
Nothing more, to see them, to be with them,
To speak with them and to listen to them;
And this desire had been
Stronger than the cold, stronger than the snow
And the distance!
It was just that at last somebody had come!

And now their eyes
Were gay and tender.
They spoke very fast,
They spoke together
To try to keep him,
They stood beside him
And betrayed a childish need
Of joking and of shaking hands . . . .

          .   .   .   .   .

He promised them that he would come back.

But before reaching the door
He fixed well in his memory
The spot where their life was sheltered;
He noticed well every detail
And finally the man and the woman,
Because he so feared in the bottom of his heart
That he would never come back.

*Our May-June number, 1920, was devoted to W. H. Hudson, and
was entirely composed by Ezra.*

W. H. Hudson—Some Reminiscences

FORD MADOX HUEFFER

I.

For a long, long time—I dare say for twenty-five years—I have been
longing to say something about Hudson. But what is there to say?
Of things immense, tranquil or consummate, it is difficult indeed to
speak or to write. . . .

Suppose one should say that one would willingly cancel every one
of the forty or so books that one has published if one could be given
the power to write one paragraph as this great poet writes a paragraph: or that one would willingly give up all one's powers of

visualising this and that if one could be granted this great naturalist's power of looking at a little bird. . . . But of course that would not be enough. Or rather it would be nothing at all. For I suppose that if one had the power to frame one paragraph one could frame others: and if one had the vision of the poet one would be the poet's self. One might say—and indeed I do say with perfect sincerity—that one would willingly sacrifice all one's gifts as a writer if one could give to this unapproached master of English ten years longer of writing life. . . . But even that would be selfish—for one would have the pleasure: one would read what he wrote.

For me, then, Hudson is the unapproached master of the English tongue. There are no doubt other English writers—though English as a language is woefully lacking in prose towards which one need not be kind—in unassailable prose. Still there are possibly other English writers. But there is no other English writer that you cannot say something about. One derives from Sir Thomas Browne—but is not as good; another gets his effects from a profound study of the Authorised Version but falls short of the resonance of the Inspired Original; another has caught the jolly humor of Rabelais; when Mr. Peskith writes you might swear it was Montaigne speaking; someone else puts down the thoughts of Dante in the language of Shakespeare. . . . Well, we know the sort of stuff that English prose is. Only Hudson is different.

The only English writer with whom I have ever had the luck to discuss the "how" of writing was Mr. Conrad. (I *will* say this for Americans that, if they practice letters, they are much more usually devoured by curiosity about what is called "technique." I have heard Mr. Owen Wister talk for quite a time on several occasions with Mr. James about the written word as a means of expression. I have talked for hours with members of the editorial staff of New York magazines—as to how to write a short story!—and I used to talk for hours with Stephen Crane—why is poor dear Stevie forgotten; the finest poet that two continents produced in a century? —just about words! And Crane made the most illuminating remark about English prose that I ever heard). But the only true-blue English writer that I ever heard discuss how to write, as apart from how to make money by writing or who was the best Agent or the worst Publisher or the meanest Editor or the Best Seller—was, then, Mr. Conrad.

And, once, Mr. Conrad looked up from reading *Green Mansions* and said: "You can't tell how this fellow gets his effects!" And, a long time after I had agreed that I couldn't tell how Hudson got his effects, Conrad continued: "He writes as the grass grows. The good God makes it be there. And that is all there is to it!"

And that is all there is to it. *Green Mansions* is the only English novel of passion; the *Purple Land* is the only English novel of Romance (and I don't except Mr. Conrad's and my own Romances), *Nature in Devonland, Hampshire Days, Birds in a Village* and the *Shepherds' Life* are the only English books about England. And you must remember that Mr. Hudson is an American of New England stock.

I suppose the chief characteristic of great writers—of writers who are great by temperament as well as by industry or contrivance—is self-abandonment. You imagine Mr. Hudson watching a tiny being and his whole mind goes into the watching: then his whole mind goes into the rendering. Probably there is some delight in the watching and more austerity, more diligence, in the act of recording. That no doubt varies. Turgenev is such another as Mr. Hudson and I can recall no third.

Turgenev, I mean, watched humanity with much such another engrossment as Mr. Hudson devotes to Kingfishers, sheep or the grass of fields and rendered his results with the same tranquility. Probably, however, Turgenev had a greater self-consciousness in the act of writing: for of Mr. Hudson you might as well say that he never had read a book. Still, in the *Sportsman's Sketches* and in the *Singers*, the *Rattle of the Wheels* and in *Bielshin Prairie* above all —you get that note:—of the enamoured, of the rapt, watcher; so enamoured and so rapt that the watcher disappears, becoming merely part of the surrounding atmosphere amidst which, with no self-consciousness, the men, the forests or the birds act and interact. I know, however, of no other writers that possess this complete selflessness.

It is no doubt this faculty that gives to Mr. Hudson's work the power to suggest vast very tranquil space and a man absolutely at home in it, or motionless vegetation, a huge forest and a traveller who wishes to go nowhere, or ever to reach the forest bounds. . . .

II.

It is twenty-five—or twenty-four, or twenty-three!—years ago since I sat with Conrad, one day in the drawing-room of my farm; the

Pent it was called. We were deep in the struggles that produced *Romance* and Conrad was groaning terribly and telling me—as he has told in several kingdoms, shires, duchies, countries and languages—that I did not know how to write. Of course I didn't know how to write as Mr. Conrad did before he became a true-blue Englishman. . . . At any rate we were engrossed. . . .

A man went past the window: very tall, casting a shadow across the pink monthly roses. These commonplace Kentish flowers peeped over the window-sill of the deep living-room whose low dappled ceiling was cut in half by a great beam. So the tall man's shadow flickered across them. . . . .

It is disturbing when you, a man of letters, engrossed in the *Heart of the Country,* see a shadow fall from a very tall stranger across your room and the monthly roses. You think of duns, bailiffs, unpaid butcher's bills. . . . But Conrad, always sanguine, hoping for the best (I never had many hopes when strangers approached me) exclaimed: "That will be the man who wants to sell a horse!" Panic, anyhow, seized us. Dans un grenier comme on est bien a vingt ans! (I suppose I was twenty-four!) A panic! The immensely tall stranger repassed the window.

Conrad went to the door. And I heard:

Conrad: You've come about the mare!

Voice: I'm Hudson!

Conrad: She's out with the ladies.

Voice: I'm Hudson!

Conrad: The mare will be back in about half an hour. . . .

Hudson was staying at New Romney—which is New only in the sense that William I built it in 1080 A. D. instead of Caesar in 45 B. C. . . . Hudson then, was staying at New Romney and had walked over—fourteen miles in order to pay his respects to the great author of *Youth, Heart of Darkness, Lord Jim,* and *Almayer's Folly.* . . .

I remember Hudson again—there are more reminiscences!—in one of the beastly cafés in Soho. (They resemble Mouquin's in Sixth Avenue, New York, though I do not remember Mouquin's as being beastly, at all—but very expensive by comparison!) At any rate it was the Café Riji, Soho. There were present Mr. Galsworthy, Mr. Hilaire Belloc, Mr. Edward Garnett . . . Mr. . . . Well, I don't remember every one who was present. And just as Mr. Belloc was shouting "Glorious county, Sussex!"—in came Mr. Hudson.

The dialogue went on like this:

Belloc: Glorious county, Sussex! Glorious county, Sussex! You can ride from the Crystal Palace to Beachy Head with only four checks!

"Five!" said Mr. Hudson. It was like the crack of doom; like the deep voice of a raven; like the sound of a direful bell.

Belloc: Only four checks! There's Woking, and Cucking! and Ducking and . . . .

"Five!" said Mr. Hudson.

Belloc: Only four checks! (He used a great many gesticulations, telling the names off on his fingers in the French way.) There are Woking and Cucking and Ducking and Hickley . . .

"Five!" said Mr. Hudson.

Mr. Belloc repeated the queer names of Sussex villages. Then Mr. Hudson said:

"East Dean!" Mr. Belloc threw his hand violently over his head as one used to see people do on the Western front: then began to tear, immediately afterwards, at his ruffled hair. He exclaimed: "My God! What a fool I am!" and stated that he was a Sussex man: bred and born in Sussex: had never been out of Sussex for an instant in his life: had ridden every day from the Crystal Palace to Beachy Head. Yet he had forgotten East Dean.

All the while Mr. Hudson sat motionless: grave: unwinking: gazing at his victim with the hypnotic glare of a beast of prey. Or as if he were studying a new specimen of the genus Fringillago!

III.

And I dare say that is how Mr. Hudson "gets his effects": gazing at his subject with the expressionless passion of a bird of prey: keeping as still as a tree: and then cutting down words to nothing. For the three words: the reiterated "Five" and the final "East Dean," convinced one that Mr. Hudson had lived on the South Downs all his life and that you could trust him to take you from Bramber to Findon in pitch black night. Whereas the thousands of words that Mr. Belloc poured out only made you doubt that he had ever been in Sussex in his life.

Of course Mr. Belloc *has* lived in Sussex for a great part of his life, and Mr. Hudson was born in the Argentine, of New England stock—about 1790, I should say. I have heard him allege that when he came to England he was the first member of his family to set foot on these Islands for 250 years. So maybe he descends from the Navigator. At any rate from those facts which may or may not be facts—for as to the real date of Mr. Hudson's birth I have only impressions; as for instance having heard him talk in terms of great intimacy of the Dictator Bolivar who flourished about 1820. . . . But then we can read *Far Away and Long Ago!*—so that at any rate from these facts, of Argentine birth, long absence from this country, immemorial antiquity, quietude and the exact habit of mind, we may get certain glimpses of Mr. Hudson's secret. For Mr. Hudson is a secret and mysterious alchemist just as much as, or much more than, Dr. Dewar.

Perhaps, owing to his Argentine birth and long racial absence from these Islands, Mr. Hudson has escaped the infection of the slippy, silly way we handle the language: he has escaped the Authorized Version and the Morte d'Arthur and someone's Rabelais and someone else's Montaigne and Sir Thomas Browne's *Urn Burial,* and all the rest of it. (I may as well put down here what I meant when I said just now that Stephen Crane said the most illuminating thing I ever heard as to the English prose of to-day. He was talking about the author of *Travels in the Cevennes with Mr. Colvin*—or whatever the title was, and he said: "By God! when Stevenson wrote: 'With interjected finger he delayed the action of the time piece,' when he meant 'he put the clock back,' Stevenson put back the clock of English fiction 150 years." . . . Stevenson, as you know, was the sedulous ape of Walter Pater or someone like that, and decked himself out in allusions, borrowed words, stolen metaphors, inversions and borrowed similes for all the world like Charles Lamb or a Tommy coming back to the Line hung about with souvenirs). Well, Mr. Hudson has escaped all that. You would, as I have said, think he had never read a book in his life. Certainly he never read a book and carried off a phrase like "interjected finger" to treasure it as Ole Bill might treasure an Iron Cross raped from the breast of General Humpfenstrumpfen, lately deceased. Then too, born in the Argentine in remote ages, Mr. Hudson had the advantage of seeing the light in a Latin country—at least I suppose seventeenth century Argentina *was* a Latin country—and so he was among a population who used words for the expression of thoughts. For, among us Occidentals, it is only the Latin races who use words as clean tools, exactly, with decency and modesty. You may see the same in the prose of Mr. Cunninghame Graham who was also of South American origin and is the only other true proseateur of these islands, since Mr. Conrad writes not English but literal translations from unpublished French originals. (I suppose I ought to put in somewhere, "present company always excepted"—for the sake of politeness to possible readers!)

And then again, being the first of his family to visit England for 250 years or whatever it was, Mr. Hudson has the advantage of being the first English writer to see this country—for at least that period. Just as he has escaped our slippy use of the language so he has escaped our slippy way of looking at a hill, a flower, a bird, an ivy leaf. Yesterday I picked the first cuckoo flower and the first king-cup of the year. When I got my hand well on the stem of the first I exclaimed:

"When lady smocks all silver white
Do tint the meadows with delight . . ."

I daresay I was misquoting, but I felt proud of myself and didn't look at the flower.

When I grabbed the kingcup I said:

"Shine like fire in swamps and hollows grey." And I felt proud of myself and didn't look at the flower.

When I hear my first skylark I shall spout:

"Hail to thee, blithe spirit!
Bird thou never wert. . . ."

and for the nightingale it will be: "Most musical; most melancholy!" . . . . and I shan't much look at, or listen to, either fowl. And it is the same with all us English writers.

For again there is the question of this alchemist's great age. Actually I believe Mr. Hudson lately celebrated his seventieth birthday. I have however known him for twenty-five, twenty-four or twenty-three years, and when I first met him he was eighty-two and told personal anecdotes of the Court of George Washington. What I mean by all this fantasia is that Mr. Hudson has an air of consummate and unending permanence wherever he may happen to be, a weather worn air as of an ancient tree, an ancient wag, a very old peasant. Wherever you find him he will seem to have been there for ages and to be time-stained to the colour of the hedgerows, the heather, the downs or the country folk. So he fits in and trees, birds, or shepherds are natural when he is about. Mr. Hudson himself is conscious of the fact, for he writes of Wiltshire in the opening pages of the *Shepherd's Life:* "Owing to a certain kind of adaptiveness in me, a sense of being at home wherever the grass grows, I am in a way a native of Wiltshire too." . . . And he is a native of Argentina, and La Plata, and Patagonia and Hampshire and the Sussex downlands—wherever the grass grows. . . . For simple people, shepherds, bird-catchers, girls wheeling perambulators, old women cleaning front stones, South American Dictators, gamblers, duellists, birds, beasts and reptiles, have been natural before him; and the green earth and the sombre trees and the high downs and the vast Pampas have been just themselves before him. He looked at them with the intent gaze of the bird of prey and the abandonment of the perfect lover.

IV.

Twenty-five years ago—really twenty-five years ago—I lay on my back on the top of the great shoulder of the downs above Lewes—looking into the crystalline blue of the sky. There drifted above me frail, innumerable, translucent, to an immense height, one shining above the other, like an innumerable company of soap bubbles—the globelike seeds of dandelions, moving hardly perceptibly at all in the still sunlight. It was an unforgettable experience. . . . And yet it wasn't my experience at all. I have never been on that particular downs above Lewes, though I know the downs very well. And yet I am not lying! For you see, in the 90's of last century, I read that passage in *Nature in Downland*—and it has become part of my life. It is as much part of my life as my first sight of the German lines from a down behind Albert in 1916 . . . which is about the most unforgettable of my own experiences in the flesh. . . . So Mr. Hudson has given me a part of my life. . . . Indeed, I have a whole Hudson-life alongside my own . . . and such great pleasure with it. That is what you mean when you say a man is a creator . . . a creative artist. He gives to the world vicarious experience.

I fancy that is really all there is to say—or at any rate what most needs saying as to this very great man. I believe that, until quite lately, he was very little known in the Literary World. But, outside that world, in the realm of the mute, Hudson must have had a great many readers. I talk frequently with unlikely men in unlikely places—with farriers in France, with vicars in hideous North Country towns, with doctors and chance people in mines—about books. The Great of course they won't have heard of; the popular they will have read and will have forgotten or confused. But if you mention Hudson and they happen to have read Hudson. . . . . Ah, then you will see a different expression on their faces! You will see them become animated, earnest, with eyes alive and with looks of affection —as one does of some one who is great, kind; who has taught one a great deal; who is part of one's family and of oneself. That is a very great, a very splendid position to hold.

Hudson: Poet Strayed into Science
EZRA POUND

HUDSON is an excellent example of Coleridge's theorem "the miracle that can be wrought" simply by one man's feeling something more keenly, or knowing it more intimately than it has been, before, known.

The poet's eye and comprehension are evident in the first pages of *The Naturalist:* the living effigies in bronze rising out of the white sea of the pampas. Then the uneven eloquence:

"And with the rhea go the flamingo, antique and splendid; and the swans in their bridal plumage; and the rufous tinamou —sweet and mournful melodist of the eventide; and the noble crested screamer. . . . These, and the other large avians, together with the finest of its mammalians, will shortly be lost to the pampas utterly." . . .

. . . "What a wail there would be in the world if a sudden destruction were to fall on the accumulated art-treasures of the National Gallery, and the marbles in the British Museum, and the contents of the King's Library—the old prints and mediaeval illuminations! And these are only the work of human hands and brains—impressions of individual genius on perishable material, immortal only in the sense that the silken cocoon of the dead moth is so, because they continue to exist and shine when the artist's hands and brain are dust: and man has the long day of life before him in which to do again things like these, and better than these, if there is any truth in evolution. But the forms of life in the two higher vertebrate classes are Nature's most perfect work; and the life of even a single species is of incalculably greater value to mankind, for what it teaches and would continue to teach, than all the chiselled marbles and painted canvases the world contains; though doubtless there are many persons who are devoted to art, but blind to some things greater than art, who will set me down as a Philistine for saying so."

Sunday Afternoon
MALCOLM COWLEY

(After Jules Laforgue)

Sunday in my bedroom staring
Through the broken window pane,

I watch the slanting lines of rain,
And since I have an empty purse
Turn to philosophy again:—
The world is a potato paring,
The refuse of the universe
    And man excrescent,
    Adolescent.

Oh for some drunken luxury,
For a divine intoxication,
For love that rises suddenly—
The ordinary dull flirtation
    That lasts a day
    And dies away
Leaves life too barren of sensation.

Weeks melt to weeks; the summer season
Passes without any reason,
And marriage cannot make things worse;
For some fine morning I shall see
    My progeny,
    What ecstasy!
My progeny in diapers.

At twenty they will grow to be
    Like me;
They too will cultivate the Mind
    And find
In some hall bedroom, Tragedy.
Until, unheralded by drums
At last the undertaker comes.

Creeps in this weary pace from day to day
To the last syllable of appointed time;
    Since life will play
    The dull repeater,
    I turn its meter
    Into rhyme.

In seven billion years, the sun,
Grown cold, will slaughter every one.
The cosmos, tired of innuendo,
Will play *glissando, decrescendo*—

My seven million progeny
In seven billion years
Will pay arrears
And follow me.

Boredom that had accumulated
Since Eve and the Pleistocene
Though belated
Will be done,
Leaving a constellation clean
Of grief and schism
And organism
Lying cold under a cold sun.

On Trial for "Ulysses"

In our July-August number of 1920 we published the conclusion of Episode XIII of Ulysses *and thus precipitated ourselves into our cause celèbre. On October 4th the Washington Square Bookshop was served with papers by the Society for the Suppression of Vice for having sold a copy of the "obscene" episode to someone's daughter. Our trial for obscenity was set for December 13 and we were to be defended by the eminent New York lawyer, John Quinn, friend of Ezra and Joyce (My Thirty Years' War, pages 206-226).*

But before this catastrophe the Little Review *had been working to make* Ulysses *intelligible to certain of its readers. For instance:*

Dear Little Reviewers:
Do you think the public will ever be ready for such a book as *Ulysses?* I read Joyce each month with eagerness, but I must confess that I am defeated in my intelligence. Now tell the truth,—do you yourselves know where the story is at the present moment, how much time has elapsed,—just where are we? Have you any clue as to when the story will end?

[*Ulysses* will probably appear in book form in America if there is a publisher for it who will have sense enough to avoid the public. Joyce has perfected a technique that has enabled him to avoid almost all but those rabid for literature. We haven't any advance chapters in hand, but it would seem that we are drawing towards the Circe episode and the close of the story. The question of time seems simple and unobscured. The story is laid in perhaps the talk centre of the universe, but time is not affected; the time of the present chapter is about five-thirty or six in the evening of the same day on which the story started,—I think Tuesday. Mr. Bloom has had a long day since he cooked his breakfast of kidney, but he has lost no time.—*jh*.]

. . . and Hart Crane sent in his first critical piece:

Joyce and Ethics

HART CRANE

Cleveland, Ohio:

THE Los Angeles critic who commented on Joyce in the last issue was adequately answered, I realize,—but the temptation to emphasize such illiteracy, indiscrimination, and poverty still pulls a little too strongly for resistance.

I noticed that Wilde, Baudelaire and Swinburne are "stacked up" beside Joyce as rivals in "decadence" and "intellect." I am not yet aware that Swinburne ever possessed much beyond his "art ears," although these were long enough, and adequate to all his beautiful, though often meaningless mouthings. His instability in criticism and every form of literature that did not depend almost exclusively on sound for effect, and his irrelevant metaphors are notorious. And as to Wilde,—after his bundle of paradoxes has been sorted and conned,—very little evidence of intellect remains. "Decadence" is something much talked about, and sufficiently misconstrued to arouse interest in the works of any fool. Any change in form, viewpoint or mannerism can be so abused by the offending party. Sterility is the only "decadence" I recognize. An abortion in art takes the same place as it does in society,—it deserves no recognition whatever, —it is simply outside. A piece of work is art, or it isn't: there is no neutral judgment.

However,—let Baudelaire and Joyce stand together, as much as any such thing in literary comparison will allow. The principal eccentricity evinced by both is a penetration into life common to only the greatest. . . .

The most nauseating complaint against Joyce's work is that of immorality and obscenity. The character of Stephen Dedalus is all too good for this world. It takes a little experience,—a few reactions on his part to understand it, and could this have been accomplished in a detached hermitage, high above the mud, he would no doubt have preferred that residence. *A Portrait of the Artist as a Young*

Man, aside from Dante, is spiritually the most inspiring book I have ever read. It is Bunyan raised to art, and then raised to the ninth power.

We had received letters condemning Episode XIII as "the most damnable slush and filth that ever polluted paper in print." We answered them all. The Baroness von Freytag, outraged for us, also answered:

"The Modest Woman"

ELSE VON FREYTAG-LORINGHOVEN

Artists are aristocrats.

Artists who call themselves artists—not aristocrats—are plain working people, mixing up art with craft, in vulgar untrained brain.

Who wants us to hide our joys (Joyce?)

If I can eat I can eliminate—it is logic—it is why I eat! My machinery is built that way. Yours also—though you do not like to think of—mention it—because you are not aristocrat.

Your skirts are too long—out of "modesty," not decoration—when you lift them you do not do it elegantly—proudly.

Why should I—proud engineer—be ashamed of my machinery—part of it?

Joyce is engineer! one of boldest—most adventurous—globetrotter—! to talk shop is his sacred business—we want him to—to love engine that carries him through flashing glades to his grave—his glorious estate.

If your ears are too vulgar—put white cotton into—in tufts—bunches! fitting decoration! Afflicted people should stay home—with family—friends. You are immodest—because you are not healthy.

America's comfort:—sanitation—outside machinery—has made American forget own machinery—body! He thinks of himself less than of what should be his servant—steel machinery.

He has mixed things! For: he has no poise—no tradition. Parvenu —ashamed of his hide—as he well might.

That is American! it is truly disgusting to imagine him in any "physical functions"—eating not excluded.

Eats stupidly also.

Has reason to hide—feels that—and:—because newly rich—in vast acquisition—feels also he has something to say—everything—everybody.

Smart aleck—countrylout—in sunday attire—strutting!

Yawning—all teeth—into space—sipping his coffee with thunder noise—elbow on table—little finger outspread stiffly—he knows how to behave in society!

Why—America—can you not be modest? stay back—attentive—as wellbred child? You have so much to learn—just out of bushes!

But—you are no wellbred child—you are noisy—nosey—bad-mannered—assumptive.

. . . Goethe was grandly obscene—what do you know about it? Flaubert—Swift—Rabelais—Arabian Nights—Bible if you please! only difference—Bible is without humour—great stupidity! So: how dare you strut—step out—show yourself with your cotton-tuft in ear?

In Europe—when inferiors do not understand superiors—they retire modestly—mayhap baffled—but in good manner. By that fact—that they do not understand—they know their place. They are not invited—of class inferior—the dance is not theirs.

They can not judge—for: they lack real manners—education—class.

If they are desirous of judging—sometime—they must think—study—rise—*slowly!* So society is made—in Europe—slowly—! so: culture—so: aristocratic public.

That attitude of the learner—the inferior—you should feel in regard to James Joyce.

That you do not—shows you have less inherent culture than European washer-lady.

Here—madame—every bank clerk meddles.

Ancient Romans had proverb—one of few great principles of world-structure—culture: *Quod licit Jovi, non licit Bovi.*

To show hidden beauty of things—there are no limitations! Only artist can do that—that is his holy office. Stronger—braver he is—more he will explore into depths.

Do not eat the *Little Review*.

Therein all strong angels are!

I have not read "Ulysses." As story it seems impossible—to James Joyce's style I am not yet quite developed enough—makes me difficulty—too intent on my own creation—no time now.

Sometime I will read him—have no doubt—time of screams—delights—dances—soul and body—as with Shakespeare.

From snatches I have had shown me it is more worth while than many a smooth coherent story by author of real genuine prominence.

300

The way he slings "obscenities"—handles them—never forced—never obscene—vulgar! (thank Europe for such people—world will advance.)

Shows him one of highest intellects—with creative power abundant—soaring!

Such one you dare approach—little runt?

Whatever made you read him—*Little Review*—anyway?

Back to my astonishment!

You see how ridiculous you are?

Well—if not—others will.

That is why I wrote this—!

Before the trial, Jane wrote an article for the September-December issue:

Art and the Law
jh

THE heavy farce and sad futility of trying a creative work in a court of law appalls me. Was there ever a judge qualified to judge even the simplest psychic outburst? How then a work of Art? Has any man not a nincompoop ever been heard by a jury of his peers?

In a physical world laws have been made to preserve physical order. Laws cannot reach, nor have power over, any other realm. Art is and always has been the supreme Order. Because of this it is the only activity of man that has an eternal quality. Works of Art are the only permanent sign that man has existed. What legal genius to bring Law against Order!

The society for which Mr. Sumner is agent, I am told, was founded to protect the public from corruption. When asked *what public?* its defenders spring to the rock on which America was founded: the cream-puff of sentimentality, and answer chivalrously "Our young girls." So the mind of the young girl rules this country? In it rests the safety, progress and lustre of a nation. One might have guessed it. . . . but—why is she given such representatives? I recall a photograph of the United States Senators, a galaxy of noble manhood that could only have been assembled from far-flung country stores where it had spat and gossiped and stolen prunes.

The present case is rather ironical. We are being prosecuted for printing the thoughts in a young girl's mind . . . her thoughts and actions and the meditations which they produced in the mind of the

301

sensitive Mr. Bloom. If the young girl corrupts, can she also be corrupted? Mr. Joyce's young girl is an innocent, simple, childish girl who tends children . . . she hasn't had the advantage of the dances, cabarets, motor trips open to the young girls of this more pure and free country.

If there is anything I really fear it is the mind of the young girl.

I do not understand Obscenity; I have never studied it nor had it, but I know that it must be a terrible and peculiar menace to the United States. I know that there is an expensive department maintained in Washington with a chief and fifty assistants to prevent its spread—and in and for New York we have the Sumner vigilanti.

To a mind somewhat used to life Mr. Joyce's chapter seems to be a record of the simplest, most unpreventable, most unfocused sex thoughts possible in a rightly-constructed, unashamed human being. Mr. Joyce is not teaching early Egyptian perversions nor inventing new ones. Girls lean back everywhere, showing lace and silk stockings; wear low-cut sleeveless gowns, breathless bathing suits; men think thoughts and have emotions about these things everywhere— seldom as delicately and imaginatively as Mr. Bloom—and no one is corrupted. Can merely reading about the thoughts he thinks corrupt a man when his thoughts do not? All power to the artist, but this is not his function.

It was the poet, the artist, who discovered love, created the lover, made sex everything that it is beyond a function. It is the Mr. Sumners who have made it an obscenity. It is a little too obvious to discuss the inevitable result of damming up a force as unholy and terrific as the reproductive force with nothing more powerful than silence, black looks, and censure.

"Our young girls" grow up conscious of being possessed, as by a devil, with some urge which they are told is shameful, dangerous and obscene. They try to be "pure" with no other incantations than a few "obstetric mutterings."

Mr. Sumner seems a decent enough chap . . . serious and colorless and worn as if he had spent his life resenting the emotions. A 100 per cent. American who believes that denial, resentment and silence about all things pertaining to sex produce uprightness.

Only in a nation ignorant of the power of Art . . . insensitive and unambitious to the need and appreciation of Art . . . could such habit of mind obtain. Art is the only thing that produces life, extends life—I am speaking beyond physically or mentally. A people

302

without the experience of the Art influence can bring forth nothing but a humanity that bears the stamp of a loveless race. Facsimile women and stereotyped men—a humanity without distinction or design, indicating no more the creative touch than if they were assembled parts.

A beautiful Russian woman said to me recently, "How dangerous and horrible to fall in love with an American man! One could never tell which one it was—they are all the same."

There are still those people who are not outraged by the mention of natural facts who will ask "what is the necessity to discuss them?" But that is not a question to ask about a work of Art. The only question relevant at all to *Ulysses* is—Is it a work of Art? The men best capable of judging have pronounced it a work of the first rank. Anyone with a brain would hesitate to question the necessity in an artist to create, or his ability to choose the right subject matter. Anyone who has read *Exiles*, *The Portrait*, and *Ulysses* from the beginning, could not rush in with talk of obscenity. No man has been more crucified on his sensibilities than James Joyce.

I tried to prepare the public for the coming debate by writing an article on The Judgment of the Masters. I announced in advance that I would disagree with practically everything that would be said in court, both by the prosecution and by the defense:

I do not admit that the issue is debatable.

I state clearly that the (quite unnecessary) defense of beauty is the only issue involved.

James Joyce has never written anything, and will never be able to write anything, that is not beautiful. *So that we come to the question of beauty in the Art sense,*—that is, to the science of aesthetics, the touchstone which establishes whether any given piece of writing, painting, music, sculpture, is a work of Art.

You will say this brings us to an impasse; that we now arrive at that point where two autocracies of opinion can be established—one which says "This is Art" and the other which says "It is not." And you will tell me that one is quite as likely to be right as the other,—and that therefore every man is thrown back upon his personal taste as a criterion, etc.

I answer: Autocracy? It is entirely a matter of autocracy of opinion. And the autocracy that matters is the perception of the great artists themselves,—the judgment of the masters.

To meet the public's age-old argument "But great artists often disagree among themselves, therefore who are the masters that are to judge?" I quoted passages from a book by Dr. Ananda Coomaraswamy's Dance of Siva *which had just been published by the Sunwise Turn Bookshop. The italics were mine:*

". . . Different artists are inspired by different objects; what is attractive and stimulating to one is depressing and unattractive to another, and the choice also varies from race to race and epoch to epoch. As to the appreciation of such works, it is the same; for men in general admire only such works as by education or temperament they are predisposed to admire. *To enter into the spirit of an unfamiliar art demands a greater effort than most are willing to make. . . . There are many who never yet felt the beauty of Egyptian sculpture or Chinese or Indian painting or music. That they have the hardihood to deny their beauty, however, proves nothing.*

"Beauty can never thus be measured, for it does not exist apart from the artist himself, and the rasika (the true critic) *who enters into his experience.*

"The true critic perceives the beauty of which the artist has exhibited the signs. It is not necessary that the critic should appreciate the artist's meaning—every work of art is a *kamadhenu* yielding many meanings—for he knows without reasoning whether or not the work is beautiful, before the mind begins to question what it is 'about.' *Hindu writers say that the capacity to feel beauty (to taste rasa) cannot be acquired by study, but is the reward of merit gained in a past life; for many good men and would-be historians of art have never perceived it.* The poet is born, not made; but so also is the rasika, whose genius differs in degree, not in kind, from that of the original artist. . . .

"The critic, as soon as he becomes an exponent, has to prove his case; and he cannot do this by any process of argument, but only by creating a new work of art, the criticism. His audience, catching the gleam at second hand—but still the same gleam, for there is only one—*has then the opportunity to approach the original work a second time, more reverently."*

Harriet Monroe, of "Poetry," wanted to help:

Sumner Versus James Joyce
HARRIET MONROE

I WANT to send a word of cheer for your courage in the fight against the Society for the Prevention of Vice. My father was a lawyer, and his blood in me longs to carry the battle to the Supreme Court of the United States, in order to find out whether the Constitution permits the assumption of a self-appointed group of citizens, of a restriction of the freedom of the press which only the state, through proper legal channels, should have any right even to attempt. I wish you a triumphant escape out of their clutches.

Of course we lost our case. I have recorded certain details of the trial in My Thirty Years' War *(pages 218-226), and I gave others in in the magazine.*

"Ulysses" in Court
MARGARET ANDERSON

THE trial of the *Little Review* for printing a masterpiece is now over—lost, of course, but if any one thought there was a chance of our winning . . . in the United States of America. . . .

It is the only farce I ever participated in with any pleasure. I am not convivial, and I am usually bored or outraged by the state of farce to which unfarcical matters must descend. This time I had resolved to watch the proceedings with the charming idea of extracting some interest out of the fact that things proceed as one knows they will proceed. There is no possible interest in this fact, but perhaps one can be enlivened by speculating as to whether they will swerve the fraction of an inch from their predestined stupidity.

No, this cannot engage my interest: I have already lived through the stupidity. So how shall I face an hour in a court room, before three judges who do not know the difference between James Joyce and obscene postal cards, without having hysterics, or without trying to convince them that the words "literature" and "obscenity" can not be used in conjunction any more than the words "science" and "immorality" can. With what shall I fill my mind during this hour of redundant human drama? Ah—I shall make an effort to keep entirely silent, and since I have never under attack achieved this simple feat, perhaps my mind can become intrigued with the accomplishment of it.

It is a good idea. There are certain civilized people who proceed entirely upon the principle that to protect one's self from attack is the only course of action open to a decent and developed human being. My brain accepts this philosophy, but I never act upon it—

305

any more than Ezra Pound does. I am one of those who feels some obscure need to have all people think with some intelligence upon some subjects. . . .

But I am determined, during this unnecessary hour in court, to adopt the philosophy of self-preservation. I will protect my sensibilities and my brain cells by being unhearing and untalkative.

The court opens. Every one stands up as the three judges enter. Why must I stand up as a tribute to three men who wouldn't understand my simplest remark? (But this is reasoning, and I am determined to be vacuous.)

Our attorney, Mr. John Quinn, begins pertinently by telling who James Joyce is, what books he has written, and what are his distinguished claims as a man of letters. The three judges quite courteously but with a bewildered impatience inform him that they can't see what bearing those facts have on the subject—they "don't care who James Joyce is or whether he has written the finest books in the world"; their only function is to decide whether certain passages of *Ulysses* (incidentally the only passages they can understand) violate the statute.— (Is this a commentary on *Ulysses* or on the minds of the judges?) But I must not dream of asking such a question. My function is silence. Still, there is that rather fundamental matter of *who is the author?* Since *Art is the person—!* But this is a simplicity of logic —they would think I had gone mad.

Mr. Quinn calls literary "experts" to the stand to testify that *Ulysses* in their opinion would not corrupt our readers. The opinions of experts is regarded as quite unnecessary, since they know only about literature but not about law: *Ulysses* has suddenly become a matter of law rather than of literature—I grow confused again; but I am informed that the judges are being especially tolerant to admit witnesses at all—that such is not the custom in the special sessions court. . . .

Mr. John Cowper Powys testifies that *Ulysses* is too obscure and philosophical a work to be in any sense corrupting. (I wonder, as Mr. Powys takes the stand, whether his look and talk convey to the court that his mind is in the habit of functioning in regions where theirs could not penetrate: and I imagine the judges saying: "This man obviously knows much more about the matter than we do—the case is dismissed." Of course I have no historical basis for expecting such a thing. I believe it has never happened. . . .

Mr. Philip Moeller is the next witness to testify for the *Little*

Review, and in attempting to answer the judges' questions with intelligence he asks if he may use technical terminology. Permission being given he explains quite simply that the objectionable chapter is an unveiling of the subconscious mind, in the Freudian manner, and that he saw no possibility of these revelations being aphrodisiac in their influence. The court gasps, and one of the judges calls out, "Here, here, you might as well talk Russian. Speak plain English if you want us to understand what you're saying." Then they ask Mr. Moeller what he thinks would be the effect of the objectionable chapter in the mind of the average reader. Mr. Moeller answers: "I think it would mystify him." "Yes, but what would be the effect?" (I seem to be drifting into unconsciousness. *Question*—What is the effect of that which mystifies? *Answer*—Mystification. But no one looks either dazed or humourous, so I decide that they regard the proceedings as perfectly sensible.)

Other witnesses (among them the publishers of the *Dial,* who valiantly appeared at both hearings) are waived on the consideration of their testimony being the same as already given. Mr. Quinn then talks for thirty minutes on the merits of James Joyce's work in terms the court can understand: "Might be called futurist literature"; "neither written for nor read by school girls"; "disgusting in portions, perhaps, but no more so than Swift, Rabelais, Shakespeare, the Bible"; "inciting to anger or repulsion but not to lascivious acts"; and as a final bit of suave psychology (nauseating and diabolical), aimed at that dim stirring of human intelligence which for an instant lights up the features of the three judges—"I myself do not understand 'Ulysses'—I think Joyce has carried his method too far in this experiment" . . .

"Yes," groans the most bewildered of the three, "it sounds to me like the ravings of a disordered mind—I can't see why any one would want to publish it."

("Let me tell you why"—I almost leap from my chair. "Since I am the publisher it may be apropos for me to tell you why I have wanted to publish it more than anything else that has ever been offered to me. Let me tell you *why* I regard it as the prose masterpiece of my generation. Let me tell you what it's about and why it was written and for whom it was written and why you don't understand it and why it is just as well that you don't and why you have no right to pit the dullness of your brains against the fineness of mine" . . .)

(I suddenly feel as though I had been run over by a subway train. My distinguished co-publisher is pounding me violently in the ribs: "Don't try to talk; don't put yourself into their hands"—with that look of being untouched by the surrounding stupidities which sends me into paroxysms. I smile vacuously at the court.)

Mr. Quinn establishes, apparently to the entire satisfaction of the judges, that the offending passages of "Ulysses" will revolt but not contaminate. But their sanction of this point seems to leave them vaguely unsatisfied and they state, with a hesitation that is rather charming, that they feel impelled to impose the minimum fine of $100 and thus to encourage the Society for the Prevention of Vice.

This decision establishes us as criminals and we are led to an adjoining building where another bewildered official takes our fingerprints! ! ! *

The London Times *was indulgent, though in comparing Joyce with "high examples" like Hardy, it said that he failed to compare "simply because of the comparative poverty of his mind":*

The World Moves

(From the London Times)

In some such fashion as this do we seek to define the element which distinguishes the work of several young writers, among whom Mr. James Joyce is the most notable, from that of their predecessors. It attempts to come closer to life, and to preserve more sincerely and exactly what interests and moves them by discarding most of the conventions which are commonly observed by the novelists. Let us record the atoms as they fall upon the mind in the order in which they fall, let us trace the pattern, however disconnected and incoherent in appearance, which each sight or incident scores upon the consciousness. Let us not take it for granted that life exists more in what is commonly thought big than in what is commonly thought small. Any one who has read *The Portrait of the Artist as a Young Man* or what promises to be a far more interesting work, *Ulysses,* now appearing in the *Little Review,* will have hazarded some theory

* In this welter of crime and lechery, both Mr. Sumner and the judges deserve our thanks for one thing: our appearance seemed to leave them without any doubts as to our personal purity. (Some of my "friends" have considered me both insane and obscene for publishing Mr. Joyce). When in court the moment arrived for the "obscene" passages to be read aloud, one of the judges refused, saying that he was sure I didn't know the significance of what I had published.

of this nature as to Mr. Joyce's intention. On our part it is hazarded rather than affirmed; but whatever the exact intention there can be no question but that it is of the utmost sincerity and that the result, difficult or unpleasant as we may judge it, is undeniably distinct. In contrast to those whom we have called materialists Mr. Joyce is spiritual; concerned at all costs to reveal the flickerings of that innermost flame which flashes its myriad messages through the brain, he disregards with complete courage whatever seems to him adventitious, though it be probability or coherence or any other of the handrails to which we cling for support when we set our imaginations free. Faced, as in the Cemetery scene, by so much that, in its restless scintillations, in its irrelevance, its flashes of deep significance succeeded by incoherent inanities, seems to be life itself, we have to fumble rather awkwardly if we want to say what else we wish; and for what reason a work of such originality yet fails to compare, for we must take high examples, with *Youth* or *Jude the Obscure*. It fails, one might say simply, because of the comparative poverty of the writer's mind. But it is possible to press a little further and wonder whether we may not refer our sense of being in a bright and yet somehow strictly confined apartment rather than at large beneath the sky to some limitation imposed by the method as well as by the mind. Is it due to the method that we feel neither jovial nor magnanimous, but centered in a self which in spite of its tremor of susceptibility never reaches out or embraces or comprehends what is outside and beyond? Does the emphasis laid perhaps didactically upon indecency contribute to this effect of the angular and isolated? Or is it merely that in any effort of such courage the faults as well as the virtues are left naked to the view? In any case we need not attribute too much importance to the method. Any method is right, every method is right, that expresses what we wish to express. This one has the merit of giving closer shape to what we were prepared to call life itself; did not the reading of *Ulysses* suggest how much of life is excluded and ignored, and did it not come with a shock to open *Tristram Shandy* and even *Pendennis,* and be by them convinced that there are other aspects of life, and larger ones into the bargain?

In 1933, Ulysses *in book form came to trial in New York before Judge John M. Woolsey (United States District Court, Southern District of New York) who rendered his now famous decision lifting the ban on* Ulysses *on December 6, 1933.*

Among other things, Judge Woolsey said:

"But in *Ulysses,* in spite of its unusual frankness, I do not detect anywhere the leer of the sensualist. I hold, therefore, that it is not pornographic. . . .

"It is because Joyce has been loyal to his technique and has not funked its necessary implications, but has honestly attempted to tell fully what his characters think about, that he has been the subject of so many attacks and that his purpose has been so often misunderstood and misrepresented. For his attempt sincerely and honestly to realize his objective has required him incidentally to use certain words which are generally considered dirty words and has led at times to what many think is a too poignant preoccupation with sex in the thoughts of his characters.

"The words which are criticized as dirty are old Saxon words known to almost all men and, I venture, to many women, and are such words as would be naturally and habitually used, I believe, by the types of folk whose life, physical and mental, Joyce is seeking to describe. In respect of the recurrent emergence of the theme of sex in the minds of his characters, it must always be remembered that his locale was Celtic and his season Spring. . . .

"I am quite aware that owing to some of its scenes, *Ulysses* is rather a strong draught to ask some sensitive, though normal, persons to take. But my considered opinion, after long reflection, is that whilst in many places the effect of *Ulysses* on the reader undoubtedly is somewhat emetic, nowhere does it tend to be aphrodisiac."

We had often been asked how we ever found a printer in New York willing to print Ulysses *for us. We answered:*

We found a Serbian printer, a man of education, temperament, and fantastic business methods. He and his two daughters were the shop. His mother had been the poet-laureate of Serbia and he "knew the beautiful words." He did not ask to be freed from liability in case of trouble with the post office. *Ulysses* was discussed in the shop with easy understanding and acute pride. Sometimes we were asked in troubled English about certain words. "Ah yes, I know, in Serbia those words are good for the people but in America it is not good, the people are not brave about words, they are not healthy about words; in America you go in prison."

After the trial our troubles did not end. We lost our printer—not through any moral scruples but, as he explained:

Dear Miss Anderson:

Tomorrow will be a week that I received copy with money in advance as agreed, and was not able to start and will not be able before next week. It is no use Miss Anderson to be so nervous. You want always first-class work and I cannot make. Do you not know that we had war? Workingman is now king. If you would pay me three thousand dollors I will not make good work. This is other times. I wrote you about this many times and will not repeat any more, but wish to say if you pay all in advance and two, three hundred per cent more as now, you must not expect good work or on time. I want no responsibility.—*Popovitch.*

We were forced to publish at less and less regular intervals, but nothing mattered so long as we could still find art material. The following prose piece by Jane was to me more rewarding than most of what we found:

I Cannot Sleep

JANE HEAP

IT shoots up into the air   is it an enormous paper-knife or a quill . . . it is a priest in a flat hat   his dress stays stiff   his hands stiff to his sides   he skims in and out among the trapezes

the whole row of mountains is falling over . . . it has caught the sun and is squeezing the light out of it   the houses have all fallen off the slopes and are tumbled together in the gorge   the forests have slipped farther down and join in a V

many niagaras roar somewhere under the ground

now the rat is coming in through the back window   he will frighten my green shoes.

all the tombstones in the graveyard have become peppermint hearts with fortunes printed on them in pink

seven seagulls for supper . . . an eye just dropped out of a seagull and plopped up again when it struck the water   möwe

I didn't say I didn't like the man   I said he had hips like shoulder-blades   look at him from the back

that woman's hands scare me   I am glad I shall never have to be her lover   I know they leave her arms and crawl about over things in the night   lean faded spiders

A metal horse stands up from the earth on his hind legs and bites the stars out of the sky   there is a sound of broken glass falling through the air.

the Grail!   no it is a bouquet with paper-lace edges and tinfoil stem   a greenwhite breast with wisteria nipple lies in the lace . . . there is a light in the breast   the bouquet floats high in the air   it floats past a city of candles . . . on the mountain side   It is night and the light changes to silver-green   It floats higher out over the sea   it cannot be pursued   it floats through the emptiness of the moon

my heart is an Idiot   I write my name and way and pin it on him . . . if we should become separated   With my hands I take my brain and slowly uncrumple it   I smooth out every crease and wrinkle   there is nothing to press it out upon except abysses   it is a long job and wearing   surprising how big it is smoothed out like melted silk   I will crumple it up again firmly and put it back after I have left it this way for a long time shining and clean   The years breed pain when one is accomplice with an Idiot

Autumn, 1921. The Little Review *had now become a quarterly. We published a Brancusi number, with many photographic plates.*

Brancusi

EZRA POUND

"I CARVE a thesis in logic of the eternal beauty," writes Remy de Gourmont in his "Sonnets à l'Amazone." A man hurls himself toward the infinite and the works of art are his vestiges, his trace in the manifest.

It is perhaps no more impossible to give a vague idea of Brancusi's sculpture in words than to give it in photographs, but it is equally impossible to give an exact sculptural idea in either words or photography. T. J. Everets has made the best summary of our contemporary aesthetics that I know, in his sentence, "A work of art has in it no idea which is separable from the form." I believe this conviction can be found in earlier vorticist explanations, and in a world where so few people have yet dissociated form from representation, one may, or at least I may as well approach Brancusi via the formulations by Gaudier-Brzeska, or by myself in my study of Gaudier:

"Sculptural feeling is the appreciation of masses in relation."
"Sculptural ability is the defining of these masses by planes."

"Every concept, every emotion presents itself to the vivid consciousness in some primary form. It belongs to the art of that form."

I don't mean to imply that vorticist formulæ will "satisfy" Brancusi, or that any formula need ever satisfy any artist, simply the formulæ give me certain axes (plural of *axis,* not of *ax)* for discrimination.

I have found, to date, nothing in vorticist formulæ which contradicts the work of Brancusi, the formulæ left every man fairly free. Gaudier had long since revolted from the Rodin-Maillol mixture; no one who understood Gaudier was fooled by the cheap Viennese Michaelangelism and rhetoric of Mestrovic. One understood that "Works of art attract by a resembling unlikeness"; that "The beauty of form in the still stone can not be the same beauty of form as that in the living animal." One even understood that, as in Gaudier's brown stone dancer, the pure or unadulterated motifs of the circle and triangle have a right to build up their own fugue or sonata in form; as a theme in music has its right to express itself.

No critic has a right to pretend that he fully understands any artist; least of all do I pretend, in this note, to understand Brancusi (after a few weeks' acquaintance) even as well as I understood Gaudier (after several years' friendship); anything I say here effaces anything I may have said before on the subject, and anything I say the week after next effaces what I say here—a pale reflection of Brancusi's general wish that people would wait until he has finished (i. e., in the cemetery) before they talk aesthetics with or about him.

At best one could but clear away a few grosser misconceptions. Gaudier had discriminated against beefy statues, he had given us a very definite appreciation of stone as stone; he had taught us to feel that the beauty of sculpture is inseparable from its material and that it inheres in the material. Brancusi was giving up the facile success of representative sculpture about the time Gaudier was giving up his baby-bottle; in many ways his difference from Gaudier is a difference merely of degree, he has had time to make statues where Gaudier had time only to make sketches; Gaudier had purged himself of every kind of rhetoric he had noticed; Brancusi has detected more kinds of rhetoric and continued the process of purgation.

When verbally intelligible he is quite definite in the statement that whatever else art is it is not *"crise des nerfs";* that beauty is not grimaces and fortuitous gestures; that starting with an ideal of form one arrives at a mathematical exactitude of proportion, but *not by* mathematics.

Above all he is a man in love with perfection. Dante believed in the "melody which most in-centres the soul"; in the preface to my Guido I have tried to express the idea of an absolute rhythm, or the possibility of it. Perhaps every artist at one time or another believes in a sort of elixir or philosopher's stone produced by the sheer perfection of his art; by the alchemical sublimation of the medium; the elimination of accidentals and imperfections.

Where Gaudier had developed a sort of form-fugue or form-sonata by a combination of forms, Brancusi has set out on the maddeningly more difficult exploration toward getting all the forms into one form; this is as long as any Buddhist's contemplation of the universe or as any mediæval saint's contemplation of the divine love,—as long and even as paradoxical as the final remarks in the Divina Commedia. It is a search easily begun, and wholly unending, and the vestiges are let us say Brancusi's "Bird," and there is perhaps six months' work and twenty years' knowledge between one model of the erect bird and another, though they appear identical in photography. Therein consisting the difference between sculpture and sketches. Plate No. 5 shows what looks like an egg; I give more photos of the bust than of this egg because in the photos the egg comes to nothing; in Plate No. 12 there is at the base of the chimaera an egg with a plane and a groove cut into it, an egg having infantile rotundities and repose.

I don't know by what metaphorical periphrase I am to convey the relation of these ovoids to Brancusi's other sculpture. As an interim label, one might consider them as master-keys to the world of form—not "his" world of form, but as much as he has found of "the" world of form. They contain or imply, or should, the triangle and the circle.

Or putting it another way, every one of the thousand angles of approach to a statue ought to be interesting, it ought to have a life (Brancusi might perhaps permit me to say a "divine" life) of its own. "Any prentice" can supposedly make a statute that will catch the eye and be interesting from *some* angle. This last statement is not strictly true, the present condition of sculptural sense leaving us with a vastly lower level both of prentices and "great sculptors";

but even the strictest worshipper of bad art will admit that it is infinitely easier to make a statue which can please from *one* side than to make one which gives satisfaction from no matter what angle of vision.

It is also conceivably more difficult to give this formal-satisfaction by a single mass, or let us say to sustain the formal-interest by a single mass, than to excite transient visual interests by more monumental and melodramatic combinations.

Brancusi's revolt against the rhetorical and the kolossal has carried him into revolt against the monumental, or at least what appears to be, for the instant, a revolt against one sort of solidity. The research for the aerial has produced his bird which stands unsupported upon its diminished base (the best of jade carvers and netsuke makers produce tiny objects which also maintain themselves on extremely minute foundations). If I say that Brancusi's ideal form should be equally interesting from all angles, this does not quite imply that one should stand the ideal temple on its head, but it probably implies a discontent with any combination of proportions which can't be conceived as beautiful even if, in the case of a temple, some earth-quake should stand it up intact and endways or turned-turtle. Here I think the concept differs from Gaudier's, as indubitably the metaphysic of Brancusi is outside and unrelated to vorticist manners of thinking.

The great black-stone egyptian patera in the British museum is perhaps more formally interesting than the statues of Memnon.

In the case of the ovoid, I take it Brancusi is meditating upon pure form free from all terrestrial gravitation; form as free in its own life as the form of the analytic geometers; and the measure of his success in this experiment (unfinished and probably unfinishable) is that from some angles at least the ovoid does come to life and appear ready to levitate. (Or this is perhaps merely a fortuitous anecdote, like any other expression.)

Crystal-gazing?? No. Admitting the possibility of self-hypnosis by means of highly polished brass surfaces, the polish, from the sculptural point of view, results merely from a desire for greater precision of the form, it is also a transient glory. But the contemplation of form or of formal-beauty leading into the infinite must be dissociated from the dazzle of crystal; there is a sort of relation, but there is the more important divergence; with the crystal it is a hypnosis, or a contemplative fixation of thought, or an excitement of the "sub-conscious" or unconscious (whatever the devil they may be), and with the ideal form in marble it is an approach to the infinite *by form,* by precisely the highest possible degree of consciousness of formal perfection; as free of accident as any of the philosophical demands of a "Paradiso" can make it.

This is not a suggestion that all sculpture should end in the making of abstract ovoids; indeed no one but a genius wholly centred in his art, and more or less "oriental," could endure the strain of such effort.

But if we are ever to have a bearable sculpture or architecture it might be well for young sculptors to start with some such effort at perfection, rather than with the idea of a new Laocoon, or a "Triumph of Labour over Commerce." (This suggestion is mine, and I hope it will never fall under the eye of Brancusi). But then Brancusi can spend most of his time in his own studio, surrounded by the calm of his own creations, whereas the author of this imperfect exposure is compelled to move about in a world full of junk-shops, a world full of more than idiotic ornamentations, a world where pictures are made for museums, where no man has a front-door that he can bear to look at, let alone one he can contemplate with reasonable pleasure, where the average house is each year made more hideous, and where the sense of form which ought to be as general as the sense of refreshment after a bath, or the pleasure of liquid in time of drouth or any other clear animal pleasure, is the rare possession of an "intellectual" (heaven help us) "aristocracy."

"Gardening with Brains"
JH

SCENE: *"The Little Review" in summer quarters: tiny house with large garden by the sea.*

CHARACTERS: *M. C. A. and jh. jh. working in garden. M. C. A. comes down the lawn dressed in black silk Annette Kellerman, Limited; large white coral beads about neck, bracelets, short hair elaborately trained about elaborately indifferent head.*

jh. Why don't you ever come down and have a look at the garden?

M. C. A. I don't know anything about such things— (*approaches as if entering a ball room*).—What are these?

jh. Tomatoes.

M. C. A. And these?

316

jh. Potatoes.

M. C. A. I don't see any.

jh. They grow under the ground.

M. C. A. How exasperating!

       (neurotic silence)

I don't see how you can keep your interest if everything grows under the ground.

jh. Everything doesn't. Tomatoes grow on top, potatoes under.

M. C. A. Aren't you smart to know such things?

jh. I have to—What would I do if I ever got the seeds mixed and dug into a t-o-m-a-t-o!!!

M. C. A. (turning to go, with a sweeping gesture)—Is there anything so charming as a garden by the sea!

jh. (imitating M. C. A.'s manner)—Ah! but the sea-weeds!!

I have never had any art enthusiasm for Gertrude Stein (except for her "Alice B. Toklas" and her story of the Second World War). I therefore include the following as typical of why her work didn't interest me. We also printed an article about her by Sherwood Anderson, one of her enthusiastic interpreters. If she had only achieved what her interpreters credit her with, I would have been interested in her own writing.

B. B. or the Birthplace of Bonnes

GERTRUDE STEIN

CAN anybody tell by looking which was the towel used for cooking.

 B. B. or the birthplace of bonnes.

 Jennie Poole had a story to tell. She told the story very well. She said that she had loaned her handkerchief to a man like a woman. Give me your handkerchief Poole he said. She gave it to him and she never saw it again.

 Double pink.

 Germaine came from Vannes. And where did Jenny come from. Sinny came from Chatillon, and where then did the saint say that she was going away. She was going away to Tourtegay.

 How many homes have we to visit the birthplace of

 Jeanne Sinny Poole.

 Margot Veraker Fairacre.

 Germaine.

 Saint Grille.

And the center not the center.
I do not know fairies.
I do not like water.
I do not remember quarries.
I do not care for grass.
I have not seen the sea.

The sea is water colour. I can make that joke again. Jeanne Poole knows the difference between warm water and coloured water. She had told us about her brother. He fell off the gun. Gun is the name of cannon. He fell off a cannon and was seriously wounded. He is now a cabinet maker. In recounting the glories of France she never forgets the father of her child. Her child is a girl I can not give a description of her character. I have been puzzled she said, I have been puzzled as to her character. I know now. She is a sovereign. This is not what was said. She had a brother killed not in the war.

She said to me Come to Brittany. I said I did not like Brittany. She said have you ever been there. I said I have met many people who have been there. And what do they say. They say it is a very pretty country, you can see it only in one day.

We then went together.

Godiva. Godiva is fair. She has two places instead of hair. And she moves, nicely.

I am describing Brittany to-day.

To-day there are a great many Bretons who take part in fishing hunting in harvesting, in manufacturing, and in auditing. A great many of them are in hospital. And a great many of them love women children ducks and ribbon. They nourish restriction.

We said to Sinny, Can you clean bronze. She said. I live beside quarries. But there is a lake too. Yes there is a lake and supper. We have coffee for supper. My mother makes the fire. And what does your father do. My father grows camelias. Not in Brittany. Why certainly in Brittany it is very warm in Brittany. Warm enough to learn knitting. If you have religion. If you have a wound and religion. If you have lost your hand and there are women, if you are a woman and have been teaching, you teach knitting you teach knitting to the children.

In words of pleasure resulting from a union of activity with anticipation and discernment concerning losses a great many people can be rougher.

Say policeman your ears are frozen said the driver. You go to hell was an answer.

Reading and butter there is more than one saying. Anybody can buy sugar. Any money can buy sugar.

In this country there are a great many disclosures. Let us take a calf. To breed a calf takes the feed for a cow. To wean a calf takes a stall. To learn that calf is killed is too disagreeable. Let us give it honey. Veal is all, all sunny.

Now to continue the narrative.

We have three causes for vindication. The first is France. The second is liberty and third is observation. You do observe that there is a reason.

B. B. is indicated.

When next we see the south we will not expect anybody to deny that birds fly north. Birds fly south sometime, and north all together.

When this you see remember your sisters in Brittany. A great many of them have no sisters with them. Sisters can frequently come from the West. We have guessed that others are equally caressed.

Sinny said of her brothers. I have three brothers. One is in the railroad, the other is a restaurant keeper and the third is a cabinet maker. And as to the father of my child he is a butcher. He was apprenticed to a butcher and he married the butcher's daughter.

In the meantime it is not difficult to realise that a woman who has borne eleven children can easily have a hernia. And her grand-child. He inherits it. From his mother.

Would you be equally satisfied with the queen.

Yes indeed she would. Yes very much indeed she would.

Vacaville is a place for cows. Vacaville rhymes with whip poor will.

Vacaville is a land of cows. Whip poor will is a bird. I recognize a third a third a third place to see.

When we went visiting we forgot about halos. The saint, if you take a photograph of a saint under a tree she has a halo. She said one must reinforce one's self. One must try to be prepared. One must really speak. One should speak to oneself. But in the presence of others. One is not in their presence when one speaks to oneself. Yes but if one does recognize the other. Then one must be content to take wages.

In this way she was not satisfied.

The weather was very warm, there was very little wind and no rain.

I do not neglect my dishes.

And in Paris.

I found them.

Now for a conversation.

Margot said to Sinny I do not cause terror. And as for me what can I do with my brother. He is too young.

Germaine why does Germaine toil.

Conversation to-day. Can we see meat. We prefer coffee. And how many sisters do you refuse to see. We do not refuse to see any sisters but there is one that we prefer not to visit and there is another one that we find disagreeable. And for the rest. For the rest there are a great many. Egyptians Scandinavians and Portugese, the Bretons are more regular than these. They can spread their anger about most successfully. But they are not angry. To be sure they are not.

How can you copy a letter. Read tenderly about how the saint leaving suddenly did not receive her photograph.

I often think that the Queen meant what she said when she said that they had not been so disrespectful no not for two hundred years.

How can you steal a pin. Why very easily with a hammer. I do not know how stupidity is exercised. Please me to see Please me to see Please me to see Indy.

Please me by not seeing a neglected case. How can you neglect a case. Suppose a mother suddenly sings. Supposing a wife sleeps. Supposing a brother has means. And let us suppose that a husband is cured. Do you mean by that completely cured.

I think I mean by that that a husband is completely cured. Of what. Of that to-night.

I can treat any one like that.

But now to remember what Margot and Germaine and Sinny and the same one and the saint said about plays. They each one said they knew about handkerchiefs. They also believed in comforting them. I comfort them.

Let us have that conversation together. Let us mean to be tall and strong. And indeed can we carry a tree. Indeed a tree is planted and so are irons. Irons and hills and can you drink water. Explain to me why you drink. Indeed it is so satisfactory that nearly everybody hopes to pray. I pray too.

Can you see still.

Can you still see.

It did work. And what astonishes me is that it will work again.

Suppose we think a minute.

If it wants to come again will you be indignant. No but disquieted. You need not be disquieted. A great many people shine pleasantly.

In a ribbon.

In a ribbon there is red.

Red white and blue.

Can you know why green is so is so yellow.

In a ribbon for a ribbon there is a necklace.

Do not say you do like beads.

I like shells As bells.

Not as door bells.

If they had all been born they would have said in rubbing dirt we are certain to bring out some colour but the value may be lost. The value can never be lost to me.

I am a great believer in even coloured silks.

I am almost certain that Esther was born somewhere. And Germaine. Germaine was not foolish.

Do you consider Margot foolish.

I consider that she is foolish when she can not notice the distinction between cloudy and clean water.

Water rhymes with daughter.

And so I end.

Concerning Else von Freytag-Loringhoven

Lola Ridge, New York:

Are you hypnotized, or what, that you open the *Little Review* with such a retching assault upon Art ("The Cast-Iron Lover")?

F. E. R., Chicago:

How can you who have had the honour of printing Yeats open your pages to the work of the Baroness von Freytag-Loringhoven?

[It's a bit too easy and a little sentimental, isn't it, to ask such questions? Yeats was born an old master. Do you feel that you "understand" Yeats better than you do Else von Freytag? We are not limiting ourselves to the seven arts. No one has yet done much about the Art of Madness.—*jh.*]

The Art of Madness

I. By Evelyn Scott

Apropos of the discussion regarding "The Cast Iron Lover" by Else von Freytag-Loringhoven, I feel enthused by my impressions to the point of adding a comment.

As jh says, the psychology of the author referred to is that of a mad woman. I feel an intense, horrid, and even beautiful obliviousness to all but the dominating emotion. There exists the callousness of intellectual stupidity and there is what we see here, the callousness of emotional stupidity, that of the savage under the cataleptic influence of religious suggestion. It is only in a condition of disease or mania that one may enjoy an absolutely exalted state, that numbness of the sensibilities toward everything outside the single inspiration....

II. By jh.

As jh does *not* say . . . It wouldn't be the art of madness if it were merely an insanity such as Miss Scott describes.

In the case of Else von Freytag I am not talking of mania and disease, of numbed sensibilities . . . hers is a willed state. A woman of brains, of mad beauty and *elegantes wesen,* who has abandoned sanity: left it cold. She has recognized that if one has the guts and the constitution to abandon sanity one may at all times enjoy an exalted state. Madness is her chosen state of consciousness. It is this consciousness which she works to produce Art. The artist evoking his consciousness at high power on some piece of difficult work appears to have become callous and stupid or a wild man to the layman. Else von Freytag works unhampered by sanity.

III. By Evelyn Scott.

. . . I concede it to be true that in no effort in which self-consciousness of any sort persists is the will absolutely in abeyance, and the beginning of madness is rarely an absolute state. To express life in words is to juggle with the poison that lies in the very medium, for language was primarily an attempt to arrest experience and so enslave life and do it to death that man might no more fear it. The artist often courts the speech of the madman because he desires the emotion he has ensnared to escape the petrification of intellectualization, but there is a point at which the will weakens beneath the onrush of forces it has itself loosed. Amidst flashes of insight like

322

fire in the rain perception dims and is finally extinguished in the blindness of pure sensation. Else von Freytag-Loringhoven, in my opinion, has walked perilously near (if she has not passed over the edge) beyond which the vision of delirium melts into the blank self-enwrapped exaltation of trance. . . . I certainly believe that Else von Freytag-Loringhoven is powerless to condition the disorder she has evoked.

IV. By jh.

. . . When two such different minds meet there is not even the possibility of a common understanding of word values: word values come from personal values.

"Art to jh appears to be something too sacred for analysis" . . . I fear not sacred enough. I write more about Art than anyone in the country, wasting time and energy that might be put into my proper work as an artist. It is all too foolish. The Baroness von Freytag will think *us* feeble-minded.

. . . Miss Scott has jumped in and talked about the madness in the Art of von Freytag—not the Art in her Madness. I never thought of discussing those psychological pecularities in the artist which are beyond the reach of the will. Haven't those things been recognized and summed up even by the layman in "artists are born, not made?"

. . . When I speak of disease I mean disorder. When a person has created a state of consciousness which is madness and adjusts (designs and executes) every form and aspect of her life to fit this state, there is no disorder anywhere; there is therefore no disease.

. . . Miss Scott has information, knowledge and words. All that she says is true, but it does not make sense because it does not fit this discussion. Unless I had tried to begin my discussion far beyond the cause which may be pathological and the effect which is not . . . beyond the support of knowledge and evidence and academic definition . . . I should feel that I had offered an affront and an insult to Else von Freytag.

V. By Else von Freytag-Loringhoven.

jh understands me wonderfully—perfectly. . . .

Is it not necessary for emotions to come out—is it not necessary for emotional people to be like insane sometimes?—to be more sane and steady and stronger than others, weaker people, after that? Is it not wonderful to be able to control that then, that emotion, which otherwise would throttle you?—but take it by the neck and make

Art out of it? and be free?—that is, the *master?* Only *such things* —done *that* way, are Art! It is Goethe's art. *He knew that too!*—he too had to do it. "Nur wer die Sehnsucht kennt—weiss was ich leide" . . . That is just as insane as my "Cast-Iron Lover."

Another thing: haven't all high-cultured emotional people (as even was a public custom—in old Greece, in the feast of Dionysus) to be insane for a time—like steam nozzle on teakettle? *Because Americans do not need that—they should not give costume balls!* They do not know what it is for—the *reason* for them—to let yourself go—! Europeans like myself cannot understand why they put on these costumes (they are silly enough—without inner sense); but *why* they do it anyway and stay up all night and move around when they are not different as if they were in their beds—so—why not rather go to bed—when there is no gayety to be relieved, or insanity, or anything to be let go—let loose! . . .

VI. By Evelyn Scott

. . . I cannot believe, after reading this semi-intelligent prose, that the mental processes of the Baroness ever achieve that completion of their cycle which results in thought. She—alas—appears to suffer from temperamental disabilities. She is far, far too inspired to think.

"Consciousness," jh continues, "does not mean the sum of un-governable dispersed faculties. Consciousness means complete be-ing." In one place jh refers to consciousness as "complete being," whereas in a previous paragraph she bars from a consideration of consciousness these psychological peculiarities which lie beyond the reach of the will. How can that be complete from which there is so much arbitrarily excluded? I wonder that jh, who only admits to that part of the mechanism of consciousness which is under the con-trol of the will, has persuaded herself to print Mr. Joyce's *Ulysses* which reveals so wonderfully the irresponsibility of subjective life.

jh tells us that madness is not disease. Disease is a deflection from the normal order of practical survival and in this category is undoubtedly madness. I am quite willing where possible, however, to accept revelations from a diseased mind. A person with a work-able imagination may call a man a thief in a profoundly compli-mentary sense, so when I discover disease in the Baroness it is not, from the artistic standpoint, an assertion of unqualified disfavor. "There can be no legitimate standard for valuing the order of sanity higher than the order of madness, except a moral one," jh declares, forgetting that even art has its necessities. There are, after all, practical values for the artist as for everyone else, and surely his primary need is for the condition, within and without, which will allow him to create. However luridly intense the vision of immanent madness, the culmination of insanity is the death of creation. That will which to jh includes everything in the reproductive act of the artist, disintegrates, and even if this were not true it is impossible to pass on to others the intimacies of disorder for which no medium exists.

"If one has the power to evoke he has more power than the evoked." jh gives us this dictum, but in what manner is this a contradiction of my statement that evocation implies in him who commands not an absolute but a limited ascendance?

"But if the artist wishes to show other men he has had this experience,—first he wills: intends unconditionally; then he must not choose with his mind but with his consciousness the subject matter which will best communicate his experience; and then by deliberate and intense activity of his consciousness he must produce the forms, colors, rhythm of his invention." He chooses, she says, not with his mind but with his consciousness. Is not this suggestion of faculties involved, which lie beyond the domain of orderable intelligence, a confession that jh, too, believes that ungovernable elements give the quality to inspiration? The power of willed selection only inheres in mind. In beginning her discussion she eliminates all that lies outside of mind and in this latter paragraph the order of her argument is inverted.

". . . the will is so powerful that it creates the being—the state of consciousness it desires." But how, jh? Is she not delving again into the realm of the subconsciousness which she voted to ignore? Surely this profound desire which stirs the darkness brings forth shapes which reflect those psychological peculiarities of the artist that our critic refuses to consider.

jh is in a position of vantage as she can exercise the editorial prerogative of the last word. She can refuse to publish my retort, but once admitting me to her pages she can not, I should think, rule out my statements simply because they do not meet with her approval.—

VII. By jh.

I am glad to allow Miss Scott the last word. I withdraw quietly. I feel that I have been permitted a glimpse of the gentle mystic soul of an adding-machine.

Aesthetic Meditations
GUILLAUME APOLLINAIRE

In the spring of 1922 we received from France a work that was considered in Europe a high-water mark of critical writing—Guillaume Apollinaire's Aesthetic Meditations on Painting. *The First Series contained the author's credo; the Second Series his critical appraisals of Picasso, Braque, Metzinger, Gleizes, Juan Gris, Marie Laurencin, Léger, Picabia, Duchamps, Duchamps-Villon.*

Today, as in 1922, I find in this work the two extremes that characterize so much modern writing. One produces admiration; the other impatience, boredom, revolt.

Apollinaire's first sentence, to me, falls within the latter category. I am bored by its senselessness: "The plastic virtues: purity, unity and truth hold nature downed beneath their feet."

He continues more interestingly:

"In vain the rainbow is bent, the seasons vibrate, the crowds rush on to death, science undoes and remakes that which already exists, whole worlds withdraw forever from our conception, our transitory images repeat themselves or revive their unconsciousness, and the colours, odours, sounds which follow astonish us,—then disappear from nature."

The next portion is a combination of the two extremes:

"This monster of beauty is not eternal.

"We know that our breath has had no beginning, and will have no end, but we conceive first of all the creation and the end of the world.

"Nevertheless, too many artists still adore plants, stones, the wave, or men.

"One quickly becomes accustomed to the bondage of the mysterious. And this servitude ends by creating soft leisure.

"One allows the labourer to dominate the universe, and gardeners have less respect for nature than the artists.

"It is time to be the masters. Good will does not insure victory.

"The mortal forms of love dance on this side of eternity, and the name of nature sums up their accursed discipline."

. . . the last sentence being the type of thing that nauseates me.

Since anyone who is interested can now read these Meditations *in book form, I shall amuse myself by rushing through them, choos-*

326

ing phrases that please me or elicit my admiration, irrespective of whether such random selection fully satisfies the reader.

All bodies are equal before the light ...

Each divinity creates after his own image: so too, the painters.

Today, as formerly, the aim of painting is still the pleasure of the eye, but the demand henceforward made upon the amateur is to find a pleasure other than the one which the spectacle of natural things could just as well provide.

Thus one travels toward an entirely new art, which, compared to painting as it has been looked upon before, shall be what music is to literature.

It will be the essence of painting, just as music is the essence of literature.

The amateur of music experiences, in listening to a concert, joy of a different order from the joy he feels in listening to natural sounds, like the murmur of a stream, the roar of a torrent, the whistling of the wind in a forest, or the harmonies of human language founded on reason and not on æsthetics.

In the same way, the new painters will provide their admirers with artistic sensations due solely to the harmony of odd lights.

Everyone knows Pliny's anecdote of Appelles and Protogenes. It demonstrates clearly the æsthetic pleasure resulting solely from this odd combination of which I have spoken.

Appelles landed one day on the Isle of Rhodes to see the works of Protogenes, who lived there. Protogenes was not in his studio when Appelles arrived. An old woman was there guarding a large canvas ready to be painted. Instead of leaving his name, Appelles drew on the canvas a line so delicate that nothing subtler could be conceived.

On his return Protogenes, seeing the drawn line, recognized the hand of Appelles, and traced thereupon a line of another color even more subtle, in such a way that there appeared to be three.

Appelles came back again the next day, without finding him whom he sought, and the subtlety of the line he drew that day reduced Protogenes to despair. This sketch was for a long time the admiration of connoisseurs who viewed it with as much pleasure as if gods and goddesses had been depicted instead of almost invisible tracings.

The new artists have been violently reproached for their geometric preoccupations. And yet, geometric figures are the essence of drawing. Geometry, the science which has for its scope space, its measurement and its relations, has been from time immemorial the rule even of painting.

Up till now, the three dimensions of the euclidean geometry have sufficed for the solicitude which the sentiment of the infinite arouses in the soul of great artists.

The new painters do not propose, any more than did the old, to be geometricians. But it may be said that geometry is to the plastic arts what grammar is to the art of the writer. Today scholars no longer hold to the three dimensions of the euclidean geometries. The painters have been led quite naturally and, so to speak, by intuition, to preoccupy themselves with possible new measures of space, which, in the language of modern studios, has been designated briefly and altogether by the term the *fourth* dimension.

The fourth dimension as it is presented to the understanding from the plastic point of view would be engendered by the three known dimensions; it would show the immensity of space eternalized in every direction at a given moment. It is space itself, the dimension of the infinite: it is this which endows objects with their plasticity. It gives them the proportions which they merit as a part of the whole, whereas, in Greek art, for example, a somewhat mechanical rhythm unceasingly destroys the proportions.

Greek art had a purely human conception of beauty. It took man as the standard of perfection. The art of the new painters takes the infinite universe as the ideal, and it is this ideal that necessitates a new measure of perfection, which permits the artist to give to the object proportions which conform to the degree of plasticity to which he desired to bring it.

I love the art of today because above all else I love the light, and all men love light,—above all else Man invented fire. . . .

The Reader Critic

A. S., Pittsburgh:

WHEN I first received a copy of the *Little Review* I was enthusiastic, but I was unable to renew my subscription on account of poverty and I feel as though I had lost something big out of my life because I didn't get to read the last numbers.

I have been working very hard since last September to support my husband and myself and simply could not afford to subscribe for your magazine and it makes me feel as though I ought to have revenge on something. My husband has been working for three weeks and now is laid off again but I think it will be hard for him to get another job and then I hope the powers that be will lay off me enough to send money for the *Little Review* for a year.

I was dead and didn't know it until I read "Aesthetic Meditations." Thanks and thanks! And damn money and damn all those who think only of the length, breadth and thickness of things! "God" hear my prayer!

X. Y., Los Angeles:
   Why, oh why publish the letter from the Pittsburgh woman out of a job?

We answered: Just to show who clamours for the Little Review *and buys it, besides the artists and intellectuals (who borrow it).*

Ulysses Again
   jh

WE are *Ulysses* mad. It is impossible to go anywhere or read anything without getting into some jibberish about *Ulysses. Ulysses* ran serially in the *Little Review* for three years . . . scarcely a peep from the now swooning critics except to mock it. Issues were held up by the post office and destroyed, we were tried and fined for sections of the book, but no art-sharks attended. Burton Rascoe, who runs the Bookman's Day Book in the *New York Tribune,* perhaps speaks for them all: when challenged for a past valuation of the book he explained that he didn't know it was a masterpiece when it was running in the *Little Review* because some of the words were misspelled, etc. We admit that they were, but we took the copy to the printer year after year, as it was, without a mark of our own upon it. Joyce, I have heard, rewrote, made corrections and revisions in the proofs of the book itself until the cost of perfection far outstripped all possible returns. *Ulysses* as it appeared in the *Little Review* is now in demand as a first printing.

As to the reviews, Richard Aldington's was internationally bad and unrelated to *Ulysses.* Then there was John Eglington's piercing blindness. But the praise is as unthought and as hysterical as the rejections. There aren't any critics in this place. None of these make-believe critics knows anything about the creation of a work of art. They rave with the same abandon about Cabell, a cream-puff sculptor, and Santayana.

If there had been some of this camp-meeting ecstasy about *Ulysses* when it was appearing in the *Little Review* the book might have been saved for American publication, the audience that was reading it in the *Little Review* might have been able to own the book, Joyce might have had enough in royalties to ensure him treatments for threatened blindness—and the disgusting profiteering on the part of dealers might have been less fat. (A single copy has already brought more than $500.)

From Burton Rascoe:

"On the basis of a few chapters of a garbled and inconsecutive version of James Joyce's *Ulysses,* which I had read as a serial in the *Little Review,* I formed an unfavorable and very erroneous opinion of that great work; and while I was pressing Cabell's claims to recognition as a writer I made the mistake some years ago of trying to prove that Cabell was meritorious by the fatuous process of asserting, with evinced reasons, that *Ulysses* was not. I repented of this error when I read the book as Joyce had written it. I found that it was possible to entertain a very high opinion of both Joyce and Cabell."

[Mr. Rascoe made a little mistake in the beginning about *Ulysses.* He has been informed, in print, that the version of *Ulysses* which appeared in the *Little Review* was Mr. Joyce's version and not a stray document which Joyce later doctored into a world-beater. However, I gather from other statements made by Mr. Rascoe that he wouldn't be able to recognize the Sphinx outside Egypt.—*jh.*]

Dear Editor: Is Santayana a real name or a nom-de-plume?

[Santayana is a name made up of the two names: Santy Claus and Pollyanna. . . .—*jh.*]

The Moscow Art Theatre

No one will deny that the Moscow Art Theatre is the last word in representation, but haven't we had too much representation in every branch of art and discarded it years ago? The "last word" should have been said and the echo died down long before the war. "They put life upon the stage"—where is the logic and dignity in spending years of devotion and discipline in the doing of a thing that Life can do even better? There is no more significance in life on the stage than in life off the stage. If life is the standard then the plays become a series of travelogues. Life has its satisfactions—Art has its satisfactions. The theatre must be theatric—a show—and everything must be sacrificed to its Art. The theatre, as much as any of the arts, must attest the existence of a superior order from the order of nature and the evidence of humanity.—*jh.*

The Chaliapin Craze

Chaliapin is a trained actor who has eliminated all the chi-chi of the grand-opera-italian-french schools. But the things that he does that are his very own no audience has ever seen done by any one quite so gorgeous or so gigantic. His school of gestures might be classed under secondary feminine traits. There is the "grace" of the hands, but it is the feet that are the most distinctive thing about the man,—walking from the knee with short steps, the narrow base, constantly shifting and turning on the heels, producing an effect of complete harmlessness. In the death scene the feet lie like a dead canary's.

The American audience, even an opera audience, falls for the weak turned he-man and the giant shown helpless. Safety first! Russia is a feminine nation.—*jh.*

Dialogue

MARGARET ANDERSON

Scene: The Little Review in ineffectual consultation over the major tragedies of the winter.
jh, resembling—Knut Hamsun? ? M. C. A.—Elsie Dinsmore? ?

M. C. A.   With all the exasperations of contemporary life I seem
   on the point of losing my interest in things.

jh.   Give me a few moments of your exasperated time and we'll get
  out another of our famous annuals.

M. C. A.   Known as the *Little Review?*

jh.   Not so largely known . . .
     (atmosphere of concentrated impotence)

M. C. A.   We must act!

jh.   I see a great deal of action all over the place.

M. C. A.   You must create!

jh.   I know of no commandment to create.

M. C. A.   You might do something if you weren't so neurotic!

jh.   Since when have the unneurotic been so creative?

M. C. A.   Don't be Norwegian! I shall go mad!

jh.   Don't! There are no modern asylums!

M. C. A.   *(fuming)* Just *what* do you mean?

jh.   No cells padded with mirrors . . .

M. C. A.   *(diverted—looking in the glass with satisfaction)* At least I'm good looking!

jh.   !

M. C. A.   And you are extremely handsome!

jh.   !

M. C. A.   Of course if I weren't so intelligent—

jh.   !

M. C. A.   I might be more effective. It's perfectly true. It's not logical for me to have brains. And *you* might be more effective if you weren't so diabolical. As our enemies so prettily say: Destroy if you must but don't devastate!

jh.   *(turns a Norwegian profile toward the interesting talker)*

M. C. A.   If we didn't waste so much time in good conversation we might at least be self-supporting!

jh.   *Be* self-supporting—and take the conversation that goes with it.

M. C. A.   Well, . . . it might be called an impasse . . .

jh.   *(allows her hand to droop from the wrist in the manner she is glad to know terrorizes her companion)*

M. C. A.   But thank heaven *I* can still get some ecstasy out of life!

jh.   Why limit me to ecstasy?

In May, 1923, we went to Paris (My Thirty Years' War, pages 242-274.) One of the first persons we saw was Hemingway, and he gave us one of his first stories. Here, however, I will quote a later one:

Mr. and Mrs. Elliot

ERNEST HEMINGWAY

MR. AND MRS. ELLIOT tried very hard to have a baby. They tried as often as Mrs. Elliot could stand it. They tried in Boston after they were married and they tried coming over on the boat. They did not try very often on the boat because Mrs. Elliot was quite sick. She was sick and when she was sick she was sick as Southern women are sick. That is women from the Southern part of the United States. Like all Southern women Mrs. Elliot disintegrated very quickly under sea sickness, travelling at night in a

332

railroad carriage and getting up too early in the morning. Many of the people on the boat took her for Elliot's mother. Other people who knew they were married believed she was going to have a baby. In reality she was forty years old. Her years had been precipitated suddenly when she started travelling.

She had seemed much younger, in fact she had seemed not to have any age at all, when Elliot had married her after several weeks of making love to her after knowing her for a long time in her tea shop before he had kissed her one evening.

Hubert Elliot was taking post graduate work in law at Harvard when he was married. He was a poet with an income of nearly ten thousand dollars a year. He wrote very long poems very rapidly. He was twenty-five years old and had never gone to bed with a woman until he married Mrs. Elliot. He wanted to keep himself pure so that he could bring to his wife the same purity of mind and body that he expected of her. He called it to himself living straight. He had been in love with various girls before he kissed Mrs. Elliot and always told them sooner or later that he had led a clean life. Nearly all the girls lost interest in him. He was shocked and really horrified at the way girls would become engaged to and marry men whom they must know had dragged themselves through the gutter. He once tried to warn a girl he knew against a man of whom he had almost proof that he had been a rotter at College and a very unpleasant incident had resulted.

Mrs. Elliot's name was Cornelia. She had taught him to call her Calutina which was her family nick name in the South. His mother cried when he brought Cornelia home after their marriage but brightened very much when she learned they were going to live abroad.

Cornelia had said "you sweet dear boy" and held him closer than ever when he had told her how he had kept himself clean for her. Cornelia was pure too. "Kiss me again like that," she said.

Hubert explained to her that he had learned that way of kissing from hearing a fellow tell a story once. He was so delighted with his experiment and they developed it as far as possible. Sometimes when they had been kissing together a long time Cornelia would ask him to tell her again that he had kept himself really straight for her. The declaration always set her off again.

At first Hubert had no idea of marrying Cornelia. He had never thought of her that way. She had been such a good friend of his,

333

and then one day in the little back room of the shop they had been dancing to the gramophone while her girl friend was in the front of the shop and she had looked up into his eyes and he had kissed her. He could never remember just when it was decided that they were to be married. But they were married.

They spent the night of the day they were married in a Boston hotel. They were both very disappointed but finally Cornelia went to sleep. Hubert could not sleep and several times went out and walked up and down the corridor of the hotel in his new Jaeger bathrobe that he had bought for his wedding trip. As he walked he saw all the pairs of shoes, small shoes and big shoes, outside the doors of the hotel rooms. This set his heart to pounding and he hurried back to his own room but Cornelia was asleep. He did not like to awaken her and soon everything was quite all right and he slept peacefully.

The next day they called on his mother and the next day they sailed for Europe. It was possible to try to have a baby but Cornelia could not attempt it very often although they wanted a baby more than anything else in the world. They landed at Cherbourg and came to Paris. They tried to have a baby in Paris. Then they decided to go to Dijon where there was summer school and where a number of people who crossed on the boat with them had gone. They found there was nothing to do in Dijon. Hubert, however, was writing a great number of poems and Cornelia typed them for him. They were all very long poems. He was very severe about mistakes and would make her re-do an entire page if there was one mistake. She cried a good deal and they tried several times to have a baby before they left Dijon.

They came to Paris and most of their friends from the boat came back too. They were tired of Dijon and anyway would now be able to say that after leaving Harvard or Columbia or Wabash they had studied at the University of Dijon down in the Cote d'Or. Many would have preferred to go to Languedoc, Montpellier or Perpignan if there are universities there. But all those places are too far away. Dijon is only four and a half hours from Paris and there is a diner on the train.

So they all sat around the cafe du Dome, avoiding the Rotonde across the street because it is always so full of foreigners for a few days and then the Elliots rented a chateau in Touraine through an advertisement in the New York Herald. Elliot had a number of friends by now all of whom admired his poetry and Mrs. Elliot had prevailed on him to send over to Boston for her girl friend who had been in the tea shop. Mrs. Elliot became much brighter after her girl friend came and they had many good cries together. The girl friend was several years older than Cornelia and called her Honey. She too came from a very old Southern family.

The three of them with several of Elliot's friends who called him Hubie went down to the Chateau in Touraine. They found Touraine to be a very flat hot country very much like Kansas. Elliot had nearly enough poems for a book now. He was going to bring it out in Boston and had already sent his check to and made a contract with a publisher.

In a short time the friends began to drift back to Paris. Touraine had not turned out the way it looked when it started. Soon all the friends had gone off with a rich young and unmarried American poet to a seaside resort near Trouville. There they were all very happy.

Elliot kept on at the Chateau in Touraine because he had taken it for all summer. He and Mrs. Elliot tried very hard to have a baby in the big hot bedroom on the big, hard bed. Mrs. Elliot was learning the touch system on the typewriter but she found that while it increased the speed it made more mistakes. The girl friend was now typing practically all of the manuscripts. She was very neat and efficient and seemed to enjoy it. Elliot had taken to drinking white wine and lived apart in his own room. He wrote a great deal of poetry during the night and in the morning looked very exhausted. Mrs. Elliot and the girl friend now slept together in the big mediaeval bed. They had many a good cry together. In the evening they all sat at dinner together in the garden under a plane tree and the hot evening wind blew and Elliot drank white wine and Mrs. Elliot and the girl friend made conversation and they were all quite happy.

To Mark Anthony in Heaven
WILLIAM CARLOS WILLIAMS

This quiet morning light
reflected, how many times!
from grass and trees and clouds
enters my north room
touching the walls with

grass and clouds and trees,
Anthony,
trees and grass and clouds.
Why did you follow
that beloved body
with your ships at Actium?
I hope it was because
you knew her inch by inch
from slanting feet upward
to the roots of her hair
and down again and that
you saw her
above the battle's fury
reflecting—
clouds and trees and grass
for then
you are listening in heaven.

Ornament in Jean Cocteau's "Le Grand Ecart"

AT the circus an imprudent mother allows the chinese magician to experiment on her offspring. They put the child in a chest. They open the chest; it is empty.

They reclose the chest. Then they open it; the child appears, and walks back to his seat. It isn't the same child, but no one notices that.

Our old friend, young George Antheil, was also in Paris, and Ezra met him in our apartment. Much interested in his musical talk, Ezra and I urged him to do an article for the Little Review:

Abstraction and Time in Music

GEORGE ANTHEIL

I

THE most important and least experimented-with part of music is TIME.

Music has always been the adventures of TIME with SPACE. Just in-so-far as this space is tightened is the music great music.

No superficial outward antiquity or ultra-modernity can alter this.

Beauty or ugliness which appeals to, or shocks the primary senses has nothing to do with determining a work of art. Art is determined by the voltage of its synthesis.

The ear, like the eye, is merely the outward human organ used for determining the surface and placing the line. The ear in itself can recognise no perfection. The latter quality lies solely within ourselves. When we look at a painting we can see only color and line. The eye sees nothing more than this.

The form we must feel within ourselves. If this does not exist there, it will never exist anywhere. We will then merely find enjoyable canvases with nice colors and little voluptuous lines. In music we have now known for some time that Scriabine was this kind of composer . . . in music.

No music can exist which is based upon such a superficial and primary thing as the ear.

II

I have no doubt that some day in the future vast rhythmic edifices of sound, tightened and stretched a thousand-fold through the evolving of the inner abstraction of music, will radiate a higher voltage than we can imagine today. And it may be that these sounds may not at all be what we today call "musical vibration." It may even be made by beating vast pieces of wood and steel, and attain vibrations today unknown. But this will all be by-product, in relation to the abstraction of time-space which is the first problem of musical art of the future . . . and incidentally, in a weak and often-times halting way, has been the great problem of musical art of the past . . . perhaps the sole great problem. The only men whom we call masters today are those men who got their work into some kind of form. The melodic and harmonic masters are dying rapidly. Their projections into space might have been nice and novel for the time in which they were written . . . novelty has a certain value.

The more enduring masters, Mozart and Bach, occupied themselves not with superficial beauty . . . or as we are doing today . . . with superficial ugliness, but with form. Form in music *is* TIME.

Therefore, as proved by every single instance in the past, it will be solely through a concentration on time that greater evolution will bring itself about in music.

III

Any musical mathematics which does not concern itself with the stuff of which music is fundamentally made, which is TIME, is emphatically a fraud and an imbecility. And as it is as impossible to work with algebraic and Arabian mathematics even as it is impossible to plot good draughtsmanship in painting by higher geometry . . . all numerical calculation of harmony is apt to be the sheerest futility.

IV

It is about time that we discard all bunkum about "chords" and "harmony." One cannot base criticism of painting upon light-vibration. Let us not talk about how concordant or discordant a composer appears to be. He may orchestrate a work for three thousand strange instruments . . . and still be only a "color" composer.

V

Let us not judge by external newnesses. They are easy to manufacture. Let us, rather, take the case of Brancusi who could work twenty years to make the finest abstract form that lay inert in a piece of stone.

The GREATEST ARTIST should be he who is able to bring out of THIS special and THAT special material, the finest forms that lay inert and potent in that material.

As I said before . . . the stuff of which music is made is not sound-vibration, but TIME. So it is not a question of new chords one may be inventing, or new musical resources one may be trying to glorify by a more elegant harmony (such as jazz!), but what new projections one is making into musical space, and one's own musical strength in the tightness of the abstractions you may or may not succeed in making.

VI

In music the only possible abstraction possible is the sense of TIME-SPACE, and its relation to the human body through the organ of the ear; through the spacing-off and draughtsmanship of TIME-SPACE by the means of various points of sound.

And sound merely means "vibration." Abstraction cannot be accomplished by vibration, but by the draughtsmanship of points of sound, and the musically invisible lines that go between them.

These forms find themselves entirely in TIME. It is impossible to establish any critical or mathematical consideration of music without beginning at this point. And to consider abstraction or any other true modernity in music without this basis would be the purest folly.

338

Waiting

WILLIAM CARLOS WILLIAMS

When I am alone I am happy.
The air is cool. The sky is
flecked and splashed and wound
with color. The crimson phalloi
of the sassafras leaves
hang crowded before me
in shoals on the heavy branches.
When I reach my doorstep
I am greeted by
the happy shrieks of my children
and my heart sinks.
I am crushed.

Are not my children dear to me
as falling leaves or
must one become stupid
to grow older?
It seems much as if sorrow
had tripped up my heels.
Let us see, let us see!
What did I plan to say to her
when it should happen to me
as it has happened now?

By 1924 I was beginning to lose interest in the Little Review. *It was ten years old; I felt that it had fulfilled its function, that I had had enough of the struggle to keep it alive, and that, after* Ulysses, *it would find no new masterpieces.*

Jane decided to carry it on as a quarterly, when circumstances permitted; as an annual when they didn't. She did this from 1924 to 1929.

During those years I stayed in France, and almost nothing that I read in the Little Reviews *that came to me there held any vitality for me at all, with the exception of the "notes" that Jane still wrote from time to time:*

Notes

JANE HEAP

THE INDEPENDENTS: This year the Independents did not exist—except for a small group at one end of the Waldorf Roof, more or less modern, more or less Cubist. Where were the dear wild ones? . . . gone; the show was dull,—dead.

We have always looked forward, each spring, to the Independents as we look forward to the Circus. We usually gathered a group of painters and idiots and went in a body. We rolled through the galleries, weeping with joy, shaking with fear, leaning together in pyramids of weakness before some masterpiece of the "I never had a lesson" or "I paint to express myself" schools of Art. Later we moved on to supper and spent the rest of the night in hilarious attempts to invent a name that the true artist might adopt and leave the name Artist to the intoxicated-in-paint.

"Have you seen the Independents?" I asked the Baroness von Freytag.

"It is entirely so," she shouted.

JOSEPH STELLA: Stella's exposition, at the Dudensing Galleries, gave one a feeling of great amazement . . . until one remembered Stella. In the last few years we have come to think of "New York Impressions," "Brooklyn Bridge," "Gas Tanks," "Pittsburg"—when we think of Stella. This show was like one of those wish-dreams everyone used to talk about when we were so psychoanalytic. At least, it was a complete rejection of the mechanical world of today, in its subject material; but in the treatment he remembered the colours he has seen in electric displays and in fireworks,—the lines of cities and machines. He has gone on a holiday with all the birds, flowers, fish and gentler fauna. When I was a child I once saw a print of the Christ-child out for a walk with the entire animal kingdom . . . I doubted but I thought it good sport . . . I think Stella's show good sport. His "Birth of Venus," with all the fish of the sea in adoration, could only have been painted by an Italian of Stella's fervour and gayety.

GERTRUDE STEIN—Gertrude Stein is always living in Paris now, as she might write, always writing and experimenting. There is a great stir of interest both in England and America over her work at the moment. Oxford in the shape of the Sitwells has discovered her. Gertrude is so handsome, such a mighty talker, the best host and playfellow, and a first-rate artist . . . I hope she has a hundred happy years.

The Story Teller's Story brings Sherwood Anderson back at his best story-telling pace. Half way down the first page when he begins with his "good-for-nothing" father you settle into the story with a grin of friendship for Anderson's style. I have heard that several people mentioned in the story are racing madly about raving at the untruth of some of his observations. I came upon two or three little passings of the truth . . . but why not laugh,—there is nothing like the Truth to put us in our graves. This is a story "according to" Sherwood Anderson. Is there anyone simple enough to believe that we have ever had the truth of any story from the beginning of the world? Everything in Religion, History, and Art was done "according to" someone.

BRANCUSI—He is in Paris, in his white clothes, in his white studio, with his white dog . . . working away trying to get the universe back into an egg.

A new age was beginning in the arts—one that held less interest for me than it did for Jane. She came back from Paris in 1925 and organized a machine-age art exposition.

Machine-Age Exposition
JANE HEAP

THE Machine-Age Exposition now being organized by the Little Review will show actual machines, parts, apparatuses, photographs and drawings of machines, plants, constructions etc., in juxtaposition with paintings, drawings, sculpture, constructions, and inventions by the most vital of the modern artists.

There is a great new race of men in America: the Engineer. He has created a new mechanical world, he is segregated from men in other activities . . . it is inevitable and important to the civilization of today that he make a union with the artist. This affiliation of Artist and Engineer will benefit each in his own domain, it will end the immense waste in each domain and will become a new creative force.

The legitimate pursuit of the Western World has been the acquisition of wealth, enjoyment of the senses, and commercial competition. America is supposed to have come nearer to an achievement of these aims than any of the older countries. It is beginning to be evident that no nation can progress beyond our present state, unless it is "subjected to the creative will."

A great many people cry out at the Machine as the incubus that is threatening our "spiritual" life. The aims of this race have bred an incomplete man . . . his outer life is too full, his inner life empty. His religion is either dead or seems a hopeless misfit for life today. The world is restless with a need to express its emotions. The desire for beauty has become a necessity.

When it is admitted that the general public must be educated over and over again to the simplest new thing, is it surprising that, without any education at all, it is unable to see that it is surrounded by a new beauty. And beyond that . . . who could expect it to see beauty in a thing not made for beauty: the Machine.

The snobbery, awe and false pride in the art-game, set up by the museums, dealers, and second-rate artists, have frightened the gentle public out of any frank appreciation of the plastic arts. In the past it was a contact with and an appreciation of the arts that helped the individual to function more harmoniously.

We will endeavor to show that there exists a parallel development and a balancing element in contemporary art. The men who hold first rank in the plastic arts today are the men who are organizing and transforming the realities of our age into a dynamic beauty. They do not copy or imitate the Machine, they do not worship the Machine,—they recognize it as one of the realities. In fact it is the Engineer who has been forced, in his creation, to use most of the forms once used by the artist.

. . . the artist must now discover new forms for himself. It is this "plastic-mechanical analogy" which we wish to present.

. . . No beauty has ever been achieved which was not reached through the necessity to deal with some particular problem. The artist works with definite plastic laws. He knows that his work will have lasting value only if he consciously creates forms which embody the constant and unvarying laws of the universe. The aim of the Engineer has been utility. He works with all the plastic elements, he has created a new plastic mystery, but he is practically ignorant of all aesthetic laws. . . . The beauty which he creates is accidental.

Utility does not exclude the presence of beauty . . . on the contrary a machine is not entirely efficient without the element of beauty. Utility and efficiency must take into account the whole man. Let us take one of the simplest and most obvious examples . . . the Ford car. It is a by-word, for utility and efficiency, to the unthinking. Yet the thousands of jokes at its expense, the endless jeering on the part of the millions of owners, who also brag about its efficiency,—is the evidence against it. The lack of rhythmic balance in its organization, its stupid, sterile vertical lines, frustrate all consciousness of horizontal motion and velocity. It is justly considered a freak.

The experiment of an exposition bringing together the plastic works of these two types of artist has in it the possibility of forecasting the life of tomorrow.

The Machine

FERNAND LEGER

Go to one of the exhibitions of machines, go to the automobile, the aviation show, the Paris Fair, they are the most beautiful spectacles in the world. Look at our street shows, "look well at labour," every time you find the work of an artisan it is good, every time that it is violated by a professional it is bad.

I have just seen the spectacle of "The Fair of Paris," where invention fairly springs up at every step, where the effort of execution is prodigious.

I was stupefied to see that all these men who have organized these admirable panels of detached pieces, these astonishing fantasies of letters and of light, these powerful costly machines, do not understand, do not feel that they are the real artists, that they have overturned all the modern plastic ideas. They are completely ignorant of the plastic quality which they create. Ignorance in such a case is perhaps salutary, but this vexing question of the unconscious in artistic creation is a painful drama which will long trouble the seekers of mystery.

Suppose, as I said a little while ago, the immense world of engineers, of workmen, of merchants, of shop keepers, become aware of the beauty which they manufacture and in which they live. The demand for beauty would be almost satisfied for them; the peasant would be satisfied with his beautiful mowing machine of many colours and the merchant with his melody of cravats. Why must these people go into raptures on Sunday over the doubtful pictures in the Louvre and elsewhere? Why do they go to gaze upon a poor imitation of a landscape hanging on a wall when a beautiful electric meter is at hand which they do not see? They believe in the hier-

343

archy of the arts, to them an electric meter could never be beautiful because it was not made for beauty.

Among a hundred pictures are two beautiful? Among a hundred manufactured objects, thirty are beautiful and meet the demand of art, beauty and utility at the same time.

We must live and create in a perpetual agitation, in this continual ambiguity. The one who handles beautiful things is sometimes quite unaware of them; in this connection I shall always recall the year when I installed the Autumn Salon and was fortunate enough to be next to the Aviation Show which was about to open. Through the partitions I could hear the hammers and the songs of the mechanics. Although accustomed to these shows, I had never before been so much impressed. Never had so brutal a contrast confronted me. I passed from enormous dull gray surfaces, pretentious in their frames, to beautiful metallic objects, hard, useful, with pure colours, to steel with its infinite variety, with its play of vermillions and blues. The geometric power of forms dominated all.

The mechanics saw me pass, they knew that they had artists for neighbours and in their turn they asked permission to see our show; and these good fellows who had never seen an exhibition of pictures in their lives, who were uncorrupted, who had been reared close to the first beautiful material, fell into ecstasies before works which I shall not trouble to mention.

I shall always see a sixteen-year-old urchin, with fire-red hair, a new jacket of bright blue, orange trousers and his hand stained with Prussian blue, gazing enraptured on the nude women in their gilt frames, not having the slightest suspicion that with his modern workman's clothes, blazing with colours, he literally killed the Salon; there remained upon the walls only vaporous shadows in old fashioned frames. This dazzling boy who had the look of having been brought forth by an agricultural machine was the symbol of the exposition next door, of the life of tomorrow, when prejudice shall be destroyed, when finally all the world shall see clearly and the Beauty of the true artisan and of the true artist shall be released.

The last piece of prose in the Little Review *that compelled my enthusiasm appeared in the summer number of 1926. It was by Jane and I felt that its beautiful and powerful imagery surpassed anything that the Surrealists had done. I still feel so.*

Paris at One Time

JANE HEAP

NAKED and transparent negroes, taller than the tour Eiffel, play ball with apricot-coloured cubes . . . against a cobalt sky.

A typhoon . . . purple-green, whirling . . . an inverted pine-tree. Ah! it is a Christmas tree with all our gifts upon it. It sways and is sucked into the sea—disappears.

The earth slants up in a plane to the farthest place in the sky. Open mummy-cases in exact rows . . . all the queens of the world, their heads turned to the left . . . lie listening forever to our words of love . . . a smile of unbelief upon their painted profiles.

The wind gently lifts them from their caskets . . . they become tall plume-pens of many colours . . . emerald, blue, yellow, black, cerise. They write in the sand, something that has been forgotten. No one moves them but they continue to write and slowly the Champs Elysées appears in the foreground . . . Rousseau-like people go walking up and down. A long line of carrousels slowly fades into place, down the centre of the avenue . . . from the Arch to the Concord. They are painted and golden, but silent and curtained and motionless. All at once all of the people, walking on the paths and in the groves, begin to move slowly towards the carrousels . . . when everyone has disappeared inside the curtains, a silent music begins to play. The curtains are lifted for a moment . . . there are no horses, no pigs, or chariots. There are two great spiral blades: giant augers. The people stand stupidly upon them and wait. The spirals begin to revolve. They dig themselves rapidly down into the earth . . . everything disappears. The music too is under the ground.

A pack of red rabbits comes bounding out of a grove at the right. Their ears back. Their bodies a straight line of speed. They are stopped in the air. They strain to another leap. They are compelled to remain motionless. A smile of indifference points their faces. They slowly change to glistening fish. They fall into a long line . . . abreast. They close their eyes and swim towards the river, singing softly in the night.

From this time on (1926) the virtue of the Little Review, *to me, lay exclusively in its reproductions of modern painting and sculp-*

ture. There is not a name of international fame today, I believe, that was not included in our roster—Archipenko, Arp, Brancusi, Braque, Gaudier-Brzeska, Chagall, Chirico, Demuth, Ernst, Gabo, Gris, Grosz, Kandinsky, Klee, Léger, Wyndham Lewis, Lipchitz, Marcousis, Matisse, Miro, Modigliani, Moholy-nagy, Pascin, Pevzner, Picabia, Picasso, Man Ray, Segonzac, Stella, Tchelietchev, Zadkine, etc., etc.

As for the literature that filled the pages of these last years, I will give samples only. I "was not amused."

"A Rotten Corpse"

OUR young Frenchmen (all but one of them have appeared in the *Little Review*) issued a four page sheet, on the death of Anatole France, which they called "A ROTTEN CORPSE." We will quote a few paragraphs (in translation) as a matter of contrast to the symposium on Conrad, in the *Transatlantic Review* . . . . in which no one even went so far as to say he was an unfertilized egg. The one attitude is so French, the other so US . . . . the truth is that neither group cares a "whoop" for any great man . . . . but the Frenchmen have more fun not caring.

"The brain of France is worthy of his Genius" so says Doctor Guillaume.

In any case mark well that the brain of France corresponds at every point with his genius, at the same time that it explains it—

But does genius explain itself?

ANATOLE FRANCE or the gilded mediocrity

. . . This mediocre man has succeeded in stretching the limits of the mediocre. This writer of talent has pushed his talent up to the door of genius. But he has remained at the door.

This man is a vase—empty.

He is a flat surface—a single dimension.

Memory only functions in his universe. Reminiscences assembled with taste. And certainly I do not deny the taste. I do not deny grace, quick intelligence, charming manners, limpid language, harmony and honey: but I say that deprived of substance and of marrow, isolated and sterile, I don't give a snap for these virtues.

This sceptic, this amiable sceptic leaves me cold. It is passion that

346

I am enamoured of. It is optimism, faith, ardour and blood that I rave over. I love life and my heart beats only for life.

Anatole France is dead!

Joseph DELTEIL

. . . Loti, Barrès, France, let us mark with a fine white sign the year which put to bed these three sinister good fellows: the idiot, the traitor and the detective. With France a little human servility has gone out. Let that day be a fete in which one buries deceit, traditionalism, patriotism, opportunism, scepticism, realism and the lack of heart!

André BRETON

. . . He wrote badly, I swear it to you, this man of irony and of good sense, pitifully afraid of ridicule. And it is really very little to write well if that is all one can do. All the mediocrity of the man, so limited, so fearful, a conciliator at any cost, speculating in bankruptcy, complaisant in defeat, a satisfied, optimistic booby, a thinking reed, all this is mirrored in Bergeret whose mildness you will try in vain to make me admire.

Louis ARAGON

. . . Still another one who lived in the golden age before the war, an age of which we understand nothing. This France is the frenchman par excellence of that period.

No, our piety remains with those who are dead so young, whose words were not left in their mouths like old lumps of sugar but were snatched from them in blood and foam. And I ask you—and this question asked, pardon me for the tone which must be taken here at this time so that the people who mourn shall not be the only ones heard in Europe, a tone which alone corresponds with the fundamental thought that Anatole France dead, France still lives, a France so many-sided that some would like to stifle her under this catafalque, a France mystic, credulous, obscure, brutal, marvellously insulated in an out-worn décor—I ask you, of what use was this grandfather to those children?

A strange grandfather who too much resembles French grandfathers: without a God, without a moving love, without an insupportable despair, without magnificent wrath, without definite failures, without complete victories.

Pierre DRIEU LA ROCHELLE

The night descends already. When one has the courage to run through the necrological articles one is astonished at the poverty of the eulogies given to the dead France. What sad celluloid wreaths! The word of Barrès is regularly repeated: "He was a maintainer." What cruelty! the maintainer of the French language: that makes one think of an adjutant or a very pedantic school master. It seems to me a singular idea to lose several minutes addressing farewells to a corpse whose brain has been removed! Since all is finished let us say no more.

Philippe SOUPAULT

Noces

TRISTAN TZARA

à Igor Strawinsky

WHEN the sun with gold and priceless gold, had encumbered enough the shops of ardency and swollen the breasts of the earth, these began to throw to the sky their food of fire and unfathomable depth.

God's hand feels the pulse of the earth. Even the fearless the blood whips the music, while ascends from the parents of the betrothed, the dignified lament. Suckled with vigor, with the ticking of time and of the passing train, it's here that life is cut as the worm and that the child falls in the column which follows the eternal moaning of the flesh. Within each pore of the skin, there is a garden containing all the beasts of the jungle of anguish.—One must be able to look with an eye as big as a city upon the glass through which one dances, takes one's love out boating, sports about and gambols. From each note it mounts, from the lines of the palm into trees, it descends from animals to roots, for each note is big and sees.

Sowing songs over earth's epidermis

under the tree overloaded with musical symbols

crawling over the calcareous knoll among lizards and tombstones, resinous and chalky sheds, cemetery exuding turpentine devoured by the eager claws set in semi-circle open like a grin.

The hairy breeze will sweep the shores, the molecules and the horns. And the essence which is wrung from the cloud and trickles, transforms the whole country into an eye weeping away its mournful destiny in the ocean. On the velvet of dreams, night aloof, gives birth to a ship.

Morning morning.

Morning of crystal, morning of bread baking, morning of maddened hives, morning smelling of stables, morning of squirrels and streamlets of cool brook water. Morning that smells good, breath suspended from the lips of life.

If you are very weak—if you are very strong—if you are ill—if you are little—if you are bored—read my books—they will heal you—you will see that all the world is mad—you will see why logic should be suppressed—every secret will be revealed to you—my manifestoes will tell you that nothing is of any importance—that there is neither good nor evil—that everything is permitted—and that man should reach out toward nothingness—indifference is the only legal and effective medicine—indifference without effort, indifference without importance—twenty centuries of history have served only to demonstrate the truth of my manifestoes—because truth does not exist—language is a play for children—morality and the laws of causality have divided life into fragments for us—under different forms: art—philosophy—sociology—politeness—justice—ethnography—politics—pyschology—etc.—if you wish to become men again who hear with your ears and speak with your mouths—if you wish to know why one must not take seriously art morality religion politics grammar which were only pastimes in the beginning—simple songs like the sport of nightingales—read my manifestoes—you can write me that I am mad.

The Last Number of the "Little Review"

In 1929, in Paris, I decided that the time had come to end the Little Review. *Our mission was accomplished; contemporary art had "arrived"; for a hundred years, perhaps, the literary world would produce only : repetition.*

I didn't want the Little Review *to die a conventional death, so I discarded all the material that had been amassed for a Last Number and decided, instead, to ask the artists of the world what they were thinking and feeling about their lives and work. We drew up a questionnaire—ten simple but essential questions—and sent it out to all our contributors.*

Questionnaire

1. What should you most like to do, to know, to be? (In case you are not satisfied).
2. Why wouldn't you change places with any other human being?
3. What do you look forward to?
4. What do you fear most from the future?

5. What has been the happiest moment of your life? The unhappiest? (if you care to tell).

6. What do you consider your weakest characteristics? Your strongest? What do you like most about yourself? Dislike most?

7. What things do you really like? Dislike? (Nature, people, ideas, objects, etc. Answer in a phrase or a page, as you will).

8. What is your attitude toward art today?

9. What is your world view? (Are you a reasonable being in a reasonable scheme?)

10. Why do you go on living?

We should have added another—an even more essential one:

11. Do you know what has been the motivating force behind all your actions?

Nearly everyone responded and the answers showed, in most cases, that they sprang from two of the undying human characteristics—vanity and unawareness. My own are a typical illustration:

Jane and I both wrote editorials. Ben Hecht wrote: "I never pass the Fine Arts Building in Michigan Avenue, Chicago, where the Little Review *once lived but youthful and exuberant ghosts say hello to me. And just as soon as I get rich enough I will buy the building and have Margaret's and Jane's pictures made out of electric lights spread across its face and over them the slogan, to be visible as far as Hegewish, Indiana:*

WHERE IS ATHENS NOW?"

Gertrude Stein sent an appreciation of Jane. Sherwood Anderson and William Carlos Williams wrote articles.

I quote as much of the May 1929 number as possible, eliminating a few names, some answers that are over-long, and omitting entirely the answers of Edith Sitwell who has written that she prefers not to be re-quoted.

Editorial

MARGARET ANDERSON

I BEGAN *The Little Review* because I wanted an intelligent life.

By intelligent I didn't—and don't—mean (1) the ability to follow an argument, (2) the capacity for documentation, (3) the gift of erudition, authority, strong physical vibrations, or any of the other primary signs by which people seem to get labelled intelligent at the moment when I am finding them particularly uninteresting.

By intelligence I meant=creative opinion.

There was no creative opinion in Indianapolis, Indiana, in 1912. So I went to Chicago and tried to produce it, in 1914, by founding *The Little Review*.

It was the moment. The epoch needed it, the modern literary movement needed it. But this was of relative unimportance to me. I really began *The Little Review* the way one begins playing the piano or writing poetry: because of something one wants violently. The thing I wanted—would die without—was conversation. The only way to get it was to reach people with ideas. Only artists had ideas . . . and of course only the very good ones. So I made a magazine exclusively for the very good artists of the time. Nothing more simple for me than to be the art arbiter of the world.

I still feel the same way—with a rather important exception. As this number will show, even the artist doesn't know what he is talking about. And I can no longer go on publishing a magazine in which no one really knows what he is talking about. It doesn't interest me.

I certainly couldn't live my life today among people who know nothing of life. It would be as if some one asked me to live seriously all the redundant human drama that undeveloped people like to put you through. Oh no.

So I feel that way about *The Little Review*. I can conceive starting another kind of review. It would not be devoted to literature, drama, music, painting, sculpture. It would have to do with the psychology of these things. It would have to do with people.

Books are interesting. They are written because people know nothing about themselves. I can read books today only to see what an author thinks he knows and doesn't, what he knows and doesn't know he knows, what he doesn't know he has revealed at all, what he is sure he has concealed, what he would like to be and isn't, what he is and doesn't like. . . .

So, if any one feels he should like to buy *The Little Review* and go on publishing all the first-rate creative expressions of these confusions, I am perfectly willing to sell it. And I will read it with interest—because of the confusions and because of the beauty of their expression.

Only, don't let me hear any more about "it's the artist who transforms life." I know it. But I'm not particularly interested at the moment in transformation. I want a little illumination.

Of course I won't start that other kind of review. I wouldn't really have the patience: every one becomes too angry when expert opinion is brought to bear upon his pretenses, his satisfaction in living the human clichés. It would take years to get down to a little decent discussion of the world psyche.

In the meantime I shall search=psychological conversation.

Lost: A Renaissance
JANE HEAP

I AM bringing the *Little Review* to an end, for my part, because I have found the answers to some of these questions.

It is a matter for speculation whether any one who has tried to get at real answers would dash into print with the results. I at least am keeping my answers for my own use and enlightenment. Instead, I am going to indicate the difference between the *Little Review* and other magazines, and try to show that this same difference is carrying us into quite other activities.

The revolution in the arts, begun before the war, heralded a renaissance. *The Little Review* became an organ of this renaissance. Later magazines, perhaps, had somewhat the same intellectual program, but the *Little Review* had the corresponding emotions; and consequently an energy that nothing has been able to turn aside . . . except itself.

No doubt all so-called thinking people hoped for a new order after the war. This hope was linked with the fallacy that men learn from experience. Facts prove that we learn no more from our experiences than from our dreams.

For years we offered the *Little Review* as a trial-track for racers. We hoped to find artists who could run with the great artists of the past or men who could make new records. But you can't get race horses from mules. I do not believe that the conditions of our life can produce men who can give us masterpieces. Masterpieces are not made from chaos. If there is confusion of life there will be confusion of art. This is in no way a criticism of the men who are working in the arts. They can only express what is here to express.

We have given space in the *Little Review* to 23 new systems of art (all now dead), representing 19 countries. In all of this we have not brought forward anything approaching a masterpiece except the *Ulysses* of Mr. Joyce. *Ulysses* will have to be the masterpiece of this time. But it is too personal, too tortured, too special

352

a document to be a masterpiece in the true sense of the word. It is an intense and elaborate expression of Mr. Joyce's dislike of this time.

Self-expression is not enough; experiment is not enough; the recording of special moments or cases is not enough. All of the arts have broken faith or lost connection with their origin and function. They have ceased to be concerned with the legitimate and permanent material of art.

I have not come to this opinion hastily nor through any habitual pessimism, but only after years of observation, revaluing, and learning. I hold no disappointment, despair, or fears for the future. I hold no negative emotions. The actual situation of art today is not a very important or adult concern (Art is not the highest aim of man); it is interesting only as a pronounced symptom of an ailing and aimless society.

This is the situation as I see it. My "luminous certitude" that it could be changed made of me a victim of the *Little Review*. In spite of logic, deprivations, financial catastrophies and Mr. Sumner, we have gone on running the *Little Review;* or I thought I had until I found that it was running me. I was a victim as much as any saint, savant, or business-man. But my idea of victimization has been enlarged. It is this that now needs my attention.

I am not going out to try to reform or reorganize the world-mind. Nor am I going to sit and brood about the passing of the arts. The world-mind has to be changed, no doubt; but it's too big a job for art. It is even quite likely that there will have to be reorganization on a very large scale before we can again have anything approaching great objective art . . .

Perhaps the situation is not so hopeless as I have described it. Perhaps it doesn't matter. Or perhaps it would be more than an intellectual adventure to give up our obsessions about art, hopelessness, and *Little Reviews,* and take on pursuits more becoming to human beings.

Confessions—Questionnaire

1. What should you most like to do, to know, to be? (In case you are not satisfied).
2. Why wouldn't you change places with any other human being?
3. What do you look forward to?
4. What do you fear most from the future?
5. What has been the happiest moment of your life? The unhappiest? (if you care to tell).

6. What do you consider your weakest characteristics? Your strongest? What do you like most about yourself? Dislike most?

7. What things do you really like? Dislike? (Nature, people, ideas, objects, etc. Answer in a phrase or a page, as you will).

8. What is your attitude toward art today?

9. What is your world view? (Are you a reasonable being in a reasonable scheme?)

10. Why do you go on living?

RICHARD ALDINGTON

1. A. To write a poem.
   B. Greek.
   C. Ninon de Lenclos.
2. Because 'tis better to endure those ills we know than fly to others that we know not of.
3. Telling England what I really think of it.
4. Having to take a job.
5. A. Losing my virginity. B. Lying with a virgin.
6. A. Honesty. B. Independence. C. Ha! ha! D. He! he!
7. A. Women's. B. Puritans.
8. Enlightened benevolence.
9. Despair.
10. Pour écraser l'infâme.

SHERWOOD ANDERSON

I am in receipt of your letter. There are some of your questions which I do not know whether I can answer or not. Naturally I will try to help out by giving the best answers I can.

1. *What should you most like to do, to know, to be? (In case you are not satisfied).*

I should like to do and know everything and to continue to be myself, with various improvements to the property.

2. *Why wouldn't you change places with any other human being?*

Because, after a good deal of experience and experiment, I have found out a few minor things about myself and would have to begin all over if I were someone else.

3. *What do you look forward to?*

I look forward to every bit of life I can manage to squeeze out or hold on to.

4. *What do you fear most from the future?*
Death.

354

5. *What has been the happiest moment of your life? The unhappiest? (If you care to tell).*

I have never been anywhere near happiness except in work or in love and have only been unhappy when these things did not happen to me.

6. *What do you consider your weakest characteristics? Your strongest? What do you like most about yourself? Dislike most?*

My feeling of optimism and this stands for all these questions.

7. *What things do you really like? Dislike?*

My chief interest is in people and most of my likes and dislikes lie there.

8. *What is your attitude toward art today?*

I really do not like to talk about it.

9. *What is your world view? (Are you a reasonable being in a reasonable scheme?)*

No.

10. *Why do you go on living?*

Because I like to.

GEORGE ANTHEIL

I hope this will be all right. Meanwhile I send every bit of admiration I have to both of you for your great courage in founding and taking so far the greatest and most historical review of our country and hope that you might accept my love and thanks for all you have both done for me at the most vital period of my life—when I was twenty.

1. To write the music I hear within and attain perfection.

2. Because then someday that other human being would get the benefit of the many battles I have fought single-handed.

3. To have barely enough to live without poverty and to have my music performed as I write it, not years afterward.

4. Ignorance, sickness, poverty, mostly the first.

5. When I went to the Ballet Russe in the spring of 1927 and realized that my *Symphonie en Fa* had not only been written but performed several times the year before. Another happy moment was when I abandoned this style of composition before most others had started it,—1928.

6. The Pole's love of birthplace, in my case U.S.A. My strongest point is that in spite of this weakness I do not live there. This answers my most strong like and dislike.

355

7. I like the last works of Picasso, the last works of Strawinsky, Miro, Chirico, the Surrealist painters, Breton, the young critic Gui Bernard, Stendhal, Gogol, *The Star of the East* of which Breton speaks, the American play "Broadway," American crookdom, newspapers, and politics (not seriously, but as a marvelously created circus), the north coast of Africa, Confucius.

I dislike intensely people with a little knowledge of music, as, for instance, New York music critics. The little knowledge they have overpowers them. I also dislike American conductors who wish to do everything for the American composer. Bitter experience has taught me to regard all American institutions originally created to finance American creative work, with disdain. The reason I live in Europe is that America prefers to encourage 10,000,-000 dollars worth of mediocrity than 75 dollars worth of courageous effort at one time.

8. I am not one of those artists, who having been sidetracked into religion, suicide, sex-snobbism (as a career), or the Divine-Essence, proclaim that there is no more art today, etc., etc. worth while fighting for. Perhaps that will be when I am older and tired, not wishing to give in by deriding the younger artists. At present I believe in creation and creation, ever anew creation, ever changing, with a prayer that I may be the first to change.

9. My world view is that outside of artists I am interested in great men of action, alive and moving today, regardless of what political faith or movement. I find that great men differ from ordinary men in that their sense of *Time* is more alert and sensitive than the ordinary political drudges who apply several sure-fire political formulas with moderate success age-in and age-out. *Time* is the great formula of the future, but someday ages away, that too must be abandoned.

10. Because of an insatiable curiosity concerning tomorrow.

DJUNA BARNES

Dear Little Review:

I am sorry but the list of questions does not interest me to answer. Nor have I that respect for the public.

HAROLD BAUER

Yes, I received your circular, and now receive its duplicate with your letter.

356

This is what happened. I spoke to my Psyche about the question-naire, very cautiously, for she is quite an old-fashioned female and has prejudices against peek-a-boo garments. She immediately burst into tears, saying: "so THIS is what you think of me!" and threat-ened to go home to mother if I ever referred to the subject again.

Put yourselves in my place, M. A. and J. H. She may be an ill-favored virgin, but she is mine own and no one else's. I can't af-ford to lose her, as I am too old to get another mistress.

All cordial greetings.

BRANCUSI

Yes, yes. Je trouve le questionnaire en arrivant du bout du monde. Je cherche un traducteur, si ce n'est pas trop tard. Donnez-moi un rendezvous ou passez me voir dans mes trois baraques.

Vous embrasse affectueusement.

Brancusi finally said: "I want very much to answer, but I have no time."

JEAN COCTEAU

1 and 2. If I did not love I would change places with someone who did.

3. To creating love.

4. A diminution of the forces of the heart.

5. The moment when I loved most. The moment when I loved least.

6. *a)* My heart. *b)* My critical sense. *c)* My capacity for friend-ship, as great as other people's for love, and my talent for displeas-ing. *d)* My talent for pleasing.

7. I like lights on faces, what people bring to one, shadows of things and of places.

8. I believe that the aesthetique of visual judgment has been replaced by a moral aesthetique, of which the criterion is emotion.

9. This is a question to be answered by the intelligence. I don't understand you very well.

10. Because of love.

NANCY CUNARD

1. To Be: Impervious, egocentric, concentrated, secret, unques-tionable, and yet all things to all men.

2. Because impossible—as the thought of projecting oneself into someone else *not* oneself *and yet* oneself at the same time.

3. Change, always—and to "set one's lands in order."

4. Lack of change, repetition of and similarity to the past.

5. The happiest moment: perhaps one childhood day on sands, thinking: this anyway through life will have to have been the 'happy day' (something finite);—or perhaps any one of certain visual moments in Italy.

The unhappiest: one death, and, each time, any important prolonged deterioration.

6. Weakest characteristic: sense of inability.

Strongest characteristic: sense of latent endurance (when not annulled by weakest characteristic).

Like most: sense of going on, and the capacity of escape.

Dislike most: inexactitude, insufficiency in all or any conditions, all forms of nebulousness, ignorance, and not being able to get things over.

7. Like: the blend of abstract and physical—such as the effect of wine, new turns in the reactions of emotion set going by a new person, influence and character of music, of dancing, of elegance, of new places, faces in the street, ends, beginnings, laced with reminiscence. Words, and eloquence; entire freedom of words.

Dislike most: War. Governmental tyrannies and intolerance to individual *mœurs* (whatever they be) in daily life or in expression. And what I take to be the general character of the french, the rawness of the americans, the mainly self-contented platitude coupled with uneasiness of the english.

8. That if "Art" means a scheme, a vocation, a series of revolutions, of campaigns, an album, or some demonstrators, there's too much of it all round—which doesn't matter—and that, as ever, the few authentic names grow permanent as fine old stone, for all that's said.

9. To answer these other nine questions must imply that one does consider oneself a reasonable being, though as to the reasonableness of the scheme . . . largely a matter of days, when not moments—on the whole loathesomely unreasonable in present times.

10. To go on living? Abstractly, or sub-consciously, because there may be something coming. But materially because nothing is known to exactly or even approachably replace it.

TRISTAN TZARA

C'est avec plaisir que je réponds à votre enquête:

1.
2.
3.
4.
5.
6. } Qu'est-ce cela peut bien vous foutre?
7.
8.
9.
10.

Always faithfully yours, Tzara.

DEMUTH

What girls you are! But here goes!

1. Lay bricks. What It's all about. A brick-layer.

2. . . . . . .

3. The past.

4. That everything will be, more or less, alike.

5. Of course, you got away with *Ulysses* but you couldn't, really, with my answers to these two.

6. *a*) . . . *b*) Lack of ambition; *c*) my hands; *d*) my health.

7. *a*) Things in which form and matter are one. *b*) Anything concealing a "cause."

8. What it has always been.

9. If the scheme is reasonable then I'm a reasonable being,—but, I hope not.

10. Most of the time I don't think that I do.

Yours sincerely.

HAVELOCK ELLIS

It will take a long time to consider all your questions and the answers will fill many volumes, some of which I have already written during the past forty years.

Meanwhile I send my best greetings together with a snapshot just taken.

Faithfully yours.

1. *a*) I should like to have been a writer—to have been Sterne or any of the Brontés. I should like to be a writer—to be even Hemingway since he is better at being Hemingway than any of the other Hemingways. *b*) I should like to know everything. Once it was simply God, now it has become departmental. It is therefore still beyond one brain. *c*) I should like to be a traveller proper to this century: a knapsack and diary is no longer enough. A voyage suitable to the 20th century is like no exploration into visible space ever taken before, must be conducted with elaborate knowledge, scientific data, vaccinations and most particularly, the superb modern mechanics which only a millionaire can rent. Poor people should not travel now. The day of pilgrims is over.

Most of all I should like to have found my date, to have been born, mentally, physically, aesthetically all at one time. Synchronization is an ideal I have not attained. My tomb if any will read, "Hic jacet, 600 B.C. Greece; 1100 A.D. France and Italy; 1700-1800 England."

2. It being impossible to change places with another mortal, the idea would never have occured to me. Anyhow we are all alike: the attainment may differ but the problem remains the same.

3. I always have a bundle of hay tied to my nose like a donkey: small hopes, only slightly out of reach and which keep me moving. Looking forward to big hopes I have given over as adolescent.

4. The most frightful thing of the future is the end of the future —senility.

5. I have been happy. I have been unhappy. The superlative of both of these has not been contained in moments. I take time.

6. If by strong you mean dominant, these are my strong characteristics: fear, loyalty, cowardice, pride, honesty, inertia (I think it's organic) and a passion for justice which is intolerable and unimaginative. My weak characteristics are the same, though I had hoped to find them different.

7. I like level ground, land, birds and flowers (and I don't care who knows it), peace, security, the front page of newspapers, light labor, prose, glass, grill-work, scents, semi-precious stones including marble, dolphins, architecture, and ideas. I dislike fiction as a theory and usually as a practice, height, depth, oceans which I find exaggerated—six inches of water being the same as six miles—, feminine women, masculine men, organizations, nationalities, chau-

vinism, credulity, missionaries, confused thinking, dogs, the ends of elephants and cows all over, public metal objects such as door handles and the sound of a stone squeaking on tiles.

8. This is not the year to discuss art of today. This century has seen one of the great pushes. It is not necessary to name names, they are being imitated. For the last ten years modern art has merely become a *placement d'argent*.

9. My world view would demand pages of explanation after hours of labor. I am reasonable, it's the others who are mad.

10. I go on living because loving ourselves and loving life are the same loves. The Narcissus myth was not made up out of whole cloth. I go on living because it is an instinct I am not able completely to conquer. I have seen it conquered but only in circumstances which were intellectually unreliable. There seems nothing to do about death except life.

ELSE BARONESS VON FREYTAG-LORINGHOVEN

This letter was written from Berlin, where the baroness had gone in 1923 to find ease and the leisure to write. She found poverty and desperation: to keep alive she sold newspapers in the streets. She came to Paris in 1926 where, a few months later, she died tragically and alone.—M. C. A.

My heart is abode of terror and a snake—they stare at each other, always, even when asleep I carry it around, I harbour it like embryo in womb—it grows. Is it the spiritual cancer that I am to die of? My mother perished from physical disease. She waited too long. Am I to wait too long? Suicide is more decent! I am not afraid of death. Ah not! It is my home—sweet—as I always said—since long—since I have become wise. Yet I am scared—like snake victim. I feel it not belonging to me—not my way—but where is my way! See, maybe I will get acquainted with it, gradually it will stroke me, as nice and familiar, even petting me and it will be my door to home. I am buried alive—I fear bed for spectre shape enters with me—there it has leisure to torture, tweak, pommel me, weaken my heart, pounding on it, pounding, pounding, pounding, until I sleep in faint. In morning it is stiff, heavy in me—even for suicide one has to arrange, to go up, to lie down forever.

You will love, even over my possible destruction, as over this letter—which would be sin if it were not written in holy purpose —irrespressible anguishcry—as Christ's in Gethsemane (I understand that now!) But I never, never thought I were Christ. I hate Christ—that is I did hate him—that is I was suspicious, perhaps because he is my fate. I hate myself as Christ! So did he! Can one tremble, writhe in Gethsemane? I am shadow-heavy . . . Yet I love the earth still. . . . Consider me a fish that is left on bonedry beach by crazy time's tide. Put me into the sea again. I will swim again . . . to bring my mother's noble, precious, highly painful bought blood to honour. I can be Raskolnikow from absolute angle, for I am optimist by nature, not melancholic pessimist as he is.

I have just discovered that I am not, and why I am not made for suicide—unless it could be done gaily—victoriously—with flourish, I think that is death in battle, or tournament—self-destruction by God—but to act God is weakness and will be punished and can never be strong—gay. He punishes his weakness in members weak, he is terrible.—I am dead already. Death cannot commit suicide. I am safe . . .

I need, for a few quiet hours—human sympathy—talk—love—in my terrible plight—because it is terrific. No joy, no light, not the satisfaction of the pride of my faculties—my art that carries me. I am beset by great multitudes of small worries—I am poor and deserted—if I had not to stand the experience of my person—my country is slowly wearing me to rags—body and spirit . . . many ants can kill the strongest, proudest life if it is fettered to ant heap—as I am to life in Germany—to life—to terrible poverty and its obligations—one may perish on a formality—winter approaching—rain, hail—cold,—I on the streets—freezing—to boot, in such weather people do not buy. I wish you would give me some time for comfort—once! Stroke my hands—and give me "cheer up." Talk with me, listen to me. I am human, and I am not newspaper seller! I have no more time—must go to sell—I should like to laugh with you—to be gay, I can be that! It is my nature—that sounds ghastly now . . . that is the tragedy . . . Tragedy is written on me . . . I almost despise myself for the trouble I make and the trouble that troubles me. But what shall I do? I am stunned nearly to exhaustion. Forgive me but I am mourning destruction of high quality—as I know myself to be . . . That is the tragedy—I still feel deep in me glittering wealth. . . .

EMMA GOLDMAN

I have not written sooner because I find the questions really terribly uninteresting and do not know what one is to answer to them. Do you really think *The Little Review* would gain by such material? I mean, since the questions are so ordinary the replies can be naught else. What interest would there be to go to the labour and expense of bringing such stuff in *The Little Review*? I should think you'd not want to republish it at all, if you have nothing more striking. However for your sake I'll try to think of some answers. If I can formulate them I will send them on.

1. I should like most to be able to travel a few years without any necessity of keeping lecture dates, writing books, being interviewed or answering questions.

2. No, I should not want to change places with any other human being. Dull people do not attract me, interesting ones are probably just as uncomfortable in their skins as I am in mine—so why change?

3. I look forward to a time when human beings will be engaged in creating beautiful things rather than being satisfied with the substitute of publishing idle magazines full of idle questions.

4. For the future I fear most the continued sluggishness of the human mind.

5. There have been two happiest moments of my life; the first, when Alexander Berkman was resurrected from a living death of fourteen years in the Western Penitentiary; the second, when I came back to Russia in the glowing hope of the Russian Revolution. My unhappiest moment was when I realized that the Russian Revolution had been crushed by the Communist State and when I had to leave Russia.

6. My weakest characteristic as far as one knows oneself is that I love my friends too much. My strongest is that I do not hate my enemies enough.

7. I love nature, interesting people—I love my ideal. I dislike above everything else dull people, petty and envious souls and gossipers in pants and skirts.

8. Inasmuch as I consider modern art in the experimental stage I welcome its restlessness, its discontent and its desperate effort to find itself. Above all, I admire the arrogance and the reckless indifference of the modern artists. My world-view is Anarchism—a social arrangement where each can express himself to the fullest without fear or favor from his surroundings.

9. No, I am not a reasonable being, nor do I consider our scheme reasonable. Who the hell wants to be reasonable?

10. I suppose because my will to Life is stronger than my reason, which tells me the stupidity of going on.

"H. D."
HILDA ALDINGTON

I have your second letter and want to say I would have answered the first but was a little startled by the list of questions. They are the sort of questions that one must answer very solemnly, like Proust, going in and over and into and around the subject, each question being a volume, two volumes or a series of a half dozen, "to be dealt with as seen fit by my executors" sort of volumes. Now reading your list a second time and being so to speak in "intellectual carpet slippers" for the moment, it doesn't seem so really very dreadful. To begin:

1. Just at the moment I am involved with pictures. We have almost finished a slight lyrical four reel little drama, done in and about the villages here, some of the village people and English friends. The work has been enchanting, never anything such fun and I myself have learned to use the small projector and spend literally hours alone here in my apartment, making the mountains and village streets and my own acquaintances reel past me in light and light and light. At the moment I want to go on in this medium working with and around pure types, pure artists, pure people, experimenting with faces and shadows and corners. All the light within light fascinates me, "satisfies" me, I feel like a cat playing with webs and webs of silver. I should like for the moment to be what I am, to know a lot more about camera work and to have a little more sheer brawn for the lugging of things up hills. Yes, I should like more than anything to have some sort of workable little car that I could work myself and go off and on, on my own, more or less to Italy and wander in and about Italian and Swiss hills making light do what I want. I should like to work the Debrie camera which I can't. I can do a little work on the small cameras and some of it will be incorporated in the big film that we are busy on . . .

2. I don't think I want to change places with anyone else because surely each one of us is a world to himself, a shell-fish of his own making. "We" are all the same at root, all just one of those protoplasmic germs or spheres or globes that Plato talks about. "We" differentiate one from the other only by the shell and as the shell is MY shell and as I have made this particular shell for my own par-

364

ticular line of defence, I can't see what I should or could want with anybody's shell but my own.

3. I think I look forward to . . . some state of being, I was going to say, and then got self-conscious. WHAT does anyone look forward to? I look forward to freedom as I grow older, more freedom as I grow still older, strength and strength and more and more and more freedom as I get still older.

4. I fear always from the future and the present the fear of fear, I suppose you would call it claustrophobia. I fear the being caught in any one set formula or set of circumstances, I fear poverty in that it might catch me up in some ugly web of the wrong sort of things and the wrong sort of attitudes. I fear people from the future who may "trap" me. From the future, I have no fear but fear of fear. I fear illness only in that it might shut me in or under.

5. The happiest moment in my life was when I stood on the deck of a second class boat called the Floride and saw the beauty of New York above me and knew the beauty of New York was part of all beauty and that I was part of all beauty being free . . . free, my first trip to what we then called "Europe" in 1911, going with a friend I loved and going straight with little luggage and a Dante (that was hers) and a few old dresses.

I am trying to think of the unhappiest moment of my life and nothing rises to the surface. There is something there, I am sure, that is too, too dreadful and destructive. I can't REALLY think of the unhappiest moment, there have been grim moments . . . certainly.

6. I am very vain and have an inordinate inferiority complex. I am loyal literally to death.

I like one straight grain in me that is pure rock, that is set under my feet when I am most febrile and flabby.

I don't know what I dislike most . . . yes, I do know . . . vide psychopathic journals.

7. What do I really like? Sun and sun and sea and sea. I like moths terribly. I like a cuckoo who sings here just at the minute and the half minute the sun rises (about four) and changes his time just at the minute and the half minute that the sun changes *his* time. I like the pine trees in winter.

What do I dislike? So many things . . . chiefly treachery.

8. Art to-day is what art always was and has been, what you or "we" choose to make of it. There has never, I am certain, been

a more vibrant, a more exciting era for the pure artist, to anyone who wants to make something out of nothing, something (to be more explicit) out of Chaos.

9. Are you a reasonable being in a reasonable scheme? Oh, yes. Certainly. Sometimes my own reason conflicts with the relative reason of the general scheme. That is not my fault nor their fault. If one perfected one's scheme one would be able to live a life "there" and a life "here" like two sets of wheels going round and round, each churning away to some purpose. Things get "unreasonable" when the wires or wheels get tangled.

10. I go on living now because I am happy and want to get the most there is to be got out of existence. I did go on living for years out of spite or pique.

Always with best wishes and thanks for everything.

(We sent our questionnaire to a single financial genius, Mr. Kahn having distinguished himself as a patron of the arts and having often helped the Little Review *through difficult times.*

It apparently pleased him to send the following response, instead of being interesting. Sorry.)

OTTO H. KAHN

I appreciate your suggestion, but, pursuant to a general rule of mine to which I have invariably adhered, I regret to say that I must ask to be excused from filling out the questionnaire which you sent me.

I am sorry to learn that you have come to the final number of your Review.

With kindest remembrances and best wishes

Very faithfully yours.

From Ezra . . .

Print what you've got on hand.—Ezra Pound.

P.S. This refers to mss. of mine suppressed by you or "jh," when I last assisted you in preparing a number of the L. R., and never returned to the author.

(Suppressed by me, dear Ezra, and conscientiously thrown into the waste basket; and a very good thing for you. Such a collection of stale witticisms it has rarely been my lot to receive. You really couldn't have hoped to get away with them in a magazine published in New York City, U.S.A., in the year 1926.)—M.C.A.

ERNEST HEMINGWAY

Enclosed please find a piece for the Final Number of yr. esteemed weekly.

I hope this will meet with your qualifications that it should not be literature.

I have been working on this day and night since your letter came and wd. greatly enjoy your acknowleging receipt of same and whether you will use same as there is a great demand for my work by the Atlantic Monthly and kindred periodicals and wd. not like to disappoint these editors when I have a piece so immenently or emminently saleable.

Yrs. always, HEM.

Valentine

For a Mr. Lee Wilson Dodd and Any of His Friends who Want it.

Sing a song of critics
pockets full of lye
four and twenty critics
hope that you will die
hope that you will peter out
hope that you will fail
so they can be the first one
be the first to hail
any happy weakening or sign of quick decay.
(All are very much alike, weariness too great,
sordid small catastrophies, stack the cards on fate,
very vulgar people, annals of the callous,
dope fiends, soldiers, prostitutes,
men without a gallus)
If you do not like them lads
one thing you can do
stick them up your . . . lads
My Valentine to you.

GEORGETTE LEBLANC

1. My life.
   Myself.
   Conscious.

2. Yes, I would change with that person who has realized himself the most completely.

3. A few moments of reality.

4. To lose what I love. To die before having been a little satisfied with myself.

5. The moment which destroyed what I believed to be my life. That interval in which I passed from infancy into the *mécanique humaine*.

6. *a)* I lack impatience, intolerance, anger, rancor.

b) Pity, bounty, gentleness, patience, indulgence, and inadaptability.

c) My wish to hear truths and to perfect myself, my scorn of public opinion, my indifference to material things.

d) What do I really hate? : The plantom which, in infancy, I set up in my place.

7. To live, understand, and know. To laugh, sing, play, listen to good and bad music.

Society, calumny, vanity, irreducible opinions, futile conversation, what is known as "character"!

8. One of man's most interesting illusions.

9. I am a being I am trying to understand, in a scheme I do not understand.

10. To live more, and better.

MINA LOY

Dear Little Review:

I sent you all my answers when you first sent the questions and I heard you had received them. It's most difficult to speak the truth twice—but here goes.

1. Quite satisfied.

2. No room.

3. The release of atomic energy.

4. Fear.

5. Every moment I spent with Arthur Cravan. The rest of the time.

6. Compassion. My capacity for isolation. My eyebrows. My inability to live without sleep.

7. Everything once. I never dislike—I forget.

8. I never take such attitudes.

9. I am reasonable and the scheme may catch up with me.

10. Inevitably—as time and space are an intellectual hoax.

I am frightfully looking forward to your last number, it ought to be electrifying if everyone has been as truthful as

Yours faithfully

JACQUES LIPCHITZ

It's almost a confession you're asking.

Here are my answers in the order of your questions.

1. For me to do is to be and the possibility of knowing.

2. But quite simply because I am incapable of being anything but what I am.

3. I don't think of the future. Only the present concerns me.

4. I repeat—the future doesn't concern me.

5. Probably the happiest moment is the moment I was born. It seems I smiled. As to the unhappy moments they're too long to relate.

6. Ah, if only I could know that, but I think I am like everybody else weak and strong, cowardly and brave, good and bad, and really there's no cause to be satisfied with oneself.

7. I have a formidable appetite. I really like many things.

8. The question is too vast—all that is being done in our time is "the art of today." I myself like only a certain art which gives me the illusion that we are not altogether abject animals and which gives us the hope of some day becoming men.

9. I am a Jew and I carry in my veins the revelation of unity.

10. I have told you already: I have a ferocious appetite and a curiosity without bounds.

ALDOUS HUXLEY

1. To know more about human beings and to be a better novelist.

2. Because I believe in leaving well alone.

3. I do my best not to look forward or backward, but to live in the present.

4. Already answered in 3.

5. *a)* I can't decide. *b)* I do not wish to say.

6. *a)* Detachment. *b)* Again detachment. *c)* Obstinacy. *d)* Detachment.

7. I like nature but not too much of it or too inhuman; I dislike mountains except at a certain distance. I am extremely unsociable and only like a few people; parties bore me extremely and even

the most intelligent conversation maddens me after a little while. Ideas—I am much too fond of ideas. I am naturally little attached to objects and do my best to discourage whatever leanings toward possessionmania I may have.

8. I profoundly disapprove of the tendencies of a great deal of modern art. The trend away from the human and the organic toward the geometrical and mechanical seems to me horrible and also for all the superficial brilliancy of the art in question, extremely unintelligent.

9. A partially reasonable being in an irrational scheme.

10. Because I enjoy being a partially reasonable being in an irrational scheme.

WYNDHAM LEWIS

I have just received your circular. Here is the photograph you ask for. The examination paper is too difficult for me I am afraid—if you like I will write a few lines that might answer the purpose.

You have my best wishes for the special number of the *Little Review* and the results, I hope, may inspire you to start again, from your Paris address.

Yours sincerely.

JAMES JOYCE

I have been away in Toulon and have been overloaded with work since I came back. Can you both please come here for tea on Monday when we can talk over the questionnaire? . . .

Sincerely yours.

Mr. Joyce decided to produce his answers after tea, or during his evening walk along the rue de Grenelle. Later he telephoned that he really could find nothing to say.

GORHAM B. MUNSON

I am sending my answer to question 8 and you may use it if you wish to run it without the answers to the other questions. I worked hard on answering them once upon a time, and I'm not going to make it any easier for other people to decipher me than it was for myself.

8. Would anyone today seriously claim that modern painting was the equal of the greatest period of Chinese painting or that contemporary British and American literature could compare with the Elizabethan period? My view is that the arts in the Western

World have sloped steeply downwards since the seventeenth century. Since the arts are merely man-made, this is the same as saying that western man has been descending during this time. If in literature one wishes to see precisely what has happened, place Ben Jonson's *Volpone* and Stefan Zweig's version of *Volpone* side by side. There you have a picture, given by just two books, of the decline in literary style, in psychological understanding of types, in human values, that has been occurring beneath our illusion of progress and evolution. My endeavor is to regard the arts neither sentimentally nor superstitiously but as what they are: the manifestations of human beings who resemble risen animals more than fallen angels.

MARGARET ANDERSON

1. *a*) To play the piano, as my imagination (excess of desire over ability) tells me I can.

b) What is the universe?

c) Pleased.

2. Because no one else would fight so hard to get what I want.

3. A complete breakdown.

4. The death of three people.

5. *a*) The moment I realized there was a human being like . . . in the world.

b) When I realized (very lately) that I think I fight for what I want, but that I will probably never fight to make an effort.

6. *b*) Strong in vanity, love of contest, capacity of interest, excitement, exaltation; in laziness, combativeness, love of ease and pleasure, psychic vitality, all types of inertia, moral courage, physical cowardice (burglars, dentists, not sports), stamina to carry out convictions, horror of causing pain; selfishness (though not enough to be admirable), parasitism, stability, equilibrium, power of attention, critical judgment (best in the world), love of justice (what is it?); strong in reasoning power, cerebral sexuality, organic generosity (unimportant), in imposing my ideas on others; in desire of change, need of privacy, capacity to create illusions, to decide quickly and be sometimes right, to live without material necessities . . .

a) Weak in control, in concentration, in capacity to lie, in resistance to physical pain (no, I resist having it); weak in flexibility, in supporting the manifestations of others, in doing things that have no immediate reward, in direct sex traits, in capacity to earn money. . . .

c) That I have no *amour propre* or other ulterior motives; that I can resist at all my sense of pity. I like my conception of life, my critical judgment, my discrimination, my prejudices, foibles, illusions, enthusiasms; my left hand, my handwriting, my body (almost entirely), my tact (I mean it), my brain, my ability to think in flashes, my vision, my enjoyments, impatiences, quickness of assimilation, capacity of decision (and the decisions), ability to live on nothing, passion for having everything (beautiful), what I have instead of optimism, ditto for pessimism, my love of sleep. . . .

d) My insistences, exaggerations, false emphasis, my right hand, my honesty, openness, my preoccupation with other peoples' suffering, disease of wanting every one to be happy (a pathology), my lack of important selfishness, having to learn certain things by experience (very few, thank heaven). . . .

7. *a)* I dare not begin . . .

   b) Dare even less . . .

8. Art (today as always): the superlative human pleasure.

9. Never have been able to produce a thought on this subject.

10. Because I can sometimes play the piano so beautifully.

MARIANNE MOORE

1. To do the kind of work that I am doing; to know what might lend it impetus; to be more efficient in it.

2.

3.

4. Unless I delude myself, I am not conscious of fear with regard to present or future.

5. My life has not been signalized by catastrophes or triumphs and has been for the most part happy.

6. Weakest characteristic, unsociability; strongest, perseverance.

7. (Like) reading; outdoor sport; (dislike) selfishness, affectation, inquisitiveness, acquisitiveness.

8.

9. International fraternity.

10. The surrender of life doesn't seem to be demanded of me.

A. R. ORAGE

I doubt whether you will get any sincere answers to these questions. After all, the stuff of the answers is the stuff of which "literature" is the disguise,—and as your questionees are mainly literary, they will naturally preserve their private capital. I wouldn't answer the questions in public myself for anything. Why? The public doesn't deserve my confession. And couldn't make me any equivalent return. In a small group, sworn to secrecy and eternal friendship, these mental confessions would be salutary and, in fact, necessary, —but where, even, is such a group? It can scarcely exist outside a monastery isolated for life. I shall be interested to see what, if any, replies you receive.

As for . . ., why do such answers surprise you? It's characteristic of world-reformers that they take themselves for granted. Under the pretense that they are too trivial a subject for question, they really mean that they are above it. These ass-gods of reform!

Anyhow, best of wishes.

EVELYN SCOTT

Dear Editors:

I am sincerely sorry to hear of the "final" number of *The Little Review*. It will take a long time for any mustiness to adhere to the tradition it has made.

May I offer to the Editors, who have so often been in advance of their age in recognizing the qualities of a living art, my good wishes for whatever they may undertake in the future?

Faithfully yours

DOROTHY M. RICHARDSON

1. Build a cottage on a cliff.

   How to be perfectly in two places at once.

   Member of a world-association for broadcasting the goings-on of metaphors.

2. Because I can't separate future from present.

3. Can't separate future from present.

4. Can't separate future from present.

5. A recurring moment. Another recurring moment.

6. Lack of concentration. Ability to concentrate.

   A certain changelessness. Superficiality.

7. Dancing, an English valley in mid-May an hour before sunset, sun behind seer. Seagulls high in sunlight. Shafts of light.

   Most people under the age of three. Beautiful women. Ugly ones. Such hippo-hided men as guess they are half-truths. Most Irishmen.

   Synthesis.

Line engravings. Gothic. Daumier. Sisley. Blake. Brzeska. Alan Odle. Rossetti. Dumas père. Balzac. Jane Austin. Hugo. André Gide. Wilde. The books Osbert Sitwell will write, and *After The Bombardment*. The plays Noel Coward will write between forty-five and sixty.

Poetry of Buddha, Jesus, Paul, Francis, Quaker Fathers, Hebrews. Keats. Alfred Lawn Tennyson, T. W. H. Crosland. Jean Stratton Porter. Wassermann. Proust. Smuts of South Africa. H. D., Marianne Moore, Elizabeth Madox Roberts.

The cinema. Cafés. Any street. Any garden. Mornings. Sundays. Brown bread and Cornish butter. Soap. The cinema. Onions. Split greengages. Cigars. Berkshire bacon. The cinema. Münich Lager. Conversation. Dry champagne. Planter's punch. Gilbert and Sullivan. Bach. Antheil. Bach. Wagner. Beethoven. Beethoven. Beethoven. Bach. Bach. The cinema. Quaker meetings.

Villas. Flats. Bungalows. Lapdogs. Diamonds. The sight of a moist-ended cigarette, of anyone lighting a cigarette in instead of above a flame, of anyone tapping off ash before it is ready to fall. Archness. White china and glass-ware. Satin. Plus-fours. Marcel waves. Trousers. Sinuosity. Aquilinity. Dogmatic eccentricity. North London. Burne Jones. Sound and Colour in cinema. The idea that every thing has an evolutionary history.

8. Regret on behalf of literature in so far as it allows the conjectures of science to stand for thought and of "art" in so far as it is slick, clever, facile and self-conscious.

9. That humanity is the irreducible minimum of life, and affirms it by denying the existence anywhere in "life" of anything corresponding to what it finds in itself.

10. Because I only just begin to see how to begin to be fit to live.

BERTRAND RUSSELL

I rather like your ten questions and I am therefore proceeding to answer them. I must warn you, however, that I am making my answers truthful rather than interesting. I have a rooted belief that the truth is always dull; nevertheless, I suppose it is what you want.

1. I should like to do physics, to know physics, to be a physicist.

2. There are about a dozen human beings with whom I would gladly change places; first among them I should put Einstein.

3. I look forward to watching the development of my children.

4. I fear most from the future that I shall become the sort of person whom people will find tiresome to be with.

5. The unhappiest moment of my life was birth; the happiest will probably be death.

6. My weakest characteristic is respect for bigwigs; my strongest an impersonal intellect. I like most about myself the fact that many people like me; I dislike most the fact that I hate myself.

7. I like the sea, logic, theology, heraldry. The first two because they are inhuman, the last two because they are ridiculous. I dislike fools, tyrants, and women who speak of children as "little darlings."

8. I have no view about art to-day.

9. My world view is that I am a moderately reasonable being in a totally unreasonable scheme.

10. I go on living because I enjoy life.

GERTRUDE STEIN

Good luck to your last number. I would much rather have written about Jane because I do appreciate Jane but since this is what you want here are my answers.

1. But I am.
2. Because I am I.
3. More of the same.
4. Anything.
5. Birthday.
6. 1. Weakness, 2. Nothing, 3. Everything, 4. Almost anything.
7. 1. What I like. 2. Hardly anything.
8. I like to look at it.
9. Not very likely or often.
10. I am.

PHILIPPE SOUPAULT

1. I am not at all satisfied to be a writer, and, a few years ago, I should have liked to be a mechanician on a locomotive. At the moment I should like to be a jockey, to be handsome, and to know how to drive an airplane.

2. I would certainly change places with a great many people, for instance with the president of Mexico. There is one thing, however, that disturbs me a little in this: at the same time, I might exchange the little freedom which I have aquired with great difficulty for less freedom.

3. I wait for happiness with impatience.

4. I fear death very much.

5. The happiest moment in my life was one evening in Urbino, in Italy, when I thought that I was really happy. The unhappiest; the one in which I realized that I am a very weak man.

6. My weak point is that I am very sentimental; my strong: that I am not too limited. That which I like about myself is my curiosity, that which I dislike is my sadness.

7. The things that I like: love, children, cigarettes, airplanes, and horses.

The things I dislike: misers, cats, art-objects, and uncleanness moral and physical.

8. My attitude toward the art of today is complex. I distrust it because it is art and I trust it because it is of today. This depends on the day.

9. I believe in *mystère*. **But** I fear reason that is nothing but mis-understanding.

10. I go on living because I believe in miracles.

JOSEPH STELLA

1. I am thoroughly satisfied to be a painter. I never repent to be one. I love, of equal love, all the other ARTS—and I may dip, now and then, into LITERATURE, but PAINTING remains my chief concern: PAINTING IS MY CONGENITAL DESEASE.

2. I would not like to change place with any other human being, because impossible—and even possible, I would not move, for I agree with Baudelaire that all our misfortunes happen because we want to change place. Gladly I accept and enjoy fully my own identity, and gladly I place it in the center of UNIVERSE, to gratify the wishes of my friends and enemies alike. Marvelous identity! Not quite clear to me, rather, a perpetual mystery. But trying to discover myself and realize all the possibilities that possibly I can bring to light, is my very grateful spiritual sport.

3. I look forward to the full realization of all my desires in Art —to find my Rose of Bakawali—to attain Serenity: Life, trans-figured by Art, descending into the glow of sunset with the calm rhythm of a rainbow.

4. To become weak and dependent. I would like to fall in the plenitude of Strength, like an oak struck by lightning.

5. The moment that I have felt that, at last, I could proceed alone, really independent, without any support, spiritually and financially speaking. I do not care to remember, and to relate, any unhappy moment: memory of pain is pain itself, and pain is a pest to be avoided at any cost.

6. The belief, still firm, never shaken, in the Blithe Myths that rose-colored our youth to provoke the march of our life; TRUE LOVE—TRUE FRIENDSHIP—REAL HUMAN GOODNESS, I consider my strongest characteristic the bull-dog tenacity of mine in clinging to what my desire leaps upon, never relinquishing its bite to the bleeding possession of it.

The most I like about myself is that ever growing indifference of mine for the opinions of the others. What I dislike the most is that quick following, because taken unaware to exercise any control, of those blind impulses which lead fatally to bitter disappointment.

7. I like everything which can procure the greatest enjoyment to all my five senses, not one excluded. Our senses are the only sure means that we have got with which to apprehend the treasures of Life. Joy, as vital as the Sun, unseals the golden massive plasticity of Life for the solid base of Art. Only through Blue Serenity can Art weave the airy luminous sonority of its music.

I abhor anything that humanity—for the sake of its salvation —has invented and is using with the lamentable result of fostering unhappiness. Like Diogenes, I may ask one simple thing: to be left free to face the Sun, for the sipping of life, without the massive support of any Alexander the Great to obstruct light. To be broken then, all those ties of sacred lies that crucify us as ridiculous Lachohoonts.

8. My attitude toward Art to-day is for independance:—independance of schools, of great names, past and present alike, used as stumbling blocks to hinder personal endeavour; of any chaperoning and patronizing by the self-appointed guides and judges —recruited among the most boisterous failures—squeaking at the entrance of Art;—and above all, of the missionary work, of all the useless advices lavished by our dear friends acting as uncalled-for sponsors.

Art escapes any definition: theories are only appropriate to the *vient de paraître* advertising artistic trash.

A masterpiece cannot be a final word, even for a generation: it is only a phrase of the continuous speech running through the centuries. Innumerable are the roads leading to Art—but great is the joy of venturing through virgin soils.

9. St. John says that men prefer obscurity to light. Truth is a jewel to enjoy in secrecy. Compromising with our dear brothers is compelled by our vital necessity to secure and preserve peace.

10. I abandon myself to the flow of Life, without asking any *quo vadis:* Life is the only tangible good thing that we have got after all. The future will take care of itself: experience proves that events destined to us cannot be checked by our will.

After spending a beautiful day, sleep comes easy. Let us hope then that our worship for Beauty makes our Life decline gently, close up quietly, like those water-lilies folding silently their splendors at twilight, at the waning mumblings of leaves and birds falling to sleep. AMEN.

SOLITA SOLANO

1. *c)* A conscious, developed human being. *a)* Function fully in the physical, emotional and mental systems. *b)* Myself.

2. Because my ego would forbid such a change.

3. My development.

4. Death.

5. Finding what I wanted in love. Believing I had lost it.

6. Weakest characteristics: Stupidity, indifference, lack of imagination, immaturity, tolerance. Strongest characteristics: courage, will-power, fidelity, respect for order, selfishness (unmaterial), intolerance, tenacity, sensibility. Like most about myself my strong characteristics and perfect health. Dislike most my weakest characteristics, my physical details and my handwriting.

7. I like new ideas, love, science, travelling, work, the sun, a few human beings, a very few examples of the arts, perfume, wine, airplanes, Spanish dancing, France, the Orient, the tropics, chess, cigarettes, kittens, the sea, illusions, Christmas trees, chic women, money, monocles, excitement, privacy, good manners, volcanos, deserts. I dislike the stupidity and vileness of all human relations, educational systems, pomposity, stories (dirty *or* clean), vagueness, what passes for art, clichés, injustice, reality (except laboratory data), not knowing anything, unattractive people, provincial life, masculinity, the cold, actors, and singers, reproaches, the theatre, novels, restraints, old age, banal conversation, games, mountains, poverty and cigars.

8. It's pleasant but unimportant.

9. Which one?

10. I have enjoyed it at times. I may again.

WILLIAM CARLOS WILLIAMS

1. I'd like to be able to give up the practice of medicine and write all day and all night.

2. Because I don't think any other sees the necessities of the moment as clearly as do I.

3. Companionship with those I love.

4. That it will keep me tied—and that I shall grow old before I shall have finished with writing.

5. I do not care to tell.

6. My weakest: my human sympathies. My strongest: my sight. I like most my ability to be drunk with a sudden realization of value in things others never notice. I dislike my dogged patience.

7. I like flowers, plants, trees and would have a private hothouse for my amusement if I could afford it. I like nearly all children especially when they are in misfortune. I like women as contrasted with men. I dislike almost everybody between the ages of eleven and fifty-eight. I like old people. I detest the triumphant stupidity of American critics. I like Ezra Pound. I like oranges.

8. Art is the thing of greatest importance in the world today.

9. My life is devoted to a belief that I am a reasonable being in a possibly reasonable scheme.

10. Because I have an enjoyable body for my pleasure.

O. ZADKINE

1. I want to do sculpture, to know sculpture, to be a sculptor. These three desires exclude any trace of dissatisfaction.

2. And *of course* I shall never change places with any other human being.

3. I want to be a good workman.

4. That the future humanity would not see such a simple thing: to be a nice and real artisan.

5. When, disgusted with clay, I started my first stone.

6. Difficult to answer, but look at all my work and you will see which expresses my weakest and which my strongest characteristics. I shall be as late as possible to sign my death sentence, or kiss myself in front of the obelisque.

7. I do not dislike anything. I really like every scrap, the tiniest, as the largest of existence. Everything *is* good, *is* right.

8. No attitude. I do my job. And I want to do it well. Time will do the rest. *We have no time to spare.*

9. Here, Miss Jane Heap, please answer for me, you *will* oblige me *so* much.

10. Do you laugh at me?

Letters

T. S. ELIOT

I am distressed by your letter. I have been pallbearer at the funeral of several periodicals and have, like the speaker in Tom Moore's famous poem, become used to the expectation that anything in which I am interested should die. But although I have not had the honour to contribute to *The Little Review* for some years, it is very hard to have such a landmark disappear. In fact it makes me feel that I am approaching old age. I have, I believe, a complete file of *The Little Review* of the days in which Pound was foreign editor and both he and Lewis and I were occasional contributors, and the serial parts of "Ulysses" were eagerly awaited. In those days *The Little Review* was the only periodical in America which would accept my work, and indeed the only periodical there in which I cared to appear.

If it is certain the *The Little Review* is no longer to be controlled by Margaret Anderson and yourself, may I express the hope that it may disappear altogether? *The Little Review* did stand for so much that was important that I should not like to see the same title used for other purposes.

With all best wishes.

Sincerely yours

Living or Dead

SHERWOOD ANDERSON

You say that I wrote a letter about "Art" in the first issue of the "Little Review." Did I then answer all of these questions you now ask me? They are too searching for me now.

I thought I wanted fame. I have had some of that and want no more of it.

I want not to be professional, smart, intellectual, stupid.

I fear most that I will achieve nothing.

The days will slip away. I will keep on having little moments of self-satisfaction.

I would like to bury myself deep in life again and stay there.

Art is too feminine. That must be why men pursue Art.

It becomes more and more a vague word to me.

All the thrills I have got have come from love—of women, men, certain days, events, places, moods, work sometimes.

Work accomplished is like a woman no longer sweet.

A book written, mulled over by the critics—what is that to a man?

I went to see an old love, half forgotten. She was still sweet and alive. The experience was worth more to me than all the fame I have got from books—worth more to me than all my books.

Why would I rather be myself than another? I am a little used to myself. I am growing a little tolerant. Let it go.

This body is perhaps as good as another. If I were to grow young again there would be too much absurdity to be got through.

I shall never have the wisdom of an old woman, although I think I grow to look more and more like an old woman. People tell me so.

Sometimes they tell me so lovingly. I do get little flashes of tenderness in voices, in hands, in eyes.

Someone I once knew well and loved, like this one who has written me from *The Little Review*, writes me a letter and says:

"You never belonged to the intellectuals. You are better where you are old woman man.

Well, that is all right. I get a thrust from that.

Of course I write. It is often no more than making marks on a wall you have to face. The marks grow ugly and confused and then, sometimes, seem to have a kind of meaning.

I would hate to read now what I wrote in the first number of *The Little Review*. At least I do not have to do that.

And this, you say, is the last thing I shall ever write for it.

Farewell, then. I do manage to have a pretty good time out of the show.

FORD MADOX FORD

Your letter with its enclosure puts me in a disagreeable position. I can't—now *could* I?—reply seriatim to your rubric. The few shreds of dignity that remain to a writer who has for so long rolled his hump around the world must obviously preclude that. And gratitude calls for repayment more in kind. What you ought to expect—and in huge measure to get—from us who for so many years supported, when we weren't supported by, your enterprise—what you ought to expect and get is not revelations as to our unworthy selves but expositions to the world of what you did. And what you did was for years to supply something that was the only thing of its kind in the world. In a world where nothing good is sure of a place anywhere—certain, dead sure!—you supplied a certain, dead sure, place for really good, unusual writing. And almost more valuable was the moral support that your mere existence in the world afforded to us.

It is not, that is to say, at every moment of the day that one is urged to write with great originality, but that which is the most depressing thought in the world—that which is the final condemnation of humanity, the *bête humaine*, Anglo-Saxondom, the industrial system, the Nordic races—is the thought that if one ever did write anything original or limpid or beautiful in form, or new—there would be in the immense world no single place in which that piece of writing could appear. Think of our immense cosmogonies, ninety odd millions of you parading under Old Glory and two hundred fifty millions of us under the banner of Empire—and all those three to four hundred millions incapable of putting up the few hundred dollars a year that are needed to form a place for the printing and publishing of merely elementarily good stuff. As far as I am myself concerned there is not one periodical in the British Empire that would publish my writings or still more that I would care to see publishing my writings—and it is only very, very lately that that has not been the case in your own vast agglomeration of states. You will say that that is a good thing seeing the nature of my effusions. But that does not take away from the fact that for years and years whilst one was putting on one's collar in the morning one felt more composedly ready to face the uncomfortable happenings in the day merely because at the back of one's mind one had the thought that you existed. It was in effect the difference between the feeling of having capital in the bank that one might use—and having none. None at all. I mean that one had the feeling that, thanks to you, if one did hit on something real to write one might afford oneself that luxury that is for the writer at once the Rolls Royce and the month on the boardwalks of Atlantic City—the luxury of finding publication for unprofitable work.

I don't know if, whilst in the ugly belly of the enterprise of shoving the LITTLE REVIEW along the idea that that was what you were doing for the hearts of your confrères in the world of letters ever occurred to you. If it did, then *when* it did, that, I will wager, must have been the happiest moment of your lives. And the more to rivet in your consciousness that assurance I will present you with at least one personal confidence. You are immoral young women in that you attempt to extract from your contemporaries confessions as to past blisses. For either your contemporaries will present you with some pompous insincerities—in which cae you will have caused them to lie; or you will have incited them to kiss and tell, which is not done in the best circles. So, in order to save you from that millstone round the neck and that deep sea which are the province of such *agents provocateurs* of Satan as corrupt us little ones I will not profess to tell you what was the happiest sensation, of my battered but composed existence. But I will tell you of one of the happiest that comes back to me. It was when, during the heaviest days of the war, in France, our Ezra sent to me, cut off by ages and miles from all remembrance of ever having written anything and from all seeming possibility of ever again writing anything—when, then, our Ezra sent me in France, the copies of THE LITTLE REVIEW in which you were serialising something of mine. One had seemed, for those aspects of life, to be for so long dead that watching one's progress through your polychromatically enclosed and speckled pages afforded one some of the pleasure and curiosity of gazing down on one's post-humous literary self. Oh yes, pleasure! For it was as if one discovered that after three years of death one's work had for so long survived.

The LITTLE REVIEW Credo

To express the emotions of life is to live.
To express the life of emotions is to make art.